Case Studies of Teacher Development: An In-Depth Look at How Thinking About Pedagogy Develops Over Time

Case Studies of Teacher Development: An In-Depth Look at How Thinking About Pedagogy Develops Over Time

Barbara B. Levin

The University of North Carolina at Greensboro

LEA LAWRENCE ERLBAUM ASSOCIATES, PUBLISHERS

2003   Mahwah, New Jersey   London

Lawrence Erlbaum Associates, Inc., Publishers
10 Industrial Avenue
Mahwah, New Jersey 07430

Cover design by Kathryn Houghtaling Lacey

Library of Congress Cataloging-in-Publication Data

Levin, Barbara B.
  Case studies of teacher development : an in-depth look at how thinking about pedagogy
    develops over time / Barbara B. Levin.
      p. cm.
  Includes bibliographical references and index.
  ISBN 0-8058-4197-0 (cloth : alk. paper) — ISBN 0-8058-4198-9 (pbk. : alk. paper)
  1. Teachers—In-service training—United States—Longitudinal studies. I. Title.

LB1731 .L474 2002
370'.71'173—dc21   2002019618
                                                                    CIP

Books published by Lawrence Erlbaum Associates are printed on acid-free paper,
and their bindings are chosen for strength and durability.

Printed in the United States of America
10 9 8 7 6 5 4 3

Contents

PART III: ANALYSIS

Preface

This book represents the results of a 15-year longitudinal study based on in-depth case studies of the development of four teachers' pedagogical thinking. These studies illustrate how teachers' thinking—about children's behavior, development, learning, and teaching—develops over time based on their personal and professional life experiences. This book is especially significant because no other in-depth, longitudinal case studies of teachers' thinking about pedagogy are currently available.

At a time when teacher induction and retention are critically important, this book can help teacher educators, school and district leaders, and policymakers better understand how to support and retain novice and experienced teachers by supporting their growth and development. Understanding how pedagogical thought develops over time and how these ideas are put into action in classrooms can be used to improve teacher education, teacher induction, and teacher retention programs.

This book is based on data gathered from regular, periodic interviews and observations of four educators who are graduates of the award-winning Developmental Teacher Education (DTE) program at the University of California at Berkeley. The common thread is that they were all 1987 graduates of the DTE program and spent 2 years in the same cohort of preservice teachers. Their case studies are rich with direct quotes and vignettes that capture the atmosphere in their classrooms and their teaching styles. Their own reflective writing adds another facet to our understanding of their thoughts. In-depth analyses explain their pedagogical development and the changing metaphors they use to describe their thinking about teaching and learning. A particular model of teacher development, the Ammon and Hutcheson

Model of Pedagogical Thinking, is used to frame the development of the teachers in this study, and several other models of teacher development are provided to offer additional perspectives on teachers' thinking.

Of course the individual lives of the four educators who are the focus of this longitudinal research are unique. Nevertheless, we can learn some important lessons about ways to support teacher development from studying the interaction of these teachers' personal and professional thoughts and actions over 15 years in the field. In fact, the professional experiences of these four teachers are a microcosm of the career paths of many typical teachers. Readers may even recognize their own stories, or the stories of teachers whom they have known in whole or in part, while reading the case studies of these four professionals.

Case Studies of Teacher Development: An In-Depth Look at How Thinking About Pedagogy Develops Over Time:

- combines narrative with scholarship, highlights the voices of four educators through the use of extensive quotes from their interviews, includes vignettes of their classroom teaching, and also incorporates their own writing;
- contributes to the field of teacher education and teacher development because of the long duration of these four case studies (1985–2000) and the accompanying in-depth, scholarly analysis of internal and external influences on their lives as teachers; and
- addresses changes in the nature of qualitative research as it influenced this longitudinal study over time, and provides insights into reasons that some teachers remain and others leave the teaching profession.

In Part I of this book, I situate this longitudinal study in theory and research on teacher development and describe the theoretical perspective of the DTE program that grounded this research. I also describe the qualitative research methods that I used during the 15-year span of this study, and I discuss the changing nature of doing qualitative research in education over the past few decades. In addition, I try to illuminate my own stance regarding this research, provide details about how this study began, and explain how it evolved over time.

In Part II, I offer four longitudinal case studies that are based on my analysis of the entire data set collected during this 15-year study. The purpose of these case studies is to illuminate how each person's pedagogical thoughts and actions developed over time and show how each teacher's thinking played out in the classroom. Embedded in each case study are extensive quotes that allow these teachers to tell much of their story in their own words. Descriptions of their teaching contexts and vignettes that capture their classroom practices are interspersed throughout their case studies.

Each case ends with the teacher's own words based on recent reflective writings about his or her current pedagogical thinking. The first three case studies (those of Sandy Brumbaum, Julie Devine, and Ralph Elder) are presented in chronological order and include an analysis of each person's thinking about behavior, development, learning, and teaching across time. One of the case studies (Rick Kleine) is a synthesis of more recent changes in this teacher's pedagogical understandings because analyses of his development during the first 6 years of teaching are published elsewhere (Levin & Ammon, 1992, 1996).

In Part III, I look across the four cases to answer these questions:

- When teachers face the reality of classroom life and become socialized into the profession and school culture, do they lose what they learned during a teacher preparation program?
- How do the pedagogical understandings of teachers grow and change over time?
- What influences a teacher's thinking about pedagogy? What personal and professional influences in teachers' lives influence their understanding of teaching and learning throughout their careers?
- What do other theories of teacher development have to say about the lives of teachers?
- What lessons can be learned from longitudinal case studies of teachers' thinking about pedagogy?

In the final section of this book, I offer my take on answers to each of these questions by looking over all four case studies across 15 years of interviews and observations of the personal and professional lives of the teachers highlighted in this book. Obviously, my answers are not the only answers to these questions, so I challenge my readers to think about what makes sense to them given their own experiences with teachers in their own context and based on their own perspectives. I also invite my readers to think about what I might have missed, but most especially to think about how they can make use of what they have gleaned about the development of teachers' pedagogical thinking from reading about these teachers' lives.

ACKNOWLEDGMENTS

First and foremost, I would like to thank the four educators whose professional lives are chronicled in this book: Sandy Brumbaum, Julie Devine, Ralph Elder, and Rick Kleine. Many children have been lucky to have them as their teacher, and I am pleased to call them my friends and collaborators. I have learned a lot about teaching and learning from my conversations with them over the years. I would like to thank the following family members, friends, and colleagues of the teachers in this book who offered important insights into their lives and careers: Annie Alcott, Heidi Bachman, Allen Black, Jim Bolar, Jim Bullock, Margaret Golden, Linda Kroll, Della Martinez, Julie McNamara, Elona Meyer, Della Peretti, and Lani Ramos. I would also like to thank Dr. Paul Ammon, cofounder and codirector of the Developmental Teacher Education at UC–Berkeley, for his support and encouragement early on in this research. My thanks also go to two educational scholars who reviewed this book: Selma Wasserman of Simon Frazier University and Daniel Liston of the University of Colorado at Boulder. I appreciate their time and thoughtful suggestions. However, I take complete responsibility for the final version of this book, and I thank Naomi Silverman, my editor at Lawrence Erlbaum and Associates, for her steadfastness throughout the process of its development. Finally, I would like to thank my husband, David Brown, for his love and encouragement while I completed final data collection and analyses for this book.

—*Barbara Levin*

Part I

CONTEXTS

Chapter 1

Situating This Study in Theory and Research on Teacher Development

No person is more influential in the day-to-day life of students than the teacher in the classroom.
—California Education Policy Seminar (1998)

Teacher quality and teacher qualifications are keys to improving student learning. Effective teacher preparation is a major component of teacher quality, along with ongoing opportunities for teacher development and effective induction and mentoring for new teachers (National Commission for Teaching & America's Future [NCTAF], 1996). Effective teachers know their content, understand how their students learn, are able to develop and teach curriculum, and also know how to determine and support their students' needs. Accordingly, effective teacher preparation includes:

- A coherent curriculum that tightly intertwines theory and practice;
- Fieldwork that is integrated with class work, coupled with support from carefully selected mentors;
- An extended clinical component, with a minimum of 30 weeks of student teaching;
- An emphasis on learning-theory and child development, with extensive training in the ability to address the diverse needs of students. (California Education Policy Seminar, 1998, p. 10)

These characteristics of effective teacher preparation describe the Developmental Teacher Education (DTE) program at the University of California at Berkeley, a postbaccalaureate master's degree program that began in the early 1980s and continues today to prepare elementary school teachers. The four teachers who are the focus of this book are 1987 graduates of the DTE program. Three of them are still teaching today. Their stories are the heart of this longitudinal study, which chronicles the development of their pedagogical understanding across 15 years. In this book, I offer longitudinal case studies of their lives as teachers in the hope of providing insights about how teacher thinking develops over time and how it is influenced by personal and professional factors, including their preparation for teaching in the DTE program.

Although current standards for teacher preparation are offered by policymakers and other experts (California Education Policy Seminar, 1998; National Council for Accreditation of Teacher Education, 2000; NCTAF, 1996), there is little longitudinal research into how effective teacher preparation plays out in the lives of teachers once they begin their careers in the classroom. For example, although teacher preparation standards call for a coherent curriculum that tightly couples theory and practice, the conventional wisdom is that theory taught in education schools is disconnected from the reality of the classroom. The prevailing belief is that when prospective teachers graduate and go off to their first jobs, the theory quickly washes out. This so-called *wash-out effect* is documented in the teacher research literature (Lortie, 1975; Veenman, 1984; Zeichner & Liston, 1987; Zeichner & Tabachnik, 1981; Zeichner, Tabachnik, & Densmore, 1987). Yet is this necessarily the case? Is everything learned during a teacher preparation program lost or changed when a beginning teacher faces the reality of classroom life and becomes socialized into the profession and school culture? Does the pedagogical understanding of a teacher grow or change over time and how does that happen? What influences a teacher's thinking about pedagogy? What personal and professional factors in the lives of teachers impact their understanding of children's behavior and development and of teaching and learning throughout their careers? What do other theories of teacher development have to say about the lives of teachers? What lessons can be learned from longitudinal case studies of teachers' thinking about pedagogy? These questions form the core of this longitudinal study of the pedagogical understandings and professional lives of four educators highlighted in this book: Julie, Ralph, Rick, and Sandy.

BACKGROUND FOR THIS STUDY

Since the beginning of my own teaching career, I have been interested in understanding what teacher thinking in the pedagogical domain looks like, whether it continues to develop, and how this happens. As an elementary school teacher for 17 years, and now as a university-based teacher educator for 13 years, I have often thought about my own development as a teacher and particularly about my own understanding of pedagogy. The opportunity to observe and study the development of other teachers' thinking, especially their understanding of pedagogy, over 15 years also allowed me to see if the wash-out effect is true or if teachers can and do use what they learn in their teacher preparation program once they are established in the classroom. However, another question driving me throughout this longitudinal study was trying to understand how teachers' thinking about pedagogy develops over time.

As a doctoral student at UC–Berkeley between 1998 and 1993, I had the opportunity to supervise student teachers for the DTE program. As I attempted to support the development of many prospective teachers who spent 2 years in this postbaccalaureate elementary teacher education program, I wondered how what they learned about children's cognitive, social, and moral development would play out in their classrooms when they were on their own. As I observed the supervising teachers of DTE students during my 5 years as a graduate student instructor, I marveled at how well they translated and integrated their understanding of child development into their pedagogical practices. Many of these supervising teachers were DTE graduates, which is how I met Julie, Sandy, Ralph, and Rick. Although I never taught or supervised these four teachers while they were preservice teacher candidates in the DTE program, I got to know them as they mentored and supervised the preservice teacher candidates placed in their classrooms.

Of course, my biases are obvious. I believe that the DTE program was and still is an exemplary teacher education program (California Education Policy Seminar, 1998; Snyder, 2000). Furthermore, I have been fortunate to maintain regular contact with these four educators over the years due to our mutual connection to the DTE program and our shared interest in helping people learn to teach. In 1989, when I first decided to follow these four educators by conducting regular, periodic observations and interviews, they were all eager to be my subjects of study, and I was interested in learning to do qualitative case study research to understand more about how teachers' thinking develops. At that time, all DTE students participated in entry and exit interviews, which were used for research purposes and to continually develop the DTE program. I had access to these tapes and the transcripts of these interviews, and all of them used the same clinical interview protocol. Such a rich source of data was a boon to me as a novice researcher, and I could not pass it up. That was the beginning of this longitudinal research study.

As I maintained contact with Julie, Ralph, Rick, and Sandy over the years, even after leaving California in 1993 for a career as a professor and teacher educator in North Carolina, they graciously agreed to continue being interviewed and observed whenever I asked. Because my parents still lived in California, I was able to get back to see them every few years. Our relationship over the years developed into one of mutual respect as we looked forward to our conversations about their most recent thinking about behavior, development, learning, and teaching. Even the length of the clinical interviews (often over 2 hours) was no deterrent because they willing gave me many hours of their time. I believe they answered all my probing questions openly and honestly, thus providing me with a window into their thinking about pedagogy at the time of each interview. In fact, at the end of each interview and after day-long observations, they all expressed how thought-provoking it was to talk about their current thinking and recent practices, and about how our conversations probably impacted their development by stimulating their thinking about pedagogical issues and about their classroom practice. Finally, after 15 years, six sets of clinical interviews conducted every 2 to 3 years, and extensive classroom observations, this book was born. It was time to stop collecting data and time to share their voices, perspectives, and stories as developing teachers.

As I chronicle the development of the pedagogical thoughts and actions of these four educators, I do so by taking periodic snapshots of the development of their pedagogical understandings based on a series of interviews and observations conducted over 15 years. I use their own words to create a montage to represent their professional lives as teachers. Because true development takes a long time, this research needed to span a number of years. In fact, if I had interviewed and observed these educators in a tighter time sequence, I would not have had the opportunity to capture many of the personal and professional factors that influenced the development of their lives as teachers.

In three of the case studies (Julie, Ralph, and Sandy), I start at the beginning—when they entered the DTE program in 1985. I then work forward chronologically to the present to discuss how each person's thoughts and actions, their understanding of teaching and learning, and their thinking about behavior and development developed over time. In Rick's case study, I provide a synthesis of more recent changes in his thinking and his personal and professional life because I have written about his earlier development in other places (Levin & Ammon, 1992, 1996). Readers may note in these case studies that each person's relative ability to articulate his or her thinking early on makes these case studies more clinical sounding and less rich with lengthy quotes than in the later years. As they developed their thinking, as they became comfortable with talking to me, and as I became more adept at probing and asking them open-ended questions, in addition to using just the clinical interview protocol, their stories became richer and their voices shone through. I also include personal and professional influences on their thinking as they shared them with me and conclude each case with their own reflective writing.

I offer these case studies as symbols of the lives of many teachers. Although each story is unique, perhaps you can recognize elements of your own story in the lives of these four educators or perhaps the stories of teachers you have known. Fortunately, such a chronicle of the lives of these teachers from the beginning to the midpoint of their careers makes it possible to highlight some important lessons about teacher education and teacher development, which I do in the chapter that follows the case studies. I also offer a detailed description of the methodology used during this study in a chapter preceding the case studies.

THEORETICAL FOUNDATIONS AND DEVELOPMENTAL TEACHER EDUCATION

It is rare in teacher education for a research project to have the continuity and longevity of this study. Most longitudinal studies follow a single teacher or a few teachers during their student teaching experiences or into their first 1 or 2 years in the classroom (e.g., Ayers, 1993; Ball & Goodson, 1985; Bullough, 1989; Bullough & Knowles, 1991; Clandinin & Connelly, 1996; Connelly & Clandinin, 1990; Goswami & Stillman, 1987; Hollingsworth, 1994; Kane, 1991; Knowles, 1992; Powell, 1996, 1997; Ryan, 1992; Sears, Marshall, & Otis-Wilborn, 1994; Zeichner & Tabachnik, 1981). With a few notable exceptions (Bullough & Baughman, 1997; Huberman, 1989; Nias, 1989a), other biographical and autobiographical works about teachers' lives usually chronicle only a year or two of their classroom experiences (e.g., Codell, 1999; Freedman, 1990; Johnson, 1992, 1995; Kidder, 1989).

Because the common thread for all of the people engaged in this longitudinal study is our connection to the DTE program at UC–Berkeley, it is important to provide some background about the program. Although more extensive descriptions of the DTE program are available elsewhere (Black & Ammon, 1992; Snyder, 2000), I briefly explain the structure and goals of the DTE program and then describe the theoretical perspective that underlies the entire program.

The DTE program is a 2-year, postbaccalaureate teacher education program that leads to an elementary-grades teaching credential (formerly called a *multiple subjects credential,* but now a Cultural, Language, and Academic Development [CLAD] credential in California) and a master of arts degree in education. Students in the DTE program are expected to develop a deep understanding of how children develop, focusing on the perspective of Piaget and other constructivist theorists (Ammon, 1984; Ammon & Levin, 1993; Black, 1989; Black & Ammon, 1990; Snyder, 2000). Students are also taught the importance of understanding the reality of teaching and learning in our diverse society, including the economic, language, ethnic, and racial diversity of children in schools today.

At a time when most teacher education programs in California were 1-year postbaccalaureate programs, the DTE program proposed that a second year of study combining a master's degree with a credential would allow for more in-depth study of children's development and teaching methods, along with extensive field experiences undertaken concurrently with university coursework (Black & Ammon, 1992). In other words, what the DTE program has been doing since the early 1980s is now considered best practice for teacher preparation programs: a coherent curriculum that intertwines theory and practice; extended fieldwork integrated with class work, coupled with support from carefully selected mentors; a minimum of 30 weeks of internship or student teaching experiences; and an emphasis on learning theory and child development, with extensive training in the ability to address students' diverse needs (California Education Policy Seminar, 1998; NCTAF, 1996).

The DTE program emphasizes coordinating an understanding of children's cognitive, social, and moral development with in-depth knowledge of content and content pedagogy. With this background in understanding children, curriculum, and instruction, the DTE program founders hypothesized that teachers would continue to develop their thinking in each of these areas (behavior, development, learning, and teaching) as they continued to teach and reflect on their teaching experiences. A primary goal of the DTE program is to provide a strong foundation on which teachers can develop their pedagogical beliefs through experience and by reflecting on their experiences (Levin & Ammon, 1992).

The DTE founders also believed it was important to develop a model that could be used to understand the development of teachers' thinking in the pedagogical domain. This model would help teacher educators understand how people learn to teach, and it could be used to scaffold the progress of DTE students as they became skilled in a developmental-constructivist process of teaching (Black & Ammon, 1992). Beginning in the early 1980s, DTE researchers proposed such a model based on data from journals and interviews of preservice and inservice teachers associated with the DTE program (Ammon & Hutcheson, 1989; Ammon, Hutcheson, & Black, 1985; Ammon & Levin, 1993; Black & Ammon, 1992; Hutcheson & Ammon, 1986, 1987). The Ammon and Hutcheson Model of Pedagogical Thinking is a cognitive-developmental structural model; it suggests that sophisticated, multidimensional thinking about pedagogy evolves from simple, one-dimensional thinking in an invariant sequence. Appendix A provides a version of this model that describes goals for instruction, the role of students, and the role of teachers at various stages in the development of teachers' thinking about pedagogy.

The Ammon and Hutcheson model, as originally proposed, suggested five qualitatively different ways to think about pedagogy in four areas: behavior, development, learning, and teaching. This model describes the quality of teachers' thinking about pedagogy as it develops over time and with experience and reasoning about one's praxis. As with other developmental stage models (Turiel & Davidson, 1986), progress in the four strands that make up the pedagogical domain may be inconsistent, asynchronous, or uneven, although there should be no real regressions. The essential qualities of pedagogical understanding that teachers go through as their understanding of learning and teaching develops from the perspective of Ammon and Hutcheson's model are described in Appendix A. According to this model, teachers' thinking about pedagogy begins with associationist and behaviorist conceptions (Levels 1 and 2) and develops toward constructivist conceptions that are initially quite global (Level 3), but that eventually become more differentiated (Level 4) and finally more integrated (Level 5). Black and Ammon (1992) described the teachers' role in the learning process in this way:

> With regard to the central role of how teachers bring about learning, for example, the expectation at level 1 is that children will learn if teachers simply show or tell them what they need to know. At level 2, the teacher attempts to remedy the shortcomings of reliance on showing and telling by involving students in the practice of what is to be learned and by providing corrective feedback and reinforcement.
>
> At level 3, the teacher is concerned that a level 2 approach, with its emphasis on closely monitored learning of specific skills, does not necessarily lead to understanding and may even impede it. Thus it becomes the teacher's role to permit the learner to engage in self-directed discovery through interaction with concrete materials that the learner is developmentally ready to understand, that is, to understand "correctly." Developmental readiness is understood only in relatively global terms—for example, in terms of Piaget's general stages.
>
> In contrast, level 4 thinking differentiates between the various domains of knowledge, in which development may occur at somewhat different rates [physical, cognitive, social, moral], and it attends to the key conceptual advances that must occur within each domain. The teacher may once again assume a more directive role, except that the teacher now follows the learner's lead and attempts to provoke progressive thinking on the learner's part.
>
> The differentiations achieved at level 4 provide the foundation for a final, more integrated level of constructivist pedagogical thinking at level 5. Now the teacher appreciates both those aspects of development that are unique to each domain and those that cut across domains, such as logical operations,

that have a potentially wide range of applications. From this perspective, the idea of integrated curriculum becomes a functional concept, as an approach to instruction with mutual support for the development of understandings in different domains and as a way of assessing the learner's capabilities across domains. (pp. 331–332)

The upper levels of the original model developed by Ammon and Hutcheson in the 1980s were somewhat hypothetical early on because data were available mainly from less experienced teachers, and there were few experienced program graduates to interview and observe. Since that time, the model has been evaluated empirically in several studies and with more experienced teachers (Ammon et al., 1985; Hutcheson & Ammon, 1986; Levin & Ammon, 1992, 1996). These studies found evidence to support the description of the developmental trajectory of teachers' thinking about teaching and learning, behavior, and development offered in Ammon and Hutcheson's original model. The longitudinal case studies presented in this book also support this model, although the intent of this book is not to validate this model, but to describe personal and professional factors that influence the lives of the teachers featured in the case studies.

The Ammon and Hutcheson Model of Pedagogical Thinking provides the theoretical framework for this longitudinal research and offers a way to compare the pedagogical development of the four educators in this study with each other and across time. Much of the data collected for this study are based on the same set of clinical interview questions on which the model was originally developed and tested (Ammon et al., 1985; Hutcheson & Ammon, 1986; Levin & Ammon, 1992, 1996). In other words, the Ammon and Hutcheson Model of Pedagogical Thinking provides an *etic*, or outside, perspective on the longitudinal data collected in this study.

However, due to the changing nature of qualitative research over the past two decades and increasing recognition of the importance of context and life history in understanding the development of teachers' thinking, the original clinical interview protocol was modified slightly in 1997. This was done to gain an *emic*, or inside, perspective from the participants. At the start of the interviews conducted in 1997 and 1999, each educator was asked, "Tell me what has been going on with you since we last talked," before responding to any of the clinical interview questions. Combined with classroom observations that began in 1989, the two kinds of interviews (open ended and structured) used in this study form the basis for in-depth analysis of the development of teachers' thinking about pedagogy over time. I describe and discuss the methodology used in this study in more detail and chronicle both my own development as a researcher and changes in the field of qualitative research during the 15-year time period of this study in chapter 2.

RELATED RESEARCH ON TEACHER DEVELOPMENT

In Dan Lortie's seminal study published in 1975, lives of schoolteachers were described based on extensive interviews, observations, and surveys. Lortie examined how teachers were recruited, socialized, and rewarded. He concluded that their work led them to feel isolated in their classrooms, forced to rely on their apprenticeship of observation for understanding how teachers teach, with weak support during the induction period and a strong emphasis on learning by doing. Although these findings were representative of the state of teacher education, teacher induction, and of many teachers' lives and careers in 1975, teaching and teacher education has changed in the past 25 years, and Lortie's findings have never been updated. Nevertheless, Lortie's research continues to be cited extensively and has become part of the vernacular about the state of the teaching profession.

In the mid-1980s, Stephen Ball and Ivor Goodson edited a book called *Teachers' Lives and Careers*, which attempted to add flesh to the bare bones portrayals of teachers offered by earlier studies. Ball and Goodson (1985) sought to include personal and biographical data about teachers in their book. They hoped to better understand teaching by learning who teachers were. Their work helped us begin to see the complexity of teachers' lives and careers and offered more contextually sensitive portrayals of schoolteachers. No longer were studies of teachers' lives represented solely through surveys and statistics, and the importance of understanding the complex nature of teaching began to pervade the research literature in the 1980s and 1990s.

Ken Zeichner and his colleagues (Zeichner & Liston, 1987; Zeichner & Tabachnik, 1981; Zeichner et al., 1987) also conducted studies of teachers that captured some of the complexity of their lives. They often used case studies to describe the development of teachers' reflective orientations toward the problems of teaching and schooling. Zeichner and his colleagues also studied the teacher education program at the University of Wisconsin–Madison, including its theoretical and practical contributions to the thinking of its graduates (e.g., Zeichner & Tabachnik, 1987; Zeichner et al., 1987). In their often-cited paper, Zeichner and Liston (1987) concurred with other researchers (Lortie, 1975) who found that preservice teacher education washes out during the induction years, and they suggested several factors that impede the development of reflective teaching. Among these other factors are reliance on apprenticeship models of teacher preparation and the ideological eclecticism and structural fragmentation found in many teacher education programs then and now.

Jennifer Nias' (1989a) 10-year follow-up study of 54 primary teachers in England and Wales, which was mainly based on individual, semistructured interviews, offers a longer term view of how teachers' conceptions of their work changes from the beginning of a career to its midpoint. The major strength of Nias' longitudinal work is that it offers insight into how internal, personal factors and external forces impact teachers' lives. In particular, Nias' research provides information about how individual teachers in her study developed a sense of self as teachers, how they viewed the centrality of the tasks of teaching to their lives, and the importance of their schools and classes to their perceptions of themselves as teachers. In her work, Nias made extensive use of teachers' voices to provide us with a long-term view of how teachers change and develop over time.

Robert Bullough, Jr., published a case study of a first-year teacher named Kerrie in 1989 and a follow-up study, which he co-authored with Kerrie 8 years later (Bullough & Baughman, 1997). These book-length case studies offer us a detailed view of the life and career of one teacher based on ongoing, extensive, and intensive interviews, observations, and conversations from the beginning to the end of Kerrie's 8-year career as a teacher. This single case study provides insight into the ups and downs of Kerrie's development as a teacher, changes in her beliefs with increasing experience in the classroom, and the influence of her personal life on her professional one. Unlike the present study, Bullough's work with Kerrie was a true collaboration from the outset, including the codevelopment of both authors' interpretations of Kerrie's life as a teacher. Like this longitudinal study of four teachers, Bullough and Bauman's case study provides details about the context of Kerrie's life and experiences and is based on prolonged engagement (Lincoln & Guba, 1985), which helps support the credibility of a researcher's interpretations.

Findings from the first 6 years of the longitudinal research described in this book (Levin & Ammon, 1992, 1996), based on periodic clinical interviews and classroom observations, indicated that the development of the four teachers' thinking in the pedagogical domain was not smooth or linear. Furthermore, the wash-out effect suggested by earlier researchers (Lortie, 1975; Zeichner & Liston, 1987) was not evident in these earlier analyses (Levin & Ammon, 1992, 1996). In fact, Levin and Ammon's (1992, 1996) findings suggest that the teacher preparation experience of the four educators described in this book was a theoretically coherent program of study that later provided opportunities for graduates of the program to mentor student teachers and to teach and supervise student teachers for the program. These opportunities apparently encourage DTE program graduates, including the four people who are the focus of this longitudinal research, to think, rethink, and articulate reasons for how they teach as they do and for understanding why particular pedagogical practices are effective in helping children learn.

In the next chapter, I describe the research methods employed throughout this 15-year study, including my own role and my perceptions of how changes in qualitative research methods during this time impacted this study.

Chapter 2

Research Methodology

In this chapter, I discuss the methodology I used throughout this longitudinal study and provide some additional information about the teachers who are the heart of this study and whose stories were told in the following four chapters. This chapter also contains a rather traditional discussion of the data sources, data collection methods, and data analysis procedures employed during this research. However, because this study spanned 15 years and the field of educational research changed during that time, I discuss changes in approaches to research with teachers at some length. Furthermore, during this study, I developed my own skills and increased my knowledge base as a qualitative researcher, so I also discuss how some procedures changed during this study.

When I began this research, I was a beginning doctoral student in the Graduate School of Education at UC–Berkeley; I had just left the classroom after 17 years as an elementary school teacher. Now, over 15 years later, I am a tenured associate professor with different perspectives on and understandings of what it means to undertake qualitative research. Therefore, I begin this chapter by describing my role as the researcher and interpreter of the pedagogical development of the people who participated in this study. I elaborate on the story of how this study came about, and I identify my biases, which have certainly influenced this research from its conception to its conclusion.

ILLUMINATING MY OWN STANCE

It could be argued that this study had its genesis long before I entered UC–Berkeley to work toward my Ph.D. in educational psychology. Although I taught elementary school for many years, it was not until a decade into my career that I felt I had developed into a good teacher. During that time, I was continually learning and refining my ideas about pedagogy. That is what sparked my interest in teachers' thinking and teacher development. Realizing that my own development as a teacher and researcher is ongoing, I was curious about how other teachers develop and how they employ—or abandon—what they learn about children's behavior and development and about learning and teaching based on their experiences in college and in the classroom.

As a doctoral student at UC–Berkeley in the late 1980s, I heard lectures and read about research *on* teachers and teaching and *on* learners and learning. Teachers were definitely the subjects of research. At the time of my Ph.D. program (1988–1993), researchers in the field of teacher education were beginning to include the voices of their subjects—the teachers—in the research literature. However, they still protected teachers by giving them pseudonyms and describing their teaching contexts generically—a large, urban school in northern California. They used third-person pronouns, and there was little research written in the first person, much less anything written by practicing teachers (with the notable exception of Vivian Paley's wonderful stories about her teaching experiences and the children she taught as a preschool teacher). In the main, the researcher's voice was the primary voice in the literature, and teachers were still the others and the objects of research in the mid-1980s.

Some researchers were beginning to conduct research in a more collaborative manner, sometimes engaging teachers as partners in their research, and giving teachers more voice and visibility by supporting research by classroom teachers and encouraging their participation in conference presentations. However, the "Teacher as Researcher" movement was just coming into its own in the United States in the late 1980s and early 1990s, and teacher research was still not considered real research by the academy, where most educational research was *scientific*—meaning experimental and quantitative.

During my doctoral program, I worked as a graduate student instructor (GSI) for 20 hours a week with the Developmental Teacher Education program at UC–Berkeley. At that time, there were also two or three other GSIs and a program coordinator, who managed the program along with the program codirectors. The program admitted 20 to 25 students each year, so everyone knew each other on a first-name basis. My job as a GSI was to supervise six to eight different students every semester. For 5 years, my responsibilities included: finding field placements for students and consulting with their cooperating teachers, whom we called *master teachers*; giving the students verbal and written feedback after observing their teaching; and engaging them in ongoing dialogue about their teaching and learning through weekly written responses to their journals, which we called *dialogue journals.* I also helped plan and lead weekly seminars with the other members of the DTE staff and attended weekly program meetings. Each week we typically met with an entire cohort of students, the first-year group, for 2 hours 1 day a week and then with the second-year group at another time. Some weeks I only met with small supervision groups of six or seven people comprised of the students whom I supervised directly.

HOW THIS STUDY GOT STARTED

When I began this study, I sought to understand how teachers' thinking developed. I wanted to use what teachers told me to explain this to others. I also wanted to understand the impact of the philosophy and pedagogy of the DTE program on its graduates. Recent graduates seemed to be a wonderful group of teachers, judging from my observations in their classrooms when I went out to supervise student teachers we had placed with them (this was and continues to be one of my biases). When I became aware that every person who had gone through the DTE program since 1980 had been interviewed using the same clinical interview protocol I had used with my own groups of entering and graduating students, I realized that a goldmine of data was available. Not only were these interviews transcribed and available to me to listen to with the original tapes, but every dialogue journal and copies of every classroom observation of all DTE graduates were stored in file cabinets in my office.

Because every doctoral student in the Graduate School of Education at UC–Berkeley has to write three position papers before taking comprehensive exams and proposing a dissertation study, I thought I could write one of my position papers around my interest in understanding teachers' thinking and learn more about how teachers develop. My first position paper was about the field of supervision because it was a new experience for me. For my second paper, I decided to interview and observe some of the recent graduates of the program who were already teaching. These were teachers I had never supervised, but I knew many of them as master teachers from my observations of student teachers in their classrooms.

I first thought about making this a longitudinal study during my second year in graduate school, although I certainly never envisioned at that time that I would continue collecting data for more than a decade or be analyzing data that spanned 15 years. My original intention in 1989 was to interview and observe members of the 1987 graduating class who were in their third year of full-time classroom teaching. I wanted to compare their pedagogical development since they started in the DTE program in 1985. I had the original tapes of their interviews, which Barbara Hutcheson had conducted in 1985 and 1987 on their entry into and graduation from the DTE program.

Dr. Paul Ammon, who was my advisor and the codirector and a cofounder of the DTE, encouraged me to begin this study and to follow four or five of the 1987 graduates into the field. He suggested five names from the 1987 cohort whom he thought would make good subjects because, in his judgment, they *got* what the DTE program had to offer. I took this to mean that they showed an understanding of the theoretical underpinnings of the program, which was based on providing a deep understanding of developmental-constructivist theory from the perspective of Piaget. Dr. Ammon is an expert on Jean Piaget and had done much of the original thinking about how Piaget's (1952, 1963, 1972) ideas could be applied to teacher education. He and other faculty members (Dr. Allen Black, Dr. Elliot Turiel, and Dr. Nadine Lambert) founded the DTE program as an experimental teacher education program about 5 years before the participants in this study started in the program. In the early 1980s, Ammon and others conducted some systematic research to establish a theoretical model describing how teachers' understanding of pedagogy would be expected to develop (Ammon & Hutcheson, 1989; Ammon, Hutcheson, & Black, 1985; Hutcheson & Ammon, 1986, 1987). The result of this research is the model I described briefly in chapter 1, the Ammon and Hutcheson Model of Pedagogical Thinking, which is also described in Appendix A. In keeping with Piaget's work and using their own expertise about development, a hierarchical, hard-stage model was developed, which suggested that teachers' thinking about pedagogy would develop in an invariant sequence through five qualitatively different levels of understanding (see Black & Ammon [1992] and Ammon & Levin [1993] for more background about how Piagetian theory and research has been applied to a model of teacher development).

During the 1989–1990 school year when I began this research, I decided to recruit the four DTE graduates teaching in the San Francisco Bay area who I knew because they served as master teachers for students I had supervised. At the onset, Dr. Ammon and I agreed that if we could not see development in these four teachers, who seemed to be successful graduates of the program, then we would not be able to see it in others in their cohort, who might not have as good a grasp on the cognitive developmental theory underlying their teacher education program. Traditional researchers at the time would have cringed at this biased sample of convenience. However, because I was learning to do qualitative research and planning to develop case studies of these teachers, I persisted. In fact, I began this study and collected and analyzed my first set of interview and observation data with the benefit of only a single qualitative research methods course, which I took from Dr. Judith Warren-Little at UC–Berkeley. To say that I began this study as a naïve researcher would be an understatement.

Nevertheless, one of the advantages I had in beginning this study was access to a set of clinical interview questions that would allow me to ask these four teachers the exact same questions during their third year of teaching (1989–1990) that they had responded to in 1985 when they first started the DTE program and in 1987 when they graduated from DTE. I also had a set of guiding questions that had been used to analyze earlier interviews and a tentative model of the development of teachers' thinking in the pedagogical domain developed by Ammon and Hutcheson, which was based on data collected from earlier interviews and students' journals (Ammon & Hutcheson, 1989; Ammon, Hutcheson, & Black, 1985; Ammon & Levin, 1993; Black & Ammon, 1992; Hutcheson & Ammon, 1986, 1987).

That is the story of how this study began, although I have only mentioned a few of my biases. First, I began this study believing that DTE grads were *good* and *successful* teachers from my perspective, and that the teachers I would interview had a good understanding of how Piaget's theory of child development could be applied in the classroom. In addition, I also began this study with the belief that I was a better person to do research on teachers than many other educational researchers because I had been an elementary school teacher for many years—not just a few, but 17 years. I felt I knew teachers, understood their concerns, and would be an expert observer because of my own familiarity with elementary schools and classrooms as unique environments. I was also biased toward the theoretical perspective of the DTE program because I found it gave me a language to understand teaching and learning and children's behavior that I did not have as a classroom teacher. My own learning about Piaget's theories in graduate school helped me make retrospective sense of my experiences with children's learning and behavior over the years. I also thought it made good sense to think that if children develop, then teachers must also develop. It had taken me over a decade in the classroom to feel like I knew what I was doing, so I believed that teachers could develop and that not everyone was a born teacher. I felt that I had a slow start and that there is a large learning curve in the process of learning to teach well, so I was anxious to understand what influences teachers' development and how this happens. Finally, I had moved to California from Wisconsin, where I had earned a master's degree and a teaching credential from the University of Wisconsin at Madison in a postbaccalaureate credential program that was structurally, although not at all philosophically, similar to the DTE program. Furthermore, I had served as a cooperating teacher for many student teachers and practicum students from UW–Madison, which has an undergraduate teacher education program that emphasizes teachers as critically reflective and culturally competent practitioners.

Having taken a year of doctoral level work in the Curriculum and Instruction department at UW–Madison prior to going to UC–Berkeley, I was well aware of the work of Dr. Kenneth Zeichner and his colleagues. I knew his research on teachers graduating from Wisconsin's elementary teacher education program indicated that they abandoned what they learned as they became socialized into the profession during their beginning years as a teacher (Zeichner & Liston, 1987; Zeichner & Tabachnik, 1981; Zeichner, Tabachnik, & Densmore, 1987). My personal take on their findings, based on my perspective as an experienced cooperating teacher, was that these findings were probably true. After all, they were studying 20- to 22-year-old undergraduates who were trying to become adults while learning to teach. I also believed that we needed to follow teachers much further into the field than just their first year or two if we expected to see true pedagogical development and not just beginning teachers operating in survival mode. Finally, I believed then, and still do, that so much goes on in the first few years of teaching that beginning teachers have no time or mental space to reflect on or apply theories they might have learned in their teacher education program. My own experience had been one of survival mode, and I assumed that was the case for most other beginning teachers.

Just as teachers bring their prior beliefs with them into their teacher education programs, and often hold onto many of them throughout their preparation and induction years (Feiman-Nemser & Buchman, 1989; Richardson, 1996), so did I bring my own beliefs and biases to this research study. I even held onto my naïve ideas about what constituted good qualitative research for many years, as you see shortly when I describe the data collection methods I used in this study. Nevertheless, I wanted to understand how teachers think, how their thinking (particularly about pedagogy) changes over time (and I believed that it would because of my personal experiences), and the mechanisms and influences that occur when teachers' thinking develops.

LOCATING THIS STUDY IN THE CONTEXT OF THE EVOLUTION IN QUALITATIVE RESEARCH METHODS

In many ways, the story of this longitudinal study is like a parable for the changes in educational research about teachers and teaching over the past 15 years. At the beginning of this study, most doctoral candidates were required to take several quantitative research methods courses as part of their program of study, but only a single qualitative research methods course was required. The intellectual arguments in our graduate classes in the late 1980s were over validity and reliability issues in doing quantitative versus qualitative research, and many educational researchers were just beginning to understand the ontological, epistemological, and methodological differences between quantitative and qualitative research. One of my personal goals for my graduate education was to acquire knowledge of both quantitative and qualitative research methods. However, I think I graduated with very little real understanding of either, and I was only just learning how to be a researcher when I began collecting data for this longitudinal study.

This study spans a period of time when acceptance and use of qualitative methods for educational research underwent a great deal of change (Denzin & Lincoln, 2000). When Barbara Hutcheson conducted the first interviews for this longitudinal research in 1985, interpretive research was just becoming accepted as a mode of inquiry in many universities, and it was difficult to publish the results of qualitative research studies in many educational research journals. The norms for educational research at the time were embedded in positivist traditions, and we were still studying the results of process–product research that emphasized such things as time on task and teacher-proof curriculum that would work in any classroom with any group of students to achieve predicted results. Correlational and experimental research studies prevailed in the educational research journals, although research methods from other disciplines such as anthropology and sociology were influencing educational research in some universities. Case studies were rare, and we were only beginning to shift from doing research *on* teachers and considering both teachers and students as subjects to considering teachers as participants in research on teaching.

CHANGES IN THE NATURE OF DOING QUALITATIVE RESEARCH

In the early 1980s, when the founders of the DTE program developed the theoretical framework that underlies this study (Ammon, Hutcheson, & Black, 1985; Hutcheson & Ammon, 1986)—relying on clinical interviews and weekly journals of early DTE students, entering and graduating students, and beginning and experienced teachers—such grounded theory was new in the field of educational research (although not in other disciplines). Early on, the Ammon and Hutcheson Model of Pedagogical Development served as a scoring guide for analyzing the clinical interviews and journal data. However, in keeping with the times, these data were scored numerically, and median and modal responses for individuals were graphed and reported in early reports of this research (Ammon et al., 1986; Hutcheson & Ammon, 1986). In later studies (Levin & Ammon, 1992, 1996), this model was replicated and validated using both quantitative and qualitative data (Levin & Ammon, 1992, 1996) in an effort to elaborate on what the numbers might actually mean. Later I realized that, in my own writing about findings from the early years of this longitudinal research, I had drawn one-dimensional pictures of the four teachers who are at the heart of this study (Levin & Ammon, 1993). For example, I only described the participants' teaching lives in my early conference presentations and publications from this study, and I used pseudonyms that I selected without consulting them. In these early papers, these teachers were not portrayed as whole people with lives outside the classroom, and it took me several years to realize that I was only telling half the story of these teachers' lives. In a paper highlighting Rick's case that I wrote in the early 1990s (Levin & Ammon, 1996), I still used a pseudonym for him (Ron) and the other teachers in this study, and I did not ask him to read my interpretations of his teaching until after they were published.

Around that time, however, I realized that I was way behind the curve in my thinking about how to conduct this kind of research. I needed to know and say more about these teachers to paint a fuller picture of their thinking because so many factors were influencing the development of their thoughts and actions. I realized in analyzing the data collected from the Time 4 interviews in 1993 that these teachers had full lives outside the classroom that influenced what they were doing and thinking as teachers. I was unable to conduct observations or interviews in 1995, so it was not until the Time 5 interviews in 1997 that I changed the interview protocol to ask these teachers more open-ended questions to get them talking about things they felt were important. I did not want to abandon the standard set of clinical interview questions because these allowed me to compare their thinking across time about specific pedagogical issues, but I did start the interviews by asking them to tell me what had been going on with them since we last talked. This allowed them to talk about whatever they wanted to before I asked my questions, and it provided me with more of an *emic*, or inside, perspective than the standard set of questions had provided. This was a revelation for me as a researcher, and I was pleased with what I learned by listening even more closely to what these people had to say about their personal and professional lives.

My research evolved and changed in other ways over 15 years. Looking back at the earliest manuscripts reporting the research based on Ammon and Hutcheson's model, it is interesting to note that results are reported for Student 1, Student 2, Student 3, and so on (Ammon et al., 1985). Our subjects were anonymous in the 1980s, and that was the norm. Furthermore, data in these early studies were reported numerically as descriptive statistics. As mentioned previously, in early conference presentations and in the first two papers published from this longitudinal study (Levin & Ammon, 1992, 1996), I used pseudonyms for the four teachers, which was also standard practice at the time. Although I did try to give voice to these teachers by using extensive quotes from their interviews, they remained anonymous and not fully dimensional. In addition, they did not read articles written about them until after they were published and I sent them copies. My rationale at the time was that I did not want to bias my data by letting them see differences in the patterns of their development. I also told myself that I knew I wanted to keep interviewing and observing them, and I did not want them to give me the *correct* answers, so I never showed them Ammon and Hutcheson's theoretical model, which I was using to interpret their thinking. Much more recently, I asked these four teachers whether I should use their real names or keep the pseudonyms I had chosen for them over a decade before: Julie, Sally, Ray, and Ron. Sandy and two other teachers permitted me to use their real names: Sandy Brumbaum, Ralph Elder, and Rick Kleine. Julie, however, preferred to keep her pseudonym: Julie Devine. Nevertheless, they have read *their* chapters in this book and have made additions and corrections to drafts I sent them. Most changes were made to correct details I had wrong and to add clarity. In addition, they have all willingly written additional passages to round out their stories. Finally, 15 years later, we are beginning to really collaborate to tell the story of their development, although I take full responsibility for any misconceptions that readers might make based on my interpretation of their interviews and observations. Obviously their stories are still filtered through my lenses by the fact that I am the one who asked all the questions, selected excerpts to include from their interviews, and determined which lenses to use to focus in on while describing their lives as teachers.

I understand now that my own one-dimensional view of teacher development is a flaw in this study and an example of my own development as a researcher. Just as the early stages of the Ammon and Hutcheson model indicate that teachers understand pedagogy in rather one-dimensional and global ways, and that teachers' thinking can develop into multidimensional understandings of pedagogy, so too has my own understanding of qualitative research developed and become more complex. My goals in this book are to (a) illuminate multiple factors that have influenced the development of these teachers' understanding of pedagogy across 15 years, and (b) provide a multidimensional look at the pedagogical thoughts and actions of each of these teachers. In doing so, I hope to capture some of the complexity of teacher development in the pedagogical domain. I believe that I now understand that a multitude of things influence the development of teachers' pedagogical conceptions, and that each teacher's life is quite complex. I strive to represent some of that complexity in their case studies.

So why did this take me so long? My development as a qualitative researcher and movement from a positivist perspective to a more constructivist view of how qualitative research can and should be conducted *with* teachers has obviously been slow. Perhaps it was influenced by the period of time when I was introduced to qualitative research as a graduate student, or perhaps I was too influenced by the majority of published research about teachers that I read in mainstream educational research journals at the time. During this study, the prevailing paradigms in educational research shifted from positivist to postpositivist views and then to poststructural and postmodern perspectives, but my own training as a researcher was rooted in an earlier time. Many educational researchers began to reject findings based on positivist and even postpositivist criteria (Goodson, 1992) and instead embrace critical theory, constructivist, postmodern, and poststructural ways of thinking throughout the time period of this study. A wide variety of qualitative research methods have proliferated, and each is based on different ways of interpreting truth. Many of these methods only started to be accepted by most doctoral committees during the 1990s. The role of context became more important, and the value of understanding *emic*, idiographic, and case-based perspectives has become more valued in the academy during the course of my longitudinal research. Representation has become a critical issue for educational researchers to tackle. I had to learn about these things on my own, and I am still learning them.

DESCRIPTION OF METHODOLOGY USED DURING THIS LONGITUDINAL STUDY

In this section, I return to my early roots and take a more traditional approach to describing the methods used during this study. I do this partly for clarity and for the benefit of students of qualitative research methods and others who want to understand how one researcher conducted a longitudinal study about the development of teachers' thinking in the pedagogical domain. I believe the evolution of the methods used in this study may be clearer if I follow a more traditional format when describing the participants, data sources, data collection, and data analysis methods used in this study.

Participants

This study focused on four educators—two males and two females—who began the DTE program in 1985. I believe that the teaching careers of the participants in this study are fairly typical of the range of professional experiences of elementary school teachers. That is, their classroom teaching experiences since their graduation from the DTE program in 1987 range from 5 to 13 years and cover a variety of grade levels and school contexts, although they all remained in California. For example, Julie, one of two female educators, taught for just 5 years before leaving the classroom. However, she continued to work in education-related jobs as a curriculum developer and math specialist for a variety of educational enterprises, including a large textbook publishing company and a small multimedia software company. The other female teacher, Sandy, taught in public schools for 10 years before moving to teach in a small private school in Berkeley that her children attend. During her time teaching in the public schools, Sandy had two daughters, taught full-time and part-time at a variety of primary and intermediate grades while job sharing with other teachers, and also served as a reading specialist. One of the male teachers, Rick, has taught the same grades in the same classroom in the same school since graduating from the DTE program. The other male teacher, Ralph, taught several different grades in two very different schools and school districts for 8 years—one public school for 5 years and then in a private school for 3 years. Ralph then spent 3 years as a supervisor and teacher educator for the DTE program. Ralph continued to teach part time for 2 of those years before returning to teach full-time in a large, urban, multilingual school in Oakland, California. All of the participants are married or in committed relationships with children or stepchildren. All are in their late 30s or early 40s, having completed their teacher education program while earning a master's degree at UC–Berkeley while in their mid- to late 20s. However, each person's story is unique and reflects the influences on their lives as teachers.

Data Sources

The data sources for this longitudinal study included: (a) transcripts of responses to the same set of clinical interview questions administered to each participant six times (1985, 1987, 1989–1990, 1993, 1997, and 1999); (b) responses to an open-ended interview question in 1997 and 1999: *"Tell me what has been going on with you since we last talked?"*; (c) classroom observations of at least two mathematics and reading or language arts lessons conducted around the time of the interviews beginning in 1989; (d) additional interviews following each classroom observation to clarify the researcher's interpretations of these lessons; (e) my field notes during observations, which include detailed floor plans, narrative descriptions of the classrooms, and running records of my observations of their lessons; (f) additional writing and e-mail correspondence from each participant responding to questions I posed; and (g) interviews of teaching colleagues, principals, former supervisors, and family members to provide additional insights about each participant.

Clinical Interviews. The clinical interviews, each of which took 2 to 3 hours to complete, were conducted individually, tape recorded, and later transcribed for analysis. These interviews originally took place at the university, then in each teacher's classroom or at his or her home. Each participant was asked the same set of questions every time, and additional probes were used when necessary for clarification or elaboration. Because development is a slow process, periodic interviews serve as snapshots that can capture each person's thinking about pedagogy at regular intervals throughout his or her teaching careers. More frequent interviews might have captured new learning based on the participants' experiences, but not true development. A copy of the clinical interview protocol can be found in Appendix B.

Open-Ended Interviews.   In 1997 and 1999, the interviews were expanded to gather data supplementary to the standard clinical interview questions. All four educators were asked to talk extensively about what happened in their lives in the time between interviews. This question was posed at the start of the interview and before any of the recurring clinical interview questions were asked. This change in the interview protocol yielded additional data about the personal and professional lives of the participants, which they felt were relevant to reveal. All open-ended and clinical interviews were transcribed for use in the data analysis process.

Classroom Observation Instrument.   Classroom observations, using the Developmental Teacher Observation Instrument (DTOI) developed by Kroll and Black (1993), were also conducted for at least two lessons in math and reading-language arts during 1989–1990, 1993, 1997, 1999, and 2000. Lessons were scripted and later analyzed using the DTOI instrument, which identifies the extent of developmental and constructivist praxis in evidence during the lesson. A summary of the kinds of teacher and student activities captured by the DTOI instrument, which are expected in a developmentally appropriate and constructivist classroom, is provided in Appendix D.

Follow-up Interviews and Field Notes.   Classroom observations were followed by additional interviews, usually at the end of the day or directly following the lesson, to help clarify the observations and make explicit the thinking and decision making of the teachers during their lessons. Notes from these sources, along with the researcher's field notes during site visits, provide additional data to triangulate the actions of the participants as these related to their thoughts and beliefs expressed during the interviews. Photographs, classroom maps, and lists of items found in the classroom and on the walls were also collected.

Participants' Writing.   Additional data were collected from each of the participants in the form of written responses to questions posed by the researcher via electronic mail. For the most part, these writings were in response to specific questions I asked them to reflect on (Butt, Raymond, McCue, & Yamagishi, 1992) or in response to queries for specific information I needed as I finalized their case studies.

Informant Interviews. I also asked each participant to give me the names of people they talk with regularly about teaching. I suggested that these people might include family members, friends, current and former colleagues and principals, or anyone else who might provide additional insights on their thoughts about teaching. These additional perspectives were also used to help triangulate findings from the interviews, classroom observations, and the participants' own writing.

Data Analysis Procedures

The qualitative data analysis methods employed in this study were designed to provide both *emic* (insider) and *etic* (outsider) perspectives on the development of these teachers' thinking and pedagogical practices over time. The techniques of constant comparative analysis (Glaser & Strauss, 1967; Strauss & Corbin, 1990), pattern matching (Merriam, 1998; Yin, 1994), and triangulation of data sources (Merriam, 1998; Miles & Huberman, 1994; Strauss & Corbin, 1990) were used to develop four case studies (Merriam, 1998; Stake, 1995) and a detailed cross-case analysis (Yin, 1994).

To develop each longitudinal case study, content analysis procedures (Merriam, 1998; Miles & Huberman, 1994; Yin, 1994) were applied to all classroom observations, field notes, interviews with the participants and informants, and the participants' writing. The purpose of the content analysis was to develop rich descriptions of the participants' classrooms, influences on their pedagogical thinking, and how their thoughts play out in their actions in the classroom from the *emic* perspective.

As described earlier, the theoretical framework for this study, the Ammon and Hutcheson Model of Pedagogical Thinking (Ammon, 1984; Ammon & Hutcheson, 1989; Ammon et al., 1985; Ammon & Levin, 1993; Black, 1989; Black & Ammon, 1992; Hutcheson & Ammon, 1986, 1987; Levin & Ammon, 1992, 1996), offered a method for describing data from an *etic* perspective. Ammon and Hutcheson's model also (a) offered continuity to the assessment of the participants' level of pedagogical understanding across time, (b) afforded a measure of internal validity for the clinical interview data, and (c) served as a rubric for comparing pedagogical development across the four case studies. The clinical interviews were scored using a multiple coding scheme (Strauss, 1979) so that each instance of talk was coded with a level ranging from 1 to 5, corresponding to the levels in the Ammon and Hutcheson model. Additionally, each instance of talk was assigned to one or more of the four strands of pedagogical thinking in the Ammon and Hutcheson model (behavior, development, learning, and teaching). From this analysis, an overall modal response level for each interview was determined in each of these four areas as defined in the Ammon and Hutcheson model (see Appendix A). By using these coding procedures consistently, responses to identical questions could be compared for each individual over time and across the four cases (see Levin & Ammon, 1992, 1996 for examples).

The DTOI developed by Kroll and Black (1993), which was used to analyze the classroom observation data reported in earlier studies from this project (Levin & Ammon, 1992, 1996), was employed throughout the study to analyze classroom observations. Classroom observations were triangulated with the interviews to determine the extent to which the participants' thoughts and actions were congruent at each juncture and over time. This instrument afforded an additional measure of internal consistency and continuity to the study because it is derived from the same theoretical constructs as the Ammon and Hutcheson model.

Based on the data analysis procedures described earlier, individual case studies were constructed to highlight the way each teacher's pedagogical thinking developed over time. Member checking (Merriam, 1998; Miles & Huberman, 1994) was used to verify my interpretations of the interviews and observations with those of the participants and strengthen the validity of the research findings. Each participant read his or her case study and made corrections or additions for accuracy and clarification. Minor changes regarding details or for clarity of expression were suggested by the participants.

Case studies of each of the professional educators highlighted in this book were written to detail the development of their pedagogical thoughts and actions based on interviews and observations collected since 1985. The case studies provide a montage of description and analysis of the personal and professional lives of these four educators and an analysis of their pedagogical development over a 15-year period. Included in each case study are an analysis of each person's current and past thinking about pedagogy, their metaphors for teaching, and vignettes that describe their teaching practices. These case studies are presented chronologically so that readers can see the progression of their thinking over time. Finally, each chapter concludes with reflections in each teacher's own words.

Part II

LONGITUDINAL CASE STUDIES

Chapter 3

The Story of Julie Devine

I just got burned out. A year came where I said, "I've just got to go." I had two students who were really tough and took a lot of my time and were emotionally draining. I remember one day I was involved in a district training program for cognitive coaching and I was learning about that so I was out of the classroom and had a substitute for an hour or two. I remember I came back and he had rigged up the jump rope over the door and had a chair and was putting a noose around his neck and talking about killing himself. I just was totally overwhelmed by his needs and feeling like I was stressed out all the time. I heard myself reacting to things in ways that I didn't want to be. I thought, "This is not the way to talk to these kids." I felt like I needed to get some better perspective. I needed to take a break.

(Julie, open-ended interview, Time 4, 1993)

Julie Devine is of Hispanic heritage. She is the mother of two young children and is married to an editor. The story of Julie's pedagogical development and life as a teacher is different from the others that follow. One of the main reasons for this is that she left classroom teaching after 5 years to enter the private sector. Although Julie remained in fields related to education, working first at a national textbook publishing company and then for a small educational software company, the development of her pedagogical understandings differs somewhat from the others who remained in the classroom. Her story provides wonderful insights into why some teachers leave the teaching profession while others remain in the classroom. Nevertheless, we start at the beginning when Julie first entered the DTE program at the age of 23, after graduating from University of California at Davis with a degree in psychology and working for a year as a substitute teacher in Grades K to 12.

JULIE'S 1985 INTERVIEW (TIME 1)

When Julie began the DTE program in 1985, her thinking about behavior and development and about learning and teaching was rather tentative. In fact, it seemed that, while she was answering many of the questions in her initial clinical interview, she was trying to figure out what she believed about certain issues. Many times during this first interview, Julie started out saying one thing and ended up saying something else. Sometimes Julie seemed to be trying to figure out what she believed about a certain topic as she talked. At other times, she was uncertain by the end of her response to a question, and her ideas changed throughout the interview. Apparently Julie did not come into the DTE program with a lot of fixed ideas about teaching and learning or about behavior and development.

Julie's tentativeness and uncertainty during her first interview are not particularly surprising given that she had no idea what she was going to be asked in the interview. Furthermore, she had just begun the DTE program and had limited experience working with children in educational settings. She had some experience as a playground leader, substitute teacher, and teacher's aide in a 5th-grade class, but she had no formal preparation for any of these positions. As Julie said during this interview, she was uncertain about many of her responses and found herself changing what she thought as she responded to the interview questions.

It's been interesting. I've enjoyed thinking about these different things because in the course of talking there've been little lights going on. A couple of times I realized that something I said I didn't really believe. And then I kind of went back and changed it a little bit. I think it is interesting to be thinking about certain things and to kind of force yourself to have an opinion or to think about something. You kind of learn from that. I thought I'd be real nervous, but I don't feel that. I think I talked pretty freely.

At the start of her teaching career, Julie seems quite interested in helping students feel good about school, and several times she mentions the importance of building self-esteem:

My goal as a teacher would be to do the best job I can helping children to learn and to be successful in school. Not so much to have the smartest class or to get through the most materials, and do the best things but just to help kids feel good about school and give them skills that they need to do the best they can in life. And just to feel good about what I'm doing and to enjoy the kids and to enjoy teachings . . . I would like to see them have an appreciation for learning and to understand why schooling is important so they can be better people. I would hope that they would . . . feel good about themselves. . . . I think I would probably, in my classroom I could see myself focusing a lot on self-esteem, tying self-esteem to a lot of things just because I think that's so important for people. . . .

In addition to valuing the importance of building children's self-esteem, Julie also seems to hold mostly behaviorist views of teaching and learning at Time 1. For example, she talks about how she would build self-esteem by showing and telling children that she appreciated them and by modeling positive attitudes about learning. Julie also indicates that she believes teaching is mainly providing successful experiences for children and modeling a positive attitude about learning.

> . . . *just by having an open attitude myself, I think, and them seeing that and by saying encouraging things. I think they would just gather that attitude, which has come from my own attitude, and from giving them experiences that help them be successful in the classroom and just showing them that they can do it.*

At Time 1, Julie's understanding of factors that affect children's behavior include internal factors such as their personality, level of independence, and feelings. She also mentions that position in and stability of a child's family might influence behavior. Julie also believes that children's peer relations and their ability to do different things are factors that affect behavior. Although Julie believes that peer relationships become more important with age, she is uncertain about why or how this occurs. Many of Julie's beliefs about factors affecting children's behavior are based on memories from her own childhood.

> *I just remember when I was in 4th grade, there were lots of tears if someone didn't like you, or so-and-so went to play with somebody else. I just remember it [social groups] being real important at that point. . . . I'm not sure why it's so important at that point. Maybe just that the kids are getting older—I don't know.*

Several times during this interview, Julie expresses concern about children's self-esteem in that it is important to prevent children from putting each other down to protect their self-esteem. Julie's concern about children's self-esteem is one of the main themes she reiterated throughout her first interview in 1985.

> *If someone said, "Well, that's really stupid." That's sort of putting the other person down. I think it's good to discuss what the other child is saying, but you don't want children to be putting each other down. . . . You want to emphasize that everybody is different and what's right for one person might not be right for another person. So I think you want to avoid damaging anybody's self-esteem, which is, I think, being real judgmental, saying things like, "That's wrong."*

Julie also indicates that she is interested in teaching fourth graders, and many of her answers have to do with children's behavior at this age. Despite her expressed preference for teaching fourth graders, some uncertainty can be seen in this quote:

> *I feel like I can have an influence on them . . . I think at the fourth grade level they are really aware of their teacher or . . . role models that they look up to and they're younger and more in awe maybe. And when they reach 6th, 7th grade, high school . . . they're into being their own person or they don't think the teacher is, you know, god or something. They're more independent from just believing everything the teacher says, whereas the younger kids are more, I don't know if the word's obedient, . . . maybe they just think more of the teacher, revere the teacher. But when they get older the teacher isn't as important or whatever. The teacher is still important, but in their mind other things are more important. . . . I'm not sure if that's what I mean . . . I know in my childhood the teacher was always the figurehead in my school, and you know, the teacher was always very important and respected.*

Julie's understanding of development, including factors that affect development and what the developmental process is like, is rather unsophisticated and unidimensional in her first interview. She believes that skills develop and that children become more independent "*through experience, their experience in development . . . ,*" and with more time in school. She also says that they "*Become more adult-like . . . ,*" but she shows a lack of understanding about how development happens, how children become more skilled, or how they become adults. In fact, saying that, "*They've had more experience in school, they've had more life experience, and they're just able to do more things than younger ones . . . ,*" shows somewhat circular reasoning about the developmental process, which is not surprising given that Julie is just beginning to learn about theories of development in her teacher education program.

Julie also believes at Time 1 that, "*some people are more equipped for understanding certain things and for doing certain things than others.*" Belief that ability is an entity, which you either have or do not have, makes understanding the developmental process difficult for some people. Although Julie values individual differences, she appears to think that these differences are immutable, hence resistant to change. If as a teacher Julie holds onto this entering belief that ability is fixed, it may be hard for her to believe she can teach all children everything they need to learn. However, because Julie's understanding of development is quite nascent at this time, which she readily admits at the end of the interview, it will be interesting to see how her thinking about children's development changes over time.

> *Yeah. I don't think I have a real grasp of it yet, but I think that it does make a lot of sense in dealing with different kids and individual differences and that's why you can do some things with kids and you can't do them with other kids. So, I think I've got a lot to learn though. I don't think I understand the whole picture yet, of course, I'm just beginning.*

Later in her initial interview, Julie elaborates a bit on her current understanding of development in response to questions related to how children learn. For example, she states that readiness to learn and a child's stage of development are factors that affect the learning process. She also says that physical maturity, mental maturity, and a person's attitude all affect the learning process. Although she originally says that children develop just by having experiences, she qualifies this when asked if there are particular kinds of experiences that are most likely to bring about learning, which is another example of her trying to figure out what she thinks as she responds to the questions in her first interview.

> *I think it's more than just the experience. It's a combination of things that bring out the learning. It might not only be the experience but the stage of development that the child is in too. Somebody might not be ready to learn something and you might do a lesson on something and they're not going to get anything out of it, but if somebody is ready to learn that, the experience might enhance their learning. . . . Sometimes it's not just the experience, but maybe the child's timing, the timing that experience occurs.*

Later in the interview, Julie's understanding of the learning process is somewhat better articulated when she says that, in addition to having experiences, the learning process is a matter of taking risks and making mistakes. However, in the following quote, it seems that Julie is talking about both herself (as someone learning to be a teacher) and the process of learning in children. Julie reminisces about her fear of making mistakes and taking risks in math as a child, which is ironic given that math becomes Julie's area of special interest and expertise throughout her career as an educator.

> *If you are always doing things you know you can do, you're never going to get very far. You're going to keep doing the same things and you're going to make little progress. But if you try things you're not so sure of, you'll make mistakes and you'll learn from your mistakes and move ahead. So, I think that's real important for the child to know that if they make a mistake it doesn't mean they're stupid or whatever, it just means that you're learning when you make a mistake. You're going to find out why you made that mistake and you're going to go ahead, hopefully. So it's important for the child to feel comfortable, to feel okay to make a mistake, and that's all involved in learning. Because I remember when I was little that making mistakes was real tragic (laughs). I always felt, you know, really badly if I did something wrong or I wasn't very good in math and I always felt I didn't want to take risks in math. I hated going up to the board to answer problems and things and I don't want kids to feel that way. I don't think it's necessary for kids to feel that afraid of being wrong and taking a risk.*

Julie's initial understanding is that teaching is mostly showing and telling. For example, she says she would teach about sentences by telling her students where to put a capital and a period, showing them examples, and explaining that this is one of our rules for communication in reading. Although she says the teacher is more like a guide than a fountain of knowledge, what she describes in her interview is mainly showing and telling with little guiding. However, Julie also says that the teaching process is a combination of the teacher imparting information and letting the children do things to learn. This combination hints that Julie may be open to allowing children to do more exploration and experimentation, which would be consistent with a constructivist view of learning, in contrast to the more behaviorist and teacher-directed teaching style she talks about throughout most of her first interview.

> *I think the teacher is more of a guide than a fountain of knowledge. I think the teacher is someone there who offers materials and the environment for the learning to take place. And it's a combination of both sharing knowledge, specific facts and things like that, but also setting the groundwork and making the environment there for the child. So the teacher sort of manages the room and decides what the different activities are going to be and . . . what areas of the curriculum the kids are going to be working on, and shares knowledge. And, then it's also the children, they're doing, the children are experiencing different things, and that leads to learning. So the teacher is doing two different sorts of things, I guess, imparting knowledge and then also letting the children do things to learn.*

Perhaps Julie's belief that people are different and learn in different ways, which she describes next, helps her begin to think about including guided exploration rather than teaching as only showing and telling.

> *Children have different ways of learning. One child may be able to sit really still and listen to the teacher lecture and tell them about this and that. And that might be a good way for that child to learn, but another child might not be able to sit so still and they might need to get their hands on different things to learn and to experience different things to learn. So I think it's important to cover different learning needs and to be able to share knowledge and facts, but then also let children do things to learn. I think not just because of the different learning styles but for a well rounded experience. I think people need to not only take in facts but also to be able to do things, to be able to manipulate things . . . so there's a combination that's necessary.*

Julie goes on to say, "*I think it's just that some people have a different brain. People just have their individual differences that account for why some people learn one way and other people learn another way. I think that's just the way it is.*" This comment expresses a rather limited understanding of the connection between teaching and learning and harkens back to her belief that ability is fixed. So, at Time 1, Julie's understanding about teaching and learning is more consistent with behaviorist than constructivist views.

JULIE'S 1987 INTERVIEW (TIME 2)

Julie's second interview at the end of her teacher preparation program at UC–Berkeley shows a lot of growth in her thinking about pedagogy, particularly in the area of development. Her thinking about learning and teaching also developed over this 2-year period, although there is still a mix of everyday behaviorist beliefs that teaching is telling and learning is practicing, with some new understandings expressed that teaching includes providing hands-on experiences so that students can learn by exploring. Some of the main themes that emerge in this interview include the importance of the teacher modeling along with the teacher acting as a facilitator.

Julie's understanding of how children's lives outside of school can influence their behavior in school broadens at Time 2, based on both direct experiences with children and learning from the master teachers in whose classrooms she worked throughout her teacher education program at UC–Berkeley. Her deepening declarative knowledge about factors that impact children's development and the developmental process seems to have been acquired in her teacher education courses and field experiences, although her ability to apply this knowledge appears limited.

Julie's understanding of factors that affect children's behavior at Time 2 still includes the role of peers, but she also expresses a new awareness of the influence of the family and home environment. At Time 1, Julie thinks that only internal factors influence children's behaviors, including their personalities, level of independence, and feelings. However, after 2 years of coursework and five field experiences, she now sees experiences such as divorce, a death in the family, or children going back and forth between two parents as factors that impact children's behavior. For example, she says that if something is going on at home, it usually correlates directly with changes in behavior at school:

> I think that whatever's going on at home affects what they bring to school. I just think there's a real direct correlation. I've seen in my student teaching placement right now that I just finished, the master teacher . . . tells me it never fails that whenever there's a change at school in behavior or work or something, she'll write a note to the parents and say, "Is there something going on at home?" and they almost always say, "Yes, their grandmother just died, or their pet just died, or we're getting a divorce or something." There's always a connection. . . .

Julie's awareness of factors that affect behavior is apparently influenced by her experiences in schools, both indirectly by her learning from what her cooperating teachers tells her and directly from her own observations of and interactions with students. For example, in response to questions about how she knows what and how to teach at Time 2, Julie talks about how she observes behaviors to help her know how to respond to children.

> I don't think you know that right away. I think that is something that comes with a little bit of experience with the child, with you spending time, you looking at the child's work. It's hard to know. It's not hard to know, it's something that comes just sort of intuitively, I think. I don't think there's any formula or anything . . . and it might be trial and error

sometimes too. . . . You can get clues from just watching the child, and also from talking to the child about what you're seeing and what you'd like to see, and then read what their response is to gauge whether or not you should push, or expect what you're getting.

Julie's understanding of factors that influence development and how these factors operate also changed during her 2 years in the DTE program, which is not surprising given the focus of the program's philosophy on teaching about children's development in the cognitive and social domains. Although her ability to apply this knowledge to her teaching is not as well developed, her declarative knowledge at Time 2 includes understanding that children's independence, ability to understand language, sensitivity to and awareness of their peers, and cognitive skills all develop as they move from being concrete to more abstract thinkers. Furthermore, Julie also understands that there is a range in development in a given grade level or age group.

Probably there's always a range of kids. In that age level there are children who are still functioning, maybe not yet concrete, where they don't understand unless you really show them something. Or like in math, they might not understand the concepts unless they're right there, moving beans and things around. And then there're other kids who are more developed and they're moving out of—and they're ready for abstract information. So you're dealing with a wide range of cognitive development in there. There're kids who are at one stage and then other kids at another stage, but they're all in the same age group—a lot of transitions too.

Julie's understanding of how children develop, however, is still concrete at this time, as can be seen here in her somewhat circular attempt to explain how children become more independent between second and fourth grade.

Because they've just developed the capacity to understand things on a different level, rather than just the level of seeing things, which is more concrete, they're now into thinking about things, thinking about their own thoughts and feelings, which they don't do when they're five or six years old. It's come through just experiencing the world around them and relationships with other people and just developing those thinking processes, through the same things, through experience and being with other people and all of that.

Although Julie has an adequate understanding of factors that affect development and a less sophisticated understanding of how development occurs, she appears to be figuring out how children's development impacts learning and what the learning process is like. Her thinking about learning at Time 2 still contains a mix of behaviorist and constructivist notions, although more often than not her responses to the interview questions show a developing understanding of learning from a constructivist perspective.

For example, most of the time Julie appears to believe that learning comes from allowing students to explore and manipulate their environment and to interact socially, which is consistent with what she was taught in the DTE program.

> *I think experiences where children have the opportunity to do things, where they have the opportunity to move things around and feel things and touch things and see things, that's where a lot of learning occurs. Opportunities where children can ask questions and feel comfortable talking to their neighbors. When kids can interact with each other about what's going on, they're going to get information from each other, because the teacher isn't on their level. The teacher, we are adults and it's hard to get back to a 7-year old brain or a 10-year old brain. I think kids can learn a lot from each other, from listening to each other's responses or reactions to what they're doing. So that those are good learning opportunities.*

> *I think when you're doing something, you're going to find it works or it doesn't work, and you have to figure out how to make it work or what to do. If you're doing it, then you're in control, and you're putting together, you're making connections in your brain. You're saying, "Oh, this does this and this does that," rather than if someone was just telling you something about something, then you don't have to interact with it and you don't know for sure if you really understand it until you have to move it around or work with whatever it is. . . .*

> *I think that when you ask a question about something, it causes you to take in the infor-mation. It just promotes a different level of thinking. If you're asking a question about something, then there's something in there that's puzzling you and you're interacting with whatever information it is. . . .*

Several times during the interview, however, Julie seems to cling to ear-lier thinking that learning comes from practicing and that the teacher needs to show and model, which reflects remnants of earlier behaviorist be-liefs. This seems to occur more often when Julie talks about the social do-main rather than the cognitive domain. In this example, Julie is talking about how children learn to be respectful of authority—a social issue. Here she still emphasizes that teaching is showing and telling kids that they should respect authority figures.

> *They have to be respecting whoever's the authority in charge or things don't work out. You help kids learn that by showing them. You're explaining to them why it's important and you can't be part of the group until you can behave this way. I think kids need to feel respected themselves before they're going to respect you as an adult, you need to show them respect in turn. You yourself show respect to other adults. . . . So just modeling and explaining to kids the benefits of respecting authority.*

Nevertheless, at this time, Julie has a good understanding of many fac-tors that affect the learning process. For example, she seems to understand

the abstract nature or complexity of what is to be learned. She also understands that learning should be connected to something personal or made
more concrete in some ways, and that children's varying learning styles influence how they learn. These understandings should help her adapt her
teaching to meet individual student needs in the classroom. In addition,
when asked about whether there is a certain sequence or order for the ways
things should be taught, Julie's response at Time 2 indicates a good understanding of how she might approach teaching in a way that is consistent
with constructivist theories of how people learn:

> *I think there's a certain sequence for learning, in that you need to start out by making*
> *some sort of connection to whatever you're going to be teaching to what the kids know.*
> *This isn't just something you pulled down from the sky and that this fits over here or this*
> *relates to what you're learning. Sort of help them organize what they're learning, why*
> *they're learning it. Then there needs to be some sort of activity. They need to interact with*
> *whatever it is that's being learned. And there needs to be afterwards a time for them to*
> *talk about what it is, to share whatever it was that they learned or what they experienced*
> *when they were doing that. And then a time for them to use it on their own somehow so*
> *that it becomes something they can use and not just an isolated exercise, but then some-*
> *thing that they see that they need to use. And that that's what they need for learning, to*
> *be able to learn something.*

When talking about the role of the teacher, at Time 2 Julie says that the
teacher should create an environment for learning and be a guide, although she still believes there is time for telling and setting the attitude and
tone for the class through modeling.

> *I think the teacher should be more of a guide than somebody who is pouring knowledge*
> *into their heads, but somebody who is creating the environment and setting the attitudes*
> *and the tones in the classroom for learning, and providing the materials and organiza-*
> *tion that enable the kids to learn by doing and learn by experiencing different things that*
> *the teacher has provided. Rather than the teacher telling all the information, the teacher*
> *is the person who creates the environment for the learning. Sometimes, there are times for*
> *telling, but I think that learning is a lot more than just listening and taking in from*
> *what the teacher says. Learning is doing things and experiencing things and making*
> *sense of what's there, rather than being told that this is what you're seeing and this is*
> *what you should be learning. I hope that I can do that.*

However, although Julie says that teaching is not just telling, she apparently has not found a replacement in her practice. For example, in the following response to a question about how she would teach the concept of a
sentence, she talks about teaching as mostly "*just talking about it*" and hoping the kids will understand what sentences represent and how they are
formed.

> *If I were working with third graders, I would probably have them write something. We would write a story or we would have some sort of writing that they'd done. Everybody would look at their own writing and we would just talk about how people write and that they need to understand their own writing and to understand each other's writing. And maybe have the kids share some of their writing with someone else, and see if there were any difficulties in understanding their writing, and talk about what made that difficult to understand. Maybe there was a period missing and you didn't know that the sentence ended, and we would just talk about why we need capital letters and periods and things like that, that we need those so that we can communicate to other people our ideas. We would just talk about what they were for. Let's see, is there another way? We would talk about it and then do it. After we'd talked about it, then they would take their own writing and go through it and make sure that they all had capitals and look to see if they had periods. How else could we do that? We'd just talk about what makes a sentence. We could somehow set up a situation where they had to explain something or write something to somebody and talk about how a sentence is an idea, then just talk about what the conventions are that we use for sentences. That's about it.*

This excerpt and the next example demonstrate Julie's residual thinking that teaching is mostly showing, telling, modeling, and reinforcing, which are ways she would teach the concept of a sentence and also how she believes you become an independent thinker.

> *You explain to them that we need to have these things so that we can understand what we're trying to communicate to each other. Just showing them this is a period and this is a capital letter. Now go back and look through your writing and change what you've done. I think the sixth graders understand that too, and that supplying a reason for that and a need for that would make sense to them.*

> *I think you need to give them the environment and show them, you need to be a model. You need to show them how to . . . what thinking is. How can I explain it? Rather than just to follow along, but to stop and think about what they're doing and be able to formulate questions about what it is, be able to summarize what it is that they're doing, and to, obviously, to ask questions, just to have their own understanding, to feel that it's okay whatever they're thinking or doing is just as valid and acceptable as what anybody else is doing.*

So Julie appears to be in transition and poised to continue developing her thinking about learning and pedagogy as she gets ready to take her first full-time teaching position. At the time of this interview, which took place just before her graduation from the DTE program, Julie's thinking about the learning process and factors that affect learning includes experiencing, doing, practicing, and exploring. Her thinking about teaching includes a mix of behaviorist and constructivist views about the teaching process. Given the apparent mix of theoretical beliefs in Julie's thinking at this time, it will be quite interesting to see how this plays out as she begins teaching her own classes. A blend of behaviorist and constructivist thinking is not unusual to see in beginning teachers; based on my personal experience, teachers often think about teaching math or reading from a constructivist perspective, but think about classroom management or handling discipline problems from a behaviorist perspective. Until these conflicting notions are coordinated and resolved, however, there is often confusion in classrooms where students receive mixed messages about when they can socialize and work with a partner, for example, and when they are supposed to work independently and quietly.

At Time 2, one of Julie's strengths is her understanding of how she will go about figuring out what and how to teach. She also displays confidence in her ability to evaluate and change what she is doing when needed. Julie's self-knowledge and self-confidence should serve her well as a beginning teacher who is still learning to teach, but who is going to be on her own making decisions about her own classroom. As far as knowing what kinds of students she is working with, Julie says she will observe her students' work, talk to parents, and also talk to previous teachers.

I think there are several different ways. One way is just to make it a point to make a little conversation with kids. Like pick a few kids a day that you're going to focus on, like during recess or clean up time, or just during some time when you're not interacting with everybody in the whole class. Just make some conversation with that child and try to find out what they're like, who they are, what they like to do, who lives at home, those kind of things, so there's an informal time that you get to know a child. Then, through their work—if you have a writing assignment, I might ask the children to tell me about themselves or something. Or just to look at their work and see what kind of work they're doing, I think that tells you something about the child, what kind of math or whatever their abilities are on an academic level. . . . Talking to their parents, too. If you have a question about something, calling up their parents to find out is a great source. Talking to previous teachers, if you're concerned about the way someone is behaving or something like that, you could find out who had the child last year and say, "What was it like with this child in third grade or whatever?" in order to find out their previous history in school.

As far as her strength in finding answers to her questions and her confidence in her ability to self-evaluate and make adjustments, Julie concludes her interview at Time 2 with these comments, which indicate a strong sense of personal self-efficacy:

I think my ability to work well with other teachers and other adults in administration—I think that's a resource that I feel that I have. Knowing where to get information and get materials and get help. Understanding the different services in the school, that's a resource. Knowing about different places in the community to get information and materials and resources, is a resource for teaching. . . . Probably the ability to evaluate what's going on in my classroom, and to evaluate myself, how I'm feeling about what's going on and the ability to analyze. If the kids weren't responding to this, could it be that I didn't present it in the right way, or they're not ready for it? Just the ability to analyze the learning situations and what I'm doing, and the ability to look at myself and see what I might change, and all that kind of thing—through just thinking about what's going on in the classroom, observing things in the classroom.

I think I know a lot more about what teaching is all about, and that it's more than just going into the classroom and teaching from the materials that I'm given. . . . But I feel like I have a real basis of understanding what it is that kids learn and why they learn and how they learn and what to do to encourage their learning. So I feel a lot more confident about understanding the curriculum and why we do certain things and what to do if certain things aren't happening and how to look at things that kids are doing, how to evaluate kids. I think those are things that I wasn't aware of before I came in. . . . But now I feel that I've got all the knowledge and abilities, and now I just need to put them to use in a classroom, to feel, "Yes, I am a teacher now," and all that. So I feel like I've reached that point. . . . Now all I need is the classroom experience on my own. . . .

Nevertheless, Julie is also realistic and quite aware of things she thinks could be obstacles in accomplishing what she wants to as a teacher. In fact, what Julie says here seems to foreshadow her future:

I think it will depend maybe on the school environment that I become a teacher in. If the administration or the parents didn't want me to spend a lot of time on certain things that I felt were important, that would be an obstacle. I would feel like I wasn't able to do what I wanted to do. Unsupportive parents or administration would be an obstacle. It will depend on the kind of kids maybe that I have. If there's some child in my class who disrupts everything and that I can't handle, then that would be an obstacle to my goals as a teacher. Then I would have to do something about changing the way I was treating that kid or finding another place for that student. Well, if I got in an environment where I didn't feel confident in doing what I wanted to do, or if I felt unsure or something like that, then that might be an obstacle for me. I would have to be in a place where I felt comfortable doing what I was doing, and felt confident. I would have to feel good about everything, otherwise that would be a problem.

JULIE'S 1990 INTERVIEW AND AN OBSERVATION (TIME 3)

Given this background information about the development of Julie's pedagogical understandings during her 2 years in the DTE program, let us now turn the clock ahead nearly 3 years to glimpse Julie's classroom during the spring of 1990, near the end of her third year of teaching in the San Francisco Bay Area in Northern California.

East Bay Elementary School (a pseudonym) is a relatively small neighborhood school located near Berkeley, California, in a lovely, tree-filled area at the foot of the East Bay hills that form part of the Coastal Range. If you continue driving east from East Bay School up into what is known locally as the Berkeley Hills, you eventually enter Tilden East Bay Regional Park. Looking west from this vantage point, you can view San Francisco Bay with Alcatraz and the Golden Gate Bridge in the middle of your view, Angel Island on the right, and the Bay Bridge that connects San Francisco and Oakland to your left.

Today, East Bay Elementary School houses about 460 kindergarten through 5th-grade students. There are 20 regular classroom teachers and a dozen specialists on the staff. As with all California schools, the class sizes in K to 3rd grade have been reduced to 20, and the 4th- and 5th-grade classes have about 27 to 28 students in each room. Because of this state-mandated reduction in class size, there are now several trailers on the school property serving as classrooms. Half the school's library is converted into a classroom as well. However, when Julie taught at East Bay School between 1987 and 1993, there were no trailers and her classes always had 28 to 30 students.

The teachers at East Bay School have an average of 14 years of experience. Every teacher at East Bay is fully credentialed, and district salaries range from $30,500 for beginning teachers to $60,000 for the highest paid teachers. East Bay School is part of a small, unified school district, which has approximately 3,000 students attending three K–5 schools, one middle school, one comprehensive high school, and one alternative continuation high school. This district also has an adult school and a children's center.

East Bay School draws from a stable neighborhood of upper middle-class families where 90% of the parents have completed college or graduate school, as well as from married student housing that serves the UC–Berkeley campus. The price range of the homes in the neighborhood averages $350,000, which is typical for most real estate in this part of northern California. The demographics of the school's population include students who are White (55%), Asian (18%), Hispanic (12%), Black (5%), or other ethnic origins (8%). Only 12% of the students at East Bay are on free or reduced lunch, and only 6% of the students do not yet speak English fluently. This population is atypical for most California schools, which are usually much more ethnically, linguistically, and economically diverse.

East Bay is only slightly more diverse today than when Julie taught there. In fact, if Julie visited East Bay School today, it would look and feel much the way it did when she taught there during one of her five student teaching placements and also for 5 years as a fully licensed teacher—2 years as a second-grade teacher and 3 years as a third-grade teacher. Although the administration is different than when Julie began there in 1987, many of the same teachers are still there today. Perhaps the only real difference Julie might see would be a few trailers and primary grade classes of only 20 students.

The only time I observed Julie was in early March 1990, when I spent two full mornings observing in her third-grade classroom. I observed her teaching reading, language arts, and math lessons all morning on both days. Over a decade later, rereading my notes and listening to my tapes brings back vivid images of those visits, which included our efforts to complete the clinical interview questions in the hour before school started on those 2 days. It seemed hectic, which is how both Julie and I both remember those times.

OBSERVATION AT TIME 3 IN 1990

When the first bell rang at 8:30 a.m., Julie stood at the door and greeted each one of the 8- and 9-year-olds who entered the room. There was a lot of chatter as the early group came in because Julie had moved all their seats around and no one knew where to sit. They were also excited about a play they were practicing, and several students had brought in props and parts of their costumes.

These students, called the *Early Birds*, were a group of 11 girls and 4 boys on an 8:30 to 2:30 schedule, as opposed to the 9:30 to 3:30 schedule the *Late Birds* kept. Most teachers grouped their students by reading ability so that the Early Bird and Late Bird groups would be more homogeneous with regard to their instructional level in reading. Julie chose not to do this kind of ability grouping and instead let the parents decide on a preferred schedule for their child. This split schedule was common at the time in area schools because it allowed teachers to teach smaller numbers of students for at least 1 hour a day. Today, because the state of California has mandated smaller class sizes for the primary grades, this Early Bird/Late Bird system has been abandoned.

Many of the classrooms at East Bay School are in the shape of a pentagon. As I looked around the room, I noted that the students' flat-topped desks were arranged in five groups of six in an area toward the front of the room, where Julie had positioned an overhead projector, a chalkboard, and a large brown chair. Around the edges of the room, there were several open bookshelves with lots of math manipulatives, including geoboards, centimeter cubes, tiles, unifix cubes, 100's boards, Cuisenaire rods, pattern blocks, beans and other counters, as well as several commercial math games in boxes. There were also class sets of several children's trade books on shelves, including *The Secret Garden, The Trumpet and the Swan, Paddington Bear, Pinocchio, Greek Myths*, and *Aesop's Fables*. There was also a class set of *Junior Great Books* for third graders. Julie told me she had taken a special class about ways to use *Junior Great Books*. Scanning the room, there was a set of encyclopedias and a class set of dictionaries, a record player and a tape recorder, two large work tables in different corners at the back of the room, and two sets of cubbies for the students' backpacks and lunches near one door to the classroom. There were chalkboards at the front and back of the room, smallish windows on opposite sides of the room, and several bulletin boards. Most of the light in the room came from high windows on two sides of the room. The bulletin boards displayed samples of students' writing, a list of the class rules, a poster of the U.S. presidents, and another poster about famous Black Americans. On another wall, Julie had placed a world map and *Good Homework* board that displayed math homework completed during a unit on perimeter and area. Another bulletin board in the back of the room by the door was labeled *Wishes for 1990*, with students' written wishes posted on it.

As the students began to find their desks, Julie reminded them to use their clothespins to mark attendance and make their choice for hot lunch. As the second bell rang at 8:35, Julie directed the students to "Meet me at the brown chair." As she moved toward the front of the room, Julie clapped a pattern to get attention and praised individual students who were getting settled on the floor by her brown chair. When everyone was settled, Julie led a discussion about the new seating arrangements, told them they could not change seats for a couple of days, and said they would have to talk with her privately if they wanted to move. Julie then moved on to discuss plans for the day, which included practicing their plays in groups and finishing their scenery. The students brought up problems they were having in their groups, and Julie *lectured* them about following along and using their scripts so they would know when it was their turn. However, her stern tone changed quickly as she asked them questions including, "Does anyone have any ideas or any solutions?" and "What can you do to help?" The class spent the next 15 minutes discussing possible solutions to the problems they were having in their play groups.

At 8:55, the students moved around the room gathering up their props and Julie handed out play scripts. One large group moved to rehearse just outside the classroom door. Julie circulated around the room answering questions from individuals in the other groups. Before agreeing to listen to one small group of girls present their play, Julie stuck her head out the door to check on the group rehearsing outside. She tried to quiet them down before coming back inside to monitor the rest of the class. Following their performance, Julie complimented this group of all girls and discussed their props with them before moving onto another group that was practicing their parts and going through their script for a second time.

After about 20 minutes, a few members of the outside group came back in the room rather noisily and the group Julie had first listened to began to act a bit silly. Julie ignored them as she continued to listen to another group practicing their lines. Some students complained to Julie about the behavior of the outside group. They told Julie that some group members were not cooperating, and Julie went back outside to talk with them. Another 15 minutes passed noisily before it was time for recess.

As the students cleared the room, Julie and I talked a little bit about the resources she has available for teaching math and reading. She told me she uses three resources for math: *Family Math* from the Lawrence Hall of Science, Kathy Richardson's *Number Concepts*, and Marilyn Burns' *Math Solutions*. She also told me that her school district guidelines for math are very loose and that she plans her math lessons based on how she feels the students are doing with the concepts she is teaching. She is not sure how much time she should spend on each topic. The plays, she tells me, came about spontaneously based on some filmstrips about Chinese New Year that she showed them earlier. The children wrote their own scripts and chose their own groups and the parts they wanted.

When the recess bell rang at 9:40, the entire class of 30 students entered the room. There are now 17 girls and 13 boys, and the room vibrated with their energy. The Late Birds also moved their clothespins to mark their attendance and make their lunch choices. Once again, there is a lot of noise as they find their new seats. It takes about 10 minutes for everyone to get settled, and Julie has to ask several times, "Let's see who is ready to listen."

Penmanship is the next order of business. Julie asks, "Does anybody know what letter we're on?" The letter for today is "Y," and Julie shows them on the chalkboard how to form a cursive Y in both upper- and lowercase. Before these third graders begin practicing their cursive letter Ys, Julie asks them, "What should you do with finished papers?" and "What should you do after you are done with your handwriting?"

Julie then remembers that she has some new books to show them, so she postpones their handwriting practice to do this and reads riddles from one of the books. She then assigns new helpers for the week and asks them to pass out paper so that everyone can get started on their cursive writing practice. By 10:00 a.m., the students are working quietly on their handwriting as Julie tunes in a classical music station on the radio in the front of the room. Handwriting appears to be a 2-day process. They spend just 5 minutes today practicing the new letter and will spend time another day writing sentences that use the new letter they are practicing.

At 10:05, Julie asks the students to put their math homework on top of their desks, and the next hour is spent correcting their math homework and playing a math game that requires them to use strategy and perform mental math computations in their heads.

* * *

When I interviewed Julie for the third time in 1990, she was in the middle of her third year of teaching full time at East Bay School. She talked about how she first taught second grade, but then requested a move to third grade because she felt it would be a better fit for her interests and talents.

Well, for my first year it was pretty horrible in the beginning and I just had a really rough class. I stepped into a classroom that was supposed to be, well the teacher who was there had all these requests . . . and I had a lot of high-powered parents. So I felt a lot of pressure in a lot of different areas, and I had some difficult kids. So, that was rough my first year. And then my second year was easier, but not a whole lot easier, and I was just thinking, "What is it about this?" And I would go and talk to another teacher all the time and just complain about everything. And she said, "I think you should try third grade. You should teach third grade." And then another teacher took a leave, so there was a third-grade opening. And I went and told the principal that I would like to try third grade and he asked, "Why?" And I said, "Well, I just feel like, it seems like at the end of the year the kids are ready to go, they seem to fit better with the things that I want to do with them." Maybe to me that meant that third grade might really be a good place for me. So he said, "Okay," and it does feel like it fits better.

JULIE'S INTERVIEW IN 1990

Based on her interview and observation during her third year in the classroom, Julie appears to be struggling to figure out classroom management and seems unsure of how to teach her third graders. She is beginning to find ways to improve her classroom management, but she is concerned that she is not communicating well with all the students in her class. She seems to understand many of the factors that impact children's behavior and development, but seems unsure of how to apply these consistently in her classroom. These things appear frustrating to Julie, and she says that she might not stay in the classroom, although she wants to stay in the field of education. Perhaps Julie's need for the children to like her and her prior belief that they will treat her with respect if she models respect are unrealistic in a classroom with 30 students, but they are consistent with her continued desire to build children's self-esteem.

At Time 3, Julie seems to have a good grasp of factors that impact children's development and of how the developmental process works, but she seems less able to apply her developing understandings consistently to her practices. This is a good example of how teachers' thoughts and actions are not always in sync and how what teachers know intellectually is not always applied consistently in the classroom. Perhaps the mix of behaviorist and constructivist beliefs about learning and teaching that is still apparent in Julie's thinking at this time makes it difficult for her to teach in a manner consistent with her beliefs.

Among factors that affect children's behavior, Julie mentions age and the teacher's comfort level with a particular age group. She also talks about the curriculum for that age group and the fact the she particularly enjoys the openness and honesty of her third graders. She especially likes the girls at this grade and feels that she has difficulty communicating with the boys. She is pleased that her students still like the teacher and want her approval.

I like the fact that they're honest about things and about their feelings. They're real straightforward. Sometimes they hurt each other's feelings but they're just so open and honest. They still really like the teacher! They really want your approval, which works for me in a way for management. But I just like the little girls that are affectionate and come to you and give you a hug . . . I don't know why but it seems like the boys are harder to, when you're talking about discipline or management or something you're trying to get them to do, I feel like it's harder to get them to do it. I never have a feeling that they know what I want them to do or that they understand why I want them to do something. . . .

Interestingly, Julie is the only one of the four teachers in this study to mention any classroom management problems during any of the interviews. She is also the only one who responds to any of the interview questions in ways that equate children's behavior with discipline and management issues rather than with describing characteristics of children at various ages. Classroom management seems to be a struggle for Julie, although during her third year of teaching she feels that holding weekly class meetings where the children can discuss behavior problems is paying off in improved behavior.

We've done something from the beginning of the year called class meetings on Wednesdays. And we have this thing we call the agenda and the kids can write down if they're having problems with somebody. We always open the meeting, everybody sits in a circle, and we open the meeting with giving one another compliments and then discussing the problems. I hear some of the kids sometimes talking about things we've talked about, or saying things to each other like, "Is that something you should write on the agenda?" I don't know, they seem like they're handling their problems better and not relying on me. I don't know if it's because of the agenda, or because they can just write things down on the agenda and then it doesn't matter, or if they're really internalizing some of the things we've talked about in the meetings.

From the first interview, it has been important to Julie that her students like her and that she have an influence on children's behavior. Hence, it is apparently frustrating to her to be struggling with classroom management and having trouble communicating with the boys in her classroom. Julie feels that if she treats students with respect and models good behaviors, they will internalize these things and respect her in return. However, she still believes that what is learned at home also influences children's behaviors in school.

I think in treating them fairly and treating them with respect you get that in return, I hope. That's the way I look at it—is if I treat them fairly and respectfully, they'll treat me that way. Part of it happens earlier at home I hope, and the other part is reflective of how I treat them.

Aside from understanding at Time 3 that children's cognitive skills and abilities continue to develop, Julie now understands that children's social skills and abilities develop as well. Some factors she mentions as developing in the social arena include children's awareness of what is socially appropriate, awareness of their own feelings and those of others, their self-consciousness, and some ability to self-monitor. Her thinking at this time is that children's intellectual and moral sides develop as they become less concrete in their thinking, and she alludes here to what she learned in the DTE program about Kohlberg's theory of moral development:

> *There's the intellectual and moral developmental differences too. . . . The 2nd and 3rd graders are more concrete in their understanding of things. The 5th and 6th graders are becoming more formal operational. . . . They can go beyond physical understanding of things and can abstract ideas or understand things that they don't have to have a picture of or touch something. They can think of three or four things at once that interact with other things. They can describe something, whereas the 2nd and 3rd graders need to see physical models or have experiences that are real to them. . . . We were reading this weekly newspaper and it had a letter to Dear Kitty about something that happened at school . . . about cheating and we were talking about why that wouldn't be a good idea. And this one child came up with the response that you wouldn't want the teacher to catch you. I was thinking about their moral understanding of things—you do things to avoid punishment or avoid authority or being in trouble. Whereas, I think 5th and 6th graders think that doesn't affect them. They don't think of things that way.*

However, when I asked how children make that shift in their thinking, Julie gave the following explanation, which is based on social learning theory, rather than relying on her knowledge of Kohlberg or Piaget's theories of development in the moral domain.

> *I think it's a combination of things. Probably the environment, your family, . . . role models, your conscience—whatever conscience is all about. . . . Who knows how that is developed—through experiences.*

Julie's understanding of the learning process developed from being fairly behavioristic at Time 1 to being a mix of behaviorist and constructivist beliefs at Time 2. Now at Time 3, she is more consistent in her constructivist beliefs about how children learn, although there are still some occasions in her interview where she says that learning means practicing and the teacher's role is mainly to show, tell, and model. However, this happens mainly when she is talking about teaching behaviors in the affective and social domains, rather than when she is talking about teaching cognitive skills, concepts, and content material. Julie also believes that children like making things and creating products, which in turn motivates them to learn, which is consistent with a global understanding of constructivist theories of learning.

*I think when kids have to make something or construct something . . . when they actu-
ally get involved in something. And it's easier for me to know where they are with understanding something. . . . So, I think if kids actually have to do something or produce
something, then I think that experience really becomes theirs. They own whatever it is
and they seem to enjoy things better too, when they make something or work with a group
and have a product. That's just more engaging and more fun. . . .*

*As a teacher we need to set things up so that they learn. . . . For example, every month in
my classroom there's an independent project that the kids do at home. It usually involves
making something, creating a model of a home or a habitat, or doing a little science experiment, or something. When I first started . . . I would remind the kids every week,
"OK, you should be just starting on your project. You should have collected all the materials. Okay, this week you should be halfway through your project. OK, now stop working on your project and put it away for a few days and then come back to it and think
about it and see what you need to change." So I was actually helping them along with
each step and showing them how to manage it in increments, teaching them how to approach it slowly, and helping them be successful in finishing it. So, I think that's one
way—to actually coach them along something. I think as a teacher you're setting things
up so the kids, so they can be successful and manage. . . .*

*I don't always give the kids one way to do something, to do an assignment. I give them
options about using different materials. They can always choose their own topic on
something, for writing something. Whenever there's an opportunity for choice, I try to
give the kids a choice. If they have their own ideas, they can always do their own ideas
rather than the one I present.*

So at Time 3, the learning process for Julie includes doing, making, and
exploring things independently or in a group; it also includes making
choices and being coached and reminded by the teacher so that the learning experience is a successful one.

Along with Julie's more constructivist understanding of the learning
process, she also shows a good grasp of many factors that affect learning,
such as children's developmental differences, various learning styles, and
interest in what is to be learned. She understands that how concrete something is and how connected it is to the learner will impact learning. She recognizes individual differences in children, and she seems to believe that
certain abilities are influenced by their experiences or the way their brains
are organized.

*I don't know if it's just with kids this age but sometimes it just seems like there's a wide
range of abilities. We've got someone that might take an hour to do half a page of some
written work and then somebody else is done in about ten or fifteen minutes.*

*I think people are either good spellers or they're not. . . . Something in the brain, I don't
know. Part of me wonders if it's kids who read a lot, kids who are very literate and have
read a lot. But there are people who are doing wonderful successful things but can't spell
at all. So I don't think it has anything to do with IQ. It's really concerned with organi-*

zation or some functioning in your brain. . . . So it really depends on the subject and maybe what kind of a learner you are. . . .

Julie is against grouping children by ability, which is something she acts on by not grouping her Early Bird and Late Bird students. Instead, Julie's groups are heterogeneous with regard to ability levels and formed by parental preferences for different schedules. Julie feels grouping children by ability is not good for their learning because it is not good for their self-esteem, which is something she still values as highly at Time 3 as she did in earlier interviews.

Ability. The one thing I really don't like about it is predisposing kids to feeling like I'm a great reader or I'm horrible in math. So I don't like that because I think it has long-lasting effects that aren't true and appropriate, especially for kids who are younger because of developmental differences. I wouldn't want to have a child who's not catching on to reading think that they're a horrible reader because I've seen lots of kids between second and third grade, their reading clicks. . . . So for that reason I think it would be inappropriate to group kids by ability and more damaging than anything else because they are labeled as something and they might not be.

Julie's understanding of the teacher's role in the learning process at Time 3 includes building children's self-esteem as it did at Times 1 and 2.

One of the things I really feel important is just helping kids feel positive about learning, So, I think that's really one on my most important jobs . . . any one thing I teach them isn't going to make or break their academic career. . . . Something I feel really good about is being able to help kids feel good about their accomplishments and what they can do and just to enjoy my class. . . .

In addition to having the students engaged in a lot of activity, Julie still believes that good pedagogy should include a lot of modeling and direct instruction by the teacher. In this example, Julie explains her thinking about what the teaching process is like as she talks about teaching writing and how she would teach the concept of a sentence to third graders and then to sixth graders. She says that students should do the writing first and then be shown what is correct and formally acceptable, thus putting activity before showing and telling.

I think it's important for them to just be able to write a lot and write and write and write. I think when they are beginning to learn how to write they shouldn't have a lot of interference with what they're writing. . . . And then gradually show them what is right, more and more and getting more formal about what you call certain things, putting more and more limits . . . on what they're writing.

Although Julie's description of how she teaches writing is reminiscent of her thinking at Time 2, she has broadened her pedagogical repertoire from *"just talking about it"* to include peer interaction and some coaching along with direct instruction.

> We would write a lot and listen to each other's writing because I think when kids hear what it sounds like then they recognize the problems. . . . So I think they need to write a lot and then hear their writing, what it sounds like. I think they need the interaction. I sit down with kids when they're done with something if they want to and we talk about editing . . . we read it and talk about it . . . we point out things that aren't right. . . . And then I actually have this little book that I dittoed off for the kids that talks about rules for writing. So, we not only do the editing, we talk about the rules for writing, and they can read one or two topics per page and there's an example and then they have to write their own example. So we formally talk about what sentences are too.

However, when I asked what she would do if a sixth grader still did not understand the concept of a sentence, Julie falls back on modeling, showing, and telling instead of more constructivist teaching practices, such as helping students figure out if their sentences make sense or allowing them to work with their peers. This indicates that she is still not completely consistent in her thinking from a constructivist perspective at this time.

> I would be worried about whether they have a learning problem, I think . . . I would do all the same things, but I think I would really work with that child specifically by modeling and showing and talking, maybe talking more formally about how a sentence needs a verb . . . and all the different parts that are necessary.

Julie also believes that it is the teacher's job to provide an environment for learning, ask good questions that advance students' learning, be flexible, and show students how they might find an answer when they do not know one. Julie wants to be the kind of teacher who does not feel like she has to have all the answers, which are actions more consistent with a constructivist perspective.

> To provide those experiences—to create those kinds of things . . . and questioning them. I know sometimes I feel real uncomfortable if I can't think of a good question to ask somebody who's doing something or if they seem to be finished. . . . It's like I want them to think about the next step . . . to get them thinking about something beyond, to stretch, or extend what ever the activity is. So, I think it's important for you to be questioning, and to provide opportunities for flexibility too. I think that's part of a good teacher's role too—is to be able to allow kids to do things that fit, not to be too rigid, . . . And I think it's great not to have all the answers, to show kids, "We'll let's go to the encyclopedia." So they can see that teachers aren't totally perfect and don't know everything and that there are tools for learning things—to show them the ways people learn.

Despite some inconsistency in her pedagogical thinking at Time 3, Julie understands how she knows what to teach. She is able to articulate that she has a variety of resources, such as her experience in the classroom over time, experiences in different grade levels, skill in observing and interacting with individuals, and input she solicits from parents to help her understand what and how to teach.

What they actually do in class and then judging from that . . . experience with kids and knowing what kind of a child might need to be pushed. And then talking with their parents. . . . Good observation and good listening just during regular activities . . . talking to kids. . . . Experience in the classroom definitely . . . and then also the things that I learned during DTE, different parts of the program, like the developmental theory, Piaget's theory . . . Things I've read and my own pulling together of the information and making sense of it. Things that I've learned, theories I've learned, and things that I've done in the classroom—it all fits together.

She also seems confident that she can make adjustments as needed in her teaching based on her good observation and listening skills:

When I'm actually teaching something, I respond to how they're reacting to what I'm saying. Like if I see a lot of confused faces or a lot of people aren't raising their hands, then that's feedback to me that whatever I'm saying isn't making sense or they're not ready for it. And then when they make comments, or the specific questions they ask are definitely feedback to what's going on. So questions, comments, if I walk around and overhear something. . . . I look at their papers and see what kinds of mistakes they're making, what kinds of answers they're giving, how thorough it is or can I get any clues from that about how they're thinking about what we're doing. Questions that they're asking . . . when they ask certain questions—that helps me understand their thinking . . . I think I'm a real reflective or introspective person so that's something that helps. Sometimes it hurts too, but it helps me process things and think about what's going on and how come that didn't work, what can I do next time. So having that inner dialogue with myself helps too. . . .

However, even with her increasing ability to think about and understand children's behavior and development, and her confidence in being able to assess her students' learning and make adjustments in her own teaching practices, Julie does not always feel successful. When I ask her what goals she has for herself at Time 3, Julie responds:

To feel successful and to feel like I know what I'm doing and be efficient at doing it, which I don't feel right now. I'm still, in the third year, trying to get things together and figure out how to teach writing and how to do this and how to do that. So, I guess feeling pretty much on top of things . . . I don't see myself always teaching in the classroom. I think I'd like to be involved in something that helps education in another way . . . maybe developing curriculum materials that I recognize as not being out there, or some-

thing like that. So maybe something a little bit beyond the classroom that I haven't al-
ready identified. But I don't think that I'll be forever teaching in the classroom.

Julie says she feels effective when the class is humming and everyone is involved and on task:

I just love it when they . . . remember something we talked about 2 or 3 days ago. That's
really exciting to me . . . And most of them are at that point where they're just drinking it
all in and they just love to learn and find out new things. It just feels so good when the
class is, you can just sort of sense this humming or whatever, where everybody is in-
volved. And it might be noisy but they're all excited and on task.

She also says that it still feels like she is on a roller coaster ride, which is
her metaphor for teaching at Time 3. She also feels like she has to be an actor.

Teaching has just been incredibly, I don't know what I ever thought it was going to be,
but it's more . . . I compare it to being on a roller coaster. You're like up in the air, then
you're down at the bottom, and you're up in the air. It's just so many different things. It
just pulls so much from you. You're like an actor. You have to be dramatic. You have to
be patient. . . . You're just so many different things, it's just mind boggling sometimes. I
guess I didn't realize that teaching was going to be such a varied, have such varied de-
mands, I guess.

JULIE'S INTERVIEW AT TIME 4 IN 1993

As it turned out, Julie stayed in the classroom 2 more years. She remained at
East Bay Elementary School until the end of 1992, when she resigned to do
some traveling and then find something else to do besides classroom teaching. When I interviewed Julie in May 1993, she was working as an editor for
a new math program for a large publishing company. More specifically, her
job was to look—from the perspective of a teacher—at the proposed first-
and second-grade curriculum, which would serve as a replacement for their
basal series and reflect the California Mathematics Frameworks to be
adopted in 1995. When I asked if she liked this position and thought she
would continue on, her response was positive.

Yeah, I think, . . . that's an opportunity that I can't pass up, you know. I can always go
back to teaching but I can't always, I'm not always going to find a job like this with this
kind of a program. . . . But I think it's heading in the right direction. And just the other
day one of the project managers said she'd made a decision that we're not going to teach
a standard algorithm for second graders, and that was great. Ever since I've been here
. . . they were talking about how they were going to do it, and it was kind of a battle be-
cause a couple of us editors . . . really know Piaget and are really developmental and we

were saying this isn't what we're used to, you know, we're not really sure about this. But they, the other people that were in charge weren't ready or willing to take risks.

When I ask Julie when she decided to take a break from teaching, she describes her feelings and thought process to me:

I would say probably off and on in my fifth year, probably the end of December or January. . . . I had these intense periods of frustration. It just seemed like I wasn't happy with the job I was doing. It felt like I was just kind of cruising. I had lost my enthusiasm. And I heard myself saying things to the kids that I . . . didn't want to be. I didn't like the way I sounded. And I just thought I've got to take a break. I had a couple kids that . . . took a lot of my energy, and . . . I would just get so mad at these kids and then, inside of myself I was just saying these horrible things and I thought, you know, this isn't right. I'm not having a good time right now, and they probably aren't either, so I should take a break.

It wasn't until like June that I actually officially asked for it, so I hadn't really made up my mind [about what I was going to do], so I almost wasn't thinking about it. But I think it was maybe a week before that that I'd gotten a letter from CMC [the California Math Council] about some job, there was also a letter from a big textbook publishing company [about a job there]. So, I thought, here are some math opportunities, because I've really been involved a lot in mathematics curriculum development. I really put a lot of emphasis on math. So, I applied for those jobs, but if I didn't get those I was going to go on a trip. I'd saved enough money and I was going to store all my stuff at a friend's house and pack up and leave. I didn't get the job right away. What I actually did, I went to Colorado for a couple weeks and just traveled.

Julie started working just 5 months before the Time 4 interview in spring of 1993. When I ask her if she is going to go back to teaching when her contract is up, she talks at length about her recent thoughts about returning to the classroom. During the course of the interview, she also talks about what she thinks about teaching children of different ages and why specializing in math appeals to her.

I still don't feel real ready to go back. I'm just going to kind of wait and see what happens. I think I will at some point, but I just don't feel that enthusiasm to go back. Maybe, working with this publisher, maybe I'll get really tired of sitting and imagining hypothetical situations and I'll want to, you know, get excited about curriculum and go back.

    I've been thinking more about how nice it would be to focus on one subject, and like the idea of going back to middle school, maybe, to, to really focus on fifth and sixth . . . I've thought about whether there were any kinds of jobs to just teach math or something. . . . For me, in the classroom, I never felt satisfied with the balance. I felt like I was doing really well in some areas and just sort of getting by [in others]. . . .

    Well, I mentioned, you know, thinking about working with middle school kids, so that's something I'm thinking about now. I taught second and third grade and I was re-

ally happy when I made my move from second up to third because I just felt like finally I can talk a little bit longer and they can sit a little bit longer, and they're not, you know, crying on my shirt all the time about who hit who. So, I really enjoyed the third graders. But I have a feeling that, that my style might be more appropriate for ten or older, you know, because I feel like I really want to engage in a lot of discourse . . . because then they are able to engage in more discourse. Maybe their, their developmental level is in formal operations instead of pre-operations or concrete operations. They're able to start to think, you know, a lot of metacognition, think about their thinking . . . but I think they are a little bit easier to relate to. You can, you can share more of your adult feelings. . . .

I don't know. I haven't thought about specific things. I think I would be a different person. And probably be easier on myself and not think that I have to do everything right. I've learned a lot more about mathematics at different levels, so I would have more understanding of the mathematics curriculum, largely because of my experience with the publishing. I'm not sure. Hopefully I'd be more organized. I always felt disorganized, with the curriculum, just doing this, doing that, hopefully I'd be able to see sort of the global picture better. I'm not sure why that would happen. I don't know, I mean just taking a break and stepping away from it for a certain amount of time. To get just kind of away from it, and forget what you were doing, 'cause I think you get into these habits and patterns, and we forget what some of those were and create new ones.

Maybe if I could just teach one or two subjects, and not everything, that would be exciting, to really focus. . . . That goes with the pressure I put on myself. I would trust in myself more, to go back and sort of believe that I'm doing this right and well and kids are learning, feel like a success. It's like the year ends and I think, gosh, did they learn anything? You know, just to have more confidence in, yes, they did learn. . . . You know, one child struggled, and didn't seem to make any progress, but just to feel that if I could just kind of let go of all the pressure I put on myself.

When Julie mentions the pressure she put on herself, I ask her if she felt that being a graduate of the DTE program also put pressure on her to be a certain kind of teacher. This was her response:

. . . I don't know if . . . I would use those words, but I think all the information . . . I think about how the students learn and, that that's how they do things and develop. I think those, those methods, good methods, the way kids learn best, aren't always the easiest ones to deliver. So I think in that respect you can feel awful in the classroom and you know that this is the appropriate way and this is what you want to set up for kids, but you don't have enough energy or resources or whatever just to do that all the time. So you do feel, you do feel the pressure . . . I've heard other DTE people who are also unhappy or are struggling, and I often say you know, we just know too much. We know so much about how kids learn and about the best way to do it, so we do, we put a lot of pressure on ourselves to do these developmentally-appropriate methods. So I think in some respects, yeah, there is, because of all that information, there's a pressure. . . . I think that is part of it . . . we know so much. We know what it takes and the good methods. But on the other hand, . . . I wouldn't want to give that up. I wouldn't. I felt like I learned so much and my knowledge is so much deeper than other people I know who go through a one year program and just student teach the whole time, and I wouldn't want to trade

that. I value everything I've studied and everything that I learned. . . . So I wouldn't want to trade that. . . .

As we proceed with the interview, Julie begins to answer the same set of questions she has answered three times before over the past 8 years. In my analysis, I notice that Julie's thinking about behavior, development, teaching, and learning had changed in some ways, but not in others. For example, I note that she did not say a lot about children's behavior, although she did have a lot to say about their development. Her understanding of factors that affect development and of the developmental process continued to develop over the past 3 years, especially her understanding of how development occurs in the cognitive and social domains. However, she also tells me that she had student teachers during her last 2 years in the classroom, had taken part in a math leadership group, and recently had been rereading Jean Piaget and Constance Kamii because of her new job. All of these factors apparently influenced her thinking and impacted her own development. Furthermore, her current job allows her more time for reflection.

Julie's thinking about factors that affect children's behavior at Time 4 include individual, internal factors and family influences as well as social, external factors including school influences. However, in this interview, she emphasizes the social factors that impact children's behavior, such as their social interactions in groups, the size of the group, their interactions with others, the consequences of those interactions, feedback from others, rules and conventions of the group and consequences for breaking them, and school climate. Although Julie emphasizes that these social factors affect how children learn to behave, she also mentions that internal factors such as ability to self-monitor, self-control, attention span, sense of responsibility, cognitive development, and maturation all impact children's behavior as well. She also says that children learn to behave naturally through their interactions with others, by making mistakes, and that all of their experiences help children become adultlike and more responsible. However, Julie also says that this just happens and that children learn to behave based on their experiences and by osmosis based on their interactions in their surroundings. Her response to my question about how children learn things like responsibility, respect for authority, and self-discipline shows her current thinking about how children learn acceptable behaviors. Ironically, this view of how children learn to behave leaves little room for the role of teachers or adults, which is a different perspective than Julie expressed in earlier interviews:

And if they learn that this is the way things work and how this is supposed to happen. And then in their interactions with others they learn, you know, if I take someone's pencil [then] that person's not going to like it, so you know you are going to fight or some-

thing over it. They just learn through mistakes . . . by interacting with other people and getting feedback from others. . . .

Instead of attributing development solely to having more experiences in life and school, as she had in her previous interviews, Julie emphasizes the importance of cognitive structures and their markers and talks a lot about children having more time to develop more interests. In fact, at Time 4, Julie seems well able to differentiate and articulate that factors such as children's physical ability, learning experiences, and social experiences all combine to impact how they think about things and view their world. For example, when I ask Julie how children develop their ability to think metacognitively, she mentions two factors:

Well, I think there are two things. One is asking those kinds of questions, to think about how they're thinking. Like part of it is just training and the other I think is just intellectually they're internal structures aren't, I mean they're not capable of separating the doing from the thinking. They just do, and they just are, it just is, they're just not organized yet . . . I think if you ask those kinds of questions often enough then yeah, they'll start to sort of incorporate that into [their way of thinking].

Julie's thinking about learning at Time 4, much like her thinking about behavior and development, seems more abstract than concrete. There are also fewer examples from her practice, which does not seem unreasonable given that she had not been teaching for almost a year at the time of this interview. However, her current thinking about learning seems to be more internally consistent and better consolidated, which indicates that she had continued to think about how children learn since our last interview. For example, at Time 4, Julie says children learn best when they learn a process or something that is going to be useful for them, when they have to create or construct or demonstrate something, and when they can make connections with what is to be learned. In addition, she thinks it is important to put the responsibility for learning in the hands of the students, and that they should do the thinking required, rather than the teacher telling students what they should do, think, or learn. In elaborating on her statement that her "*biggest goal is to help kids feel good about learning and to feel good about themselves,*" Julie says she would accomplish this by:

Well, by making learning, making it reasonable. Not asking them to do unreasonable things, things that don't make sense—boring, repetitive, and dry learning—all those things. By avoiding those kinds of things. Provide situations where kids can do things and create things and learn all the things they are interested in learning. And, by making the classroom a fun place to be. Helping kids be responsible for their own things in the classroom, part of the classroom routines, all of those things. That it's a place for

*them to be. It's not my place where you can come in every day, but this is our place—
those kinds of things.*

Although Julie readily articulates many factors that affect the learning
process at Time 4, she clearly understands that the concrete nature of
something and how personally relevant it can be made to children affect
the learning process. However, in talking about how she would achieve her
goal of making learning fun for students, Julie discusses this in general
terms rather than by giving any specific examples as she did in earlier interviews. In fact, the same kind of general, abstract response seen before can
also be seen to the question about what kinds of experiences Julie thinks
are most likely to bring about learning. This nonspecific response makes
sense because she is not teaching anymore.

*Experiences where the kids have to come up with, where they have to create something,
where they have to demonstrate something—rather than me just telling them something.
Having them, like if I wanted to talk about questioning I would say that the kids have to
maybe come up and present to the class with a partner to share something, and the kids
would come up with a couple questions and the kids would respond to the class. I think
when you put the responsibility back on the child to do all the thinking and to create
something that it's going to stick more into (their heads), in their mind than just hearing it from me instructing them.*

Nevertheless, Julie's goal for student learning at this time still relates to her
earlier beliefs about promoting self-esteem over teaching content, as this
response indicates:

*I think for me, more than anything else, more than any particular content, my biggest
goal is help kids to feel good about learning and to feel good about themselves. So it does-
n't matter what happens. If they feel capable and they enjoy learning, that's the most important thing. And as a teacher, if I would get down on myself and think we didn't
cover this, we didn't cover that, I would just try to remind myself that if they're enjoying
school, then that's important right now. At the elementary level, I think that the teacher's
most important goal is to help them feel good about learning because that's going to be
more important later on, and if they are ready for it and feel good about it [then] they
can do it.*

Not surprisingly, there is not much difference at Time 4 compared with
Time 3 with regard to how Julie understands the teaching process. For her
the teacher's role in the learning process is still to create learning opportunities and then serve as a guide and model, rather than tell them the answer
or give them an algorithm to use:

*Well, through guiding them, through modeling some of the kinds of questions, behaviors
that would lead to obtaining information. How to ask the questions that would get more
than just a yes or no answer, and just modeling and talking about it.*

Giving them the situation and creating, recognizing the good problems or the situations that are going to be worthwhile for kids to explore. So having the ability to do that, to create those kinds of things and to recognize what's worthwhile and what's important. But then also to be there as the guide. To recognize, to observe and to watch and see who needs more help and who needs information. Rather than, [telling them everything], imparting all of the algorithms, walking around and kind of guiding kids.

When I ask for an example in the field of mathematics, however, Julie's understanding about how children learn mathematics seems more advanced than at Time 3, although still not detailed or supported by specific examples. Here she describes a situation where she thinks children will learn by constructing their own understandings and even realizing their own misconceptions:

When creating a situation where the kids have . . . to create, construct something, where you give them a situation, but they have to sort of put it together. I think that's where connections are made, and where the learning sort of reaches a different level rather than just . . . memorizing something. I think there's more learning done when they actually work with something and organize it, or construct it. To give them a situation where they have to plan a fundraiser and they have to figure out what they want to sell . . . I think that's where the kids create and, . . . when they're in that meaningful situation that's when they learn a process or something that's going to be useful because it's there . . . your mind puts together something that makes sense. And if it doesn't make sense then you realize it. . . .

However, when talking at Time 4 about how she would teach the concept of a sentence, Julie still has not completely stopped thinking about teaching as telling, nor completely embraced constructivist pedagogy in the field of language arts, as can be seen in this example:

It would be fun to make it a puzzle to give them, just throwing out a bunch of words out of order and see if they could put them together and make sense of them. We could talk about. With some of them it's convention, so we say we do this and we do that, you know, you put a capital here and a period there. I used to do something where I would write something on the board that was out of order and had no capitals and no periods and they loved correcting me. That would be the big deal. How many mistakes did I make and can you find them all? And can you write it properly? And they loved that . . . I don't think they're going to discover those kinds of things about a sentence. Although, I guess we could give them, everybody could get a book, and say, "What are the things you notice? What do you notice about this sentence?" Look at a bunch of sentences and they could sort of discover it. I never did that, but it's an idea. So you could have them make observations about how do you know a sentence from a paragraph? But then, because of the conventional nature of those things, you just kind of say, "This is what we do. Okay, now can you find all the mistakes that I made over there?"

When I ask Julie to explain how she makes the distinction between when she should just tell students something and when they should discover it, she replies with some hesitation that she believes you should tell students basic facts but let them discover concepts.

> *I think conventional things, like there are twelve inches in a foot, I mean that's the kind of thing that you tell kids—information, that's social information that you need to tell, tell people. . . . But, deeper concepts are the ones that I would make kids to construct on their own. . . . Well I wonder too, myself, if I, if I'm making clear distinctions or if I'm sort of, like saying both and not really, you know, meaning too much. I hope I'm making some distinctions.*

So while Julie's thinking about teaching, learning, and development has continued to develop at Time 4, she also continues to hold onto some of her earlier beliefs, especially the importance of building children's self-esteem. In addition, Julie's metaphors at Time 4 indicate how difficult the whole teaching and learning process is for her. Furthermore, her current metaphor seems to contradict other statements about how important it is for the students to do the work with her guidance.

> *You're like an octopus. You know, you've got all these different arms and you're just trying to do all these things. That's the thing that pops into my mind. And there's also being a conductor, where you have this section over here and they're supposed to be playing lightly, and you've got the drums in that corner. And you know, you're trying to like, I'm trying to watch everybody and I'm in charge. I'm responsible for them and I'm trying to pull them all together.*

JULIE'S INTERVIEW AT TIME 5 IN 1997

I interview Julie again in 1997. At this time, she is working for a small software development company and is recently married. I ask Julie to tell me what has been going on with her since the last time we talked and she fills me in.

> *I was teaching in the Bay Area last, teaching third grade and then in 1992 I left and went to a textbook publishing company. They wanted to begin their new math program with California in mind and so they wanted to hire classroom teachers. I took a job as a project editor working on this new program for California, a basal program for math for elementary. I was there for about two and a half years and then the woman that hired me there . . . called up and said, "Hey, we need somebody—a print publishing person, editor, teacher type." So I've been here [at this software development company] for about two years. . . . We do what we call multi-media curriculum and curriculum software. We have computer activities and we also have hands-on activities. We do print materials for the teacher and CD-ROMs and I help develop the activities, both with the hands-*

on and the computer activities. I'm part of a learning content group, we call it. I also co-ordinate the writing and the editing of the activities. . . . It's very enjoyable but I do miss the teaching, especially last year for some reason. I suddenly thought, well, I'm missing those kids because I think that there's only so long that you can do this kind of thing, de-velop materials, without being with the kids again.

I ask Julie how she liked her job at the textbook company and she remi-nisces about how valuable that experience was and how she thinks she learned a lot.

It was a great learning experience. It's a pretty big company compared to this company. There were two hundred employees. But I really learned a lot. I reflect back on what I knew as a teacher, how panicked I was when I first started. I remember feeling over-whelmed by the whole year's curriculum, thinking, "Oh my gosh, what am I going to do for math?" because the district that I was in didn't have a math series. It's just so inter-esting now to reflect on what I have been doing and how much I know about the kinds of experiences you want to give children at almost every level but particularly we've been working on products for kindergarten to grade three. I feel like I've got just such an amazing sense now of the different areas that are important there. . . . I think I've had some wonderful experiences, some amazing experiences. I feel like I can always go back to teaching. I think that what I'm doing now is only going to prepare me for more opportu-nities if I want them. I was thinking recently that it might be nice to go back and be a math specialist because I've got such a perspective now on all the different programs and resources that are out there for people.

I also ask Julie how she got so interested in developing math curriculum, and she responds by talking about the influence of her teacher preparation program at UC–Berkeley.

It's interesting. I really attribute it to Allen Black [who was co-director of the DTE pro-gram from 1980–1995]. I grasped or was attracted [to math and math curriculum] be-cause I feel like I had such a thorough foundation in DTE of how children learn mathe-matics. I think that that gave me a much broader knowledge base than I feel that other teachers that I know.

Julie also describes her current role as the math specialist in her learning content group at the multimedia company, which includes developing cur-riculum products, planning activities, and designing software programs. She also tells me that they field test their prototypes, which allows her to be in classrooms periodically.

We sit around and talk. Before we actually design the activity or think about the activ-ity, we focus on the math and we figure out, we talk about what are the important con-cepts that we want to get across and what are the considerations that we need to have re-garding the learner that we've targeted this particular activity for. Because we work with people who don't have an educational background, we communicate that to the pro-grammers or the artists, designers who are going to be working with us. We often bring in manipulatives to demonstrate concepts and we often take the team through activities so they can understand what we mean by equal parts with fractions or rotating a shape. So we actually engage people in doing these things so that they understand what we are doing. . . .

Once we get a rough idea of what the activity is going to be, whether it's on the computer or a hands-on activity, then we would go to the classroom and try it with kids and see what their understanding of the activity is and try and assess what they're learning. Is this teaching what we want it to teach? Are the kids getting something out of this? It might not be teaching exactly what we want to teach but do we think that they're engaged in mathematical thinking when they're doing it.

Then we go back and revise things depending on what we saw and then once we've got it revised we take it out again and see if we've made [it better]. Often we need to make a big change if the kids are really bored, or if they were just comparing things and they weren't doing the mathematical thinking that we wanted them to do. We did a number series recently and we found, that with some of the activities, the kids could just solve the problems by looking, visually, and we wanted them to be doing some mental computations. We discovered that when we had the kids actually doing stuff and we were there to observe them and talk to them. So we came back and set problems up so that they had to think about something mentally and do that before they could get feedback from the computer by doing something and seeing what happened. . . . I think that's my favorite part, putting something out there in front of the kids and then observing what they're doing and trying to figure out how they're thinking and what they're getting out of it.

When I ask Julie to talk about why she left teaching after 5 years, she describes being stressed out and overwhelmed. She shares an incident with two students who had particularly difficult behavior problems, which caused her to feel emotionally drained.

Following this conversation, I ask Julie all the same interview questions she had answered four times previously during the past 12 years. It is interesting to see how her thinking about children's behavior, development, learning, and teaching developed since her final two years in the classroom and then over 4 years working on math curriculum in two different positions outside of teaching. Most of the examples Julie offers in response to the clinical interview questions relate to mathematics instruction and the elementary math curriculum, which was not surprising given that she had been immersed in this area for several years.

In response to the clinical interview questions, Julie offers little insight into her thinking regarding children's behavior, although she expresses a preference for teaching older elementary age students. Because Julie had not direct responsibility for children since she left the classroom 5 years before this interview, her lack of development in her thinking about student behavior is not surprising. Nevertheless, based on her experiences with students in several grades, Julie does say that she prefers teaching older students because of their social behaviors, discourse skills, and increasing cognitive abilities.

> *I really do love third grade but I would probably be open to a higher grade. I don't know that I would want to go younger. I always felt that kindergarten was a little bit too . . . I like the discourse in the classroom too much. I think socially they're a lot of fun. When I taught second grade, the second graders were always tugging on me and when recess was over, it was always the kind of stuff, "Well, he did this and she did that." All those kind of things that take away from your other time and I just got tired of all that kind of interaction. I really enjoyed third grade. The kids were really fun and able to read longer and get more into projects. We started doing some longer writing assignments and working on writing reports . . .*

During her interview at Time 5, Julie indicates that she understands how children's individual differences influence their behaviors as well as the decisions a teacher makes about learning and teaching. For example, in this statement, Julie said she knows what and how to teach based on her experience and her knowledge of children's development. She also reiterates her belief that individual differences are important to consider.

> *I think some of that sort of practical stuff comes from experience. I think in general if you know something about their development. . . . You can read things in books that are going to give you some guidelines about what to expect but I also think that your expectations shouldn't be too rigid because you need to acknowledge that kids come with different experiences and different abilities and different interests and that not everybody is going to be able to sit still for twenty minutes in the second grade to read a book. You need to have some latitude in that. You need to be able to allow for individual differences.*

Although Julie's thinking about children's behavior appears to be unchanged since her last interview, her understanding of child development has advanced and is consistent with a more differentiated understanding of constructivism. Although Julie has not been teaching during the past 5 years, she has observed in classrooms as part of her current job. These experiences seem to have focused her thinking on children's development and children's learning, especially with regard to mathematics, problem solving, and logical thinking. This quote shows that Julie has a good understanding of the developmental process, especially how it relates to how children understand mathematical concepts at different ages. Here she explains how first-, third-, and fifth-grade children develop the ability to coordinate and keep two different attributes in mind, which has to do with their developing ability to take more than one perspective. She also talks about her understanding of *class inclusion*, which is understanding that something can be a member of more than one set.

With our product, let me think. Our first product was geometry. We have lots of shapes, pattern blocks that the kids can manipulate. I think for both of those levels it's still important that kids actually have the concrete things to move around. I don't think that changes with concrete versus preoperational [thinking]. But I know that as far as things that we think about when we're developing different activities, things like, we were going to have kids compare the length of something. With the preoperational children we know that they're not going to be able to maintain a baseline to compare things, that they might be distracted by one attribute or another and not be able to coordinate those, so that if we gave them a series of sticks to order that they might do them in a random order or pay attention to the one end and not the other end and not the base. Whereas the third graders would be able to coordinate that and would be able to keep in mind those two different attributes. The other thing we thought about when we were doing geometry was their ability to perceive space and take a different perspective. I think that the younger kids aren't able to assume a different perspective. They can only take their own perspective when they're looking at something, whereas the kids in third grade can anticipate what another person's viewpoint or perspective might be. Just in general, the notion that the younger kids can't keep more than one thing in their mind. They can't coordinate different concepts. That something might be a member of this set and that set at the same time. They just focus on one aspect or property. . . . In general the fifth graders are going to be more capable of multiplicative thinking. That's something I've been thinking about recently with some of the projects we've been doing—fractions, in particular. I went to a workshop at the NCTM (National Council of Teachers of Mathematic) conference and we were talking about some of the operations that we do with fractions and I was thinking about how the traditional ways that we teach, where we do a lot of algorithmic stuff, really relies on kids abilities to see the multiplication or the additive sets and the younger kids aren't able to see that.

Julie also talks about her observations of children's increasing ability to think about their own thinking—that is, to think metacognitively—and their increasing ability to articulate to others what they are thinking. This is not something Julie talked about in her first three interviews while she was teaching, but it is something she is interested in understanding. Her current understanding of how children's metacognitive thinking develops is apparently a result of opportunities to observe children during the field testing of math activities she designed. Here Julie talks about the difference among first, third, and fifth graders completing math activities.

They might be a little bit better at articulating what they're thinking because that's another thing that's difficult sometimes—working with these younger kids at an early stage when we're trying to develop an activity. They can't always talk about what they're thinking. They don't always articulate what they're thinking. But the older kids often can remember what they were thinking and can communicate that to you. . . . The kids in first grade don't have as much of a vocabulary as far as logic goes, making connections between things, and understanding differences about things. I think when you get to third grade the kids are able to do that but in first grade they're not quite there yet. They just haven't had as much experience, as wide an experience, to talk about.

Thinking about where they are in cognitive development, being preoperational versus third graders would be more into concrete operations.

At this time, Julie seems to understand how children's vocabulary, logical thinking, cognitive processes, and ability to think metacognitively develop in the area of mathematics. She also understands that this happens at different times for different children, which is a more multidimensional way of thinking about cognitive development than Julie displayed in earlier interviews. However, her knowledge seems to be crystallized in the area of children's mathematical thinking, and she does not say much about how children's development might be similar in other disciplines (language arts, science, social studies, etc.) or in other domains (social, moral, ethical, or physical). Mainly she talks about children's cognitive development, especially about how their logical and mathematical thinking develops; she talks very little about children's development is the social domain, which makes sense given her professional responsibilities in recent years.

Julie's current understanding of children's cognitive development is quite consistent with her thinking about the learning process at this time. She says that learning comes from trying to make sense of one's experiences, which is a change from her earlier thinking that learning comes from exploring and doing.

I think in general the brain, just as a human being, that we're naturally curious and the brain wants to make sense of the world, so in that sense, we are all learners. We are all trying to make sense and learn things, but I guess there are some attitudes toward learning that I think that we could teach children, and that is things like it's okay to make mistakes so that we can learn from them, if we didn't do something the first time the way we wanted to or we didn't get an answer that we wanted to. Not that there's always one right answer but to recognize that there might not always be one right answer and that there are other ways to get an answer or to create a final product. So, I would want children to have that understanding. I think that's an important understanding because someone who is learning something should realize there isn't just one way to do it, but that there may be more than one way to do it, or more that one way to get to something they're trying to learn. Part of being a learner is being able to ask questions. So, those are the kinds of attitudes and things that I would want kids to engage in to be learners.

Julie's thinking about learning is also more multidimensional than in earlier interviews; she now understands that a variety of factors influence the learning process, including children's interests. In fact, when I asked Julie about what she would want to know about her students at the start of the school year, she gave a very different response than in previous years. In every other interview, Julie said she really did not want to know anything about her students before school began. She said that she would not want to be influenced by another teacher's opinions and that she likes to give children the benefit of the doubt when they came into her class. This time, however, Julie says she wants to know what children are interested in and motivated by. This difference in her thinking is probably a consequence of her current professional context, where she is trying to develop curriculum and learning materials that appeal to children's interests.

> *I would want to know something about their interests. Another thing we try to do with our products is to connect to children's experiences and create situations that they can relate to, that they can connect their learning to. So I would want to know a little bit about the kids. What are they interested in? What do they do after school? What do they do on the weekends? What sort of activities are they involved in? So that I could design the learning to appeal to them and to help them connect to what they are doing . . . I don't think that one method is going to work for anybody, I mean, is going to work for everybody, but that you need to assess the learning and see what they seem to be hooking onto or responding best to, and to know whether they need more skills, more information. . . .*

Julie's view of the teacher's role is also consistent with her current way of understanding children's development and the learning process. That is, although she thinks learning is sense-making, she also thinks that teaching essentially involves guiding children's thinking, asking them questions, and determining what they might need to advance their learning, which is different from earlier thinking—that children will learn if you just provide them with hands-on experiences.

> *The teacher's role initially would be to identify and structure what those experiences should be to determine what it is and the sequence that they might go through to teach a concept or to teach some sort of lesson or activity. To think about what the children are going to need to bring to the experience and then asking: What makes sense? What would you do first? What would you do next? I think it's the teacher's role to, while the children are doing something, to be walking around and observing what they're doing and thinking about what the children are doing and what that says about the child's understanding. And to question the child, find out information about what they're getting out of the activity. To guide the child and have a sense of what that child might need next or what you could do for that child if she is not understanding. Being able to evaluate how that experience is going for that child and determine whether she needs to go do something else or how you can help them or push them a little further. To make those kinds of judgments. The guide.*

In fact, the metaphor Julie has for herself at Time 5 is the teacher as a coach or guide, and she sees the children as being in the drivers' seats.

> *Definitely, the guide or the coach. Somebody who has a sense of what it is that they want the child to get out of the activity or what kinds of experiences they want that child to get. So, they have a goal in mind but the child has to take an active role. It's not just the*

teacher that has to do all of the teaching and presentation but that the child is just as responsible. It's an interactive thing rather than just one direction. For the kids . . . They'd be, they would they have to be the driver. When you're trying to show someone how to do something on the computer, people often say, "Do you want to drive?" And I think that when the child is the driver then they're the person who has to make some decisions and has to act on things. That that's when they're going to be learning rather than just passively doing nothing or just receiving information. It's not until they have to actually perform something, do something that they really learn. They have to take an active role.

Although Julie does not say anything about children's social development in this interview, she talks about the importance of helping children learn to get along socially, appreciate differences, and communicate with each other. She also talks in very different ways about children's self-esteem, which is something she has continued to value since her first interview. However, in response to a question about her goals as a teacher, Julie defines *self-esteem* differently than in earlier interviews. Now she says that building self-esteem is not just helping children feel good. She now says it means helping children feel capable and confident as learners who have strategies they can use to tackle and learn new things. Her goal of helping children appreciate differences and being able to communicate are also more clearly articulated than in previous interviews.

I think my goals as a teacher would be to help every child feel like they were a learner and that they were capable no matter what. I think traditionally children have been grouped and we've really done a lot of ability grouping, that some children were sort of pigeon-holed early and their whole school experience was sort of colored by that. So, I think it is the teacher's role to help children find their strengths and just really be able to capitalize and be confident in their abilities as learners and to give children strategies for learning in general so that when they come across new things, they are conscious of ways that they can take control of their learning. Another goal would be to help children function socially. That was something that I really enjoyed when I was teaching. I used the "Tribes" [Gibbs, 1994] book and we would have class meetings and talk about issues and solve problems together. I think that's really important too, helping children get along socially and learning about other children and how to tolerate differences and communicate. I think those are the most important things. . . .

Julie also expresses in her current thinking that the teaching process should be more student-centered, which is different than how she talked about it previously. This example also shows a more active view of the teaching process than Julie expressed in earlier interviews, when she talked about how to teach the concept of a sentence to third graders. In prior interviews, she described teaching as showing, telling, and modeling, which are all teacher-centered views. This example describes a more elaborated and student-centered view of the teaching process:

I think one of the best ways is to show them what's not a sentence. Give them an example that's incorrect and to talk about the difference so that you can create some sort of a contrast so they can see, "This is one, this is not one." One thing I used to do with my second and third graders was to write something that wasn't correct and to let them correct it and sort of engage them in playing the teacher and being the person who gets to decide what's wrong with the sentence. So that was always fun because then they had a more active role. And then I think actually giving children words on a card and punctuation on a card that they could manipulate and they could move around into different places and see how it feels and how it looks. I think that would be helpful for kids. I think just exposing them to good language and literature is a way for the notion of a sentence to just be present in their brain.

The next example also shows how Julie's thinking about teaching has changed after a few more years of experience in the classroom and several more years of developing curriculum materials and designing experiences to help children learn. In earlier interviews, Julie talked about experiences being important to learning, but she was unable to explain why, which she is able to do here.

I think experiences where children can connect their learning with something they already know. When the connections are explicit they're more likely to remember it and to make sense of it if it has some sort of connection to something they already know. Experiences where children are actually involved in doing something rather than just passively receiving information. It often disappears right away. So that they can actually physically construct something or mentally they have to make it fit into something, some sort of framework. When they have to use the information in some way, they are more likely to remember it.

However, when Julie talks about learning and teaching in the social domain, there are still remnants of explicit telling and modeling. Nevertheless, she does talk about setting up situations where students can talk and experience situations, such as logical consequences for particular behaviors, in a more active and student-centered way. In general, at Time 5, her thinking about teaching and learning seems less teacher-centered and more focused on students being actively engaged in learning. In this excerpt, Julie talks about how children learn to be responsible and self-disciplined:

As a teacher you model that yourself, so that just by observing your behavior. And then you can make some of those things explicit in the classroom by having children take responsibility for their actions. If they do something that hurts somebody else, then there needs to be some sort of consequence that makes sense for that. And they need to consider the other person's feelings and experience. So just in those ways, by helping children and by making that explicit. Talking about what that feels like and what that looks like. Setting up situations so that there could be a logical consequence so that they're not doing it just because the teacher said. I don't think that we want children to blindly follow au-

thority but to be able to be responsible for their actions and be able to evaluate what's right and what's wrong. . . . Yes, I guess, through modeling and making it explicit, through setting up experiences where they need to do that or they see the reason to do that. I think the best thing is just helping children to see why it's important or how it helps them.

Ironically, as Julie talks for the first time in this interview about children's developing ability to think about and articulate their thinking, she also talks about her own metacognitive thinking during this interview, which is something she did in her very first interview as well.

. . . It's interesting how just, in hearing myself right now talking to you, I know that I've said things differently. I know that there've been some more connections or something has happened from when—You know I remember the first time I did this interview . . . , I still remember that, and it's really interesting to me to see how I've continued to think about these things—or just whatever experiences I'm having now are still contributing to my understanding of these things. . . . In preparing for this next . . . product on fractions right now, I was looking at this book, Elementary School Mathematics: Teaching Developmentally *by Vanderwall. So I think some of the development stuff, it's like I'm looking at it again. I think when you're a teacher in the classroom you don't look at that stuff as much. I probably learned it in DTE and then applied it in the classroom or to assignments and things like that but it's just interesting how, looking at it again, I feel like each time it's becoming more cemented and I have more experiences to tie it to. I feel like some of what I'm able to talk more about or think about examples is just because there's been more time and more experiences to connect it to and kind of looking at it again and reading about it again.*

Julie also has a good awareness of her resources and sources of information for her own development as an educator. She says she has the time in her current position to really think about how children develop and learn, especially with regard to mathematics.

I think other teachers are a great resource. And then I've always enjoyed reading professional material, journals and things, "Mathematics Teacher" or whatever, "Teaching Children Mathematics" magazines that are put out by various professional organizations. I've always enjoyed staff development opportunities, so those are all great resources. And, I think that's probably something that's really kept me motivated and learning new things, trying other things and exposing myself to new ideas, and talking with other teachers and continually trying new things . . . I thought about classroom experiences. I thought about things that I've been doing lately, things that I've read about lately because being in this position where I don't have a class all day I do have opportunities. It is part of my job to read some of those journals. I have more opportunities to read those things and to remember these things about development, and to say, "OK, we're going to do fractions now. How do children learn fractions? Let's look at the sequence. What should we do first?" So I was thinking about some of those things that I've done recently. And I just think that I've had time to reflect over the years and I think I'm still making connections with things that

I learned. You almost forget at some point where you learned something but I think the connections still are being made to the experience that I had teaching . . . and I'm still sort of putting things together and realizing things.

JULIE'S 1999 INTERVIEW (TIME 6)

At the time of this final interview, Julie was staying home with her young daughter. Prior to the birth of her daughter in 1998, Julie spent almost 3 years working on a team developing multimedia math curricula for a small software development company. Julie's role on this team was the pedagogical and content expert for innovative products for the school market, including multimedia software, hands-on activities, and Internet resources. This position ended when her company was acquired by a larger software company at about the same time Julie discovered she was pregnant. When I interviewed Julie for the sixth time in May 1999, she was doing some freelance consulting work for another educational software company, which included writing curriculum guides for teachers to use with products already developed. However, because Julie enjoys her new job as a mother, she is not looking for a lot of projects and prefers spending time at home with her young daughter.

At the beginning of this interview, Julie reflects again about some of the reasons she left teaching after 5 years and also ponders the possibility of returning to the classroom when her daughter enters school. Her retrospective insights provide some clues about the typical pressures and stressors on beginning teachers that often lead them to move out of the classroom, although not always out of education altogether, as is the case with Julie. Some of the factors that Julie remembers as her reasons for leaving the classroom include the pressure she felt over having to develop curricula, trying to meet parental expectations, and her own lack of confidence in these two areas. These are some of the same factors she mentioned in previous interviews, but she elaborates even more during this interview. Julie also talks about the pace of the classroom and the school day, all the decisions teachers have to make daily, including trying to meet a wide variety of student needs, and large class sizes that were also stressors for her. Julie also mentions the pressure of knowing what she should be doing and feeling unable to do it all, which she thinks is something shared by other graduates of the DTE program.

One feeling that I had was that I could never accomplish everything. I remember this and I wonder if it would be different in a different setting. But, I remember when I was teaching, that we really weren't using the new textbooks and we were pretty much creating a lot of our own curriculum and the district was pretty loose about what the expectations were, so I felt a huge burden to figure out what to do with these kids and how to do it. It was kind of up to me to connect with other teachers to figure it out . . . but that was a huge thing for me. Having to plan the entire curriculum was so big. I felt pressure from the parents in my classroom. I don't know, I just felt a lot of pressure about their expectations. They always wondered about homework and especially in the beginning they didn't like having a new teacher looking after their child. Writing me long notes about things—I didn't like that.

I didn't feel confident enough. I think towards the end I did, but that was hard and I didn't like the pace of the classroom, just the unending—all the decision-making that happened. Having to deal with all the different kids. I felt like, I think that was a stress for me. I remember just being annoyed and having a headache everyday when I got home. Now I look back and wonder. Maybe that just wasn't the right place for me. I wonder what it would have been like at a different school or at a different grade level. What would I do better in? If I were to go back now, would I be better at getting the classroom in the right climate for my style or whatever? . . . The class size too, that would make a difference.

But I do remember thinking and talking to other people from DTE. You know so much about what you should be doing and what was appropriate and ways we wanted to do things, and it was just so hard to do it all. It was just too hard to handle. You know the things that you want to do this year but you should not expect that you would be able to do everything.

Julie's comments about knowing what she should be doing and her feeling of not being able to do it all sounded familiar to me based on my own experiences during 5 years supervising student teachers in the DTE program. From my perspective, this is something that seems to be both a strength and weakness of the DTE program That is, the DTE program, then and now, prepares teachers who know how to teach effectively from a developmental and constructivist perspective. They know how children learn, they understand current best practices, and they know how to develop curricula appropriate for elementary age children. When these four people were going through the DTE program from 1985 to 1987, they were learning pedagogy that was innovative at the time. However, the methods they learned to use in the DTE program in the mid-1980s became normative teaching practices in the 1990s: hands-on, discovery-based science and manipulative-based, problem-solving orientation to mathematics instruction; literature-based versus basal reader-based reading program; and a whole language approach integrated into a balanced reading program using good children's literature. However, knowing and doing are not the same thing for many teachers, and Julie was not the only one I saw or heard about who struggled with implementing everything learned during their time in the DTE program. For Julie, it was ultimately too overwhelming. Even after 5 years in the classroom, she did not feel satisfied with her ability to do everything asked of her as a teacher. Instead she felt a lot of the pressures and stressors commonly associated with teaching, but not enough support or rewards to keep her in the classroom.

It was not poor pay that encouraged Julie to leave teaching, but other factors. For Julie, and probably for others, it was frustrating to not be able to do everything she knew she should and could be doing in her classroom. For Julie, these frustrations were pressures that led to her decision to leave teaching. Perhaps she felt pressure more strongly from upper middle-class parents in her school, or perhaps she was never able to get her classroom organized in a way so that she did not go home every day feeling stressed and having a headache. Perhaps her expectations for herself were too high given class sizes that hovered around 30 students, or perhaps it takes some teachers longer than 5 years to figure out how to teach in a manner that matches their beliefs and ideals. Perhaps it was having three different principals in 5 years and not having a lot of fellow teachers to whom she could relate and with whom she could work closely. Perhaps teaching really was not a fit for Julie's preferred style of interacting with children, or maybe she was just too young at the time to be able to handle the pressures of teaching. More than likely, it was the combination of all these factors.

During this sixth and last interview in 1999, Julie says little about children's behavior in general and offered no well-remembered incidents or stories to tell as examples or elaborations for her responses to the clinical interview questions. As she thinks back on her teaching experiences to answer the interview questions, Julie has much more to say about student learning than student behavior, however. Once again, this seems logical because Julie spent the last 5 years of her professional life developing curriculum materials to help children learn mathematics. Although she periodically had opportunities to observe children in classrooms, she was not responsible for their behavior. Perhaps that memory of teaching had faded in her mind.

However, Julie mentions various social, cognitive, and developmental factors that impact behavior, especially children's differing abilities to do things. She also mentions that children's experiences influence how much they can understand something, how meaningful something will be to them, and how much attention they pay to something. At Time 6, Julie attributes children's behaviors to their abilities, experiences, and interests, although she also mentions that children's level of cognitive development and their motivation can also influence their behaviors.

Although 12 years have passed since she graduated from the DTE program, Julie continues to have a good understanding of Piaget's theory of cognitive development, especially as it relates to mathematics—her area of special interest and expertise over the years. In this interview, Julie clearly understands that both social and cognitive development influence children's behaviors, and she says she can use the language of Piaget rather facilely to describe her work in developing math curriculum materials to others.

. . . We had to interface with programmers and designers and all of that. So, people that wanted to understand what you were talking about but you knew that they didn't share that knowledge. We would try to explain that, and that was always part of the beginning of product development was talking about helping people to understand that this is the approach that we are going to take and this is why. We want kids to be able to see fractions represented physically and these bars and, you know, they had to be different colors and we would often talk about why that was important. . . . First graders would probably be definitely more at concrete operations and probably still a little egocentric. Socially, I would say they are concerned about rules, people cheating. . . . Cognitively, third graders are still at concrete operations where sixth graders are more approaching formal operations. You could talk more abstractly about ideas and things with them, where the third graders are still more hands on, concrete. Socially, the third graders are definitely in a different place. How can I describe that? The peer relations have not become as critical as they have become at sixth grade. I think that at third grade kids are still, you know, they are definitely forming friendships but not, there is a lot more stuff going on with sixth graders . . . I think that having some sort of concrete experience no matter how old the kids are, I think is a good way to start and moving from the concrete to understanding what it is that they are doing and why they are doing it. First they get to do something concrete and then they learn more about why they are doing it and then move into practicing it and applying it.

At this time, Julie summarizes her goals as a teacher by talking about what and how she wants her students to learn. Although she still believes that building self-esteem is more important than mastering any particular content or task, at Time 6 she adds that she values helping children learn how to learn and enjoy learning. She also values their learning how to get along with others and being able to operate socially.

I think that the things that are most important, rather than . . . having to master any particular thing, would be that they know how to learn and that they enjoy learning, that they know how to study something, or that they enjoy learning, that they feel confident of themselves as a learner, that it is OK to make mistakes and that is part of the learning process. I would want them to learn how to be with other kids, because I think those two things, being confident in yourself as a learner, and being a social person or knowing how to get along with other people, I think those are the two things that are important rather than mastering your times tables or reading 20 books in a year or something. So I think that those would be my goals.

Interestingly, Julie's views about the purpose of learning are much more wide-ranging and clearly articulated than in previous interviews. For example, in describing what the learning process is like, Julie says that learning happens when the time and context are right, when things make sense and are familiar, and when children are physically doing things and making mistakes that they then try to correct. She also says that learning occurs through concrete experiences, practice, and application, but makes no mention of learning as being told what is important to learn:

I think that building on what I just said, when the kids are in the middle of doing something and there is an opportunity or a need arises for something, I think that is when learning is likely to take place, because it is meaningful for the kids, it has a purpose and they can see that right there, where they need it. It obviously is something that is going to be appropriate to them because they are in the middle of it or they are creating it and it is not something that you have read in your textbook that all kids need to do these things. It is more that this kid is exhibiting this behavior or whatever so I know that I am going to do this now. So having the right context, I think that would be it. Then things that make sense and using things that are familiar to them and that has to be in context too and when that context is meaningful or familiar you can learn something better within that context. They can just fit that new knowledge into something that already exists. I think that doing something rather than just watching or being told, that always will induce more learning and the kids are physically doing something and trying it out, making mistakes and being able to correct it right there or do it differently or trying to overcome something.

Julie also understands that the complexity of the task impacts learning. For example, she understands that the number of variables that have to be coordinated makes the task more or less complex, and that how concrete or abstract something is, and the developmental level of the student, are also variables that influence learning. Furthermore, nearly all of Julie's examples in this final interview are about teaching mathematics and her experience teaching third graders, indicating that her understanding of children's learning has continued to develop in this discipline, but not in others.

I have to think back and picture a few third graders. When you start to introduce multiplication, they understand it really well when you are talking about repeated addition. Then when you start talking about two groups of three and three groups of two and a lot of those, what do you call them, different classes of groups using the same number, that is when you can lose a lot of the kids, they can't see that yet. That is something that I think is pretty typical for third grade. Some of the concepts like volume, things like that, I think are involved in the same category in that there are so many different aspects with depth and they can't coordinate all of that. Some of them still have a hard time with expressing, sort of how they were thinking about that. I would say, "How did you solve that problem?" or "What process did you go through?" They would have a really hard time, getting beyond the last step of what they did. I would say that they are still pretty concrete. They need to see something physical right in front of them or they can't really remember a series of things that they were thinking of or a step that they went through to produce something.

During this final interview, Julie seems to have completely shifted from seeing the teacher's role as one of showing and telling to one of guiding instruction based on observing and interacting with the learners:

I think that the teacher's role is to set up situations where kids are going to have opportunities to do things and learn from what they have done and for the teacher to kind of be there to watch for the right opportunity to introduce a new thing and to just be watching and seeing when it is time to add new information. To help them do it a different way or help them to learn if they did it wrong to help them do it again. To use information and make observations. Rather than catching mistakes, it is the teacher's job to turn it into, to see and interrupt mistakes and say [to yourself], "OK, this kid is doing this and it means this, not that. So and so did this wrong, but I can learn from what they have done and see what changes I need to give them next." To kind of watch and use the observations that way rather than just saying, "OK this kid cannot do this yet." To use that to say, "OK this is where they are and this is what I should be doing next." To be the guide, guiding them.

Julie also thinks giving students open-ended tasks is a good teaching strategy:

I think giving kids an opportunity to write and do some kind of journal writing, that is always a good way to see how they can write and how they can organize their thoughts and where they are, their language art skills. Then as far as math, setting up some kind of activity where the kids might have to do some recording. Organize their paper, like if we are doing something that they need to have some sort of a record. It is always very interesting to see how kids organize things and how they can write down what they have done or create some kind of diagram to explain their thinking. That was something that I enjoyed. I had math journals, I had the kids write in math journals and that was always real interesting to see how kids could write things. And another thing that would be good at the beginning of the year would be to have the kids create their own story problems, because then you don't have to say [that] everybody has to do an addition problem, but say create your own story problem and then they can chose whatever operation they want. Then you can see who is writing a division problem and who is still struggling with some kind of addition problem. You can just see a lot about where they are and what they are doing.

Julie's metaphor for herself at Time 6—the teacher as orchestra or band conductor—fits quite well with her thinking about the teacher's role, her reflections about the multitude of decisions the teacher has to make, and the complexity of meeting the needs of all the students that contributed to her leaving the classroom. She also explains this metaphor differently than at Time 5. However, although Julie says she would not necessarily be doing all the directing and telling, she still describes her image of the teacher as the one responsible for doing all the work to bring the group together and for making it sound good.

Maybe like a conductor. You have a whole range of things out there and all these different instruments and all these different groups and seeing the kids in general like that and they are not all one color or flavor or one ability. There is such a mixture you're and trying to do so many different things at once. You know, you need a little more over here and a little down over there, and just try to keep in all going. Make it sound good. That seems to fit pretty well . . . and I would be the person who is responsible for their growth and participation. Not necessarily as the director, telling them exactly what to do, but just sort of the person who is kind of bringing them together as a group.

In earlier interviews, Julie talked about the teacher as guide, which is a common metaphor: *But then to be there also as the guide—to recognize, observe, and watch and see who needs more help and who needs information* (Time 3, Clinical Interview, June 1993). Unfortunately, however, I did not probe to find out if Julie was thinking of herself as the tour guide for a whirlwind tour of 21 countries in 21 days, the guide for the trek of intrepid adventurers into the wilds of some exotic place, or the guide who scouts the trail ahead for the rest of the group to locate water and warn them of dangers. Perhaps she was thinking of herself as the teacher who is the *guide on the side* as opposed to the *sage on the stage*. All of these metaphors imply different possibilities for the teacher's role, but it is not clear how Julie envisions her role. However, given her current metaphor of teacher as *conductor*, I have to wonder how Julie would fare if she decided to go back into teaching because she apparently views the teacher as the one doing all the work. This makes me wonder whether she might still be overwhelmed by all that a teacher has to do, just as she was when she left teaching after 5 years. She certainly does not have an image of teaching and learning as a state of flow that Rick and Ralph developed. Rather, Julie's metaphors convey images of great effort on the part of the teacher.

One of the most interesting things about Julie's pedagogical understanding at Time 6 is her thinking about the purposes of technology in educational settings. From her perspective, technology is a powerful tool for teachers and students to use for learning, and she is cognizant of the importance of introducing and using various tools in developmentally appropriate ways. Her views are quite likely influenced by her experiences working in educational settings outside of schools, and her most recent job in multimedia software development certainly impacted her thinking about the purpose of technology in education. This may also be the reason that her thinking about this topic is more sophisticated than the other teachers in this study who never mentioned using technology in the classroom unless I asked about it directly. Julie, however, volunteers these comments at Time 6:

I think technology is an important tool. I have been thinking a lot about that too and thinking about how we used to use technology as just kind of something jazzy, and hey it's the newest thing, and kids like it, so let's use it. But, you want to think about the power and how it can, you know, it's kind of like the calculator. It can allow us to do things really sophisticated in an easier way. I think that it is important for teachers to see technology in that way and develop a curriculum that will give kids experiences and that are appropriate for their age levels, and . . . when they finish school we want them to be able to use these tools. So, where does it make sense to introduce spreadsheets or introduce a drawing tool . . . ? I see some of the game software as one very small part of technology. I think that some people think that's it. There are all these things that kids can do. I think that we need to think about the end goal for kids to be adults in the work-place and remember that there is a lot of power in these different tools.

JULIE'S STORY . . . IN HER OWN WORDS . . . SUMMER 2000

As Julie's story comes to a close, I ask her to reflect on her career, write about her current thinking about teaching practices and curricula as well as her past personal and professional life as it might relate to understanding her present professional thoughts, and ponder her future as it relates to her personal and critical appraisal of her life as a teacher. Julie did this during the summer of 2000 by thinking back over her 5 years of teaching experience, 3 years working for a textbook publisher, and 4 years working in software development. The final part of this chapter is written by Julie.

I am currently at home with my first child. My most recent full-time employment was with a small multimedia start-up. The company's mission was to create materials for classroom teachers that would provide powerful mathematical experiences for children. This goal was achieved by the creation of a series of units, which combined hands-on activities and a CD-ROM of multimedia activities all pertaining to a particular mathematical idea. I was initially hired for my publishing experience and my awareness of the needs of the classroom teacher in implementing the hands-on lessons. I helped design and edit the hands-on activities that went into the teacher's guide. By the time I left the company, I was the person responsible for developing the mathematical content for both the hands-on activities and the multimedia component. I worked with a group of math specialists and professors to develop the content, and a team of engineers, designers, and other people to develop the product. I also went into classrooms to test the activities, observing student's experiences throughout the development of the product. Our materials stood out in the marketplace because we used examples from everyday life to illustrate mathematical ideas using a variety of media. For example, we had a short movie on a CD-ROM about fractions showing examples of fractions found in a garden. The computer activities were engaging and purposeful. Several of our products won national educational awards!

Although I left teaching over 8 years ago, I do not think my thoughts about pedagogy and curriculum have changed all that much. I strongly believe that children learn when they feel relaxed, confident, and interested or stimulated. Children need to explore materials and concepts on their own to capitalize on the brain's desire to make sense out of the world. The role of the teacher is a delicate dance of knowing when to intervene with new information or direct instruction to help children gain new understanding, insight, or to master new skills and when to let children explore and make sense on their own.

It is important that students make connections between concepts that are related as this leads to deeper understanding rather than rote or piecemeal understanding. Students often do not make connections on their own; they must be made explicit by the teacher. I tried to do this at the beginning or ending of my lessons, but it was always dependent on how much time I had. I knew it was a good idea, but didn't realize how key it was.

One's curriculum should have meaning for the students. I tried to create activities that allowed students to draw on their own interests and abilities. For example, in my reading program, I often gave students opportunities to choose books to read, rather than have everyone reading the same book. Students did projects based on their own book. My spelling program started with a core list of words. If students spelled them correctly, then they created their own list of words based on misspellings in their daily writing and interest words. Each child's list was very individual. Math journals provided opportunities for students to express their own understandings. Students loved making up math stories or number sentences and sharing them with the class. I had math projects where students in pairs designed a survey on a question they designed and then visually presented the results to the class using graphs or charts. I held class meetings, Tribes style [Gibbs, 1994], which provided students opportunities to discuss problems they had with other students. This was an opportunity to learn and use social and problem-solving skills.

A textbook can provide curriculum, but I would probably never use any single textbook exclusively for my curriculum. Teachers need to have access to good teaching materials, and they shouldn't have to work real hard to find them. When I first started teaching in the late 1980s, I had no textbooks to use in my classroom. My district had not approved any textbooks in any subject area for my grade level. We all had a copy of Mary Baratta-Lorton's Math Their Way and that was about it. Coming out of the DTE program, I didn't believe in them—didn't think they were the way to teach students. Today there are many good textbooks (they probably aren't even called textbooks anymore) available to teachers that align with what I was trying to do 10 years ago on my own.

When introducing new concepts, it is important to give them a context to which students can relate. The context should be familiar and motivating. There are many different kinds of contexts such as fantasy, real world, or just an intriguing problem to solve. When students see a clear purpose or find an activity meaningful, real learning occurs!

I think one of the greatest challenges of teaching is meeting individual needs. One size does not fit all! Designing curriculum that can allow for a variety of approaches or experiences provides access to learning for everyone. A noisy, busy classroom will not suit all students, nor all teachers, and neither will a quiet, still classroom. Both variety and routine are important.

As a teacher, I was always trying new things. I was rarely satisfied with the job I was doing. I never felt I was meeting the needs of all my students. However, when a lesson went well or I could see that a student had learned something new, it was really thrilling and I loved my job. The year that I left teaching, I was collaborating more with other teachers, working on lessons and units together. I had started switching classes with other teachers so that we could repeat lessons and capitalize on one another's expertise and experience. Repeating lessons is such a good way to improve on a lesson and learn new things. I wish I had done more of this earlier. I might have felt more satisfied with my teaching instead of feeling that I couldn't do it all or very well. I would have been able to focus on my area of expertise, which for me was mathematics.

Mathematics was not an innate strength of mine. I struggled with math as a student, beginning in first grade all the way through to senior calculus in high school. It wasn't until I went through the DTE program that I made some critical connections to concepts and gained understanding that I never experienced as a student. It was the hands-on experiences of working with physical models and representations that caused some basic concepts to suddenly make sense to me. I was amazed that I was finally mak-

ing these connections as an adult! In DTE, we studied basic math concepts in-depth and how cognitive development relates to how students learn these concepts. I developed a strong foundation of understanding how students learn mathematical concepts. I remember as a classroom teacher how this empowered me, and I wished that my fellow staff members could understand the same. I felt that I wanted to help all students see these connections to understand math so that it wouldn't be some big scary mystery as it was for me when I was young. That mission guided me in the classroom and beyond, when I left teaching to work for a textbook publisher and then the multimedia start-up.

My experiences developing curriculum materials for a large publishing company and small multimedia start-up have gotten me to the point of thinking about larger issues in education such as equity. When you are trying to design materials for a variety of classrooms and teachers, you think about the larger world, not just your own classroom. After visiting many classrooms to test out activities and software, I look back at my own teaching and realize that I did a lot of great things in my classroom. I never would allow myself to see that when I was there as a teacher.

When I look to the future, I imagine a couple different possibilities. One is that I would work for publishers creating curricula to help teachers deliver meaningful learning experiences to their students. As I sit here thinking about this, I am recalling that long ago, before I even started teaching, I thought that creating lessons would be a lot of fun. I guess I shouldn't be surprised that I didn't stay in the classroom. I've never really enjoyed public speaking and being "on stage," which is what teaching a room full of students is all about. The creative process of designing a lesson and student materials has always appealed to me.

The other possibility would involve working with students. Being a teacher in a self-contained classroom with 28 students would not be a good choice for me. The stress I experienced day in and day out manifested in frequent headaches, and feelings of dread and anxiety lead me to believe that I just wasn't cut out for the role of a self-contained classroom teacher. However, I could see myself working with smaller groups of students, perhaps as a specialist of some sort. I really do enjoy the process of learning and teaching and the dialogue and discourse between student and teacher.

I've often wondered, too, if I entered teaching at a time and place when there was not a lot of support for curriculum, which made it an extra difficult job. The state of California was coming out with a new cycle of frameworks, and there weren't a lot of materials that addressed these approaches—approaches that mostly were in agreement with what I learned in DTE. Now that I have a larger perspective, having worked in other environments (publishing), I might go back to teaching and find that I would experience it with much more confidence in my abilities. I spent 5 years in the classroom; perhaps I was just about to leave behind the stress of being a new teacher, but certain circumstances (those mentioned above, as well as a few troubled students that sucked all of my time!) pulled me out the door, out of the profession. Who knows?

AFTERWORD

To update the reader: Julie gave birth to a second child in the summer of 2001 and is staying at home with her two young children as this book is published.

Chapter 4

The Story of Sandy Brumbaum

DTE teachers are really different than those who come from elsewhere, and I think I would not be the teacher I am without DTE. It just made me more aware of developmental education and how children develop and [how] everyone develops at their own rate, and goes through stages. I would hope that most credential programs study Piaget, but we did it in such depth. I do have to say that what we did then I did not appreciate and I don't think I got it. I wasn't ready to hear a lot of what Paul [Ammon, the codirector of the DTE program] or even Allen [Black, also a codirector of the DTE program] said, because I was coming from a really technical background in economics, math, and psychology and children were really foreign to me. I think that the people who go through the program now are a lot more experienced, and so they are ready to receive that information and probably got a lot more out of it than I did. But I think it set up that bug in my head that this is the way that children learn and laid the foundation so that everything that I learned or heard had to jibe with that or else I didn't use it or it didn't make sense to that theory. I think that a lot people when they come into teaching, they don't know how children learn, they don't have an understanding or a philosophy of how kids learn, they just do things without thinking about why and what it means for the kid.

(Time 5, Clinical interview, 1997)

Sandy is Chinese American, married to a banker, the mother of two daughters, and a teacher. She has taught in full- and part-time situations since 1987. She taught mainly primary-age students in the public schools in San Leandro, California, for 10 years, and recently began teaching in the small, private school that her daughters attend in Berkeley, California. She has been a first-grade teacher, a second-grade teacher, and a reading specialist.

Now she is a fourth-grade teacher. Her special interests include literacy and writing instruction and early literacy development.

Sandy was born in Ohio to Chinese parents who emigrated from the People's Republic of China, first moving to Hong Kong and then to the United States. Because her father worked in international business, the family moved several times. Sandy lived abroad for 16 years and went to school in Taiwan, Japan, and Korea before returning to the United States to go to college. After graduating from UC–Davis with a major in economics, Sandy worked in a bank for 2 years before entering the DTE program in 1985. Sandy had no teaching experience before beginning her teacher education program except for her experiences as a summer camp counselor and a tutor, but she knew she wanted to teach rather than remain in the business world.

SANDY'S 1985 INTERVIEW (TIME 1)

Sandy entered DTE with a strong belief that family background and how children are raised influences both behavior and learning. She felt this to be true for children whom she would encounter as a teacher as well as for herself. In her interview, she draws on "*learning experiences . . . from home and teaching, what my parents taught me,*" she says. "*So it was mostly my background.*"

Sandy says in her first interview that age, self-control, attention span, maturity, understanding of the world around them, and ability to work and cooperate with others all influence how children behave in class. She also reiterates that how children behave at home influences their behavior at school.

> They may be the only child, and their mother just babies them to death and they're always going to be, "I want this and I want that and my mom gives it to me and why can't I have it here." . . . That encourages them to be self-centered, being babied at home. Whereas if you came from a large family and you didn't get as much attention and you had to share things with your brothers and sisters, then you won't be as self-centered as the single child.

She says little else about children's behavior in this initial interview except that misbehavior might affect the teacher's performance in terms of ups and downs.

> A down would be when your kids weren't paying attention, or they just refuse to listen to what you're saying, or if they are unusually rowdy, or they just wouldn't settle down one day and you were having a hard time disciplining them. Or . . . a down would be if you were trying to teach a certain subject or help a certain student and he or she just wasn't

cooperating or just couldn't understand. I don't know, it would be more frustrating because you couldn't figure out how to help a child.

Sandy also says that the quality of early learning experiences, children's interest in or affinity for different subjects, and parental influences all influence development:

Maybe they didn't have a good experience when they were in the younger grades with one subject. Like if the teacher didn't teach math very well in first grade and so they didn't get the basics down and so they wouldn't like math later on. Or some kids just take to science naturally, and they really enjoy science and playing around with experiments, or some kids really like history and others don't. A lot of it has to do with what the parents do with the kids at home. If they read to them a lot and they work with them on their math, then the kids may like those two subjects.

This is the extent of Sandy's initial thinking about children's development. She does not discuss the developmental process or talk about what develops in children, indicating little understanding of child development at the beginning of her teacher education program. Given Sandy's limited experience with young children, this is not surprising.

Sandy has a more robust understanding of learning at Time 1, realizing that in "*first and second grade, they're still learning the basics, whereas fourth and fifth grade [students] probably should have the basics, and they're going on to more advanced learning: division and math, and molecules and atoms in science.*" Because she would rather teach content than the basics, Sandy thinks she would prefer teaching older children. However, a few years later, she changes her mind as she develops an interest in emergent literacy.

Which age group? I think I would choose one of the older grades right now because my first 2 weeks of student teaching were with first and second graders, and now I'm working with 3-year-olds. I feel like I want to work with kids who you can teach more things to, whereas the younger kids are learning the real basics, so I don't know, I think the older kids. I don't really know if I'd like it better, but right now I think I would like fourth and fifth grade.

Sandy has a rather naïve understanding of the learning process, believing it is rooted in rote memorization. She says that children learn by memorizing math facts and shows a similarly naïve conception of learning vocabulary, although she has little understanding of how this might occur except through practice.

In math you have to learn by rote memorization. I mean there's no other way around it unless you use your fingers all the time, so I think you have to do that in math. And with . . . [vocabulary], to a certain extent that's rote learning too, but you want to make it [a] more meaningful experience. You want to give the words meaning so the child will understand them, where the child isn't necessarily going to understand why he's adding 2 + 2, why it's four. . . . Whereas, if you teach them vocabulary, the word has a meaning and they still have to practice it, but it's not just pure memorization.

However, Sandy does appear to understand from the outset that children learn in different ways and that teachers should teach in different ways:

It's up to the teacher to try to teach it different ways. One child may understand it in one way but another child may understand it another way. . . . Everybody has a different way of thinking, so you have to try to relate a subject to their way of thinking, their way of understanding. So you may have to explain something two or three times before you can relate it to their thinking, to a child's thinking.

Her initial understanding of the relationship between learning and teaching is a good omen for Sandy, as it would be for any beginning teacher. It sets the stage for understanding how and why children learn in different ways, as well as how to teach to meet those different ways of learning.

Furthermore, Sandy also believes that, besides family influences, children's interests and the quality of their earlier learning experiences shape learning and behavior in school.

There are particular kinds of instances that will probably bring about not learning, like if you have a bad experience then you might turn off to whatever you're learning, and if you have a really good experience, that might get you really interested in what you're learning and want to learn more. . . . If the family situation is really bad at home, that can lead into a lot of anger and frustration in the child and that may be a reason why he or she is not cooperating well in class or behaving well in class.

A child in a dysfunctional home may not experience "*a whole lot of discipline at home, and he watches TV while he's doing his homework,*" she explains. "*So he's really bright but he doesn't learn well. He can learn, but he doesn't know how to study and how to learn,*" she adds. With that understanding, Sandy believes that a teacher can help parents improve the learning environment at home. However, she also believes that what parents expose their children to can affect children's affinity for different subjects, transcending their innate intelligence.

Some student . . . may really enjoy reading [but] just doesn't like math at all, and so she may be in the highest group for reading but not in the highest group in math. It may be that her parents read to her a lot when she was small, and she went to the library when she was a little girl. But they didn't give her the same exposure in math, so she may be at a higher level in reading than in math. . . . Some children have had exposure to a lot of things, so they can relate to a lot of things whereas another child may have [had] a limited exposure. So that one little boy, at home or at Christmas his dad bought him a sci-

ence set or a chemistry set or something like that, so he's been playing with little flasks and whatever and then another little boy didn't have that at home and was learning chemistry or science for the first time. The first little boy has already had the exposure, he understands a little, he knows what a flask is and he's worked with little tools before, so he'll learn faster than the other boy who has never had the exposure before . . . so I think it's pretty much what you've been exposed to and what you've experienced.

Beyond teaching the basics in the early grades and content in the upper grades, Sandy thinks the school should teach qualities such as responsibility, self-discipline, and respect for authority. However, she believes that these qualities are taught by telling students the rules.

You have to learn the very basics, like you're responsible for cleaning up after yourself [for example.] . . . If you do any art or something, washing your paint brushes, and that's all part of responsibility, and that just kind of expands as you get older and into the upper grades. . . . The teacher tells them these are the rules, and you have to clean up after yourself.

In discussing how she would teach the concept of a sentence, Sandy also describes teaching as showing and telling students what they need to know. To her mind, learning occurs when students acquire specific facts and rules.

I would start out by teaching them the different parts of the sentence, what a verb and a noun is . . . [with examples such as] "See Spot run" or something like that. I mean that's a very basic sentence, but you would want to start them out at a very basic level. So teach them what a verb is and what a noun is and tell them that the period always comes at the end, that proper nouns are always capitalized, and the very first letter of the first word is capitalized. But just getting them to understand the basic sentence first of all.

Like many beginning teachers, Sandy also wants to teach in a way that makes learning "*as pleasant an experience as possible to get students interested, because if they show interest in the subject, their learning will be more enhanced, or they'll try to learn more.*" For example, she says, "*So, if they're learning math, try to make it as fun as possible in the younger grades so that . . . they'll all learn it and how it can apply to something else.*"

SANDY'S 1987 INTERVIEW (TIME 2)

Sandy's pedagogical understandings at Time 1 are a good example of what the Ammon and Hutcheson Model of Pedagogical Thinking calls *naïve empiricism*. However, her pedagogical understandings on completing the DTE program 2 years later are different. In fact, as Sandy prepares to graduate from the DTE program, she realizes that she has changed a lot and is ready for a classroom of her own, although she feels a little anxious as well.

> *I've really learned a lot and just two years of student teaching and all the extra coursework that has gone along with the teaching, [has] really helped me a lot. . . . I feel really ready to have a classroom of my own and not student teach anymore. . . . I'm still really apprehensive about it, but I think I'm less apprehensive than I would be if I had just been in a one-year program. But I can see that there's still a lot that I have to learn. This year is going to be an interesting year.*

One change is that Sandy would rather teach the basics to children in the primary grades rather than teach content to older students. Another change is that, during her time in the DTE program, Sandy seems to have developed a fascination with early literacy—an interest she maintains throughout her career.

> *I'm really excited about watching them develop. I'm really excited about watching them begin learning about their reading and their writing, and just learn the basics. . . . I relate better to the younger kids, and they're still really excited about learning, which I really enjoy. For them, learning is kind of like playing in a way, so it makes my job easier, whereas the kids, when they get to fourth-to-sixth grade they've already had some bad experiences possibly. Some have, and it makes it a little bit more challenging.*

Perhaps Sandy's preference for teaching younger students also has to do with how she thinks student behavior impacts learning.

> *Usually they have behavior problems, which lend to the problems of learning. If they're in second grade, they've had behavior problems in kindergarten and first grade, and because they've had these behavior problems they haven't learned as much—they're running around the room, or they're spacing out and doing some other things, or arguing with some other kid. This takes away from their learning, so they wouldn't have gotten all that learning they were supposed to have in kindergarten and first grade.*

Sandy also believes that children's behavior and learning are influenced by the classroom environment as well as the teacher's expectations.

> *The teacher expects the kids to get along, and no put-downs, and no degrading, and no fighting, or whatever. I think the kids can read the teacher and know what is okay and what isn't okay, so the kids know it's not okay to hit or steal. Every teacher has that but some teachers, I think, are more lax about it than others, and if they know that it's real important to the teacher, then they'll learn not to do it in class.*

During the 2 years she spent in the DTE program, Sandy expanded her understanding of how children develop to include cognitive, physical, and social factors, such as their ability to communicate, their gross and fine motor skills, basic social behavior, how to talk, and how to relate to people. *"You just become more aware of things. You're not as egocentric, I guess, when you're older,"* she says at Time 2. *"Starting in preschool, the kids are going out and playing with other kids, and they're realizing that they're not the only one, that the world doesn't revolve around them solely."*

Sandy's goals for her students at this time illuminate her thinking about learning. Her goals include affective goals, such as being excited about learning, and social learning goals, such as getting along with others and becoming self-sufficient and independent learners. In fact, these goals remain quite consistent throughout Sandy's career.

> *I want them to be excited about learning, and I want them to learn to get along with other people. Those would be my two main goals for the kids. I would want them to be self-sufficient or independent, so they don't always come to me for learning. I guess that's another goal I have—for them to generate their own learning experiences instead of coming to me to always generate a learning experience for them. I would want them to be independent, and I would expect them to get along with each other well.*

Sandy also has other goals consistent with learning in the social domain, as can be seen in her response to a question about the school's role in teaching children responsibility, self-discipline, and respect for authority.

> *They have to learn to be responsible for their actions. They have to learn how to be self-disciplined. It's like being autonomous, independent, and generating their own learning. Otherwise they would go through life asking other people what to do and being a follower. Being respectful to authority, I think, that's what laws are set up for, but you want them to have a mind of their own too.*

Sandy's description of the learning process seems to match these goals. For example, she talks about the value of communicating and learning from peers and being actively involved in learning, particularly through play:

> *If they have a question, their classmates will tend to understand it and explain it better than the teacher because they're kind of on the same wavelength. But they're more involved, I think, when they're working with partners. They're just listening, and that's why manipulatives work so well, because they're able to use them and they're more involved, whereas [when it's] more abstract they'll start to flake out.*

When talking about factors that affect the learning process, Sandy believes that readiness to learn and previous successful learning experiences promote further learning and therefore influence how easily something is learned.

Something is hard to learn because they're not ready to learn it. If the child doesn't un-
derstand addition yet, then it's going to be hard for him to learn subtraction and multi-
plication. If a child really understands addition and subtraction and can add three
plus three plus three in his head, then he'll be able to learn multiplication quickly. So I
think it's just a matter of whether or not he's ready to learn. If a child isn't ready to read
yet, then reading will be hard for him. He won't get the concept of reading. But if he's
been exposed to the words a lot, if he's been exposed to letters a lot, and has had a lot of
reading with teachers and parents, or has read through books and looked through books,
then I think reading will come easier. So it's just experience and whether or not he's
ready to learn that makes it hard or easy, . . . being able to do it well, I think, or under-
standing it. If you can read well then you want to read all the time. If you can't read
well then you won't want to read at all. If you're good at math then you won't mind
math. If you don't like math, then math will be a drag every single day.

From Sandy's perspective, ability grouping also influences the learning
process by hurting children's motivation to learn, their behavior, and their
self-esteem.

Kids know when you've grouped by ability. Especially for the kids in the lowest groups, it
doesn't do anything for their self-esteem, and it makes it really hard for them to try
harder to move themselves up in the group. It also happens that, generally, the kids in
the lowest group are also the worst behaved kids in the group. It's hard for the teacher if
she has to work in a group where all the kids are discipline problems or behavior prob-
lems. Not that much learning is going to get done. If you group heterogeneously, the
(children with) behavior problems will see how to behave, and it will also give them that
boost in their esteem. "I'm not in the lowest group anymore. I can do it. The teacher
trusts me to be able to work." Just that boost in their ego really generates, makes them
want to learn.

Sandy also believes there is a lot of variability in children's aptitude for
learning different subjects, but that parts of that aptitude might be inher-
ited. Furthermore, she still believes, as she did at Time 1, that family background is an important factor in learning. In other words, both nature (experiences) and nurture (heritage) are factors in Sandy's thinking about
learning at Time 2. Perhaps her exposure to different kinds of learners
from many different kinds of families during her 2 years in the DTE program has broadened her view about factors that affect children's learning.
However, Sandy retains her initial belief, based on her personal life experience, that the family influences children's learning.

Some kids are better readers than they are mathematicians. Some kids are better mathe-
maticians than they are readers. Some kids will be in the top group all the time, and
some kids will be in the bottom group all the time. I think, generally, there will be a lot of
variability. . . . A lot of it has to do with their background, whether or not their parents
read to them when they were small. If they read to them a lot, then they would tend to be

good readers, generally. If their parents did a lot of number things and counting and whatever, then they would tend to be good at math. That's not to say that they wouldn't be good at reading, either. One might be better at reading than math or the other way around. Some people are just better in one area than they are in another. From my experience, I think that part of it might be inherent. Their parents [for example, might be] better in reading than in math and they pass it on to the kids. . . . I just know that my dad is really good in math, so I'm better in math than I am in reading and writing. Maybe it's hereditary, I don't know. I also think it has to do with exposure when you're small.

Besides emphasizing the importance of teaching social skills, Sandy often talks in this interview about how she teaches basic skills in language arts, reading, and math. Sandy thinks that the teacher's role is to establish specific tasks for learning through a whole-class lesson. Sandy follows this by having students work independently, with partners, or in small groups while she helps individuals as needed. This is a structure or style she continues to use throughout her career.

It would be just presenting the material to the group as a whole and then letting them go, . . . and then going around and seeing how each child is doing, or each group is doing. Then pulling kids individually who haven't got whatever the teacher is trying to have them do. . . . My approach would be teaching them in a large group first and then having them go and work individually or in small groups. . . . It could be [any task]. It could be write a story or it could be draw a picture, arts and crafts thing. . . . You could do it with any area.

At this time, Sandy's understanding of learning and her teaching methods seem consistent. That is, she believes that students need to communicate, learn from their peers, and be actively involved in their learning. In talking more specifically about teaching second graders how to write correct sentences, Sandy describes the importance of teaching about sentences in the context of writing stories and modeling with student-written examples.

One way I would approach it would be to tell them to write a story and then after they were done writing a story with whatever punctuation and grammar they wanted to, then we would go back and take a story . . . that a kid has written before and say, "Okay, let's look at this story" and see what one idea is and that will be a sentence, and then what another idea is and that will be a sentence. Attacking it that way, so that it's not, "Okay, write a sentence," but so that it is in some kind of context, something they're familiar with doing. They would be familiar with writing stories. . . .

I would set up activities in the classroom that would interest [them] and hopefully encourage them to generate their own learning. Like using learning centers and working with groups, so kids talk to each other and they use another kid's idea rather than (be) teacher-directed: "Today, I want you to write a story about this." Instead of that I would say, "Write something that you're interested in." In math, like patterning or free explora-

tion. They're autonomous and they can do whatever they want to do, so they don't keep coming to the teacher saying, "What do I do now when I'm finished?" This is what I'm thinking about being independent.

Sandy also believes that an important part of her role in the teaching process is to help students learn by teaching concepts in several different ways *"just because some kids will understand it one way, and another kid won't,"* she says. *"If you teach it a different way, that child might understand it."* She explains this with the example of teaching the concept of multiplication as repeated addition and by using arrays to teach families of facts.

Say you want to teach 3 × 5 or just present the concept of multiplication. You'll say, "3 × 5 is 3 rows of apples going this way and 5 rows of apples going this way and you count them all, and that will be 15." It's like saying, "You're adding 3 five times or you're adding 5 three times." That's one way of presenting it. You can present it another way, saying, "You have 15 little blocks all lined up together, and if you divide them up by 3s so you have one group of 3 and another group of 3 until you have 5 groups of 3, and you're adding it." You're doing it the same way, but I think you're teaching it differently.

No longer is teaching just telling students facts and rules; Sandy has now developed five methods to ascertain what and how to teach:

• Observing her students: *If the curriculum is a success and the kids are excited by learning, then I think it's a good curriculum. If the kids didn't learn anything from it, from a unit or whatever, or if it wasn't that much fun, then I think I would have to work on it some more. I guess I would measure it or evaluate it by how successful it was in the classroom. . . . Working with kids individually or in a small group. Just talking to them one on one, getting to know them, or having the kids write or draw even. A lot of interesting things come out of that.*

• Understanding child development: *[For example] just knowing they're still in the first stages of concrete operations, or if they're 8 years old, they'll be in concrete operations in some areas and in some areas they'll still be in a stage below that. Just thinking back and reviewing generally what age group they're able to perform at, which level of development. That would help you understand that for example, this means they don't have reversibility yet, or they don't understand addition, and they won't be able to understand one-to-one correspondence.*

• Going by the district expectations: *Like at the end of first grade, your class should have learned this, and so if I had never worked with first graders before, I would use that as a guideline for coming into second grade . . . or I will test them for those skills to see where they are.*

• Talking to other teachers and taking courses: *Seeing how they teach a certain subject or how they deal with a certain problem, courses that you can take to learn about content. But I think friends and teachers [mainly]. Especially people from this program, since we've had the same background and lot of us are staying in the same area. I would see them as being a real resource.*

- Relying on student teaching experience and observing other teachers: *I thought about Cheri's classroom and ability grouping, and I thought of Scott's classroom. Something that I could relate to and some experiences I'd had.*

Sandy does not rely on test scores, however. *"I don't think test scores really reflect what they're capable of,"* she says, which is another belief she continues to hold throughout her career.

Sandy's pedagogical understanding of children's behavior and development at Time 2 is what the Ammon and Hutcheson Model of Pedagogical Thinking calls *everyday behaviorism.* Her thinking about teaching and learning, however, contains many elements of what this model calls *global constuctivism.* This is a fairly typical pattern of thinking in many DTE students at the time of their graduation, but it is interesting to see how Sandy's thinking develops after a few years in the classroom as a full-time teacher.

SANDY'S 1990 INTERVIEW AND AN OBSERVATION (TIME 3)

I observed and interviewed Sandy several times during the 1989 to 1990 school year, her third year of teaching second grade at Washington Elementary School in San Leandro, California, a suburban community of about 70,000 people. San Leandro is located on San Francisco's East Bay, just south of Oakland. It is sandwiched between the Bay on the west and the East Bay foothills of the Coastal Range on the east.

San Leandro is one of the oldest cities in the Bay Area. The Spanish and Portuguese were the first Europeans to settle in the area, but today San Leandro is primarily a working- and middle-class, multiethnic community of senior citizens and young families. In recent years, local economic development and the construction of low-income housing have increased the economic, cultural, and linguistic diversity in San Leandro's schools. In fact, 35% of the students come from families for whom English is a second language, and more than 33 languages are spoken in the public schools. .

In the San Leandro Unified School District, about 7,600 students attend seven elementary schools, two middle schools, one high school, and one continuation school. Washington Elementary School, where Sandy taught for her first 3 years, was built in 1916. In 1999 to 2000, there are about 425 students in Grades K to 5 at Washington, although during Sandy's tenure between 1987 and 1990, the student population was somewhat smaller. When I visited Sandy's second-grade class in the spring of 1990, she had 33 students, although California law has recently limited class sizes to 20 children in Grades K to 3.

Unlike the other teachers at Washington, Sandy usually teaches math instead of reading during the first and last hour of the day, when she only has half her class. On this split schedule, Sandy teaches about 16 or 17 *Early Birds* and *Late Birds* for almost an hour a day. Because Sandy uses a whole-language approach to teach reading and language arts, she does not want to group her students by their reading ability. Instead, she groups them according to their skill level in math, which is also a compromise. Sandy's principal supports her decision to do this, although most of the other teachers in the school cannot understand how she can teach reading effectively to a whole class. Unlike the other teachers, Sandy foregoes having a teacher's assistant in favor of spending that money on reading materials, such as sets of leveled books from the Wright and Rigby Groups and class sets of children's literature books.

Although Sandy believes her pedagogical decisions are confusing to the other teachers in her school, she feels comfortable teaching reading to a large, heterogeneous group of students. She eschews basal readers in favor of using a whole-language approach to reading, writing, spelling, phonics, and oral language, although she does *Daily Oral Language* every day. When I visit Sandy, I see a typical day of teaching math, reading, and language arts to her second graders.

The classrooms at Washington seem rather small, especially when there are more than 30 children in them, but Sandy has a rug where all the children can sit if they squeeze in close together. She has also arranged 16 small tables into eight groups for four children each. Around the room, bookcases and a bookrack are filled with a wide range of children's literature, and there are cubbies for the children's jackets and backpacks. There is a sink in one corner, and Sandy also has a small storage room filled with additional materials. Bookcases lining one wall are filled with tubs of math manipulatives and school supplies, a record player, and a caged rabbit. A chalkboard fills one wall, and there are windows on another wall. Children's artwork hangs from two lengths of wire criss-crossing the room diagonally. Student projects and charts and graphs from previous lessons cover the walls and bulletin boards. A rack near the rug is loaded with poster-size sheets of poems, and a pocket chart hangs near the front of the rug area.

On the day I observe, Sandy begins with just 11 children in her Early Bird group. For about half an hour, these children are scattered around the room working independently and writing stories. Sandy and JoAnna, her student teacher from the DTE program, meet individually with the children. These conferences entail asking the second graders to read aloud from stories they are writing about what they think it will be like in 2000. Sandy and JoAnna ask questions about their writing and encourage several children to make their stories as realistic as possible. At the end of each conference, Sandy and JoAnna ask the children to read their stories to themselves one more time and circle any words they think might be spelled incorrectly.

When the rest of the class enters the room at 9:15 a.m., the students gather on the rug. When they are settled, Sandy discusses a math puzzler introduced the day before—something the children had taken home to solve with their families. The problem is the classic one about the farmer who has a bag of wheat, a goose, and a fox.

"*The farmer is going on a trip and comes to a river. But there's a problem,*" Sandy says. She stops at this point and asks one of the children to explain the problem. Sandy praises the student's explanation and asks, "*So there's got to be a way to solve this problem. How many people talked about this with someone at home?*"

Next, Sandy selects three children to stand up and pretend to be the farmer, the fox, and the goose. One child suggests building a bridge, and Sandy says, "*OK, let's try that,*" as she points to a pretend bridge.

After they try another child's solution to the problem by acting out how the farmer can get the fox, the goose, and the wheat to the other side of the river without losing any one of the three, Sandy selects another set of children to act out a third solution.

After spending about 10 minutes on this problem, Sandy instructs the students about their next task, which is to sort the materials in the junk boxes on their tables into two groups. She tells them to come up with several different ways to sort the materials, talking with their partner about their ideas. She also asks them to record the categories they decide on with small chalkboards they have often used before. She tells them that she or JoAnna must check their spelling before they go on to record their category names on a large index cards she has put at their tables.

Before dismissing the students to their tables to work together in pairs to sort their junk, Sandy also says, "*There's going to be a problem. What do you think it might be? I'll give you a hint. The problem is two teachers and 28 kids. What do you think the problem will be?*"

The children call out, "*We have to wait our turn!*"

Sandy smiles and then dismisses the children to their tables by groups and reminds the monitors for each table to get two chalkboards, two pieces of chalk, and two socks they can use for erasers before going to their seats.

As the children work on their sorting task, Sandy and JoAnna circulate around the room, talking with pairs of students who have raised their hands. After the students have worked on this task for about half an hour, Sandy rings a bell and waits for all the children to stop talking and moving before she directs them to clean up and get ready for recess.

After the 15-minute recess, the children troop back into the room and go directly to the rug where they sit, waiting for the next lesson to begin.

Sandy praises several children by name for coming in quietly and sitting patiently on the rug. Someone upsets a box of pencils, but no one says a word. Two children get up quietly, pick up the pencils, and return the box to its shelf.

On a large piece of chart paper, Sandy has printed a message, which the children have to correct. This is called *Daily Oral Language*, which Sandy uses to help her students prepare for the standardized test they take at the end of every year. The uncorrected message reads:

> maria visit me at thanksgiving and I visited her at Christmas
> I and my sister seen two dogs a rabbit and a mouse

Sandy calls on students who raise their hands with ideas about how these sentences need to be corrected. With each suggestion, she also asks them "*Why?*" For example, when Charles suggests that the M in maria should be capitalized, Sandy asks him to explain why before she makes the correction to the message on the chart. Sandy spends about 15 minutes on daily oral language before moving on to spend the next hour on other reading and language arts activities.

With the children still sitting on the rug, Sandy introduces a new Shel Silverstein poem about an old man. She reminds the children that several Silverstein books are on their bookrack and then points them to two charts they created during earlier lessons. One chart is filled with vocabulary words associated with being elderly; the other is a Venn diagram entitled, "Is it Better to Be an Adult or a Child?"

After Sandy reads through the new poem once, she asks the students to echo her by reading each line after her, one line at a time. Then everyone reads through the poem in unison several more times before Sandy asks, "*What are things the little boy does that the old man also does?*" This leads into a discussion prompted by questions the children have about why elderly people need diapers and why grownups do not always pay attention to kids and to the elderly. Sandy answers the first question by saying, "*Because they sometimes lose control of their bladders,*" but she asks for some volunteers to answer the second question.

Following this discussion, Sandy leads the children in a 10-minute choral-reading session of a dozen other poems they have learned before. These poems are either pinned up around the room or hang on the flip chart behind their newest poem. Some of the poems are also words to a song, which Sandy leads the children in singing.

Although the children are getting a bit wiggly on the rug, Sandy tells them she is going to read them a story about an old man and a little boy.

When Sandy finishes reading them Silverstein's *The Giving Tree*, one boy volunteers that his uncle had a stroke, and other children want to tell about their sick relatives as well. Sandy takes a few minutes to let these children speak. The rest of the class listens politely before she stops them, saying, "*We need to be moving on.*"

Over the next half hour, Sandy juggles one group of six children who are taking turns reading *Nate the Great*, by Marjorie Sharmat, in pairs and another group of eight students who are working together to create a report card out of poster paper for the main character in one of Marc Brown's *Arthur* books. JoAnna supervises two other small reading groups, and the rest of the children read independently. Sandy sees that everyone is settled into their tasks before meeting with the group making the report card. After consulting with each other, one person in the group begins recording their ideas on chart paper:

Subject	Grade	Comments
MUSIC	C	Arthur is terrible at music.
APPETITE	A+	Arthur eats everything in sight.

While this group works on their report card, Sandy asks the students who have been reading *Nate the Great* with their partners questions such as: "*What was the problem in this story? What was the mystery? Is there a bigger problem in the story? Did Nate the Great find the missing picture? Where was it? Look in your book if you don't remember. Everybody turn to the page where it tells you. The pictures tell us where the missing picture is, but do the words tell us?*" When the children respond, "*Not really,*" Sandy asks them to turn to the previous page and reread it silently. She then asks them, "*Does that explain it? Where are the words on this page that tell us exactly what happened to the picture?*" When they finish this discussion, Sandy tells them to get their free-choice books to read on their own until it is time for lunch.

At the end of the hour, everyone records what they have read today in their reading logs, and then they choose their books and sit on the rug or at their tables to read silently. During this time, Sandy asks one girl to read aloud to her as the others finish writing in their reading logs.

When I talk with Sandy during lunch on this day, she explains how she organizes her instructional time during the day:

I group them by ability for math [but] I'm changing it. I grouped them by ability last year for the whole year, and I grouped them this year by ability because I think it's easier to teach math. I mean there are just some kids that are just slower than others. . . . It was easier to group for math because the group that was working at a faster pace really un-

derstood the concepts, so they could really move, whereas the slower kids, I've really had to work with them on the concepts and they weren't ready to go on to adding and subtracting above 10. So I split them that way.

But, it's not good to do that all the time either because the lower kids need the stimulation the upper kids give them, and they are not getting that the way it's set up now. I also wasn't happy because we weren't doing any problem solving, . . . so I'm giving up the computation stuff.

What I've decided to do is that two mornings a week I'm splitting for math, and two mornings a week we're doing writing instead of math, and we're also going to do whole-group math with problem-solving things. I don't know if it will work. Also, last year we had math on Wednesday mornings all together, but this year because I have my class meeting on Wednesday mornings, we're not able to have that time. . . . The other reason why I'm doing writing in the mornings is that I'm not getting around to the kids, and I can't do the writing conferences the way it's set up now. So, if I split the kids up for writing two mornings a week, then I'll be able to have more individual time.

I did try last year at the beginning of the year to not have morning groups and late groups, and I tried to get it so that I could have all the kids come at the same time and leave at the same time—which means an extra hour a day for them—from 8 to 3 instead of from 8 to 2 or 9 to 3—but I think I would have had a lot of pressure from teachers if I had done that. And last year, I did make that change from splitting for reading to splitting for math, and I feel a lot happier about that. There are other teachers who don't approve of that. They split for reading—everybody else splits for reading except me. But, I think that I would have had a lot of resentment if I had gone to the whole day. Well, they all teach with the basals, and they have four groups, and you can't do four groups in one reading period. So for them it's easier to manage. . . .

I think the parents would have been fine. For the most part they would have been happy because they don't have to take care of baby-sitting problems, and that would have been part of the reason for the resentment from other teachers—the parents would have gone, "Mrs. Brumbaum is doing this, why aren't you doing it?" But the other thing is that the district, the teacher's union, worked hard about 20 years ago to get the split reading groups, [and] the staggered schedule, and then if somebody decides to go against that, then it goes against the union and what they've worked for.

Sandy has clearly given a lot of thought to how she teaches reading and writing, which she does from a whole-language perspective. She says,

I just see that as being really different from a basal reader that they're using right now. I really want to do a little more oral language, chanting, and doing things with pocket charts, and learning nursery rhymes, and poems and learning to read that way rather than memorizing words and learning from a controlled-vocabulary type structure, and doing worksheets. I'd rather just see them writing and being read to, instead of just filling in the blanks and [having] them doing phonics work—which they do need, but I'd rather just teach it to them whole, integrated with the reading, rather than separated out.

It's interesting, because I just went to the California Reading Conference in San Jose and they were talking about whole language with the fourth and fifth grade . . . but when you talk about teaching whole language, what does that mean as far as doing it

with an intermediate-grade class? I don't think it would be that different from what I'm doing with the second graders now. I'd have them in literature books. Sometimes we would do a literature book together; sometimes we'd do independent reading where everyone chooses their own book, and sometimes we'd do small groups where different kids would read the same book. I guess the activities would be the same too—"Reader's Theater," and trying to teach the skills through the literature rather than separating them out and doing worksheets. So, I guess in that way I consider that whole language right now, and that's what I've been doing in second grade too.

At the end of the day, in her responses to the standard clinical interview questions, Sandy says little about children's behavior and development, although she has plenty to say about learning and teaching.

One of the few things Sandy does say about behavior at Time 3 is that she thinks social factors influence children's behavior. Sandy singles out the following factors as influences on children's classroom behavior: how they get along together and their independence and ability to work in groups. She also thinks that, with age, most children improve these skills, but she does not explain how this happens.

Sandy thinks that cognitive factors develop, including children's problem-solving ability, logical thinking, and their ability to imagine hypothetical situations and hold more than one or two variables constant in their mind to solve problems. She also says that children develop physically and mentally as they become less egocentric, better able to understand abstract concepts, and able to think more abstractly. She has little to say about the workings of the developmental process, except that development is a natural process that happens because children have more experiences as they get older.

Sometimes things are real black and white for them and there's no in between, and . . . they either like something or they don't like it. There's no gray. . . . I guess it is just developmental and where they are. Some of them are more abstract thinkers and are able to deal with the gray, and it's not so much right or wrong anymore. . . . The older kids are a lot more honest with you, and I think they'll let you know what they like and don't like. I think they are at that point able to express their feelings. . . . They are able to think through what it is that they are thinking. They have a reason, and they know the reason why they feel this way, and they know the reason why they don't.

As this statement indicates, Sandy's thinking about children's development is rather global and nonspecific. In fact, her understanding of the developmental process is not particularly well articulated at Time 3, and her understanding of development is about the same as when she graduated from the DTE program. This is not too surprising given that, during her first 2 years in the classroom, Sandy focused on the practical aspects of teaching and learning, and her thinking about child development has not been exercised as it was when she was in graduate school learning developmental theory. It is also an example of why many researchers claim that what was learned in teacher education programs washes out during the induction years. For Sandy, and others in this study, this looks to be the case, but it may be an artifact of studying beginning teachers for only 1 or 2 years and not following them further into their careers.

Nevertheless, when asked what kinds of experiences are most likely to bring about learning, Sandy has a lot to say. She does so in the language of Piaget, utilizing the Piagetian concept of *disequilibrium*:

> *You do it to them to a certain extent, but I don't think that you can help them get to a disequilibrium point. It's just that they're there and they've got this one understanding of something and they're ready for you to come to them and to say "Well, what about this?" and they'll go "Oh!" and then at that point they are in disequilibrium, and they are ready to learn.*

Sandy also offers a concrete example of how she creates disequilibrium experiences by asking questions to guide students' learning experiences:

> *When I was working with a low group of readers . . . and we were arranging words . . . [from the Dr. Seuss book] HOP on POP, and I had them on cards, and I asked them to match all the words that rhymed together. They went through and they tried to sound out each word, but they didn't really get the fact that they were spelled pretty much the same, and that there was a pattern in their spelling. They didn't get that that made a difference to the way you say the words until I said, "Well, look at the words. What can you tell me about these words that you've stacked here? You say that these words rhyme. What can you tell me about the way they look?" And one kid said, "Oh. They're all spelled kind of the same. They all have -AT." And the other kid didn't get it. I don't think he saw it. You can lay it in front of them and you can hope that they see it, but I don't think that you can pound it in their head. So I guess you just have to keep providing them with experiences, and hopefully at some point they are ready for it. . . . It's hard for them to get it in the whole group—big groups, I mean. I think you've just got to give them as much experience as you can and hope that at one point or another the kids are ready for that "aha" experience, and then they'll get it. You've got to lead them to water as often as you can. Because if they are not ready to drink, they're not ready to drink. You can't force them.*

Sandy prefers to work with small groups rather than with the whole class to get her students into ideal learning situations, which for her is a state of disequilibrium. Furthermore, her teaching practices appear to match her pedagogical thinking:

> *I don't feel like when you are teaching the whole class you are getting everybody, so it's real hard for kids in the whole group environment to get the "aha" experience. It's got to be more in a smaller group or individual type setting. So I think writing conferences are*

good for "aha" type experiences. . . . Especially for those really low kids. . . . The active learners will learn from anything, whereas you've really got to work with the lower kids, the kids who aren't academic. . . . For them, I think that the smaller groups settings are better.

Sandy also seems to understand that many factors affect the learning process, including children's preferred learning styles, how much background or previous experience they have, and how abstract or concrete something is. In fact, her thinking about learning is better differentiated and supported by specific examples that show how her understanding of the learning process is more elaborate than it was 3 years earlier.

One kid may learn and understand how to carry and borrow [in subtraction] just by being shown how to do it with pencil and paper, but other kids may need to be shown with manipulatives, or if manipulatives don't work then they need to be shown another way. And so for different people, they will learn one thing in different ways just because of the kind of learner they are. . . . That's one of the problems with the basal [reader] is that they are just teaching the kids one way and there are kids that can't learn that way.

It's just the concept—whether it's an abstract or a concrete concept. If it's a concrete concept, it's easier to learn. Also if you have the background knowledge or experience, it makes it easier to understand. If you haven't had a foundation, then you have to build up that foundation first before you can understand what the concept is. I guess it's just like [for] a scientist or something where some things are real easy to understand because they understand everything that leads up to that one concept, but for us there's a big gap and I don't understand that at all because I haven't had that foundation.

When Sandy talks about what is taught, she includes academics, such as reading and writing, math, and problem solving, but she also stresses teaching social skills. This includes helping children learn how to get along with others and how to become independent in the classroom—two goals she had at Time 2 and still feels are important. Here Sandy describes how she teaches children to be independent thinkers and learners:

A lot of it is when kids get into trouble—by asking them, "How could you have done this otherwise? How could you have worked it out? What is something else that you could do next time this happens?" It's not something that they are going to learn overnight. But I think that the way the classroom is set up, the kids have to learn to get help from someone else, and they have to learn to help each other. I'm all over the room, and the kids are all over the room, and it's not like they are all in rows and everybody sits at their seat and can't get out, and they don't raise their hands and wait until I come to them, because everybody's going to have a problem and they just need to decide if it's a problem that I need to solve, or if it's one they can get help with from somebody else. So partly they learn it because they have to survive in the classroom, but I try to model it for them, and we talk about it a lot.

Responsibility, self-discipline, and respect for authority "*should be taught at home first, and then the schools need to follow-up on them,*" Sandy says. "*I don't think it is fair for society to say that it's the school's job to teach the kids, and not the parents.*"

Sandy's understanding of the teaching process at this time is consistent with how she talks about the learning process. For example, Sandy thinks that teaching means offering her students guided experiences they can build on before doing any direct instruction, starting with the whole class and then working in small groups and individually with children as needed. In the following example, Sandy talks about how she would teach the concept of a sentence to third graders. Note that this description is similar to what she said at Time 2, but different in that here she gives a more detailed example. She also offers her rationale:

> *The best way would be to first model it in my writing and also to take an incorrect piece of writing as far as mechanics and correct it with the class. And then for the kids who are still having problems to do it individually with their own writing. And I think that's one of the reasons why "Writer's Workshop" is really great, because you get to work with the kids, maybe in a small group or individually based on what they are ready to learn. Then they can apply it to their own writing. Because you can teach periods through worksheets until you are blue in the face and not have them apply it to their own writing.*
> . . .
> *It's nice to give them an experience to go through before you tell them what they are going to learn just so that they have a background or that they have some kind of experience so that they know in a way what you are talking about. . . . It takes a lot of preparation to do that, but I think the kids learn more. They focus more, and they understand more of what you are saying when you stand up there, talking to them about what you are going to be doing, when they have some kind of experience to base it on. Then you do the whole group and then model it for them, and then have them work through it in a group, in a small group, or individually.*

To know what and how to teach, Sandy seems to depend on her own assessments and observations of how children approach a task. In fact, diagnosing where they are in their learning appears to be one of Sandy's strengths.

> *At the beginning of the year I definitely want to read with each student and see what kind of reader they are, not so much what words they know or don't know, but how they approach reading and what their strategies are in reading. . . . As far as math goes, I do an assessment test at the beginning of the year. It's just a math sheet where I ask them to do simple addition, and missing addends, and time problems, and money problems. It's just to see what they have retained from last year. I don't know if that's the best thing to do, but it's not so much whether or not they get the answer right, it's more what they do to solve the problems. . . . Yes, something else that I do—and I can do this with second graders but I can't with first graders—I have them write me a letter on the first day of*

school just to see what their writing skills are, what their handwriting looks like, what they are able to spell, but also how comfortable they feel, and whether they can put together a sentence or a paragraph.

Sandy also has set goals for her students and herself that convey her growing interest in early literacy:

My goals for them: I want them to be independent first. I want them to not always have to come to me to figure out what to do next. I want them to love reading and writing. I've been thinking so much about these low readers and how I can help them. . . . They are so focused on word-for-word, and they try to sound out each word. I want them to get that reading should make sense. I want them to do more predictions and focus more on the meaning, and what makes sense here, rather than what does this word say. I don't care if it's right or not. If it makes sense, okay as long as it goes with the rest of the story.

Right now my goal is to really work on the language arts, reading and writing. I'd like to integrate them a little more. One of the goals I had for this year was to really do poetry with the kids, and I feel like I've really done that. The kids just love the poetry time that we have. I feel like everything is so separate still. We do writing at the beginning of the year and the kids say, "Is this reading, because we're doing writing right now." So it was integrated, but then I also have writing Workshop, and I don't know if that's something I can let go of, because it's not really integrated with reading. Yet in a way it is because during writing time, if kids don't finish up whatever they were doing in reading or in social studies, or if they're writing letters, they can finish up during writing time.

She also makes a point of getting feedback from her students:

If they are enjoying something, that's feedback. And I feel like if they have enjoyed the activity, then they have learned something. Then the chances of them learning something will be better than if they didn't enjoy it. Most of them will be able to see that they enjoyed it and learned something. A lot of time we'll do an activity and we'll stop . . . and talk about it afterwards.—"How did it go? What did you think? Did you like it? Did you not like it?" So I get feedback that way. Or even just in their work, when they read or they write, that's feedback on whether or not they've learned something. . . . Something I've played with also is doing an evaluation sheet or something, maybe in January—"What do you like to do or how fair do you think I am?" And that kind of thing.

Nevertheless, Sandy wonders if she is doing the right thing and making a difference in her students' learning, which is something she continues to ponder throughout her career as she strives to enact her pedagogical beliefs.

I've had parents say to me, either at the end of the year or the next year, "so and so really loves to read and I think that you did that for him," or "I've really seen John's writing come a long way this year." So I think that I have made a difference, but I also get concerned because I look at the CTBS [California Test of Basic Skills] score, and because I don't focus on those skills, and I don't drill them, and I don't teach them a format, their scores go down. So I worry about that. But luckily the principal, Jim, doesn't believe in them, and he doesn't put that much value on the scores.

But I think the parents do, and they wonder why the scores go down. I don't believe in the test, and yet it's there, and it is something that somebody looks at, and so this year we do little things in the classroom every day to try to get the kids ready for that. In February or something, I'll probably pull out some worksheets so the kids get used to them. You know I think part of the problem is that I haven't done worksheets at all. I don't do worksheets, and I don't ask them to fill in the bubbles, and so they don't know how to take the test.

But the other thing is that I don't worry about the skills as much as everybody else does, which is not necessarily good . . . I probably shouldn't say that. I don't think that I'm not teaching them, but I think what I'm teaching them are survival skills, real-life skills, and . . . I'm just not focusing on the skill skills. Because I feel like they'll get that eventually, because so many teachers teach skills that they'll get it. I don't know if that's a good attitude or not, but I want them to be able to think, to be able to survive when they go outside.

ANOTHER INTERVIEW WITH SANDY IN 1990

I also interviewed Sandy several times during the spring of 1990 for a project I was doing for a graduate school class. My goal was to capture Sandy's voice and focus on the issues she was thinking about at the time. This interview was open ended, beginning with my asking her what she had been thinking about as a teacher. What follows is the result of that interview, which provides additional information about Sandy as a teacher and person at Time 3 during her third year in the classroom.

I've been thinking a lot about making a change from teaching second grade here. I think I'm ready to teach another grade. I am really comfortable with second grade now, and it's fun, but I'm ready to move on. Eventually the second grade curriculum would get boring and I need variety. Another change may be to go with my principal who is going to be moving to another school in the district next year. He believes in what I'm doing and would like me to help him "spread the word" at his new school. So he will try to find me a spot at that school, if I want to go with him.

I would go with him because if I stay here, I will have to change the way I teach because of the new principal. I probably wouldn't be able to split my kids for math, and I'd have to use the staggered time for reading like everyone else rather than teaching reading with the whole class. My principal allows me to do that because he likes my program, but the new principal, I've heard, would be more by-the-book and probably not allow that to happen.

I know teaching first grade will be a lot more work, but it will be exciting. I really want to tackle beginning-literacy. I know second grade now after teaching it for three years, and I'm interested in working with children who are just beginning to read and write. I've gotten a taste for it by working with my low readers. I feel I have enough information and training. One reason it might be more work is that the kids aren't as independent in first grade. My new school will be tougher, and it is much more multicultural than here. I'm not looking forward to teaching the handwriting—but I am interested in the development of literacy. I want to check out my theories and see if how I think beginning reading and writing should be taught really works—experiencing language first by using lots of oral language, poetry, shared reading, etc. Maybe I'll find out that you have to teach spelling to first graders or they won't learn to spell, but I want to see.

I don't really think I'm all that well liked here either—well, that's not really it. There's a lot of jealousy and some alienation here between Gail [another graduate of the DTE program] and I with the rest of the staff. I think they think we are trying to be stars and impress our principal and the parents. Other staff members have even remarked on our being the principal's "favorites." But that's not what it's all about. I'm doing it for myself. We do have a lot of definite ideas about how to teach—like that learning is a process and not a product, which we learned in DTE. Most other teachers are just accustomed to using teacher's manuals, basal readers, and ditto books, and they don't really have a strong philosophy of education. People talk and lots of people here say that I'm the principal's favorite and because of that I get to go to a lot of conferences and do these Workshops like "Family Math." The principal is really supportive of us. I guess I'm spoiled, and I like the autonomy I have here with him.

I think other teachers started wondering about me my first year when I agreed to teach the "Junior Great Books" program. I was a first-year teacher and there I was taking on this extra thing for the GATE [Gifted and Talented Education] kids, but I really wanted to do some literature-based reading. It was the first time they had tried it in the district, so schools were grouping the GATE kids together for reading. Now everyone uses the program in their own way. During my first year, though, the GATE program was arranged for second and third grades, and fourth through sixth grades too. I took all the primary GATE kids during the last hour of staggered reading while the rest of my class came the first hour for their reading. What the other teachers couldn't understand was how I could teach reading to different levels of students at the same time. This became even a bigger issue the next year when I didn't do staggered reading and taught whole-group reading instead. That's when people started recognizing that my teaching style was a little different than the traditional way of doing things.

One thing I really wish I could do more about is parent involvement and parent education. This was really brought out when we did the Family Math [program] and also when we did a presentation to the parents about how whole language will look different from basal readers. Parents listen, but their expectations don't change.

Last year I went to a conference at UC–Berkeley on parent involvement, and I was talking about doing home visits when this other teacher said, "Oh yeah! Where am I going to find the time?"

I think half my job would be done if I could reach parents. I'd really like to do parent Workshops, but I don't know how to get parents there. I'd like to do something like Family Math, only with language arts. Even when you do, I guess it's like teaching a class of kids, and some will get it and some won't.

This year all the parents are really supportive. I get good feedback. Their kids like school, so they're happy. Some parent even told me they like the way I do spelling.

Parents at my new school probably won't be as involved as these parents. It's a Title 1 school in a lower socioeconomic neighborhood, and most are working parents. It's not that they care less, but they won't be able to help out at school as much.

I don't know if I'll do anything different with the staff at this new school. It's a much larger group of teachers with at least three in each grade, but there are a lot more young teachers. I think they are more open to new ideas, since some of them just finished their teacher training recently.

I think the principal's job is to set the morale, but I know it will be hard to get cohesiveness with such a large staff at the new school. The former principal there didn't provide very strong leadership. Jim has a good reputation, though, so he may get the support he needs that way. The most important thing to me is that the principal should support me in whatever I want to do because he knows that I am knowledgeable and can make knowledgeable decisions. He shouldn't just support me on blind faith. He should support me with parents too—because he knows I'm doing a good job in my room. I think other teachers would say that the first job of the principal is to be the ultimate authority with the kids, and I don't necessarily agree with that. He should also anticipate any possible disagreements between teachers.

There have been some big political issues this year, and not wanting teacher aides is just an example of another difference between Gail and I and the rest of the staff. So I have student teachers from DTE. The principal raves about the student teachers we get to the rest of the staff, and it probably creates more jealousy. The teachers just talk to us about how much work it is, and how the kids need to spend their time with just us, but I think it is important for the kids to have another teacher in the room to interact with and to help them. For me, a student teacher is better than an aide because, coming from the DTE program, they already share the same philosophy that I have.

I don't know. Gail says its hard being a pioneer, and she's right. We were just talking about this. Maybe there are some effects we've had on other teachers, like their trying to do more literature-based reading. . . . Working in another district might be easier. It is hard being a pioneer, but it is challenging for me—but then I don't have any parent problems this year like Gail, so I'm not as frustrated as she is.

What would really have helped me during my time in DTE is if someone had told [me] that what I was getting was the "ultimate" program, but that I wouldn't be able to do everything in the first year—and that this was all right. One of the supervisors did tell me that it would be okay if I had to teach from a basal reader, and that there was something to be learned from doing that. First-year teachers have to make some compromises because of time limitations and district constraints. Maybe they will have to teach spelling instead of being able to use invented spelling as they were taught. They may have to compromise because they aren't going to be as secure in their philosophy of teaching as I am now. I had to, but now I wouldn't give up my program.

You know I think it might be easier for a DTE teacher to burn out than for some other teachers from other teacher training programs. Other programs don't have as much theory, and teachers are satisfied with just using basal readers. For me there's never enough time to do everything you know you should be doing. I'm always shooting for a better program because I think I know what it can be like. It's hard when you've got such firm beliefs. I know that this is the best way for developmental teaching. They covered every area of the curriculum in the methods classes in DTE, but you can't do it all. The methods classes really didn't help. They just threw ideas at us and I wasn't really ready, and didn't get anything from them. We didn't know why these activities were given to us, and there was no continuity. Everything I learned about teaching came from the theory classes, not from the methods classes. The theory gives you reasons why things work. They really focused on the developmental schemes. The methods classes needed a more developmental perspective, and I needed to try things and then apply it to the theory.

I'm just now getting comfortable with language arts—with writing and speaking and listening and reading. One parent said I must work 20 hours a week just on re-

sponding to the children in their reading logs. I do, but then other things don't get done, like correcting all their homework papers. Last year we did a lot of publishing of their writing, and I did a lot of typing of stories. I just had to stop before burning out. The state does the same thing to teachers with their 7-year cycles. There's not enough time to get comfortable with one area before it's time to move on. I thought the DTE program was such good training, and I worked so hard that I thought life would be a cinch afterward. But it's not true. Now I'm always juggling so much.

When I think about myself in comparison to other teachers in my school, I think I have a theoretical background that others don't have. For example, I know why basals aren't developmentally correct, that kids should work in groups, and use manipulatives. Other teachers know kids but not the theory. Or, they have old theory, like the reading specialist who got her credential 10 years ago. Other teachers don't want to change what they are doing. They say, "We've seen this before. It's the same thing we did before." Or they just [ask] why should they change to this new thing because it will just change again. But I disagree with that. I think that there are more and better studies—more research—since these teachers went to school. I believe in and understand, or at least try to understand, those new studies.

Another difference between me and some of the other teachers is that the more I learn, the more I feel I need to know. I read more, and I go to more workshops. Other teachers have their classrooms the way they want them and they aren't willing to change. Change is hard. But if I think it will make something better, then I'm willing to do it.

SANDY'S 1993 INTERVIEW AND AN OBSERVATION (TIME 4)

When I made plans to interview and observe Sandy in late spring 1993, she had moved to a different school in the same district and had been teaching first grade at Wilson Elementary School since 1990. She also gave birth to her first child, Hannah, in 1991. At the time I interviewed her, Sandy was job sharing with another teacher and teaching first graders 2½ days a week.

More than 850 students attend Wilson Elementary School, which is much larger than Washington Elementary. Wilson is a Title 1 school because 48% of the students are eligible for free or reduced lunch, and therefore it is entitled to receive extra federal funding. Wilson also serves an even more diverse group of students than Washington did when Sandy taught there. The ethnic makeup of Wilson is 43% Hispanic, 16% Filipino, 15% White, 12% Black, and 12% Asian. In fact, 35% of the children at Wilson are designated as English Language Learners; the state average in California is 25%. Sixty-four percent of the children at Wilson speak Spanish as their first language, 12% speak Cantonese, 10% speak Tagalog (the language of the Filipino children and their families), and 8% speak Vietnamese. There are also children attending Wilson whose first language is Korean, Arabic, or Punjabi. The school housed one of San Leandro's "Newcomer" classrooms for children of recent immigrants, where they can adjust to American schools and learn some English before being placed into the appropriate classroom.

As I enter Sandy's first-grade classroom, it strikes me as a microcosm of the school's population, with 31 boys and girls of different racial and ethnic backgrounds, some English proficient and some English Language Learners. Her classroom looks like many other first-grade classrooms I have visited over the years, except that one of the walls is literally covered with poster-size pieces of laminated chart paper, on which Sandy has printed poems and songs that her students read and chant every day. The theme for the week's activities appears to be *friendship,* judging by the titles I see on several pieces of chart paper: "Best Friends," "With a Friend," and "Making Friends," among others. Several other large posters display word lists related to friendship or have titles such as "Winter is . . ." and "Fall is . . .".

As I look around the room, I observe six clusters of small tables arranged on two sides of a large rug. Some of these tables are grouped so that six children can sit together in a cluster, and others have room for four children. There is a large chalkboard on the wall behind the rug with self-portraits of the students posted above it. Hanging on either side of the chalkboard are a calendar and chart paper for the daily message. Between the rug and students' tables, a low bookshelf holds small chalkboards, chalk, and erasers. Opposite the rug are more bookshelves with many colorful tubs full of books. These tubs are labeled with topics such as weather, color, poems, animals, and friends. More books are arranged on shelves forming Sandy's class library.

Below high windows, low shelves contain tubs full of math manipulatives, including pattern blocks, Unifix cubes, dice, geoboards, plastic counters, and other kinds of manipulatives used for learning math. There is also a listening center with a tape recorder and several sets of earphones, a small chalkboard, a small whiteboard, a file cabinet, and more bookshelves under the windows. Several graphs and charts also hang below the windows with labels that read: "Graph of the Week" (how many teeth the children have been lost each week), "Monthly Chart" (how many students have birthdays each month), "Weather" (a daily weather record), and "Class History" (events that occurred each month). In front of the window wall, a rectangular table holds materials for writing and signs reading "Sign up for Author's Chair," "Sign up for a Conference" and "Publish Here."

In the corner of the room opposite the large rug and in front of the sink is a kidney-shaped table with five chairs for small-group work and a second small table. Teacher materials and school supplies are stored in wall cupboards covered with children's math art projects. A file cabinet and closets for the students' jackets and backpacks are near the door. One bulletin board next to the door is labeled "Parent News," and a second bulletin board is apparently just for things that are red, yellow, and brown.

The morning begins with half the class, the Early Birds, engaged in a 10-minute spelling lesson with Sandy. Fourteen first graders are writing on small chalkboards and trying to figure out what goes in the middle of words that begin with the letter W, which Sandy has written on the large chalkboard. The students copy these partially complete words onto their chalkboard, leaving a space between the first and last letters. Sandy asks them to try to make words they know by adding a letter in the middle and using the sounds of first and last letters to help them.

w	d	w	g
w	g	w	n

After filling in the missing letters to make words, Sandy asks the students to say them several times. She then asks them to erase and make four more words that also begin with the letter of the week. On the large board, she writes the following:

w	f	w	l
w	r	w	m

This time Sandy pronounces the words one at a time: wolf, wail, war, and worm. She asks the students to figure out what letters go in the middle. After going over these new words, emphasizing the beginning and ending sounds, Sandy asks them to erase and write five of their best Ws. As they finish, the students bring their chalkboards to the rug. They sit in a circle and show their work before student helpers collect the chalk, erasers, and chalkboards and put them away on the nearby shelf. [Note: Sandy says that she does not remember this and thinks she might have had her students write the first and last sounds of words with an initial or final "w," but not the middle letter.]

It is now time for math. Sandy reminds them about a game they played the day before with dice. She then explains a new dice game that requires both dice, one with numbers on it and one with the traditional dots on it to represent numbers. Sandy demonstrates how each student will roll both dice and add the results in the proper place on their recording sheet, which she lays out in front of her on the rug.

		1 + 2		2 + 3		4 + 3			
1	2	3	4	5	6	7	8	9	10

One student asks how you could get 11, and Sandy asks the class if anyone knows. Several hands go up and Sandy tells them they can add 11 and 12 to their record sheet if they want. She also tells them that this game is just like another game they have played before called "Shake the Beans." In both games, she tells them, you roll, count, and write your equation.

Sandy then explains that the new dice game will be at the triangle table while the game they played yesterday will be at the circle table. The junk boxes will be at the diamond table, and the pattern blocks and "Shake the Beans" are also out for them to use today. Sandy then asks one student to get the number sheets, which have target numbers on them for each student to work on. Some children are working on larger numbers than others, and Sandy tells them to work on a new number today—one they have not worked on before. Sandy dismisses the students, one table at a time, to choose different math activities to work on for the next 20 minutes. Sandy spends this time circulating around the room to observe and help students as needed. Most of the students change tables or a different activity at least once during this time, but everyone is actively engaged—rolling dice and recording the numbers, shaking and counting beans, or making patterns with the pattern blocks.

With about 10 minutes left in the Early Bird hour, Sandy asks the children to clean up, put away all the math manipulatives, and come sit on the rug. This happens very quickly. Sandy then asks them to sing the words to the story she has displayed on a rack, *The Five Little Ducks*. The students do this enthusiastically twice through before Sandy dismisses them by name to go outside for recess.

When the rest of the class returns after recess, the seats at the tables are nearly filled. I count 28 students now, 14 boys and 14 girls. Four students are absent. It gets quiet in the room because this time is designated for silent reading, and most students are in their seats or sitting on the rug with their books. Sandy helps some of the students find new books to read and collects several notes that students hand to her.

After 10 minutes, Sandy rings a bell and asks the students to put their books away and come to the rug. She waits for them to get settled before saying anything. Sandy spends the next 7 or 8 minutes on the morning calendar routine. She tells them that today's date can be written as 3-5-93 and that this is a secret code for March 5, 1993. She asks the students to repeat the date after her, count by 5s, and give her some math sentences for the number 5. She records all the equations they volunteer on chart paper, including: $4 + 1 = 5$, $7 - 2 = 5$, $5 + 0 = 5$, $2 + 3 = 5$, $10 - 5 = 5$, and even $1 \times 5 = 5$, which one child offers. The next part of the morning routine is something Sandy calls *Daily News*, which she prints on a large piece of chart paper headed by today's date. Sandy asks if anyone has any news, and when she is finished writing what they tell her plus a sentence of her own, she and the students read together:

> Today is Friday. It is March 5, 1993. One of
> our buddies in Ms. Lewis' class wrote a poem. We
> have many versions of *The Little Red Hen*. We are
> going to have an earthquake drill today.

Sandy asks the class if anyone can tell her why she put a line under *The Little Red Hen*, and one student tells the rest of the class that it is the name of a book. Then Sandy talks with the class about today's earthquake drill. The students get all excited and want to share their experiences with earthquakes. Sandy allows a few minutes of this and then settles the class down to explain the drill procedures.

After this, Sandy leads them in reading the poems and songs posted on the walls. She stands and uses a pointer to point to each line. The students do choral reading, reading and chanting them together as a group, with Sandy leading. Some of the students appear to have memorized several of the poems and songs, but all seem to be able to participate.

After about 10 minutes, Sandy sits back down to read them a book called *The Little Yellow Chicken*. The students are attentive to the story, which Sandy reads with great expression. A brief discussion ensues about the characters in the story, and then Sandy asks the students to read it with her one more time. The students clap in excitement over this. Sandy then asks them to think about this story and *The Little Red Hen*, especially how they are the same and how they are different. Sandy then draws two large, overlapping circles on a clean piece of chart paper. She labels one circle *The Little Yellow Chicken* and the other *The Little Red Hen*. She asks them to tell her about things that happened in both stories. She writes these in the place where the two circles overlap. She also writes things that are not the same about each story in the other parts of the two circles. Finally, Sandy reads *The Little Red Hen* aloud to the class one more time before it is time to get them ready for the earthquake drill and then recess.

SANDY'S 1993 INTERVIEW (TIME 4)

Although Sandy tells me she really enjoyed teaching first graders for the past 3 years, she also tells me she has been struggling to balance her personal and professional lives. As a new mother, she is job sharing and teaching part time, but this is problematic in some ways. Perhaps it is best to let Sandy explain this herself.

> *It makes it harder. There are a lot of things going on. Part of it is that I have a baby, so I don't have as much time at home in the afternoons, and evenings, and on weekends to*

spend planning for school. The other part is teaching part time and job sharing. . . . I'm not completely free to do what I want to with the curriculum, and so I'm kind of tied down that way. . . . Right now I'm thinking of possibly taking a leave next year and doing something related, but I don't want to give up everything that I've done the last seven or eight years [since] DTE. And I'd like to do something related to teaching, . . . work in a preschool or go back and take some more classes, or do something somewhere else that's related to teaching, because I've got all this stuff at home, and I don't want to give it up, and I want it to be used. . . . I like being with the baby, but I don't know if I could be there full time. So that's the other thing . . . part of me doesn't want to get out of teaching because I think it would be hard to go back into teaching once I leave, because I think that the classroom dynamics are changing so fast.

As a follow-up, I ask Sandy to explain what she means by *changing classroom dynamics* and what she would have to readjust to if she left teaching.

The kinds of kids that we're getting into the school. Just in 6 years of teaching there've been a lot more non-English speaking kids and a lot of kids that come from broken up families, and . . . it just seems like the kids have gotten needier and needier and needier, and the classes have gotten bigger and bigger and bigger, and the demands on the teacher have gotten to be more and more and more. . . . I can deal with it if I stay in teaching, but I don't know if I can deal with it [if I] leave at one point in time and then come back and find that . . . all these demands have increased on the teacher.

When I ask Sandy to say more about the changes in public education and the demands on teachers, she voices concerns that continue to frustrate many teachers today.

The money's not there, so the class sizes have gotten bigger. The support for the teachers has gone out the window. You don't get the psychological help that you need for the kids, and the support from the parents isn't there, and you're getting a lot more non-English speaking kids, like I said before, in your classroom. And you're not getting help for that, and then we've got some kids in there that need a lot of psychological help and the special programs aren't there to take them into the special day class or the emotionally disturbed class. Those programs aren't there, so everything's being done by the teacher. . . . So there're just a lot of demands being put on us, the public school system, and the teachers can't deal with it by themselves. Or like, I shouldn't say they can't, just that it's very demanding, and it's hard to meet everybody's needs.

But what would she do if she took a year off? I ask her if she would like to get into staff development and teaching other teachers given her interest in the whole-language approach and her earlier desire to do more with involving parents in programs like Family Math.

I don't like doing training. I don't like doing classes, giving classes. I'm not comfortable in front of adults. . . . I do okay, but it's not something I enjoy. My teaching partner, on the other hand, just loves it. And she can get up there, because she's got that kind of per-

sonality . . . and she enjoys doing that. I like to do the planning and all that stuff, but I don't enjoy standing up in front of a group of people.

I also ask Sandy whether she thought about teaching at a private school, where class sizes are typically smaller. This prompts Sandy to talk extensively about her feelings about education from her dual perspective as a teacher and new parent.

That goes against my philosophy . . . and all your training from DTE to work in public schools. We're going through this dilemma now that Hannah's a year old. What are we going to do when she gets to be school age? Are we going to send her to private school or to a public school? . . . My husband is pretty frustrated with the whole process . . . [and] I think if she were going to school next year we'd be sending her to a private school. . . . I believe in public education, but I also think that there have been a lot of changes and a lot more demands put on the teacher that make it more difficult for the teachers to teach.

Before beginning the clinical interview questions, Sandy also talks again about her frustrations with job sharing, with trying to juggle her roles as a teacher and mother, and with her thinking about taking off a year, all of which weigh heavily on her mind as her sixth year of teaching comes to a close.

Part of me is thinking that it takes a certain personality to be able to job share and that I'm not one of those personalities. I guess you have to be more easygoing about things. And I feel like I'm pretty easygoing, but I think that for me, I have a lot of expectations of myself as a teacher, and in that way I'm not so easygoing about my teaching. In that way it's harder to let go.

And it's especially hard when you've got two people in the classroom. . . . We have two different teachers with two different styles. Barbara's expectations and her goals may not be the same as mine, and the way that we deal with them might not be the same. We never sat down and said, "These are my goals," but I think that philosophically we share the same ideas and the same goals. I think that we approach them differently.

I wouldn't job share if I didn't have the choice. . . . That's why I'm thinking of taking a leave. I'm thinking that there's something else that I could do. I would really love to be teaching full time if I . . . felt like I could do a good job and yet not take away from my being a mom. But I can't. So, I have to give that up.

It's frustrating, that part of it, not being able to do what I want to do because I'm job sharing. That's frustrating, and not being able to plan, . . . Even if I did have my own classroom, which I could do, then I wouldn't be able to plan for it like I wanted to do, because I have a baby at home. So, there's all these things going on, and. . . . It's hard to know, which one is weighing more heavily.

When talking about children's behavior in the classroom during this interview, Sandy compares social and cognitive differences between the first and second grades she taught for 3 years each. She explains how a host of factors influence behavior of first and second graders differently. By extension, these factors affect what a teacher can do with children in these grades, which she attributes in part to their experiences with the school routines.

> *It's real hard to teach 32 kids [first graders] in a classroom with all these other needs. . . . The classrooms need to be smaller so that you can work with them independently, because everybody's got a different need, and they're all at different levels, but they're not yet able to work independently. Whereas the second and third graders, you can give them something to do, and they can sit down and do it while you're working with a small group. With first graders it's really difficult to do, especially at the beginning of the year. But at the end of the year, the second half, it's easier. . . . And actually the second part of first grade is the most interesting because they've developed and they've matured a little bit, and they're also on their way to becoming readers and writers, and so they've become more independent. And they've also been in school a lot also, so that they know what the routines are and what to do. So that becomes more interesting to me, but the first part of first grade is the hard part, I think.*
>
> *But I feel like the classroom management system that I had set up in second grade, it worked with them because they were able socially and cognitively to deal with it, whereas first graders are still too immature to deal with it. So then you have to deal with them on a different level, and I'm not sure that that's what I like doing. You have to do little rewards constantly with them, whereas [with] the second [graders] and the older kids you, can do self-government or other things like that.*

Sandy talks about development mainly in response to the question about how their development might influence how they understand a timeline. She also mentions several factors that influence children's development, such as their ability to think logically, their social skills, and their diminishing egocentrism and increasing independence. "*First graders are still very egocentric and the second graders also, although not as much,*" she says. "*But sixth graders, they're not egocentric anymore, they're more into this peer acceptance thing, and they want to be accepted by their peers.*"

Sandy's response to the timeline question at Time 4 indicates she is thinking about learning and development as more integrated than separated. For example, she says that first and second graders would not benefit much from using a timeline because they have a limited concept of time at this age.

> *They have a hard time with today, tomorrow, yesterday or much less . . . when I was born or when I was one, or when I was two, or once I'm going to be like, 10. I still have kids who ask me after the morning recess if it's time for lunch. So I just think that that they need to deal with those things first before they can understand a timeline. I don't think that it would hurt, but I just don't think that they would get a lot out of it.*

She goes on to say that, as children age, their experiences with time help them develop the concept of how a timeline works and what it represents,

which is the closest she comes in this interview to expressing her thinking
about what the developmental process is like.

> They'd just have more experience with life. Every day they've had more experience with
> time. They've been alive for a longer period of time, so they know when Christmas is, and
> when Christmas comes, they know when their birthday comes, and so they know what a
> year is, they've had that experience. And so that's their concrete experience to apply to a
> timeline, and so the more experience that they have, I think, [it] will get easier for them
> to understand what is a timeline.

With more relevant knowledge and life experiences, junior high or high
school age students benefit most from timelines, she says.

> They've had some math skills that would teach them what a number line is, and they're
> learning history. They're learning more about the history of life, and so they can apply
> when it is to the timeline. That's not to say that you can't apply your own life to a
> timeline. I think that makes it more interesting. And I think that developmentally they
> could understand these things in more abstract terms.

Although Sandy apparently thinks that both learning and development
occur as children have life experiences, she also thinks that, by setting up
the proper environment, teachers can promote learning.

> But you cannot force them to learn. Some just are not ready to learn, and some kids may
> be beyond that concept that you're going to teach. So it's more your environment and
> how you structure the learning that enables the children to learn if they're ready to learn.
> I just don't think that you could tell them something and they'll learn it, or say this is
> what we're going to do and everybody would get something out of it. They would get
> something out of it, but they might not get what you wanted them to learn out of it.

Sandy also thinks that practice is important in learning to read, write,
and do arithmetic. She is not so sure about the role of memorization in
learning, however.

> You're not going to become a good reader or good writer if you don't do both of those
> things. And for spelling, that involves a certain amount of memorization. I don't know
> if spelling tests are necessary. . . . They need the math concepts of what addition is or
> what subtraction is before they are asked to sit down and memorize all the number
> facts—same thing as in multiplication and division. That's a real debate right now,
> whether or not the kids should be taking speed tests in math or spelling tests. Spelling is
> . . . not as big an issue for me as math is. . . . Memorization is a big thing. I think it's
> important to know your math facts, [but] I don't know how much you should force the
> kids to sit down and memorize the facts and take speed tests.

Sandy also believes that writing is not merely a skill, but an important tool for further learning. In this excerpt from the Time 4 interview, Sandy talks about using learning logs, in which the students have to write about what they have learned from a science lesson or about what they have been reading.

> *It helps us learn. I know what the kids are getting out of it. It helps the kids reinforce what they've learned to write it down on paper or to draw a picture. And it's also good for the parents. It shows the parents that this is what we're doing in school. So I think it's a really good tool.*

Regarding factors that affect the learning process, Sandy still believes children's prior experiences at home and at school, and how abstract or how concrete a concept is, affect how hard or easy it will be to learn.

> *If they've had a lot of experience with reading, with words, and with seeing it done at home, like being read to, then it's easier for them to become readers and writers than it is for kids that haven't had that experience. I think the same is true in math. If they're constantly counting at home or doing word problems with stuff at home, then it's easier for those kids to learn because they have the experience at home, or somewhere else, than the kids who haven't had experience.*

Sandy also thinks that children for whom English is a second language may initially be delayed in learning their letters and reading while they master language orally.

> *But it doesn't take them very long to catch up with the other kids. I think some of them have problems with the writing part because of the sounds. . . . I've seen problems with the spelling, and I think it's because they use different sounds and different letters to make sounds. The non-English speaking kids have a harder time learning the letters than the English-speaking children. I'm still not sure why that is.*

Sandy believes at Time 4 that what is taught should include social as well as academic skills. As a first-grade teacher, she is especially interested in teaching her students to be readers and writers, but she says they need to be able to work with others as well.

> *If they can do that at the end of the year, then you feel like you've succeeded as a first grade teacher. But you also want them to work independently, think for themselves, solve their own problems before they come and search you out, or try to figure out how to solve a problem, or they might try asking somebody else, or figuring it out by themselves . . . I guess I want them to enjoy school and work with the other kids.*

In fact, Sandy's teaching goals remain the same as they have been since Time 2, when she graduated from the DTE program. To accomplish these goals, Sandy understands that the teacher's role in the learning process is to be a good observer and to know her students well enough to create

> *this environment or this experience for them in a way that everybody can gain something from it. And the teacher's role is also to try to see where each child is at and which level they're at so that she could kind of target this experience towards the biggest group of kids that are ready to learn. . . .*

She also understands that the teacher has to be able to evaluate her students' work and get feedback in other ways so she can adjust what she is doing and reteach when needed.

> *The biggest feedback is whether or not they're doing what I'm asking them to do. Like if I introduce a lesson and then they go back to their seats, and they're doing the job, then they were listening and they understand what to do. If they don't, if they're not doing what they're supposed to do, then something missed and I have to explain it over again. They have learning logs where the kids draw or write whatever they learned. I watch to see if they understand, just from their actions, and if we have a discussion, whether the kids are asking the right questions, or whether they're just way off of what we're talking about.*

Sandy's beliefs about the advantages and disadvantages of teaching students in homogeneous and heterogeneous groups influence how she accomplishes her teaching goals—a subject she discusses at length in this interview. Although she philosophically opposes grouping students by ability when they all know how to read, she does split her beginning readers by ability so she can teach specific, fundamental skills.

> *You need to do that [group them] so that you can teach them the tracking concept or whatever to the same . . . group. But we only meet for 5 or 10 minutes every day in that group, and then they go off and they work in other groups. So that's the only time we group for ability. . . . It makes it easier to teach the kids that are on the same level, especially the kids that don't know how to read. It's unfair to group them with a high reader if you're trying to teach both kids how to read because you're going to be too low for the readers and you're going to be too high for the kids that don't get tracking yet. . . .*
>
> *But I don't think that you should do it once the kids are able to read. Once the kids know how to read, then I think that it's important to mix abilities. The advantages are that . . . it helps the lower kids to have a higher kid in the group because they could help each other, and they have modeling for what the reading is. And it helps the higher kid because it reinforces what they're learning to help somebody else learn to read. And I think that just because the kids aren't able to read as well, or even if you're a good reader, it doesn't mean that your ideas about a story are any better ideas.*

In addition to using groups sparingly when teaching skills, Sandy employs a Workshop approach to teach reading and writing, rather than whole-class direct instruction. Within the Workshop structure, she believes the teaching process includes modeling, asking lots of questions, providing mini-lessons, and meeting with individuals to help them improve, for example, their writing in third grade, as she describes here in response to the question about how she would teach the concept of a sentence.

> *I would just have them write in writing Workshop, and then during the lessons either borrow somebody's story or use somebody's from the year before and go through and talk about how you need to stop, and model putting in the periods. That will just be an intro-duction to it, and then in my conference with the students, if they're publishing, I'm publishing with them. Then go through and go over with them again. . . . Some kids will understand what I'm talking about, what I'm doing. Some kids won't. And with those kids I have to sit down and really model it with their own writing. I can't give them somebody else's writing and say, "Here, fix this. Put the periods in the right place." . . . Well if I were modeling it for the whole class, some of the kids would be sitting either in their seats or on the rug. But if I'm doing it one-on-one or in a small group I would take somebody's paper and I would say, "Okay, let's read this. Where did you stop? Let's put a period there, and let's read on. Where did you stop? Let's put a period there." And then I'd have the students try to do it by themselves.*

Sandy believes that structuring and guiding are part of the teaching process. She also believes that a sequence or order is important when teach-ing discrete concepts, although not necessarily for broader concepts.

> *Take something like math. The kids have to learn to add before they can multiply. So there's a certain sequence of events. But you don't have to wait until the end of the year to do measurement, or time, or whatever. So in a broad subject area . . . there may or may not be a sequence. . . . Even with reading and writing. I think they both go hand in hand, so . . . you don't always have to introduce reading before you introduce writing. In fact I think that writing possibly should be taught before reading. If you're introduc-ing a specific topic, like a subject or a unit about dinosaurs, or plants, or something like that, then you need to give the kids the background information before you go into a les-son.*

Asked about how teachers know what and how to teach, Sandy names these four factors:

- Experience teaching a grade: *You know that this is kind of the range of kids that you're going to get, and this is what they should be doing.*
- Attending Workshops and reading education books: *Which I haven't done lately [because of the new baby], but going to Workshops and reading books that have to do with teaching, education books.*
- Talking to other teachers: *Wilson just started this language arts support group, which has helped me talk to other teachers about writing Workshop, publish-*

*ing, evaluation, portfolios, things like that. . . . They usually get, like, 10 teachers—
8 to 10 teachers, I'd say.*

- My training at DTE: *The terminology gets lost sometimes, but I have to say
also that it's easy to get caught up in the everyday stuff, all the everyday worries that
we have to think about, and to forget about the developmental stuff. I was thinking
about this the other day because I think one of the reasons why . . . , it's made me
think, maybe, more developmentally is because I've had student teachers. I hadn't had
a student teacher in a year and a half, and it was easy. I felt like when I talked to
Carli [her current student teacher from the DTE program] that she was bringing me
back to thinking about some of these issues that I tended to lose track of over the last
year and a half. [But also,] I still have a basic philosophy that I develop about education, in which I assume a lot of the terminology and jargon and stuff.*

When I probe to ask why a student teacher makes her rethink her practice,
Sandy's responds:

> *It makes you think about what you did and why you did it. And they also ask you ques-
> tions about what you're doing . . . in class, or why are you doing this. And you have to
> be more responsible for what you're doing.*

However, toward the end of her sixth year of teaching, Sandy seems to be
at a crossroads and is seriously considering taking some time off from teaching to spend with her young daughter. In fact, she offers a metaphor that
reflects her conflict about teaching at this time:

> *I'm thinking of something like the tide, where it goes up and comes back down. Some-
> times you're just really excited about what you're doing and so the tide is up, and some-
> times . . . it's harder to go forward and you just get fed up with things. . . . It's a really
> bad metaphor because it's not very encouraging. It's my present state of mind, so things
> aren't happening and the tide is down, so when it comes back, then I'll go home and I'll
> read a book about teaching and think, "Oh yeah, I could do this with someone," and the
> tide comes back up, and it's constantly going back and forth.*

SANDY'S 1997 INTERVIEW AND AN OBSERVATION
(TIME 5)

As it turned out, Sandy did take 2 years off from teaching following our last
interview. She stayed home for 2 years with Hannah and gave birth to her
second daughter, Ellie, in 1994. Although she wanted to spend more time
with her children, she was feeling down about teaching. Here is how she
tells it:

When we last talked, I was feeling really down on teaching and I wasn't happy with what I was doing. . . . I felt like at Washington, my last year I had a really good program, and my first year here [at Wilson] I had a really good program, and then when I started job sharing I was making a lot compromises. The person I was working with was great, and we're still really good friends. She's very outgoing and animated, and I'm more low-key I think, so our teaching styles [differ], and then we had a couple groups of kids that were difficult. I don't think it was unusual. It was just in my frame of mind and having to adjust to a new schedule and all that stuff. I was just really down on teaching. . . . I left and I wasn't going to come back to teaching at all.

Sandy began volunteering with an adult literacy program at the Berkeley library, but left when her second daughter was born. Meanwhile, her husband was considering returning to school. That pushed her to return to work. She also attended the Emergent Literacy Institute, which offered a new direction for her—"a second wind," as she put it.

When I visit Sandy again in 1997, she is back at Wilson Elementary School, where about half the students qualify for the Title 1 program. Her job as a part-time Title 1 literacy specialist is to help children with delayed literacy development. This job requires Sandy to pull students out of the classroom to work with them individually or in small groups and to do demonstration lessons for teachers in the regular classroom. Sometimes she also works with small groups in the classrooms at Wilson.

Last year what I did was work with 16 kids, and they were all second graders who were in the bottom 10% of the second grade class as far [as] reading ability, and I pulled them out and did small group "Reading Recovery"-type activities with them. I felt then that the amount of time that I spent with them was not worth the amount of growth that I saw because, yes, you have a small group of kids, but each one has his or her own individual needs. It was really hard for me to do individual work in a small group, and then on top of that, only three times a week for 30 minutes, and I wasn't seeing the growth.

What I was trying to do with them was counter-productive because they went back into their classrooms and they were doing something that was completely different or counter to, or completely opposite of what I was trying to teach them to do, so I felt I was not helping them and in some ways the opposite. They were not getting that learning time and I was confusing them.

So I thought about it over the summer and read both of [Richard] Allington's and [Patricia] Cunningham's books, Classrooms That Work *and* Schools That Work, *and we talked about how "pull out" wasn't the answer, so "push in" was the answer. We needed to work with teachers in helping them develop skills to work with low kids and having those low kids in the classroom at the same time, and that would reach a greater number of kids.*

So it's allowed me to go into classrooms and to work with teachers. I see a lot of different classrooms, which I didn't get when I was a classroom teacher because I was very isolated. It has allowed me to understand what their needs are and what the roadblocks are to getting them to move further and getting them to move away from ability grouping and moving away from telling them a spelling word if they don't know a word.

But all this has been in literacy, so it's really helped me think about literacy and what the best practice is, or what balanced literacy is, or how to put together what I think is a good literacy program for students, which is very different from being in the classroom where I have all these demands, not just language arts but math and science. But I've found that what I've done with literacy and everything I've learned about kids and the learning and teaching . . . can be applied to math and science. . . . It's frustrating in some ways and it's hard working with different kids, and I go into classrooms where things aren't the way I would do them, but I have to bite my tongue and do what I can do to help those teachers at that time. And it's hard to conquer the world.

The thing that has been good is that I have been able to work part time, but I haven't had to split my time with someone else and coordinate, because that kind of wore on me. Next year the teachers are saying we need somebody to work with the kids and them, so they want more time, and they want to look out for the kids so they're talking about pull-out again and working with the kids, not the teachers, and probably more a full-time position, 80% or 100%, and I don't want to work that much yet, so . . . I'm in flux again.

I'm willing to work up to 80% but that's my limit. If they want more I'll have to share with somebody, which will then get me back to that same situation. On the one hand I'm pretty independent, and I like to do my own thing, and [although] I see the value of working with other people, . . . it's just how much time that takes and whether I am on the same wavelength. Because if I'm working [with] somebody who doesn't do things the same way I do or think the same way I do, then it's difficult . . . so . . . I'm kind of waiting to see what's going to happen next year.

Sandy also told me about another role she has this year—mentoring two first-year teachers through the Beginning Teacher Support and Assessment (BTSA) program in California.

I meet with them every Tuesday afternoon, about 45 minutes with each of them, and then with Sean I go into his class and with Stuart sometimes I go in to observe. With Stuart it is more a management thing. . . . He's had real highs and real lows, and so for him it's more a confidence thing, . . . whereas with Sean it is more talking about the teaching, what's going on in the classroom, the curriculum as opposed to classroom management. . . . It's kind of the same thing I've already been doing this year, working with teachers, but as I said before, change is really hard for teachers. The nice thing in working with new teachers is that I can influence them at the beginning and kind of put bugs in their ears for them to think about at the beginning, so I can get them off to the right start.

Sandy then talks about how, in California, the current politics of education dictate the method for teaching reading—a method diametrically opposed to Sandy's own training, beliefs, and experience. She also implies that this is one reason she has considered leaving teaching.

California has gotten really political, and I don't know if you want to get into that, but it's really scary. . . . The Packard Foundation has given school districts a huge grant to purchase [the] Open Court [book series] to teach reading, which the California State Board of Education is pushing. They are hiring 30 literacy coordinators to be in the schools. There are 60 schools, so they are going to be halftime in the schools training the teachers and making sure they are doing Open Court. This is just the big thing now in California and it's amazing to me. We're going around in circles. . . . [The previous spring, the California legislature passed a Phonics Bill]. So now the State Board of Education saying it's against the law to use their money to train teachers in using emergent literacy. . . . The state is saying, "Now you can't do that, you can't use your money for that [or] you'll have to pay back this money, and we'll audit you to find out if you've been using this money to do in your class."

If that's the case, then I won't be able to do these trainings because that's not my message. The state legislators are going around and saying that they don't want the teachers to train the kids to look at the picture or use context cues to figure out words. We want them to sound it out and better yet, we can't give them literature to read until they decode it and give them decodable books first. . . . The district, I hope, understands where we are at, and I think there are enough teachers here that understand and believe in what we're doing, and we won't let it affect us, but you know if the state comes in and says you can't be doing this, then I don't know what that'll mean. I don't think it will get to [be] Big Brother looking over us. I don't think it would get that far but if they do, then that's a very scary thought.

Sandy also talks about her goal of helping the teachers at her school feel more successful and less overwhelmed by all they have to do. She says she places a high value on having time for reading and reflection for continual learning.

It's really hard. People are overwhelmed. I give them articles to read and they don't have time to read it. They've got demands coming at them from all different directions, and I could say that my papers are most important, but they have more immediate things that they need to think about, and they can't deal with metacognitive stuff if they have papers to grade, or field trips to plan for, or an art project to prep for. So it just takes a lot of staff development, and I think it also has to do with going after teachers and saying what is important. But I think for the first 2 or 3 years it is really hard to see beyond the next day or next week. . . . One way we can help the teachers is to give them time. I know they go to Workshops, which is a great thing, but they are so busy going from that Workshop to the next lesson that they don't have time to reflect and synthesize or to process or prepare what they learned and apply it, and so all that information just gets stashed away. I try to help work with the teachers to think about it on their own time. Then I think there is a lot more transfer. Things that I read 5 years ago make a lot more sense now, because I read it but didn't know what it was saying, and it's the same thing when we read Classrooms That Work. The teachers have all read that, but how they apply it will depend on where they are at and what they are ready to take in. You just have to find different ways, knowing where the kids are at, knowing where the teachers are.

Sandy also offers a metaphor that represents her understanding of pedagogy at this time. It has to do with making quilts, which is quite apt because her thinking about behavior, development, learning, and teaching at this time is pieced together to create an inseparable whole. Her final comment about never being finished with teaching is also quite apt because Sandy continues to be a learner as well as a teacher.

> *I started a new hobby when I took my two years off. Quilting is challenging because you have to take pieces of fabric and assemble it into something, hopefully beautiful. In teaching, there are also a lot of materials and resources available to you and it's what you take and how you apply it and how you put it together that will determine the outcome, so I kind of see that as a metaphor. On the other hand, when you are done with the quilt, it's finished, but with teaching, I don't think you are ever finished.*

SANDY'S RESPONSES TO THE CLINICAL INTERVIEW QUESTIONS AT TIME 5 (1997)

Sandy's experiences as a parent add to her understanding of children's behavior and development, which she describes as, "*Seeing just how they develop is fascinating, how they grow and change and make sense of their world and starting to read and write and watching it develop and talking.*" In fact, Sandy no longer believes that traits and abilities are inherent in children only because of their family background, as she did earlier in her career. Instead, she sees that all children have unique personalities, abilities, and characteristics that influence their behavior. "*They are who they are because of who they are and not entirely their family.*" Although she knows how difficult it is for teachers to meet the needs of every child in their classroom, she understands how important this is. As a parent, she has developed more empathy for the perspective of her students' parents.

> *You look at kids as your students, not as somebody's children, so that now that I have my own children I think well, gosh I really want their teacher to know this and that about them. It's not that I didn't think about it, but when you have so many kids, it's really hard to think about each child when you have the whole class, and what you can do for the class. Of course there were individual children that would stick out and you would worry, but as a teacher you worried more about the group and not the individual child, so [having a child] just made me more aware of these kids as people. . . . It sort of makes me appreciate the parents' point of view, which I didn't have that perspective.*

Sandy's perspective as a parent has also changed how she thinks about the purpose of sharing time in the classroom. In past interviews, Sandy was not keen about spending class time on sharing and thought that the main benefits had to do with enhancing children's communication skills (listening and speaking). "*Nobody talked about looking at your kids further and bridging that gap between home and school,*" she says now. "*We're part of the class, and we need to know who our family is and what makes them tick, what makes them happy, and validating what they do and who they are.*" Not only does it help make each student feel a part of the class, but sharing time helps her get to know her students better.

> *I never used to like sharing because I always thought that it would be something that they brought from home, and it would be materialistic and . . . [I] thought it took time away from academics. Being a parent, you realize how important it is for kids to bring something to share. My daughter always wants to bring something to school, a toy or whatever. And I never wanted toys in my classroom, but I think that it's made me realize that they need something to help them bridge that gap from home to school. . . . I read an article about this recently, it was just [about] how sharing is a good thing because it does bridge that gap for the younger kids. But then for the older kids, it doesn't have to be something from home, but something about them or something that they have done at school, and it could be academic or not. This year we had conflict-resolution training, and a lot of teachers are doing circle time to share. I think that just makes the kids more personal, and you get to understand and see them and see things from their eyes. Everybody has their time to speak, and if they don't then that's okay too. But getting other people to see who they are, too, because kids just don't choose to learn about each other, and I hadn't looked at it that way before. . . .*

Everything Sandy has to say about children's development at Time 5 is tightly coupled with what she says about how children learn and what she thinks about teaching. For example, in this passage, Sandy explains that many factors influence the learning process, including possible learning disabilities, student motivation, the context for learning, individual rates of development, readiness to learn, the role of practice, and learning styles.

> *You could get into a big discussion about reading disabilities and dyslexia and all that, so that aside, if the kids are surrounded by friends, and they are motivated, and they have books available, and they want to learn how to read, then once they've adopted strategies, . . . it's the practice. I think some kids have trouble reading because everybody has their own rate of development. Some kids are ready to read at a younger age and others at an older age. My daughter is 5½ and she is writing before she is reading. That's just her learning style. It's just part of who you are. It's not like I deprived her of books and reading. She loves that and has all the experiential stuff, but she is not ready to sit down and learn these books or put the letters together.*

Sandy also mentions the importance of hands-on learning experiences and age-appropriate curriculum as benefits for students, especially concrete learners who are not able to think about things in the abstract.

> *There have to be hands-on manipulatives for them, whereas the third-through-fifth graders are able to do a little more abstract thinking, not that hands-on manipulatives wouldn't benefit them too. They do that stuff too, so you know they are still very egocen-*

tric, and everything is still new. . . . . I think that everything you do in K–2 can be done
in 3–5, so I don't think there has to be a different curriculum for the two age levels.

As Sandy continues to talk about teaching and learning throughout the
elementary grades, she describes the learning process as engaging in
higher order thinking, making inferences, and refining skills once children
have developed the basics, as well as while they are learning the basics.

People like to say that in K–2 you are learning to read and in 3–5 you are reading to
learn, and I kind of have a problem with that because it's not like the kids at K–2 aren't
reading to learn because they are. . . . Some are still learning to read, whereas in 3–4,
hopefully they have learned how to read and now you are refining those skills and doing
more inferential and higher order activities. . . . Well, higher level thinking activities
are things you want to do in K–2 also . . . like for example writing, you want the kids to
approximate—just write, squiggles or drawing or whatever and then 3–5 you want to
refine their skills and how to develop a story or working on the flow of the story or think-
ing about the beginnings, endings, character development, plot and tying it together.
But some of these skills can be taught in K–2, and in 3–5 they are learning to write in
different genres.

In talking about learning and teaching at Time 5, Sandy uses concepts
from the theories of Jean Piaget (disequilibrium) and Lev Vygotsky (the
zone of proximal development [ZPD]) to explain how she views the learning process:

There's that whole concept about disequilibrium and presenting the student with a dif-
ferent scenario that will get them to change their thinking. Then that's an optimal time
for learning, but it's really hard to find those times. Another way to say it is Vygotsky's
ZPD and knowing how to pull the student along. And that means knowing the kids
coming into your classroom and what they need, like directionality, or if they have it,
then move on. Just having that structure set up in your classroom so that if you have
that information, you can go with the program and make that a teachable moment in-
stead of having an explicit, systematic phonics program, and saying okay everybody is
going to go through this list of sounds whether you know it or don't know it or are ready
for it. . . .

Sandy also reiterates the importance of asking the right questions at the
right time. "*Some questions will get kids or adults thinking more . . . not a yes or no*
question, but a 'What would happen if?' . . . Those kinds of questions tend to cause
disequilibrium, more than 'Did this happen?' or 'Let me tell you the answer.'" Several times in several different contexts, Sandy stresses that a teacher has to
know her students as well as many different ways to teach them.

Everybody has a different learning style. I learn differently than you or anybody else and
so they don't all learn in the same way—chronologically either—and so I think that as

many different ways that you can explain ideas or present curriculum or make things available to the children, that's when you increase the number of kids that are learning.

While understanding that because everyone learns in different ways she must teach in many different ways, Sandy also believes in the value of practice and repetition as long as it comes with a purpose and a context.

You have to practice to get better. It's just like practicing the piano or bicycle or practicing reading. . . . They talk about writers and how they have to write a lot, and some writers just write pages before they sit down and write something good. In sports you have to practice whatever. I think practice has [a] place.

Repetition is wonderful when you are singing songs and chanting rhymes because that's the way that you learn, by repeating things over and over again. Repeating books over and over is how you become a better reader. So that's a good thing, but that's in the context of something meaningful.

In describing how children learn, Sandy also talks about how she would teach. For example, she says she would set up an environment that encourages students to learn through discovery and choice, but with the teacher guiding and directing the students' learning often by working with small groups. In earlier interviews, she talked about the teacher's role in creating an environment for learning, but now Sandy emphasizes the importance of the teacher knowing students well enough to effectively guide their learning.

A teacher needs to set up a classroom where . . . kids can move around and work in areas where they want and need to. Also the teacher needs to know which kids need to go [where] and what their needs are and how to direct those kids into those areas. Also, if you have that kind of arrangement, then the teacher also needs to know who needs the information, how to pull small groups to work together also. So . . . kind of the coach, kind of the facilitator, that is the role of the teacher.

Sandy also says she thinks teaching should start with the whole and go to the parts, which reflects her preference for a more holistic or balanced approach to teaching reading (as in the whole-language philosophy for teaching reading) rather than in the opposite direction, as in a phonics approach that would mean starting with the parts before moving to the whole. In practice, Sandy addresses the whole and the parts in her classroom simultaneously. That is, she uses a lot of children's literature, songs, chanting, and poetry with the whole class. Yet she also employs a lot of word study, spelling, and phonics based on patterns in the language she finds in the books and poems she selects and the skills her students need to learn, as judged by their progress as readers and writers. For example, she explains here that she thinks it is unnecessary to teach reading using a specific order or sequence because students should read literature and chant poems and songs at the same time.

> *For example, the phonics thing, they say there is a sequence of teaching kids how to read, and you start with phonics, and you teach them sounds and then you give them sight words and all that, and then you can give them a literature book. I don't see that [that] sequence is useful, and I don't think it's good for kids because they lose the context, they don't know what they are doing with it. You can tell them that these are all the sounds, but why are they doing it? To read, and so why not start with literature and do the chanting and reading and all that fun stuff, and then say: "O.K., let's look at this word."*

Perhaps describing what I observe of Sandy's teaching at Time 5 in 1997 will show how her thinking about teaching and learning plays out in practice because her beliefs and practices, her thoughts and actions, are synchronous.

AN OBSERVATION OF SANDY'S TEACHING AT TIME 5 (1997)

When I observe Sandy during the spring of 1997, her new role as the Title 1 literacy coordinator takes her into several classrooms where she works with small groups or does whole-class lessons that serve as models for the teacher and learning experiences for the students. In one combined class of 28 second- and third-grade students, she begins a weekly Writer's Workshop with a 10-minute mini-lesson about how writers get ideas for their stories. During the next half hour, Sandy conducts a whole-class fourth-grade spelling lesson while the teacher observes. Sandy later tells me that this lesson is based on a presentation that she and the teacher attended earlier in the year. Earlier in the day, Sandy also meets individually with several students whom she has pulled out of class; at the end of each day, she works in a fifth-grade class with a small reading group. I only describe the Writer's Workshop mini-lesson and the fourth-grade spelling lesson here.

In a combined second- and third-grade class where the children are using the Writer's Workshop approach, Sandy reminds the students that last week they discussed the kinds of writing they typically do in the classroom and points to a poster they developed together that lists different genres of writing: fictional narratives, descriptive writing, letter writing, poetry, directions, summaries, opinion pieces, and notes. Sandy then shows the class some children's magazines, including *Cricket* and *Lady Bug*; she says, "*I really like these magazines. I brought them in for you to look at because they take one topic and show how you can write all kinds of stories about it—like water, for example.*" She asks the class, "*When I say water, what do you think of?*" The students call out answers such as sprinklers, swimming pools, a fire truck, and a water slide. Sandy then shows them examples from one of the magazines, including poems, picture stories, and games that all relate to the topic of water. For example, the magazine has a realistic fiction story in it about a child taking a bubble bath. Sandy then asks, "*Why do you think I am showing you these?*" One student raises her hand and responds, "*To get ideas.*" Another student says, "*When you are reading you get ideas.*" Sandy then asks the class, "*What kinds of stories do you usually write?*" The response she gets is, "*True and not true,*" to which she adds, "*Fiction and nonfiction, right. Well, you can do all different types of writing about things you know about and experience every day.*"

Following this exchange, Sandy reminds the students that they can use these magazines to get ideas for their writing and that she will pass them around so they can look at them during Writer's Workshop. She then calls the roll, conducting what is known as a *status of the class* so that she can get a feel for where each child is in the writing process and what he or she is going to be working on during Writer's Workshop today. The students respond to their name in turn by briefly stating what they are planning to do, including starting new stories, continuing with works in progress, meeting with a peer or teacher to conference about their writing, revising a story, or doing final editing of a story before publishing it. Sandy comments on some of their responses, but makes her way through the class roll in about 5 minutes. She then asks designated student helpers to pass out writing folders as she places the children's magazines on tables around the room. Both the classroom teacher and Sandy then circulate and check in with several students as they settle into Writer's Workshop. For the next 10 minutes, Sandy confers with one student about his writing while the classroom teacher does the same with another. The classroom teacher then sets a timer for 15 more minutes and reminds the students that this is now a silent writing time.

When the timer goes off, the teacher reminds the students that they have 5 minutes to finish up what they are working on before sharing the day's writing. Although the noise level goes up slightly, the children actually look disappointed that this time is coming to a close for the day. As Sandy gathers up her things to move to another classroom, the teacher invites several students to read aloud from their writing—a traditional part of Writer's Workshop called *Author's Chair.*

In the fourth-grade class we go to next, the students have obviously been studying ocean animals, and Sandy tells me that this week is "Ocean Week" at the school. This classroom is even decorated to look like an ocean, with paper seaweed and kelp hanging from a wire strung across the room and large, three-dimensional drawings of sea animals hanging among the kelp. In fact, every class at every grade level participates in this all-school theme each year, and their studies culminate in a trip to a Pacific Ocean beach where they observe seals and sea lions and learn more about their habits and habitat.

Sandy begins the lesson by writing a sentence on the board that reads: "*Sea otters keep their coats clean by* _____ *licking and combing their fur.*" She says, "*Please read this silently and see what you think is missing.*" The students raise their hands and guess that words such as *rolling* and *grooming* should go in the blank. Sandy reexplains: "*No. I am looking for words that describe* how *otters lick and comb their fur and not things that otters do.*" Someone suggests that the word *carefully* could go in the blank. Sandy then asks each student to write the word *carefully* on the 3 × 5 cards she has passed out. Next she asks, "*Can some of you tell me how you spelled* carefully *on your cards?*" Sandy writes their suggestions on the chalkboard:

| carfully | cerfully | careflly | carefully |

Sandy then asks the students to tell her how they know how to spell this word. Most of the students say they sound it out, and one student says that she knows the word *care* and sounded out the rest of the word. Sandy suggests that these are good strategies; she also asks them to think about how they see a word spelled out when they look in a dictionary. When no one responds, Sandy goes on to show how to break a word down into chunks called *syllables* as she writes the word on the chalkboard: *care ful ly*.

Next Sandy asks, "*Can you suggest some other words you know that have the word* care *in them?*" The students give her the following list, which she writes on the chalkboard:

| careless | Care Bears | careful | caring | cares | care more |

The classroom teacher interjects at this point to remind the students that they had learned words earlier that end in *-ly*. Sandy picks up on this and expands on the *-ly* pattern by asking, "*Who can give me some other words that end in* -ly *that tell how you can do things? For example, I might do something carefully.*" The list that Sandy writes on the on the chalkboard grows to look like this:

| cleanly | quietly | nicely | enjoyably | mostly | beautifully |
| lovely | especially | quickly | slowly | seriously | likely |

The lesson to this point has taken about 20 minutes. Sandy proceeds to pass out cards to table groups so they can brainstorm words they know that have these spelling patterns in them: *ing, oat, ean, er,* and so on. At this point, the teacher and Sandy circulate to monitor various groups and to encourage them to write down words they know with these patterns in them.

The lesson closes with each group orally sharing the list of words they made with the word part given to them. Sandy leaves for a fifth-grade class, where she meets each day with seven Spanish bilingual students who are reading a chapter book.

When I talk with Sandy at the end of the day, she tells me she aims to model a way for the teacher to make spelling lessons emerge from students' writing or other subjects they are studying and then develop these into brief phonics and spelling lessons. The Writer's Workshop, Sandy explains, is also something she is modeling for this teacher. She is helping her to work out the logistics of doing Writer's Workshop and learning how to manage things like student conferences and teaching mini-lessons. Both teachers are working to incorporate new ideas into their regular practice, but need someone to show them the way before they feel confident to do it on their own. Sandy will debrief today's lesson with these teachers later and then plan the next steps with them.

As we continue to talk, Sandy explains that she gains a lot from modeling and teaching lessons in other teachers' classrooms and feels that most teachers do not get a chance to see and do things in new ways. Her job is to help them make changes in their practices, but in fact she is also learning.

Part of it is that they don't get out of their classrooms, and they don't see what the possi-bilities are. If you are a teacher who's been teaching for a while and you've been doing things, and it's worked for you pretty well, then it's really hard to change. Change is re-ally hard, I'm finding. I know that it's hard, but also teachers are overwhelmed and busy and they have things to do, and it's really hard to think of a different way. What I'm doing is talking about a different way of teaching. It's not basals, it's not ability grouping, it's not spelling lists, it's not math facts, it's a whole shift in thinking, and it's really hard for people to make that shift, to think about it and also to see how it's go-ing to work. So then that's been a really good thing for me, because I get to go out and see all these classrooms, I get to talk to people and go to conferences.

Sandy even plans to attend a summer institute in New Hampshire at her own expense to learn more about teaching writing because the more she sees, the more questions she has about how to teach writing more effec-tively. She also says she belongs to a book group at the school and connects with local and national networks of teachers on the Internet who focus on teaching language arts. All of these experiences help Sandy continue to re-fine her thinking and practice.

Having people available to talk to, a support group, is great. I think I had a lot of ideas when I was first teaching but I was by myself and nobody was doing what I was doing. Then I moved from Washington to here. I feel there is a lot more support. I have a lot more friends and people that think the same way whom I can to talk to. Yes, there's an-other woman here, this is her first year here, and there is another teacher here who went

*through the California Literacy Project last summer. There's Tracy [another DTE grad]
and Cindy [the Vice Principal], and without Jim's support [the Principal] from the very
beginning, it would have been impossible—just their confidence that we are going to do
the best for the kids, even though they don't always understand what you're doing.*

At the end of this interview, when I ask Sandy if she has anything else she
wants to say, she comments on the quality of teachers produced by the DTE
program and the value of intense study of educational theory.

*DTE teachers are really different than those who come from elsewhere, and I think that I
wouldn't be the teacher that I am without DTE. It just made me more aware of developmental education and how children develop and [how] everyone develops at their own
rate, and goes through stages. I would hope that most credential programs study Piaget,
but we did it in such depth. I do have to say that what we did then I did not appreciate
and I don't think I got it. I wasn't ready to hear a lot of what Paul [Ammon, the
codirector of the DTE program] or even Allen [Black, also a codirector of the DTE pro-
gram] said, because I was coming from a really technical background in economics, math,
and psychology and children were really foreign to me. I think that the people that go
through the program now are a lot more experienced, and so they are ready to receive that
information and probably got a lot more out of it than I did. But I think it set up that bug
in my head that this is the way that they learn and laid the foundation so that everything
that I learned or heard had to jibe with that or else I didn't use it or it didn't make sense to
that theory. I think that a lot people when they come into teaching, they don't know how
children learn, they don't have an understanding or a philosophy of how kids learn, they
just do things without thinking about why and what it means for the kid.*

SANDY'S 1999 INTERVIEW AND AN OBSERVATION
(TIME 6)

When I contact Sandy 2 years later for another interview and observation,
she had moved back into the classroom. She is job sharing again and teaching fourth grade 2½ days a week.

*I have the same arrangement that I had the last time I job shared, which was two or three
days a week. . . . So this year I am working with a different woman. I have known this
woman since I started at Wilson, which was 1990, and she had a child and we were
kind of working together last year doing Title 1 and being Title 1 specialists and working in the classrooms and supporting the fourth- and fifth-grade teachers, similar to
what I was doing when I was talking with you last time.*

*We both felt last year we really wanted to get back into the classroom and try to put
into practice the things that we were asking other teachers to do, and we missed the community of kids. . . . We decided last spring that we would job share. At first we wanted
to teach in the primary grades because those are the reduced class-size grades, but the
principal asked us to teach fourth grade because there had been some turnover at that
grade level.*

Also, our Title 1 program was trying to work with teachers and beginning teachers and changing their language arts curriculum so that it is more Workshop driven, rather than basal driven or whole-group literature studies, not even studies but whole-group literature, which is when the whole class is reading a book for 3 months [and] doing all of these different activities. So what we wanted was to have a Reader's Workshop and Writer's Workshop and have social studies and science be interwoven with the reading and the writing. I mean, we had all of these grand ideas and putting it into practice has been very challenging, partly because we had to divide up the curriculum and the consistency has been difficult to continue.

On Wednesday, what we try to do is to overlap a little bit, so Paula comes in Wednesday morning and she starts the day with them, and then I come in about 10:30 a.m. So, we overlap with a little bit of reading and writing and then she leaves at lunch. Well, we eat lunch together and just kind of check in and she passes on any news that she has and then I spend Wednesday afternoon with them. So, usually Wednesday afternoon we have math. What we decided was that I would take math and she would take social studies and science, and then we could split language arts so that we were doing Reader's Workshop and Writer's Workshop every day. . . .

The problem is that there are so many other things that you have to do during those times. . . . So she ends up doing spelling during writing time when the kids should be doing writing, and I try to do math in 2½ days instead of over a period of a week so that I am cramming everything in . . . and then they don't think about it for 4 days. Whatever we talked about 4 days ago, we start again on Wednesday and we have to go back and . . . you just lose momentum doing that. So that is the biggest problem. We had originally set it up so that we would share everything, but we also said that I would be responsible for planning math. But I had never taught fourth-grade math before, so even though I kind of knew what they are supposed to do, getting the actual activities ready for her in addition to everything else was just not doable. So finally we just said, "You do social studies on your days, and I will do math on my days."

Well, I taught second grade for 3 years and then I went to first grade, and I taught first grade for 3 years, and then I took 2 years off, and then I did Title 1 for 3 years. But that was mostly language arts, and I was working with different age groups, and mostly it was in intervention, . . . helping the second graders who weren't reading yet, or going into classrooms and helping the kids who were struggling readers in those classrooms, and helping teachers set up some kind of program that was able to meet their needs. . . . So this has been a real learning experience for me. . . . I worked with fourth graders during the last 2 years, but my whole focus at the beginning of my teaching career was all in primary grades and developing literacy. My training was . . . emergent literacy, and so in working with older kids and teaching fourth grade, I have learned a lot and I am still learning.

This whole year has just been a learning experience, for example, trying to figure out how you get from Writer's Notebooks into a writing project. We did a lot of stop and start, stop and start. We wanted to start with memoirs but . . . we were doing a lot of testing I think, so that was happening during writing time. . . . We were just trying too many new ideas at one time and the Writer's Notebooks just kind of got pushed aside. So we ended up doing a lot of creative writing, show-not-tell, descriptive writing, and little small activities, and the Notebook was set aside. In the last couple of months, we just started it up again but did not work on memoirs because . . . the concept of it was too

*much for them. We narrowed it into just family stories and that was just a little more fo-
cused for them. So we have been working on that, but just going from the Notebook, how
to choose an idea from the Notebook and turn it into a project that is something that you
want to work on for a while has been challenging. . . . I have learned a lot. I still have
not figured it out completely. Part of it was that my expectations of how it was going to
work were a little high.*

Before launching into the regular set of questions for the clinical interview, I ask Sandy what her best experience has been this year. Her response
has to do with working collaboratively with her teaching partner, Paula, to
plan and try out their ideas.

*It has been really great to work with Paula and just to talk about these ideas that we
[have] And I think that we are professionally along the same wavelength [about] what we
want to do and what our understanding of language arts [is]. So, just trying things and
talking about it . . . has been really good. I felt like I grew a lot. I mean, we talked a lot
during the summer when we had time and we would talk about curriculum and we had
these ideas of doing groups for social studies and science and having a Workshop. . . .
[But] it was just too many new things at once, and it is hard to keep that. So, we started
one project and that lasted a week, but then, to keep that going . . . took too much energy.*

Job sharing also makes it difficult to solve discipline problems, which
Sandy responds was her worst experience of the year. Because she and
Paula teach differently and at different times, it has been a challenge to
build a community in the classroom.

*We have a really hard class, and just dealing with the discipline problems has . . . taken
away a lot of our energy. I have learned a lot also from that and tried to make the conflicts a learning experience by turning it around so that it does not completely explode,
and defusing it. I'm also trying to create a community. This is the first year that I have
really focused on keeping the classroom as a community. The other years it just kind of
came together because of the way the kids were. This year you really have to work at it, because there are still a lot of strong personalities. The routine of the classroom helps build
community, and with Paula and I job sharing, that has come later in the year. We each
try to do the same thing, but we each do it differently, and so they have had to get used to
our styles. That has taken them longer than it probably would have with just one
teacher.*

Apparently, this class has a large group of aggressive boys, so Sandy and
Paula have had to work extra hard with individual students and the group
to teach the children how to resolve conflicts.

*It's just coming to understand each different personality and not blowing up when
somebody accidentally bumps you, talking about it, thinking about what your reaction
could be, what some other reactions might be, and why this might have happened? Is it*

always that they are intentionally trying to hurt you? Looking at it from different per-
spectives. [We] try to have a class meeting every morning, just some sharing, and then
we try to have an appreciation circle at the end of the day, just as closure. Getting kids to
listen to each other and not laugh at somebody else or cut them down—they are finally
starting to do that. They are finally starting to listen, and we can go around the circle
without having to stop and say, "Please listen to what somebody has to say." The school
has a conflict resolution program. I was trained in it a few years ago, but I don't feel like
I have completely been able to practice what we are supposed to be doing. We tried some of
the activities, which are to talk about conflict and how you react to certain situations
and giving I-messages, which sometimes feels artificial. We're just focusing on that
more, and trying to be more positive than negative.

Sandy has had to adjust to a whole new set of challenges and benefits in teaching kids who are older, and therefore more independent than the first and second graders she taught earlier in her career. Her fourth-grade students are more aggressive and social, but the curriculum is richer, and students take a more active role in their own learning

Most of them can read or write independently. There is a whole range as in any class-
room, but, for the most part, we are pretty lucky in that we don't have any nonreaders as
there sometimes are in fourth grade. Everybody is reading. Academically they are more
independent. . . . First graders . . . need you to work with them and kind of take them
step by step. There are fourth graders that need that too . . . [but] the attention span of
the first graders [is] not as long as the fourth graders. They are a lot more concrete and
you have to do a lot more hands-on activities. I think that there are a lot of differences
but there are of similarities too. You can't just say that fourth graders are able to think
abstractly and then not have manipulatives.

Sandy's students seem to be especially social from her perspective, even for children who are at an age when they are normally making many new social connections.

My special challenge is just having them focus on the task at hand and not be into every-
body else's business. Part of it is [that] we do a lot of group work or partner work, so in
some weeks I am encouraging it. But then there are times that I want them to be working
by themselves. I mean, it is not very often, sometimes in math. . . . But this is just a re-
ally social age and you just kind of have to go with it. But it takes so long to get every-
thing done that it makes me crazy sometimes.

Because of all the adjustments she has to make, in some ways Sandy feels as she did 12 years ago when she was just beginning her career.

Everything that I did in second and first grade I threw out, partly because I have learned
a lot more since I was in the classroom last time, and partly because I was starting with
a new partner. We just threw everything out and started from scratch. Being at a differ-

ent grade level I feel like I am just starting anew. So it has been quite a learning experi-
ence for me, and the other thing is that I don't have the time to devote to thinking about
teaching and planning as I did when I was first starting out. Now I have kids at home.
Back then my weekends were wide open and my evenings were wide open, so it is very dif-
ferent.

Despite these challenges, Sandy feels there is something she can learn
and get interested in teaching at any age or grade level, and she relishes
teaching something new. For example, she enjoys the richness of the
fourth- and fifth-grade literature and social studies curriculum. She also enjoys how older students are able to think more abstractly and talk at a
higher level about ideas and the things they read.

Because I have moved around so much, now I feel like that at any age group, I could
teach them and learn something from them, and each group has their own special need,
and not just need, but an area that I could get interested in—so like, say fourth and
fifth grade, the literature is really rich and the social studies curriculum is really rich.
But in the primary grades, like first grade, teaching them how to read and write is really
exciting too. . . . I can talk to older students as people more than as little kids, and they
are funny, and you can joke with them. You can get into some really deep issues and just
really study an idea. Like we have been learning about slavery, and they really got it—
just the injustice and that it is still happening. . . .

We can see in this interview at Time 6 that Sandy's understanding of factors that influence children's behavior and development definitely interacts
with and affects how she thinks about the best way for children to learn and
how she needs to teach them. A specific example comes from her response
to the question about the optimal age and grade level to use timelines. Sandy
now sees that a timeline could be useful at any age depending on how it is
modified to fit what children can relate to and understand.

I don't know if there is one age that is more especially useful. I think that it depends on
what you are trying to teach. I think that you can do timelines in kindergarten in talk-
ing about your week and what you did on Monday and what you did on Tuesday and
Wednesday, Thursday and Friday, a short time span which is very concrete for them,
and even then it is pretty abstract, yesterday, today and tomorrow—or even the idea of
before school, after school, and before lunch, after lunch. . . . When you were born and
what you were doing when you were one and what you were doing when you were two
and what you are doing now that you are six years old or whatever is more abstract. . . .
It kind of depends on what your purpose for using a timeline is, and I think if one were
used in fourth grade, it would give them just a historical perspective, like this happened
a long time ago, and this happened 100 years ago or this happened 150 years ago dur-
ing the gold rush or during slavery in the 1800s, about the same time as the gold rush.
. . . They need to know that every inch is equal, that an inch is a unit of measurement
that represents a time frame of 10 years. I think that is a pretty abstract concept for some

*kids to understand that. So, time is taught . . . as part of a measurement, but to replace
it with a unit of measurement as in inches, I think that is an additional concept that
they need to have.*

This kind of conditional thinking is more sophisticated than what she
displayed in earlier interviews. Perhaps this is a result of her experience
teaching students of different ages and her growing understanding of how
developmental factors interact with and influence learning and teaching.
Perhaps by working in other classrooms with novice and experienced teachers and different kinds of learners she has been forced to think about new
ways to improve teaching and learning. Perhaps it is also a consequence of
planning with another teacher and having to articulate her ideas. More
than likely, it is a combination of all these experiences that has advanced
Sandy's understanding of pedagogy.

Similarly, her attitude toward sharing time has also become more sophisticated. She has come to see it as a means to build community in the classroom
by helping students learn about each other. She believes sharing time builds
empathy, a sense of self, and self-esteem—all character traits that influence
children's classroom behavior—and therefore, in a classroom where she has
had to struggle with aggressive students, it has been a critical tool.

*We have had sharing in fourth grade, and I think that is one of the things that has got-
ten the kids to empathize with one another. . . . In fourth grade they still want to bring
things in and I don't want the stuff. I would rather they share about themselves. . . . We
have a rule that we can't talk about a movie you have seen, can't talk about TV, can't
talk about video games or gifts or anything like that. Then they really have to think,
"OK what am I going to talk about?" It builds in themselves an idea that there is something interesting about me and it is not tied to an item; it is tied to who I am. That is really important, and sharing is a good way for kids to share out and also to hear who
these kids are in the classroom. It has been great. . . . A lot of times they don't believe that
they have any worth or [believe they] are not important or that there is nothing that they
can do well or nothing important that they need for someone else to know about them.
. . . Even adults want to share out about themselves. Everybody wants to talk about who
they are, and that they have something important that they want to say, so I don't think
that it is any different. Schools don't acknowledge a lot of times what kids have going on
at home or inside and we just don't get a chance to know our kids very well. I think that
I have learned a lot about the kids that I have worked with, but a lot of kids chose not to
share.*

Sandy expresses her understanding of connection between teaching and
learning at this time in theoretical terms, using both Piagetian and Vygot-
skian concepts. First, she says that students are ready to learn when they are
in a state of *disequilibrium*, which is Piaget's term describing situations when
a learner has two different understandings about something that need to
be resolved. Second, she says that learning also happens when the teacher is

able to provide additional support for learning, called *scaffolding*, beyond where students may be able to learn on their own. Scaffolding is one of Vygotsky's concepts that refers to support offered by more experienced others in the *zone of proximal development*. Third, Sandy also understands that the teacher should provide an interactive and social learning environment that includes partner and group work because students can learn from their peers as well as from adults. Both Piaget's and Vygostsky's theories of learning support such an interactive and social learning environment.

> *Well, there is that whole equilibrium. If someone is in disequilibrium and they start coming up against these different ideas, they are ready then to learn something and move on to the next step of the I + 1 in the zone of proximal development. I think that is where learning happens, . . . when you are ready to hear and you are ready to learn. Now a lot of times, either the kids are beyond what we are teaching them, or they are not ready for that next step, so learning does not happen. So as a teacher, figuring out where those kids are, here the I is and then adding the 1 to it. There is a whole range, so the challenge for the teacher is just to keep providing them with those experiences and having them work with peers or in groups so that there is more interaction with the kids, because the teacher cannot possibly go to each kid and say "OK, now this is what we are doing."*
> *. . . Yeah, just trying to set up those experiences and also setting up an environment where it is not the teacher and 32 students but the teacher with many other teachers, [each of] them teaching each other.*

When Sandy talks specifically about teaching at Time 6, she says she likes teaching language arts and believes she can teach reading and writing to students of any age. She also hopes she can teach them to be lifelong learners who love reading and use writing to express their emotions and record ideas, observations, and questions.

> *What I like teaching the most is language arts—reading and writing. I feel that I can do that with any age group. I mean you have to change the books that you are going to use and how it is structured. Teaching them the literary elements, having discussions, discovering how a book can influence their writing, and having their writing lead to a better understanding. You can do that with any age group, I think, but you can go deeper with the older kids. Still, it is important to teach these ideas in addition to the skills.*
> *I would like them to have a love for reading and for books and to be able to use their Writer's Notebook as a place to vent or to write ideas or to keep a journal so that they can look back on who they were in fourth grade and also use it as a lifelong tool, as a companion.*
> *. . . In their writing, I try to encourage the students to use their Notebooks for reflection, for example, these are my thoughts or observations, . . . or I noticed a nest in that tree, or I noticed this as we were walking down the street—just thinking and asking questions. I guess that is something else that we try to work on, not just accepting things,*

but asking questions, like why, or that doesn't make any sense. . . . I think that all has to do with being a lifelong learner.

In talking about other things she teaches, Sandy still believes that the school should teach students responsibility, self-discipline, and respect for authority. This is something she also expressed earlier. However, her current thinking is more conditional with regard to the school's role in teaching respect for authority because she does not want to teach blind obedience. She wants to teach her students to think and question.

> *We talk a lot about being responsible for our actions and so we need to be responsible for what we say and what we do and how we say it and how we do it because it can affect other people in different ways. Also, being responsible for our homework or for our books or for turning in our papers or for getting our work done on time. . . . Those are all little things that I do in the classroom to teach them responsibility. Just being part of a community. . . . Working with kids who have trouble with time management or disciplining or being self-disciplined and controlling their anger, a lot of in-the-classroom little things.*
>
> *I want them to be respectful of authority, but I also want them to be able to question in a way that is not offensive. I guess my understanding of the question is whether it is the school's role or it is the parent's role. I feel like, yeah, it is the school's role. I have kind of a hard time with the "respect authority," because you can go too far with that and not question why people or why the government says, for example, that these are these laws. We are teaching about authority and respecting authority, but being self-disciplined and responsible, yeah, I think that we need to teach them that, and we need to set it up so that in the classroom . . . they could practice that.*

Sandy also believes the teacher's role is to provide experiences that teach students how to learn. She teaches them strategies for learning and problem solving, rather than just teaching them the algorithms for finding answers.

> *In teaching them how to learn, I am also teaching them strategies for what to do when they don't know something. So, I feel like with reading and writing and with math, I am always trying to teach them strategies. If you don't know the answer, how do you figure it out? What is something that you can do to figure it out? If you are reading, what do you do if you don't know what this word is, if you are writing, what do you do if you don't know how to spell a word, or in math what are some strategies that you can use if you don't know this multiplication fact, or if you don't know how to solve this word problem. Providing them with experiences, but also giving them strategies instead of an algorithm.*

Perhaps a snapshot of Sandy's teaching in her fourth-grade classroom at this time can bring to life the teaching practices she talks about in the interview. This is also a good opportunity to see how congruent Sandy's thoughts and actions are at this time.

AN OBSERVATION OF SANDY AT TIME 6 (1999)

I observed Sandy teaching in late spring 1999 at Wilson Elementary School. She taught math in the morning, followed by Reader's and Writer's Workshops. On this day, Sandy's fourth-grade class has 28 students—15 boys and 13 girls.

When the bell rings at 8:15 a.m., Sandy leaves the classroom to pick up her students from the playground where they are lined up. As they return to the room, Sandy stands by the door and either hugs or shakes hands with every student who enters the class. Copies of the local newspaper are on every desk for the children to read at the beginning of the day. After they put away their backpacks and take care of their lunch choices, I observe most of the students reading the comics or doing a word find puzzle on the Kid's Page while a few read the weather or some of the news articles on the front page. Some students have jobs to do at this time, but everyone is responsible for putting their own name card into baskets labeled either *hot lunch* or *cold lunch*. One student has to tally these and take the lunch count down to the office. Two other students sort and reshelve the books turned in that morning. One student sharpens pencils and another takes all the cold lunch bags that have been deposited into a large crate to the cafeteria. The students appear to be independent and self-directed. They all seem to know what is expected of them. During this time, Sandy talks to some students about their homework assignment, collects notes they have for her, and talks privately with one child she observes up sharpening a pencil for the second time instead of reading the newspaper on his desk.

At 8:30, Sandy asks the class, "*Who has one thing to share from the newspaper?*" She also reminds everyone to be a good listener. One student brings up an article she read about a fire and mentions that some children ran away from the firefighters. Another student comments that this fire was in a local restaurant and that it was set by two boys. Sandy asks, "*Does anyone know what arson is?*" No one raises a hand. After some wait time, Sandy explains, "*Arson is when someone deliberately sets a fire, when they do it on purpose. Arson is against the law and a very dangerous thing to do.*"

Sandy calls the students by name to come to the rug for their morning circle time. "*Please think about what you want to share this morning,*" she says. Once the students are settled in a circle around the edge of the rug, Sandy passes around a soft model of the earth. The students hold this object when it is their turn to speak and then pass it on. During sharing time, several students say, "Pass," and Sandy reprimands one child for not listening and sends him back to his table. Once everyone has had a turn to share, Sandy gets a clipboard that holds a list of things students have written down that they want to discuss. One child asks why there isn't a schedule on the board for today, and Sandy responds, "*Because we have the same routine every day and because we discuss it each morning.*" [Sandy told me later that her teaching partner, Paula, usually wrote the schedule on the board and that she had trouble remembering to do the same.] Some of the items on the list for discussion include plans for an upcoming field trip, books they want to read together, and a problem that happened on the playground yesterday.

By 9:00, the students have returned to their seats at seven tables scattered around the room. Sandy begins using the overhead projector to explain a math game they will play with a partner at their table. Several times, Sandy models how to play the game, called *Leftovers*, asking different students to come up to the overhead to be her partner. The game requires using wooden counters, dice, and paper for recording results. Sandy changes the game by using different numbers and shows the class how to record their results as math equations. For example, if the number is 15 and one student rolls a 6 with her die, then the object is to see how many groups of 6 are in 15 and how many are left over. If the number is still 15 and her partner rolls a 4 with the die, the object is to see how many groups of 4 are in 15 and how many remain. The students are supposed to use the wooden counters as manipulatives to form the number of groups of 4 or 6 found in 15. Using the overhead projector, Sandy shows how to create a record sheet like this:

15 / 6 = 2 R. 3
15 / 4 = 3 R. 3
15 / 2 = 7 R. 1

By 9:15, Sandy is ready to direct the table monitors and supply clerks to do their jobs. Before she does, she asks the class, "*How many dice and how many pieces of paper are needed if there are four people at your table? How many dice and how many pieces of paper do you need to pass out if there are six people at your table?*"

As the monitors pass out materials, Sandy reminds the class that the first game will start with 15; she asks each student to count out only 15 wooden counters from the bucket at his or her table. As the students begin playing Leftovers with their partners, Sandy circulates around the room and helps several pairs to correctly record their math equations. Halfway through the time she has allotted for the game, Sandy changes the target number from 15 to 20. After 25 minutes of playing time, Sandy counts out loudly, *1 – 2 – 3 – 4*, to get the students' attention and asks them to clean up, which takes about 5 minutes. Then Sandy asks the class, "*What did you notice about this game when you played it? What happened when you had fewer wooden counters than the number of the die you rolled?*"

At 9:45, it is time for recess. First, Sandy reminds the six students who are on *self-government* to go ahead and then she dismisses the rest of the class by table groups. Self-government is part of Sandy's classroom management system. She also used it with her second graders at Washington School. Students become eligible for a week of self-government by keeping out of trouble and completing their homework each day. In other words, they have demonstrated that they can govern themselves and that the teacher does not need to remind them about their behavior or responsibilities. From the pool of eligible students each week, their peers nominate students based on whether they helped someone else in the class the week before. Students on self-government are free to go to the bathroom or get a drink without asking permission, to take balls or jump ropes out for recess, and to leave for recess, lunch, and the end of the day without waiting for the teacher to dismiss their table group.

After recess, Sandy reminds the students, *"We are going to do Reader's Workshop now. And I want to thank you for being extra quiet when I am testing, just as you were yesterday. Monitors, you can pass out the reading folders now. Everyone should find a quiet place to read for the next 45 minutes."* As the students receive folders containing their books and Notebooks, they find their favorite reading spots in the room. Some students stay at their desks, others move to the rug area, while still others browse the bookshelves and bookracks for a new book to read. Sandy helps several students choose new books and then circulates to see who might want to sign up for a book-talk group. Students choose whether to form these groups; although everyone in each group is reading a different book, they all want to share what their book is all about and hear about what others are reading. Several students sign up to meet on another day.

After 45 minutes of silent reading time, Sandy says, *"Please write an entry in your reading diary today and then get ready for Writer's Workshop. You have 10 minutes."* As the monitors collect the reading folders and pass out writing folders, Sandy waits quietly. When everyone appears to have made the transition, she asks for their attention: *"I need all eyes and ears."* She waits until it is silent. Sandy then reviews with the entire class the steps in Writer's Workshop, which she has on a large poster in the front of the room. She reads:

STEPS IN WRITER'S WORKSHOP:

1. Write in your Notebooks every single night.
2. Choose an idea from your Notebook and write a draft—writing more, creating a first draft.
3. Peer conference with a friend about your first draft. Use sheet to get feedback from peers.
4. Revise your first draft.
5. Conference with teacher. While waiting for a teacher conference, you can go back to your Writer's Notebook.
6. Revise next draft and put into the Editor's box.
7. Students are the editors.
8. Teacher checks and gets it typed (or student types or retypes). Go back to #1.

Sandy then takes a *status of the class* by calling the roll and asking the students to tell her where they are in this process today. All of this takes only 10 minutes, leaving 25 minutes for the students to work on their writing before it is time for Author's Chair and then lunch. Sandy confers with one student and then talks to two students who are not on task. Two student editors work independently using their red pencils to make corrections to stories they find in the Editor's box. I also observe a few pairs of students engage in peer conferences—reading aloud to each other and talking about their writing. Most of the students remain at their seats to write in their Notebooks. Sandy seems frustrated with the two students she talked with earlier who are not writing, and she does not get to another student who has signed up for a conference with her.

Before beginning Author's Chair, the sharing time that concludes Writer's Workshop each day, Sandy says, "*Please, everyone, put away your writing folders now, so you can focus and listen to Brianna's family story about when she was a baby.*" When everyone is settled, Brianna reads her story. The students clap for her, and Sandy follows up by asking these three questions in turn: "*What do you remember hearing in Brianna's story? What questions do you have for Brianna? What suggestions do you have for Brianna's story?*" At the end of this discussion, the students applaud one more time, and Sandy dismisses them by name to line up for lunch.

ADDITIONAL THOUGHTS FROM SANDY AT TIME 6 (1999)

As we resume our conversations and the clinical interview after school, I ask what obstacles she sees to accomplishing her professional goals. Sandy seems frustrated as she responds:

> *I guess my obstacles would be that I can't be the kind of teacher that I want to be. I can't put out that much effort and have a family too. So I work part time and then I get frustrated as a teacher because I am not doing what I want to do and I don't have the systems in place, I don't have the time to plan or to think or research, or whatever it is that I need to do to be the kind of teacher that I want to be. I know that is an opportunity cost for me and that I have to sacrifice who I am as a teacher so that I can be a half-decent or good-enough parent and that once I get beyond the child rearing age I can then focus more on teaching, but also have a life.*
>
> *I guess the other obstacle is that I don't feel like I have a community of teachers that are at the same place where I am at so that I can talk to them, share ideas with them, and get ideas from them. The books that I read, like* In the Company of Children *[in which author and literacy expert Joanne Hindley describes successful practices at the Manhattan New School in New York, which is a public school where Shelley Harwayne was the principal] . . . [describe] my vision of what an [ideal] school is. All of the teach-*

ers get together, they all have Writer's Workshops, and they all use Writer's Notebooks, and they all do literature studies and Reader's Workshops. They are all doing the same thing, so instead of talking about how to set up a Reader's Workshop, they are talking about what great books support the writing and what writing supports the reading. You can talk at that higher level, instead of at the very basic level.

As Sandy explains, she often relies on attending Workshops and reading books to help her figure out what and how to teach in ways consistent with her beliefs and goals. Yet she gets the most from talking with other teachers trying to do the same things she is trying to do. She practices these new ideas—just as she believes it is important for her students to practice the things they are trying to learn.

I have a lot of books and I can read them, but I don't think that they give you the full picture. So I can try to do what they say that they have done, but I think that going and actually hearing someone talk about it and practicing it is really important for me. Talking about how things work with other teachers, so those are my resources . . . I can do a lot of learning by myself, but only up to a certain point. Then I need to go and practice with somebody else guiding me, saying, "Try it this way" or "Have you thought about this?"

When I ask Sandy if she ever had the kind of community of teachers she yearns for, she reminisces about times when a colleague or student teacher filled her need to talk about teaching. She also experienced it at a summer writing Workshop in New Hampshire, where "*we were there as learners,*" she says. At the schools where she works she can only name one colleague at Washington Elementary with whom she could exchange ideas. At Wilson, she and the other teachers do not seem to have the time to coordinate their schedules for a teachers' roundtable.

We were teaching at different grade levels, but we understood each other pretty well and we were able to share ideas, not specific ideas but more concepts. I learned a lot from her. Also when I wasn't working part time I had a student teacher. I think that student teachers push you to think more, especially DTE student teachers because they ask questions related to developmental learning, they do these projects tied to their classwork, and they pushed me to think more about why I was doing things: "Oh yeah, why am I doing that? That is not important. I shouldn't do that; this is why."

We tried [to start a group to talk about teaching] at Wilson, but when we did there were teachers who thought that they were doing what the book said. . . . So, I'm being judgmental about their teaching, but to me it was clear that they were still pretty traditional in how they were viewing Reader's Workshop or Writer's Workshop. Or, maybe my expectations were too high. I don't know how you can have a meaningful group unless you ask specific people, but everybody was just so busy, and . . . it was really hard to find a common meeting time.

I also ask Sandy about how she knows what and how to teach. Her comprehensive answer includes factors such as her experiences teaching students at different grade levels, observations of her students as they tackle the tasks she sets for them, the work they produce, and listening to them read. Feedback from her students' families also helps her understand the children's learning needs. She also describes steps she takes at the start of the school year to get to know her students.

> *I try to take samples of their work, so that if they can't write me a letter then they would draw a picture, and I think that whatever they produce is very indicative of what they are able to do and what they are thinking about. Usually what I would have them do is write a letter to me telling me what they want to learn and what they want to do this year and so from that letter I notice—Do they know how to write a letter? Do they know how to spell? . . . Which hand did they write with? . . . Do they need help? Can they write? Can they sit still and finish a project without disturbing anybody else? I really think that I learn a lot when I am observing them at work and not just their work. Part of it is that I want to see what they can do, but I also want to observe them and see how they interact with the other kids, what they do when I ask them to do something, what their reaction is to it, all of that. I get more information from that. With reading, with older kids, I have them read independently, and I will go around [and listen to them read] quietly, or I will pull them aside so that I know where they are with their reading levels.*
>
> *[Yetta] Goodman talks about being a kid watcher and just listening to them and observing them, and they will tell me what they know and what they don't know and how they feel about it and if they feel open to hearing it. . . .*
>
> *We don't get a lot of parent involvement, but we do get parents saying that the homework is too hard, or that so and so didn't understand it, or I think that you are being too tough on my son. That is all feedback and that is all stuff that we need to hear, whether we like it or not. Then we need to deal with it. I think that I need to in order to help these kids learn, so that they can learn, but I need to be open to their families.*

As an experienced teacher, Sandy also relies on a schema she has developed about what students should be able to accomplish at a given grade level (e.g., in third grade) to help her know what and how to teach. At the same time, she also understands there will be individual differences and a range of skill and ability levels.

> *I would expect them to be kind of where my second graders were when they left me. [That] is kind of the framework that I am thinking in right now. That doesn't mean that what we have here is an average third grader. But then there is such a range in the classroom, in any class, in any school, that they could be much lower or much higher. I just think that I would go along with an average third grader, that they would all come to me reading and writing and knowing their addition facts and subtraction facts and maybe some multiplication and go from there. Some of them may know and some of them may not. Some may be way off the chart. . . . I just think that at any grade level there is going to be a range so you have to be prepared to meet the ranges with different materials.*

At the end of our time together on this day, I ask Sandy if she had changed.

In the last 2 years? Yeah, I think I have changed being back in the classroom. Being out of the classroom is very different. Thinking about teaching and being out of the class-room is very different than when you are actually inside a classroom. In some ways I think that I know a lot more now than I did 2 years ago or when I graduated. A lot of it is inside, and being able to articulate it is difficult. I read a lot, and what I read makes sense at the moment, but it's difficult to be articulate. We were talking about having a community where I could talk about these ideas or having a student teacher—I feel like I was more thoughtful and more articulate about it then. Yeah, I have learned a lot and yet I feel in some ways I have regressed a little bit in not having an opportunity to discuss my teaching with others.

I also ask Sandy what metaphor she has for herself at this time. Two years ago, her metaphor had to do with a quilt and seeing herself as quilter piec-ing together all the materials that would go into making a quilt. Her new metaphor for herself is teacher as cook or chef:

When you are learning to cook you have to follow the recipe step-by-step. You have to use this ingredient and so much of this and you have to measure this out exactly and as you become more experienced you start using the cookbook less or using it as an idea more then as a recipe. I guess, as a teacher, I feel like I go back and forth. If a topic or unit is new to me then I tend to look towards a book, or another resource that is not necessarily a teacher's guide, for ideas. After I have taught it for a while I can rely on my experience. This is true not only with the curricular area but with the age level. Then it becomes more of my own recipe, as opposed to someone else's. I am in control and I write the reci-pes. But I don't feel like I am there. I feel like I am still following a cookbook sometimes . . . the ingredients are the ideas and the activities and the books to use in the classroom. . . . The teaching I guess changes from following the recipe step-by-step to some improvi-sation—or in the presentation of it. How you present it, you can either do it gourmet style or you can do it casserole style.

SANDY'S STORY . . . IN HER OWN WORDS . . . SUMMER 2000

During the summer of 2000, I asked Sandy, and each of the educators high-lighted in this book, to reflect on a few open-ended questions. What follows is Sandy's response, which serves to update her story by allowing her to de-scribe her thoughts in writing.

Before I write about my "present professional thoughts and actions," I think it's impor-tant to explain all the different teaching capacities I've been in for the past 12 years. My tenure in teaching has been varied—I've not been in any position longer than 3 years, although I was with the same school district for 10 years, not including the 2 years I took off to start a family. I taught full time until my oldest daughter was born and have been part time ever since (part time being defined as 40%–60% to 80% this year). Last year, I left the public school district where I had worked for 10 years and moved to the private school my daughter attended. Over the years, I've taught first, second, and fourth grade, and I was a Chapter 1 literacy specialist focusing on early literacy and children with delayed literacy development.

From the beginning, my focus and main interest was primarily in language arts with some attention to math. Science and social studies were taught as filler activities or units to integrate the whole curriculum. Although I have kept current with the latest "best practices" in language arts, I found it was quite challenging to implement all my new ideas after going back to the classroom; it was made even more challenging to be teaching a grade level that I was not familiar with. This past year, I have struggled with making history/social studies a meaningful part of the curriculum, and this year I will be learning a lot about teaching fourth-grade science.

In addition to focusing on the content, I am personally struggling with the idea of the classroom teacher working part time. While all my teaching partners have been wonderful, I have felt less connected to my job, and the loss of control over what happens in the classroom is unsatisfactory to me. I feel the continuity of teaching and learning is affected, as is the sense of community in the classroom.

This year (2000–2001), I will be teaching fourth grade as I have done for the past 2 years, but in a slightly different capacity. Last year, I was mainly responsible for the humanities portion of the curriculum—language arts and history/social studies. My teaching partner has left to become the director of our feeder middle school, and so this year I will be teaching all the fourth-grade curriculum except for math.

Berkwood Hedge is a small private school in Berkeley. There are six classes serving seven grades (and until recently, they were all split grades—we now have straight grades except for the oldest class, which is a 5/6 grade combination), with 18 to 21 students in each class. Teachers in a collective-style governing body administer the school. In addition to having teaching responsibilities, the teachers and one office manager are also responsible for the operations of the school.

Being a teacher is fascinating work. I love to watch the children grow and develop during the school year. Since they come from such different backgrounds and experiences, I know that no two children are the same. Therefore, I try to understand where each child is developmentally and use that knowledge to guide our work together for the rest of the year. My goal as a teacher is to instill the joy of learning in all children; to help them become lifelong readers, writers, and problem solvers; and to develop their critical thinking and reasoning skills. I give my students autonomy so that they can grow to be independent learners. I let them make choices whenever possible because they then have greater ownership in their learning. I am still very committed to developmental education and believe that instruction should match the individual learning style and the development of the student. This is my ideal, but reality falls short of this and I struggle with this a lot.

Children learn to become readers and writers by practicing reading and writing. Therefore, we spend much of our time reading and writing during Workshop time. In reading Workshop, children engage in literature studies, independent or partner reading, and small group guided reading. They explore the elements of literature, study a variety of genres (realistic and historical fiction, nonfiction, poetry, mystery, and fantasy, to name a few), learn how to select books at an appropriate level, monitor their own understanding, and apply the knowledge gained from reading to their writing.

In writing Workshop, children are writers. They keep a Writer's Notebook in which they record observations, reflections, and ideas from the books they read. They work on writing projects in a variety of genres that become "published" pieces. Taking ideas from their Notebooks, they develop a piece and move it through the different stages of the writing process, including revising and editing. Children learn about writing (style, voice, structure) from their reading and in this way reading and writing support each other.

Spelling is an important part of the writing program because we want others to be able to read our writing. Therefore, spelling becomes a major focus during the editing stage of the writing process, when children are getting their projects ready for public viewing. We also spend time studying spelling patterns and engaging in word study, actively using our books as a source for our words since it is through reading that we really learn how to be effective spellers.

Through the study of social sciences, children learn about their place in the world, past and present. Our focus is on California history, with an overall theme of "Who are we and how did we get here?" We begin with a study of our individual family histories and use what we learned as a basis for learning about California Indians, the Gold Rush, and the current immigration flow into California. During the year, children learn to look critically at the information provided in books and other resources. We consider what facts are printed, discuss from whose point of view they were written, and reflect on what is missing. We investigate the groups affected by events in history and discuss how events came about and why.

Children work in different groupings throughout the day (independently, with partners, or in small groups) to provide lots of practice working cooperatively with others. Conflicts are seen as opportunities to learn, and the children are guided to use conflict-resolution skills. Class meetings nurture a sense of community, encourage reflection, and foster empathy and respect for all people.

Hopefully, this information will shed some light on what I think and do in my classroom. I think the trait that keeps popping up over and over again in my teaching is that I like to have control over the curriculum. I have never been able to follow a textbook series in any subject, with its predetermined worksheets and teacher guides. While I have occasionally used a textbook to teach (e.g., basal readers and consumable math books during my first year of teaching), it was only to supplement a unit or focus on a particular strategy. I read a lot of professional books that I consider developmentally and child-centered and gather ideas from them to develop units of study for my students. This is very time-consuming, close to re-creating the wheel, and it would certainly be a lot simpler to follow a textbook. I read a quote recently by Donald Graves [education professor emeritus at the University of New Hampshire], which I think explains why I spend so much energy on curriculum development. He said, "Teachers must be the chief learners in the classroom, spending a significant amount of time modeling their own learning and showing students how." (Strategies That Work) I have to figure out what I am teaching and understand it before I can teach my students. It has to make sense to me if I want it to make sense to them. I think this is also one reason I left public school; I was frustrated with the mandates over what I had to teach and when and the increased control the state has over the materials teachers use to teach.

Because I read a lot about how other teachers put together a unit or what they do to teach reading, spelling, math, and so on, I am also constantly questioning my own practices and looking for newer and better ways to teach an idea or subject. This is a trait I want my students to have—to be reflective and thoughtful about their own learning—so I encourage them to be metacognitive about what they are doing. I wonder whether it's better to teach writing by having students keep a Writer's Notebook or if I should just stay with the writing Workshop I've been doing in the past. Right now I'm struggling with how to teach spelling. I've gone from not touching it at all to giving weekly spelling lists to appease the parents. This summer I've read many books and articles about spelling and am coming to a better understanding of what I can do to help students improve their spelling. Last year I learned so much about California history that I never knew before because I had to teach it. What was amazing to me was that the research and reading I did to get a handle on the content gave me more information than other teachers who had been teaching California history for several years using a textbook. This year, I will have to start again with science, but, not having a science background, I think I'm going to rely more on a published series such as FOSS. All this is to say that constructing my own understanding has been character building for me and I've been able to continue being a lifelong learner. But if I do this every time I change positions or grade levels, eventually it gets overwhelming because I can never get a handle on the content. I'm looking forward to staying put for a while so I can refine some of the units I've done the last couple years.

I'm finding that a new focus to my teaching is in the social/emotional areas of teaching and learning. I think I've traditionally been the kind of teacher who wants the students to do (behaviorally) as I say and if they don't, there is a consequence. Although I did try to understand why they were behaving as they did, I didn't work with them on ways to change their actions in a more positive way. I also thought that students who didn't like a subject because "it was too hard" just had to bite the bullet and deal with it. My move away from this approach has a little to do with being a parent and living daily with the need to find different solutions to a situation. It also has been pushed on me this last year, as the culture of Berkwood Hedge is so different from the public school system that I came from. Of course this was one of the reasons I chose that school for my daughter, and it may have been a case of the way I wish I taught. I know now that creating a sense of community is really important for the social/emotional needs of the child (and teacher) and that having a respectful relationship with the students is especially important. As I tend to be more of an introverted person by nature, I need to make more of an effort to reach out to the children to engage them in conversation. In thinking about these issues, I am also learning how cultural differences affect the teaching and learning that occur at school. Attitude has also moved to the top of my list. Being motivated improves student performance incredibly. Making learning fun and exciting has been an important lesson for me this year.

One other area that I have put some energy into this past year is in having a social justice program. Berkwood Hedge, over the past few years, has been moving toward such an approach to teaching, and the teachers agreed to look at our teaching with social justice lenses. This of course means something a little different to everybody, but for me it meant, on one level, looking at how I presented the unit on California Indians; for example, being mindful of the literature I use, respecting their culture and history, and including their side of the story when looking at events in California history. At another level, it meant talking in class about how we treat each other and those in our commu-

nity, who has the power, who has the loudest voice, who is heard most often (a big issue last year with 13 boys and 6 girls). My learning curve is steep in this area, but it seems like a natural progression of where I am moving professionally.

[When I think about the future] I would really like a 9–5 job, with a 5-day work-week!! I'm still trying to decide if classroom teaching part-time works for me (you'd think I'd know after 5 years and four different teaching partners!) and if working as part of the collective is where I want to put my extra energy since it takes away from my teaching. Thoughts of grad school enter my head once in a while as I would like to learn more about literacy, as do ideas of working in a children's bookstore where I can read books I love all day long! I would then have evenings free to quilt.

Being a parent has changed my life as a teacher. On a very concrete level, it has af-fected how much I teach and how much time I'm able to give it. I can also live like Piaget and test my theories and understandings about child development on my children. But mostly, parenting has challenged me to find balance in my life—to make time for my family, hobbies, and exercise—because teaching itself can be a 24-hour job. My hus-band, a banker, is spiritually minded. He has spent the last 5 or more years thinking about self, the meaning of life, and quality of life. Because of our evening discussions, I am starting to focus more on the inner meaning of teaching, why I teach, and what it means to me, rather than what I do or teach.

A FINAL OBSERVATION OF SANDY (FALL 2000)

Because Sandy moved from teaching primary-age students in a San Lean-dro public school to teaching fourth graders at a private school in Berkeley, I wanted to observe her once more in her new school setting. I had heard about Berkwood Hedge for many years, but never had the opportunity to visit. Berkwood Hedge is an alternative, nonsectarian, coeducational, inde-pendent school near downtown Berkeley, California. Berkwood School was originally established in 1947 and was the first racially integrated school in Berkeley. Hedge School was established in the late 1960s by a Berkwood parent and operated as a teacher collective. These two schools merged and reopened on the former Berkwood campus in 1975. The school was ex-panded in the 1980s and now has about 120 students in Grades K to 6. Al-though the tuition at Berkwood Hedge is $8300 annually, a relative bargain compared with other private schools in the East Bay area, it is still too ex-pensive for the majority of the population. Nevertheless, the faculty and families have worked hard to increase the diversity of students attending their school by keeping 30% of the slots open for scholarship students. A collective structure, social-justice curriculum, focus on the arts, and strong sense of community are all important at Berkwood Hedge School.

The social-justice focus permeates the curriculum and the philosophy about how to interact with children. This is quite evident from the first mo-ment I am in Sandy's fourth-grade class and from the school's mission state-ment.

Mission Statement

Berkwood Hedge School is more than an independent school. It is an intimate community of students, families, and educators administered by a teacher collective and committed to the recognition and celebration of diversity and multiculturalism throughout the school culture.

As a community, we model collaboration, critical thinking, and a respect for individual differences and learning styles. Our graduates have a vision of social justice and feel empowered to work for change.

Our social-justice curriculum, guided by a developmental approach to whole-child education, instills a joy of learning, academic excellence, intellectual excitement, and emotional well-being.

We believe this educational process opens us to respond fully to the ever-changing world with all its richness and diversity and all its needs and concerns.

As I walk through downtown Berkeley to Sandy's school, I pass students going to Berkeley High School and Washington Elementary School, which are less than a block from Berkwood Hedge. The two public schools display the rich ethnic and cultural mix of the population of California students. Berkwood Hedge, however, does not. About 80% of the students attending Berkwood Hedge are White or upper middle class or both. However, in Sandy's fourth-grade class, the 18 students—9 boys and 9 girls—are a more diverse group.

The first event I observe is the weekly all-school community meeting. As soon as the first bell rings, all the students file into a multipurpose room, the size of two classrooms, which is directly below Sandy's second-floor room. All but the oldest class of fifth and sixth graders sit on the floor while one of the music teachers plays a tune celebrating new life on an instrument that looks like a finger harp with a gourd amplifier. She plays until everyone has settled down, then tells the students the instrument comes from the Shona people of Zimbabwe.

Once all the children and teachers are quiet, the kindergarten teacher, the leader of the weekly community meetings, announces an upcoming read-a-thon, one of the annual fundraisers at Berkwood Hedge. She also says that the other music teacher will perform in a play opening in San Francisco that night and asks the students to send her "good vibes." She then reads a list of students with birthdays during the month. As she calls the students' names, they stand and everyone claps for them. When all the October birthdays have been recognized, the entire student body sings a special version of Happy Birthday.

Following the birthday celebration, the meeting leader asks if anyone wants to honor someone. Beginning with the kindergartners, she calls on students from each grade who want to honor another student for anything. As she advances from grade to grade, students say things such as, "I want to honor Sara for being my friend and playing with me," "I want to honor Micah for helping me with my project yesterday," and "I want to honor everyone on my winning soccer team." A teacher honors her entire class for a productive day the day before. Only students who have not honored at previous community meetings may speak, but several more students in each class raise their hands to express their appreciation publicly. After the half-hour meeting, everyone returns to their classrooms.

Sandy's room seems quite roomy and easily accommodates all 18 children. Five large tables with four chairs each surround the rug in the center of the room. Sandy tells me later that she soon expects to get two more students whose applications are pending, but the school aims to keep all the classes at 18 to 21 students.

There are windows on all four walls of this room, in the library alcove, and above the formica shelf on one wall. Sandy's desk is in one corner of the room opposite the classroom door. The chalkboard hangs on the front wall of the room.

Formica counters span the length of two other walls. Underneath these counters, open and closed shelves hold math manipulatives, school supplies, and boxes with Sandy's teaching materials. An iMac and printer that Sandy bought with $5000 annual budget, two PCs and two Macs, and two more printers sit on the shelf along the back wall. Sandy does not use the computers much, and they are not turned on today. Sandy later tells me that she has struggled with the best way to use the computers this year. Last year, she says, some students were using the Internet inappropriately. She says she is still struggling with the best way to use them with her students.

The fourth wall of Sandy's classroom is filled with bookshelves, cubbies for jackets and backpacks, storage, and below a window by the door a cabinet for school supplies. In addition, one corner of the otherwise rectangular room juts out to makes a quiet spot for Sandy's extensive class library. Shelves full of books, organized by authors and genres, line three sides. More books cover a worktable in the alcove. Most of these books belong to Sandy personally, a testament to her willingness to share her love of books and children's literature in particular with her class.

Sandy has begun a timeline to help her students relate events in California history to one another. It is displayed on one wall of her room. Above the computers, a bulletin board displays different kinds of maps, and several more charts are posted around the chalkboard and in the area near her desk. These charts all relate to reading and writing, which along with social studies and science are Sandy's main teaching responsibilities. This year Sandy teaches 5 days a week; her partner teacher is mainly responsible for teaching math, but just 6 hours a week.

Sandy's students sit on a rug in the center of the room where Sandy begins class by going over the day's schedule, which is posted on the blackboard.

By 9:15, Sandy is ready to begin Workshop. She begins by reading aloud a book called *Shortcut*. In preparation, Sandy tells the class, "*While I am reading, I want you to think about what the author, Donald Crews, does in this book to make the story come alive.*"

After asking for some children to repeat her instructions so that she knows they understand her purpose for reading, she begins. When she is finished, Sandy repeats her question: "*How does the author bring life to the story?*" She writes the students' suggestions on a large piece of chart paper she has taped to the chalkboard. The students suggest that the author has used sounds, which Sandy writes down, reiterates with some elaboration, and then rereads an example in the book where the author has used sounds. Someone else suggests that the author has people talk in the book, and Sandy writes "uses dialogue—people talking" on the chart. After rereading some of the dialogue in the book, another student suggests that the author uses a lot of detail. Sandy writes "details" on the chart and then asks if the students know what the book's genre is. They suggest that it is realistic fiction, but Sandy explains that the book is a memoir and defines *memoir* for the children as an incident in the life of the author, probably real. She also explains the word *foreshadowing* to label what another student describes as the author's attempt to hint that something is going to happen in the story. She writes the terms *foreshadowing* and *zooming in* together on the chart. Finally, Sandy reminds them about a writing concept called "show, not tell" that they have talked about before and reads some examples from the story in which the author describes an event in detail without directly telling what happened.

This mini-lesson only takes 10 minutes, and before Sandy dismisses the students to find their Writer's Notebooks she says, "*Try in your writing today to pick one small incident to zoom in on. Use details. You can use sounds and dialogue in your writing. These are all strategies that a writer uses to make a story come alive, just as Donald Crews did in* Shortcut."

Sandy then dismisses the students by name, one at a time, to get their Writer's Notebooks and move to their permanent writing places. In no time at all, the children are scattered around the room—some at tables, some in corners of the room on the floor, some on the rug. For the next half hour, Sandy talks with individual students about what is in their Notebooks. For example, I hear her talk with one student about the list of titles she has written. She explains to the girl that writers usually choose titles after they have written their stories. However, she also praises this student for the many lists of story ideas that she has written and shares that she does the same thing in her own Writer's Notebook. Sandy then moves on to talk to another student about using dialogue in her story, and consults with a third student about zooming in on just one aspect of the story he is writing. I also note that Sandy carries a clipboard around with her to these conferences and uses a form she has developed to record what the students are working on after meeting with them.

At the end of the 30 minutes allotted for Writer's Notebook, Sandy asks all the students to return to the rug for a sharing time. Some students, reluctant to stop working, remain at their tables, but Sandy encourages them to finish and listen to those who are going to read what they wrote today. She calls for students who tried something different today. Most of the students who share tell Sandy that they tried to write with more details. One boy says he is trying to use foreshadowing, one girl used some dialogue in her writing, and another girls says she is trying to zoom in.

At the end of an hour, Sandy says it is time for Readers' Workshop. "*Yesterday when we were reading about the California flag, there were a lot of long and difficult words,*" she says. "*So I want you to think about strategies you use when you don't know a word.*" On another poster, Sandy records their ideas and the completed list looks like this:

Strategies to use when you don't know a word:

* Read on, go to the end of the sentence. Go back and see if you can read it. If not, ask someone for help, but not right away.
* Think about if you've seen the word before.
* Use other books on similar topics to learn words.
* Substitute with a different word.
* Chunk it (e.g., "pro-clam-a-tion").
* Sound it out.

Sandy writes these ideas on the chart—not in the order that students suggest them, but in order of how they should be used. For example, Sandy explains that "Sound it out" goes near the bottom of the list because many words are irregular and cannot be sounded out very easily. She puts "Read on" at the top of the chart and explains that it is a good idea to read on to the end of the sentence—to think about and substitute other words that might make sense. She reminds the students of words such as *proclamation*, which they encountered in their reading the previous day, and that they might be able to "chunk" into syllables. She also reminds them that longer words may contain smaller words or have affixes in them that they already know.

Following this discussion, Sandy suggests, "*Today when you are reading, be thinking if you are using some of these strategies.*" She then dismisses them individually to get their books for Reader's Workshop. During the next half hour, Sandy once again circulates around the room to talk with individual children about what they are reading. On her clipboard she makes notes as she listens to students read aloud, questions them, and helps some choose new books. A parent who volunteers weekly arrives and listens to several children read, questioning them about their books. Toward the end of Reader's Workshop, Sandy reminds everyone to record in their Notebooks what they read and to come sit on the rug.

Every child is reading different books and has a folder where they record what they read each day. Sandy tells me later that they also read and write in their Writer's Notebook for homework each night. She also tells me that all of her fourth graders are readers, although two or three are not yet reading on grade level. Before beginning the weekly class meeting, she asks them to share what reading strategies they used today.

During the class meeting, students can bring up problems they want to discuss according to a written agenda they compiled earlier. Sandy calls their attention to the first item, an allegation of cheating during the breaktime soccer game. After several children share their views, Sandy acts as moderator, ensuring that all are heard and helping the students come to a resolution on which they can act. The next topics include pencil monitors who do not do their job, sharing books with their book buddies and teasing during the lunchtime soccer game with another class. This precipitates a long discussion about how to handle people who tease. The last topic before it is time for lunch has to do with people taking things from others in the classroom. The children tell Sandy that this has already been resolved, so they do not need to talk about it anymore.

After an hour-long lunch, the children return to the rug to hear one student recite a memorized poem. The poem is funny, and the children have a good laugh. Students volunteer to be poet of the week, one of several jobs in Sandy's class. After this, Sandy reads aloud from a chapter book, *Dragonwings*, by Lawrence Yep. During this time, the students scatter around the room to find a comfortable place to listen. Some draw while she reads. Social Studies is next, and at 2 p.m. the students scatter around the school for vocal or instrumental music or for a dance class. They return to the room just before the 3 p.m. dismissal.

AFTERWORD

To update the reader: Sandy is still teaching 4th graders at Berkwood Hedge and trying to balance multiple roles as teacher, mother, and wife.

Chapter 5

The Story of Ralph Elder

I was a dancer before I came to this and before I came back to graduate school. [I] taught dance and theatrical improvisation, and I kind of shut that all out because I was going to be a teacher and a professional. I had my videotape lesson and my first year of teaching was such a revelation because it was so boring. I was trying to be a good teacher and I couldn't be dramatic because that wasn't professional. I don't know what made me do that. It was just horrible and it was embarrassing, and all of those things, but mostly it was just boring. I said, "I think we can loosen up a little bit here."

When I was in Moraga, there was a wonderful math person who did a lot of math and art connections and did all these different kinds of projects, and it was her passion, and I just took everything that I could get and my kids went to town. They would just go with these kinds of projects. They loved it and they would extend it. So as I am reading to the class, they are working on these symmetry projects that may go on for weeks and on these individual projects, and other kids are working on other things. This was very clearly something that I had stumbled on, something very rich.

Then teaching kindergarten . . . was kind of a loosening-up process, and that made it fun. . . . It came about kind of gradually, and I gradually expanded my boundaries and, "O.K. let's try this and see how that goes," and by the end of the first year, I found a way that kids could really look, and kids were creating great stuff. I went to workshops and got some of that. So, big paintings and that kind of thing became something that I was more kind comfortable with.

Ralph Elder is White, a gay man, and a teacher. Ralph taught third grade in a public school in Moraga, California, for 5 years and then transferred to a smaller private school in Oakland, California, where he taught kindergartners for 2 years and then fifth and sixth graders for 2 more years. He also worked as a supervisor for the Developmental Teacher Education program at UC–Berkeley for 3 years before returning to teach third grade in a large, urban public school in Oakland, California, located in a poor, changing neighborhood with many recent immigrant families.

A 1975 graduate of Reed College in Oregon, Ralph danced professionally and taught dance and theatrical improvisation at his own studio before he entered the DTE program at age 33. Initially, he thought a professional teacher could not use artistic expression in the classroom, and for his first several years as a public school teacher Ralph confined his interest in art to his personal life. Yet after he saw another teacher effectively integrate art into her classroom, and once he began teaching kindergarten, Ralph came back to his artistic roots and felt freer, compelled even, to integrate artwork and the arts into his teaching wherever possible.

RALPH'S 1985 INTERVIEW (TIME 1)

During Ralph's initial interview in his first month in the DTE program, he believes that factors related to the children (their personality and temperament, likes and dislikes, and positive and negative feelings about school), their families (family background, position in family, stability of family), and the schools (as institutions with large classes taught by only one teacher) all impact children's behavior. This is because students' likes and dislikes influence how they approach school and learning, he says.

Ralph's preconceptions about schools drove him to become an elementary school teacher, where he thought he could reach children before they lost their potential. He said large classes and schools as institutions can extinguish the spark of children's curiosity or cause it to languish and go underground. He came to this negative view of schools while teaching dance and doing improvisation with adults, working with continuation high school students as a tutor, and as a regular nursery school teacher working with infants and toddlers. He found the younger children were spontaneous and fun to teach. In contrast, with high school students, he says,

> So much has already gone wrong in terms of their education, and I was working against those years of bad training, and it felt hopeless to me. . . . I want to start at the beginning before anything's gone wrong and hopefully start them out on the right track.

Ralph's understanding of development and the developmental process at Time 1 shows some insights, but there are also some contradictions in his thinking. For example, he mentions that a child's knowledge, vocabulary, and physical coordination develop over time and that he thinks older children become more academically and socially sophisticated. This seems reasonable, but he contradicts himself by saying, "*My guess is that kids start out on a certain track very early, and perhaps they don't change much.*" Such contradictions indicate some misunderstanding at this time, or perhaps a naïve understanding of child development, but they are fairly typical of most adults' knowledge of child development.

Ralph describes the developmental process as one of physical maturation, which he believes is different for each person. "*I think it comes through maturing, . . . getting older, increased capability, increased physical coordination and strength. I think different individuals manifest that in very different ways depending on the kind of input they get from the environment.*" Ralph also sees the developmental process as "*moving from just a personal consideration and themselves to a broader way of looking at the world and an interest in something outside themselves.*" That is, the developmental process is one of building new understandings and gaining new perspectives on the world based on new experiences and new information, and moving from having only personal, egocentric views to gaining broader perspectives.

He also believes that people develop through achievement and by having multiple opportunities to succeed in age-appropriate and supportive conditions. These ideas represent reasonable understandings of the developmental process, but Ralph also reveals some contradictions in his thinking, at Time 1, about learning and development in these three statements:

- *I think kids come to school with certain kinds of tendencies . . . particular sets of tendencies, not very specific but different little personalities. . . .*
- *I think it [ability] would stay pretty fixed. There might be some changing, sure, but substantially I would bet the core kind of identity will stay pretty much the same.*
- *Some people learn and some people never learn.*

Despite these contradictions in Ralph's understanding about development and the developmental process, even his conflicted notions about whether ability is fixed or changeable, such thinking can be a good beginning for a budding teacher. Confusion or contradiction in a person's thinking—a state Piaget called *disequilibrium*—can catalyze new understandings as a person seeks to resolve these contradictions in thinking. In Ralph's case, this seems to be the starting point for his emerging understanding of individual differences and the importance of providing different ways for people to learn new things.

During this initial interview, Ralph also expresses his belief that people cannot be made to learn. "*I don't really think you can force kids to do something that they really don't want to do, certainly in terms of academic work, and I think it's a waste of time.*" They cannot learn without having the basics first. "*The same thing is true in school, if you try to learn complex operations without understanding basic principles or patterns of thought, . . . you sort of do the form, but it's never really yours."*

Ralph also cited a number of factors at Time 1 that affect the learning process, including both internal and external factors: years of bad training, large class sizes, kids who already think they have failed at something, children's interests, expectations of the teacher, climate of the class, complexity and familiarity of the task, demands from parents, time constraints, and a child's responsiveness to and relationship with the teacher. These factors are all very realistic and more insightful than might be expected from the average first-year education student. However, it is important to remember that Ralph came into the DTE program with several years experience teaching dance and theatrical improvisation to both high school students and preschool-age children. These experiences and his subsequent thinking about them obviously influenced the beliefs he brought with him into the DTE program.

In talking about the teacher's role in the learning process, Ralph's says: "*Generally I think the teacher sets the stage. I think the teacher is responsible for . . . creating and maintaining an environment in which learning takes place.*" He adds that teachers teach by giving examples and nonexamples, doing some direct instruction, providing definitions, offering multiple examples to classify, and giving lots of practice. He also says:

> *There's a structure to the day that also involves providing information, exercises, questions, leading statements being made [that are] provocative [and] stimulating, and activities or exploration in a certain direction; providing materials and the wherewithal, and papers and microscopes, and instructions on how to use them, sending out problems to be solved, giving feedback. I think it is real important letting a child know that he or she is proceeding in the appropriate direction and redirecting them.*

Ralph also indicates that he believes teaching can become more inductive by eliciting suggestions from students, helping them refine their ideas into a definition, applying the definition to examples, and refining the definition to come up with a rule that discriminates among the examples. He also reiterates his belief that the teacher should find ways to make the school experience rewarding and interesting to maintain students' motivation. Finally, he expresses a belief, which is one that he holds throughout his career, about the importance of providing multiple opportunities for students to learn something

> *It is important to go at it a number of different ways . . . I don't think all kids are going to understand a broad concept with any one particular approach. . . . [The more] ways you can go about it, the better off you are.*

Although Ralph initially has a contradictory understanding of behavior and development, his thinking about factors that can affect learning, and especially his understanding of the teaching process, are fairly well developed. Nevertheless, Ralph entered the DTE program with a rather behavioristic perspective on teaching and learning, as opposed to a well-developed developmental constructivist one. He thinks teachers teach mainly by modeling, reinforcing, and giving a lot of directed practice, although he is able to describe some inductive ways of teaching as well. He also believes at this juncture that students learn new skills by first acquiring the prerequisite building blocks, but he has a limited developmental-constructivist view of the learning. Nevertheless, these contradictions in Ralph's thinking are good because, as he continues in his teacher education program and sees other ways to teach and think about learning, he is able to confront them.

Furthermore, at this stage, it appears likely that Ralph can easily develop new ways of thinking from a more developmental and constructivist perspective because he seems attuned to children and seeks to use a variety of sources, beginning with:

> *My observations of children in the classroom and mostly my experience in working with kids and being able to see what works and what doesn't work. (So far I've seen a lot of things that don't.) . . . A lot of learning for me comes from . . . being able to think about where I am going wrong or in some cases what may work. Other teachers and the experience of other teachers, people that I have that are directing me, but even more so the teachers out in the field are real important, and already I can get ideas and different approaches to try that worked for them. . . . I drew upon a lot of my experiences that I've had both as a student and as a teacher. I've done some teaching, so there's some basis [in] my experience in the world. . . . And my reflections over the last six months, particularly since I applied to this program, and considering [whether] this is something that I really wanted to do and if so why, and what did I expect to get out of it, and so . . . it's really sort of my ruminations, my thoughts about it.*

Ralph says learning is *"like solving a puzzle or problem or dilemma, a quality of opening . . . a way out of a particularly stuck place . . . understanding something that was a mystery . . . a tension that is resolved."* At this early stage of his career, many of the pieces to this puzzle are missing, but some are already in place.

RALPH'S 1987 INTERVIEW (TIME 2)

At the time of Ralph's 1985 interview, in his first year in the DTE program, he believed that factors related to students, their families, and schools as institutions all have an impact on student behaviors. After 2 years in the program, which included courses in developmental theory and teaching methods; five field experiences with increasing levels of responsibility for planning and teaching; and extensive reflective writing and discussions with instructors, supervisors, and peers—Ralph has refined his thinking somewhat.

When interviewed just before his graduation in May, Ralph had come to think that parents and the home environment impact student behavior the most:

> *The parents and the home and the kind of training that they've received and continue to receive . . . has the most profound impact. . . . I think a lot about it in terms of the kids who have particular problems in school or are having trouble in [some] way. When I can see their parents and how they interact with their parents and who their parents are, I get an understanding of where that kid is coming from and where that problem is coming from. A kid who calls out in class and [has] very little control of his or her own behavior and whose mom can't set limits, and the kid is kind of pushing her around all over the place, I can say, "Oh, I see. This kid has never had to deal with limits or has not had effective discipline and hasn't learned about that from home." So that makes sense that that's where this behavior is coming from. There may be violence at home or drugs at home or a lot of chaos or a divorce, more serious kinds of problems are going to show up in the kid and what's happening with the kid at school.*

Besides familial influences, Ralph also strongly believes that children's individual, innate personality differences affect their behavior:

> *[Because of] differences in intelligence, some kids learn more quickly than other kids. Other kids need more experience at a particular level until they feel comfortable with it. They just work more slowly. Some kids are more interested in learning things than others. They'll zoom right through because that's where all their interest and attention goes. Some kids are not as interested. They won't learn as quickly. There's some quality that's different even than intelligence. It's like this gestalt of all these different experiences and things coming together. Kids' strengths are in different areas. It's remembering that in terms of the kinds of expectations you have of kids that they're not going to achieve all in the same way.*

Ralph focuses on the primacy of parental and peer influences. "*Somehow there's a shift that I see in terms of what's important to them. Certainly their parents' values and opinions remain very important, but what their peers think begins to have a great deal more weight.*"

Ralph's thinking at Time 2 has developed from the first interview and there are fewer contradictions. At Time 1, he saw the developmental process as one of building new understandings and perspectives of the world based on new experiences and new information, and progressing from personal, egocentric views to broader perspectives. He also believed that people develop through successful endeavors and by having multiple opportunities to succeed under age-appropriate and supportive conditions. By Time 2, he still believes this, but he now understands that many factors besides the cognitive and the physical affect development. He is also better able to describe specifically how development occurs as schemes become more elaborate.

> *Because the kids have that much more experience, that much more knowledge, and it's like the fields of their knowledge are much more fully developed. In second grade or at the concrete operational stage it's sort of like the map is getting laid out, where this will be, where that will be, this organizational kind of plan. Then it becomes much richer over the years between second grade and sixth grade, and the specifics begin to be filled in and there's information in each area, so you can kind of see the patterns and how things fit together. When you get a new piece of information you can see how that kind of falls in the range of things.*

Also, whereas at Time 1 he only understood that timelines would be effective if they related to the child's personal life, in the following example Ralph shows a deeper understanding of the importance of a child's developing sense of time as an important factor in using timelines.

> *I don't know much about it, but in first and second grade I think kids' ideas about time are very fuzzy. They haven't been through enough years to really know how long a year is. There's that part of being egocentric, as not just having difficulty taking the perspective of another but also remembering what it was like 6 months ago. They're very oriented toward the moment, and what happened back then is just gone. So I don't think it's a very meaningful concept. By fifth and sixth grade I think kids can understand because [they can think], "I know my grandmother and how old my grandmother was and what, maybe, 100 years ago was, and because I've seen a building that was built in 1712, then I kind of get that sense."*

Although Ralph still considers experience and physical maturation to be important in a child's development, he is better able use developmental theory to describe the process of development. For example, he still uses general terms to describe development at this time, as in this statement: "*The child's world gradually expands, as the child matures, from themselves and Mom and immediate family and perhaps a closer–in community to a broader base.*" Yet he can now explain his current conception of development (as reorganization of schema) in more detail.

> *They're looking at the world in a different way. If they were making that shift into operational kinds of thinking, they would have a kind of new mental apparatus that would sort of want to organize the information in a different way. They're not just kind of collecting impressions, but they're dealing with the information they get in a different way.*

Ralph's understandings about behavior and development, as they relate to his thinking about pedagogy, grew from Time 1 to Time 2, as did his thinking about learning and teaching. One main difference in this interview is that he offers more details and examples about what and how children learn and how he wants to teach. At Time 1, Ralph mainly spoke in generalities, although he had some teaching experience when he entered the DTE program. At Time 2, however, he provides details and illustrations as in the following discussion of how children learn reading and mathematics differently in second and fifth grades:

> *The challenge would be in assisting them to make that transition academically from learning to read and learning addition and subtraction families and real basics to beginning to apply that. Not just learning to read but using reading to learn about something else, to moving into exploring content in a different way. . . . As kids learn to read and as kids become comfortable and confident with their skills in reading, they can use it to get information and to pass on information.*

When asked about the usefulness of a timeline, Ralph also gives specific examples, although his basic thinking has not changed from what he said in his first interview:

> *Actually, I think it could be useful at most age groups in very different ways. I think the traditional kind of timeline where you have 1492 and 1776 and 1987 could be useful at a fifth- and sixth-grade level because I think they can understand that and have more sense of past, present, and future and of what those years might actually mean. In second grade, you might have a timeline relating to a week in school or a month, the month of October and what happened when, and let's look at the history of your Christmas vacation and you might map that out. That might have some meaning if it's something that the kids have participated in.*

In discussing the learning process, Ralph is also more articulate and detailed in his thinking, although he still believes children learn in different ways and that it is important to provide multiple opportunities for them to learn.

> *There are many paths to learning anything. I think all kids learn in different ways. Part of the job as a teacher is to provide a variety of different kinds of experiences in order that kids have the equivalent access to the information or to the concepts that you want them to get. Kids learn visually, kids learn auditorily, kids learn kinesthetically. One technique will work for one kind of learner and maybe not so much for another. I think it's important to approach the same material with a variety of different kinds of experiences, as much as time allows and your own creativity can come up with.*

Ralph has developed a more complex understanding of the factors affecting the learning. At Time 2, he still seems to believe that people cannot be forced to learn, nor can they learn without a foundation in the basics. Yet he is now able to elaborate on why he believes these things.

What happens in those first 2 years, 2 and 3 years, can have a really profound impact for good or for ill. . . . If a student is going to have a good experience in first grade and not feel pressured and not feel failure and feel supported in the kinds of efforts that they make, feel on the track, it's going to be a lot easier to work with that child in second grade than if the expectations have been too high or they felt failure or they felt frustrated or the curriculum hasn't been appropriate for them or whatever and they don't like school. That feeling of liking being there or not liking being there, being a willing and eager participant or else being turned off to it, is the most important thing. If you have that, there's all kind of ways to go. If you don't, you can't do much until you can get that kind of participation from the learner. . . .

He also says:

Some kids need to practice skills and overlearn certain things to retain them. Some kids do not need to do that. I think it depends on individual learning styles.

Some things are complex and require major reorganization of information; they are broader, more inclusive kinds of ideas. Something that's more of a specific fact, you don't have to change that much. Learning is about change, and if you're just adding on a new fact to what you've already got, that's not so hard.

By now, Ralph is able to point to specific children he has taught in his student teaching to illustrate his points, as in his discussion of how children's individual differences affect how they learn.

The official recognition very much has to do with reading, writing, arithmetic, spelling and academic achievement, but for some kids that's just not where their strengths are. It's important that they are involved with that and grow with that, but I think of Paul, I think of Tyler, I think of these kids, it's just not their gift. We need to kind of broaden the range of expectations, or models, or kinds of achievement that are rewarded.

By Time 2, Ralph realizes—probably as a result of his teacher education experiences—that reading, writing, and discussing are valuable ways to learn.

With the first graders, it's experiment. We did a lot of looking and talking about and manipulating and interacting with the objects. I [had] them write down observations and this and that, but it didn't really seem right to me, it didn't seem that important to me. It seemed kind of peripheral, . . . but what was important was just having them see and talk about it and talk about it with one another. . . . I don't know if by second grade it will be more important for them to write and record, but I imagine that it might be. . . . The child might want to organize the information or write it down and see it. Might need to do that, but in first grade I, don't think they much need to do it, there's not much interest. I think that in any classroom or at any level, sharing your ideas is a real crucial part of learning. . . . To articulate what you think to another person is very different than sort of kicking the ideas around in your own head. I think the learners learn more specifically, in greater detail, more deeply what their own ideas are.

In this interview, Ralph's views of learning and teaching have progressed from a behaviorist perspective toward more developmental and constructivist views, reflecting the theory he learned in the DTE program.

It comes a lot through talking about things, discussing problems. You can model that kind of behavior in kids. As you do that, kids can see how it's done. If that kind of activity is going on in the classroom, they get a chance to see other kids doing it and they can try it in small ways. In a science lesson, you can ask the questions and they can give the answers as to what the information is, or you can find out their questions and have them talk about ideas and have them find out what the answers might be. You can have them discover information based on their own thinking rather than giving them information and then testing them about it. I think if that's your approach, then they're going to be doing some more of that kind of thinking. They'll practice and you get better at things as you practice them.

Ralph also has much more to say about the teaching process at Time 2 than at Time 1. He still wants to teach young children because he wants to help get them off to a good start in school, which at Time 1 was one of the reasons he said he wanted to teach elementary school. However, now he has some concrete ideas about how he will do that. For example, in these excerpts from his graduation interview, Ralph focuses on teaching to individual needs of students, providing the right kinds of experiences so they can each be successful, asking the right kinds of questions, and finding a balance between teacher and student input and interaction:

I'm lately big into success and failure and that the most important thing we can do as teachers is to provide kids with successful experiences, and that looks really different for different kids, and that is particularly crucial right from the beginning, from kindergarten, first, second grade. That sets the tone that kids believe that they're struggling with competence, and if they can feel competent and are provided with opportunities to be successful in their own individual ways, I believe that that will carry them through real well. There's an important balance I see with that kind of activity, between letting the child speak on their own, and really own what they're saying, and having the words come from the child, and letting the child struggle through putting it together, and providing sort of appropriate intervention and guidance. I think what's useful is asking the right kinds of questions. You want it to come from the kid, but then you can provide a little bit of guidance each time in terms of thinking about where you would like them to go with this, what's the next step for this kid in terms of becoming more proficient at this activity or learning more. There could be a different activity for different kids depending on what they would need.

Asked how he would teach second graders the concept of a sentence, Ralph describes something similar to the whole-language method, although in 1987 the whole-language movement was just ascending to its place as the dominant method of teaching reading and writing that it would hold through the 1990s.

> *It depends on what they're doing, and they're probably all in different places. I want to have kids writing their own material, writing their own stories, so I'm going to be coming from a base of students writing in journals or writing creative stories or writing about topics that they're interested in, something that they want to write about. I would try to approach it in an individual way in terms of working with individual kids or kids in small groups in terms of how to make what they're saying clear, easy to read, publishable, how things look in books, talking about conventions in that way. My sense is that most kids know what a sentence is even if they don't write them. I think they pick it up from reading because the material that they read is written in sentences.*

In Time 1, responding to interview questions designed to get at his thinking about how teachers know what and how to teach, Ralph was focused on learning from his students, his own experiences, and other teachers. At Time 2, he reiterates the importance of these sources, but also adds parents and his teacher training to his list of resources for understanding what and how to teach. From parents, he says, he can learn:

> *. . . A lot both in terms of the information that they have to give you about their child, and then also just meeting them and seeing who they are as people gives you a lot in terms of the child's background and where they are coming from, difficulties they may be dealing with or just basically what their family background is and where they're coming from.*
>
> *From the training that I've had, I have a broad kind of understanding of the developmental stages that kids go through and in general, at certain ages what kinds of skills they have and what kind of skills they don't, what's not appropriate for them. So that's one source of knowledge. Another is, of course, the child's performance and not so much what they do but how they go about doing it. I think I get a lot of information in terms of how a child is thinking, the level at which a child is thinking, by seeing how they might approach a particular problem. Talking to them, finding out what their thinking is, probing beneath the surface of what they're doing to kind of see what kind of thinking is going on and that can give you a good idea of what they're capable of. Often those kinds of things seem to set limits on what [kind] of kids are not ready for this. At the same time they are ready.*

Ralph also reiterates that his students and teaching experiences provide feedback so he can assess his effectiveness as a teacher. Many beginning teachers just finishing their teacher education program are not confident enough to rely on their students for feedback to the extent that Ralph does. Rather, they tend to look to external sources for information, including test results, their supervisors' observations of them, and perhaps parents' feedback. Ralph trusts his own intuition and feelings, as well as his observations and reflections on what he sees and feels is going on with his students in the classroom—all likely to be factors in his success in his first few years of teaching.

RALPH'S 1990 INTERVIEW AND AN OBSERVATION (TIME 3)

After graduating from the DTE program, Ralph took his first teaching position as a third-grade teacher at Rheem Elementary School in Moraga, California, which is just over the hills to the east of Berkeley. One of his five student teaching placements was in a first-grade class in the same small school district, so he knew the community. After a race down a six-lane freeway from the city, it is relaxing to slow down to the winding, pretty, strictly enforced 25 MPH streets leading to this suburban elementary school. Most of the houses in the surrounding neighborhood hide behind groves of trees and shrubs or at the ends of long driveways. The area looks very prosperous and it is. The real estate in this area is very pricey, even by California standards, and the population is almost homogeneous. Nearly all the children who attend Rheem come from White, upper middle-class families with one or two working parents. Although some families have lived in Moraga for a long time, and were fortunate to buy their houses before Proposition 14 severely restricted property taxes in California, residents who moved to the community more recently paid a hefty premium to live here. Ralph, who lives in Berkeley, will make this 25-minute drive 180 days a year for the next 5 years.

Rheem Elementary stands at the end of a cul de sac, which is also the end of the developed area. Beyond, the land rises to the grassy foothills of the coastal range. The neighborhoods surrounding the school are full, and there are no empty lots available for further development. I made this trip many times to observe student teachers in Ralph's classroom before, during, and after the interviews and observations for this study. In fact, I was quite familiar with this school and Ralph's classroom during the 5 years he taught there, which coincided with the 5 years I was working on my doctorate in the Graduate School of Education at UC–Berkeley. As a graduate student instructor (GSI) at Berkeley, I supervised student teachers for the DTE program for 10 semesters. I was in Ralph's classroom to supervise at least one student every year, and I supervised other DTE students in other classrooms at Rheem during Ralph's tenure there. I also conducted a small research project with kindergartners and first graders at this school one spring semester.

Typical of elementary schools in California, Rheem comprises several one-story buildings linked by covered walkways. Ralph's third-grade class, at the end of a wing of eight rooms, is large and carpeted, with a wall of windows on one side and two exterior doors on opposite sides. Beneath the windows, low shelves are filled with books and math manipulatives. Three-dimensional geometric figures made from toothpicks and gumdrops sit on one shelf. Large chalkboards and bulletin boards line the walls at each end of the room. One bulletin board is postered with lists and drawings of things found in the world in groups of twos, threes, fours, and on up to groups of 12. The other board has students' illustrated stories and hand-drawn classroom maps. There is also a commercial map of the United States, a sign ("Remember It's OK to Make Mistakes"), and another bulletin board with a set of class rules, group rules, an editing checklist, and the math stumper for the day. Opposite the windows are the closets, which are lined with hooks and shelves for the children's jackets and backpacks. These closets are also used for storage.

Scattered around the room are several round tables, clock, computer, sink, telephone, typewriter, boom box, and piano. The students' flattop desks are clustered in groups of five each. Ralph's desk is tucked into one corner, but he rarely sits at it. Mainly he uses it to store his teaching materials.

I observed Ralph several times at Rheem, but during this visit to his class during his third year, I saw a math lesson that exemplifies his teaching style. It is the end of the day, and Ralph is taking students' responses to several recent math stumpers. These mind benders are challenging for most third graders, but Ralph puts one up every day and makes them optional, encouraging those who are interested and those who need a challenge to try them. After several students give correct responses to one of the problems, Ralph introduces the mathematics lesson for the day to the entire class. He poses these authentic, real-world problems about an upcoming class field trip to the Exploratorium in San Francisco.

"*We have six moms and 25 kids going on this fieldtrip,*" Ralph begins. "*How can we say this? How can we write this?*"

Using answers suggested by the children, Ralph writes, "25 ÷ 6" and "25/6" on the chalkboard. "*There are 25 kids in 6 groups or 6 groups for 25 kids,*" he explains.

"*Now, I'm going to pretend that we're going on the field trip today, and we have two students absent. What's the problem now? How can I write it using math symbols, and how can we say it?*"

Again, students offer answers. Ralph writes, "23 ÷ 6" and "23/6." Then he says, "*Those are the math symbols for 6 groups in 23 kids or 23 kids divided into 6 groups.*"

He continues: "*Suppose on the day we go that two of the moms are sick, but all the kids are going. Now what's the problem?*"

After listening to the students' responses and writing down mathematical sentences to represent what they suggest, Ralph asks, "*What if all the kids are going, but each mom brings a husband? What would the problem be? How many groups would we have?*"

Following this exchange, Ralph continues with the directions for the lesson: "*Today we are going to do a lot of dividing, not by 4s or 6s or 8s, but by 2s and 3s. The question I want you to ask is how many groups of 2 or 3 are there in 28 or 16 or whatever the number is you roll using these dice. If you can ask that question, then you will be dividing.*"

Holding up the materials they will use, Ralph explains, "*I'll be giving you a pair of dice and counters to use with a partner and this sheet to record your answers. We'll do some together and then you'll do them with your partner at your table. You can choose whatever counters you want to use—Unifix cubes, chips, units—but let me show you how this might work with Unifix cubes.*"

As Ralph models how the students will roll the dice to create a number to be the dividend, he also demonstrates how they should record each problem on their sheet. He says to divide each number they roll by 2, and he shows them how to build the number they roll with Unifix cubes, then break the cubes into groups of two, count these up, and record their answer. He rolls a 1 and a 3 to make 13, and then he asks them how many groups of 2 he will have in 13 and what he should to do with the leftover Unifix cube. He shows them how to join 13 Unifix cubes, break them into groups of 2 until there are no more pairs, count up the dyads and the one leftover cube, and then record their work. After going through these steps with two more examples, he asks for questions.

After asking the students to discuss how they will share materials and take turns, Ralph passes out the materials. As Ralph circulates around the room to see how each group of students is doing, he says things like: "*No, that's wrong. Check it out. Check your groups.*" "*Yes, yes. That's great. Keep going.*" "*Count out 17 and then put them in groups of 2. Then count out the groups of 2. I'll come back and see how you are progressing.*"

After 10 minutes, Ralph asks them to do the same steps again, but to make groups of three and to ask themselves how many groups of three are in each number they roll. Again he checks on the groups, making comments to each like: "*Michelle, you need to be recording your problems like I showed you.*"

Near the end of the lesson, when students have cleaned up and put their papers in the center of the table, Ralph asks what they observed about dividing by 2s and 3s. One student notes that when there is a remainder, it is always 1. Ralph asks if that was true when they divided by 3, and the students realize that the remainders can be a 1 or a 2, but never a 0 or a 3. After 45 minutes, Ralph asks them to turn in their manipulatives and papers as they line up.

RALPH'S 1990 INTERVIEW (TIME 3)

After observing Ralph teach math on this occasion, I ask him the same set of clinical interview questions we used in 1985 and 1987. Unlike in his first two interviews, this time he is able to give many concrete examples of how he would or would not teach something and specific cases illustrating how he believes students learn and how he should go about teaching them. In earlier interviews, his comments about teaching and learning had been much more global and generalized—not quite platitudes, but not as certain, real, or grounded in practice and personal experience.

Analyzing this interview, I am particularly interested in how little he has to say about student behavior and development and how much he says about teaching and learning. That he says less about behavior and development than in earlier interviews puzzles me, although it was a pattern I saw in two of the other three teachers at Time 3. Apparently, these teachers spent less time thinking about developmental theory and, with the exception of Julie, did not seem to be concerned about children's behavior when I interviewed them. This is surprising to me given the findings of Veenman (1984) and others that classroom management is the number one concern of the vast majority of beginning teachers. I believe new teachers must focus on that which they most need to master. For Ralph, Rick, and Sandy, this is their ability to teach and find ways for children to learn. Controlling the class was not their main challenge.

In this interview, one of the things Ralph expresses is how much he values the innocence and joy of his young learners, their initiative, and their growing independence. He says part of this had to do with their "*learning some of the ropes at school,*" but a lot of it had to do with having more extracurricular experiences with various tasks in general as well at school: "*They would learn by having the experience of doing it.*" For him, experiences are key to learning and development at this time, although how he defines experiences is important to comprehending the development of his pedagogical understanding at Time 3. Ralph expresses one way he understands pedagogy and experience in response to the question about how he would go about teaching children the concept of a sentence:

> *In general, I think kids need a chance to read, and write, and read aloud their own writing, and hear other kids read writing, read out loud, and practice plays, and all this kind of thing before they sit down and capitalize and put periods at the end of sentences in the right space. In the sense that an understanding in terms of our written language, of the function of a sentence, has got to seep in before the practice comes . . . before they'll be able to do it with any fluency, they need to just practice recognizing it and doing it.*

He also refers to the importance of experience when he talks about how he teaches place value to his third graders. "*I teach it with 75 different approaches partly because it is so fundamentally important for the kids at my grade level to really understand.*" However, with 3 years of experience teaching third graders, Ralph is concerned about pushing too much content and doing things that would be too abstract for these young learners:

I'm less interested in teaching content and I'm not as good at it. . . . I'm more interested in teaching concepts in a broader sense, . . . a fundamental understanding of math and science, and in the process of writing and expression.

This concern about teaching and learning being focused on experiences that are developmentally appropriate (although these are my words and not Ralph's) comes up again in the interview when he discusses an astronomy lesson he is teaching to his third graders: *"You don't want to push the content until they have direct experience . . . but I think they'll become abstract, able to think abstractly. They may not grasp it completely. . . . Kids are pushed to think abstractly way too soon."* Besides emphasizing the importance of having concrete experiences, Ralph also describes learning as progressing step by step in small increments:

If you are starting with something new you are going to start as concrete as anyone else. . . . In order for it to be meaningful . . . I think you have to start with just as concrete as a way they can be directly involved in and begin to build the concept from the foundations. . . .

It's one little block and one little piece and we can only learn—occasionally you have tremendous insight and those are blessed moments—but usually you just see the piece. . . .

If you are going to learn about fractions, it's going to take many, many years, and there're thousands of small pieces that go into structuring that. That's how it is.

Although he certainly talks about teaching multiplication facts, language skills, and spelling words, Ralph conveys to me several times that he thinks the learning process is more important than teaching any particular content. In fact, this is a theme throughout his Time 3 interview, and he states it explicitly more than once: *"I'm still more interested in the process of learning than I am in whether they have the content. That's important, but it comes second."*

In Ralph's 1985 interview, he said one of his main goals was for children to become independent learners—a belief he brought with him into the DTE program—one he continues to hold and that guides his teaching 5 years later. Yet now Ralph is able to go beyond declaring this belief to describing several examples of how he carries it out in his own classroom. This is a good example of how his thinking about pedagogy has developed from being unidimensional, rather vague, and general to more multidimensional, specific, and contextualized. Here is one example of how he goes about teaching math and reading:

So I have a variety of different levels of material that will be assigned. I put a bunch of material out there and let the kids choose as well. I trust that at some level they'll choose something that can benefit them. I do trust that kids have . . . some sense [of what they need] and that I can take cues from them, and they can guide their own independent learning.

He also reiterates the recurrent themes of experience and process as he talks about how he sets up the learning environment.

The teacher provides the setting, provides appropriate experiences, maintains an environment conducive to learning and maintains order, and tracks individual kids to keep them moving along. The teacher provides stimulation, acts as a model, which is probably more important than I remember or think about because the actual instruction and generating material and responding to the children's material assumes 85% of my conscious effort . . . but it really is that the process is important and that kids have someone that believes in them and also that I am willing to listen to them.

Ralph says other factors that affect the learning process include not just listening to the children, but paying attention to them as individuals (a strong pedagogical belief Ralph expressed first in his Time 2 interview). Here he refers to the importance of addressing individual student needs in several comments in this interview:

It's very important for each child and it's very important for the whole tone of the classroom that kids are seen as individuals and unique . . . and because kids think differently, and some kids are very immediate and process everything immediately and the output is very immediate, and some kids take a long time to think about things and consider them and will continue to think about things long afterwards . . . and because They respond, I think, because they are ready to respond to a different kind of approach . . . so, I think responding to those kids as an individual and they had needs that were different.

He also expresses a conviction that he, in his role as the teacher, should model what he thinks is important:

That means doing what you do and not just doing what you say. . . . And that means reading when they read and writing when it's writing time. I've been able to do that this year for the first time. . . . And they can see that I do love to read and that reading is important to me and it's a great pleasure . . . that's going to mean more than maybe learning this set of skills . . . that's the bigger picture, that's what's behind it.

Ralph also talks about the teacher's job as guiding students through the steps of how to do something as well as accommodating a range of different skills and levels of development—accommodating them in some way, or at least addressing the issue of meeting the needs of kids with different abilities, backgrounds, and needs. In fact, the metaphor Ralph uses for his teaching is a *constant juggling act*. He also alludes to his understanding of developmental theory and provides some insight into how he understands and applies the developmental constructivist perspective at this time:

Starting at all kinds of levels, I try to put in as much flexibility as possible. I do have a developmental perspective, so it's not so much how I'm instructing the children as the kinds of experience that I can provide. So that's one kind of inherent flexibility. Then I'm putting an experience or a context out there, and the kids can handle it at the level they're at. . . . Then I will vary material and break kids into groups and so I've individualized material for certain kids and have them read with parent helpers, or a high school student who comes into the classroom, or an aide, or myself. So I have a variety of different levels of material that will be assigned. I put a bunch of material out there and let the kids choose as well.

Referring once again to the relative importance of content and the learning process from his perspective, he says, "*I think a teacher kind of sneaks in the content as well.*" Ralph also believes that practice, repetition, and review are important aspects of the learning process, which he tries to provide in many different forms:

The kids do need to repeat and to overlearn things because they do forget. So there is that kind of drill. In fact, they come in so many different guises, games, and it doesn't have to be just flashcards. I also think the kids need long-term repetition. They need to review and repeat things. . . . It's not enough to hit it once, that you talk about rounding numbers in October and have a test on it in the spring and that's it, you know, you need to do that throughout the year.

Part of the reason Ralph believes that practice is important is that he thinks the same things can be learned in different ways:

The same things can be learned in different ways, . . . from different angles. As a teacher you are going to pick up different kids if you approach things in different ways because some kids respond to one style or one thing and not to another.

Apparently Ralph's thinking about the role of practice in the learning process has become a logical necessity and underlies why one of his strongest beliefs and practices is that he has to provide multiple opportunities for students to learn.

Some of Ralph's obstacles, challenges, and uncertainties have to do with assessment, class size, and balancing his role in the classroom. Regarding assessment, Ralph has questions, but no answers:

Assessment, I think, is the biggest obstacle . . . to what I would like to do in the classroom. As long as you're relying on standardized testing as the gauge, as the kind of ulti-

mate gauge, I'll be running into that. How to do assessment that is practical, thorough, and accounts for individual development and the learning process is a difficult task.

Class size seems to be related to Ralph's concern about assessment, and perhaps at the root of it as well, because he feels he cannot do individual assessments and record keeping on 30 kids:

It is so hard. It is so ongoing, and record keeping is such a monumentally difficult task as it is and . . . it all comes down to class size and the fact that there're too many kids in order to really do that . . . because what's missing at this point, you know, is the follow-up. In order to be effective with a developmental program, that's got to be there. . . . Class size, of course, that's really the only issue that there is as far as I'm concerned. . . . If I had half of what I have then, I would accomplish six times what I do.

Ralph apparently feels conflicted about his role in the classroom and about how directive he should be. "*It's a constant compromise in the classroom in terms of letting the kids be responsible and make their own mistakes and not letting them make mistakes and telling them what to do.*"

From a developmental-constructivist perspective, Ralph continues to develop his pedagogical understandings at Time 3. He believes that his students need to correctly understand the concepts that underlie the facts, procedures, and skills in various subjects, and he is more interested in supporting the processes of learning than in teaching specific content. He is also somewhat conflicted about his role. He seems to lean in practice toward engaging his students in many hands-on experiences, most of them thought provoking. Yet he conceptualizes his role as one of modeling and guiding, which is more than solely offering opportunities for his students to explore and manipulate materials freely. At this time, he mainly plays a supportive role because he sees what the children need: "*They have a certain drive to be competent and independent.*" However, Ralph has to juggle and balance these issues every day with his image of himself as a teacher, whose job it is to guide children through the steps of how to do something.

From my perspective as an educational researcher and teacher educator interested in teacher development, especially how teachers' thinking develops in the pedagogical domain, and also as an elementary school teacher with 17 years experience and 13 years experience observing and supervising over 125 prospective teachers, I believe Ralph's conflicted roles, his struggle with assessment, and his beliefs in trying to provide for each individual student in his class can be a great space for a teacher to be in. These kinds of conflicts between goals and actual conditions can trigger learning and subsequent change in thoughts and actions. They can be a catalyst to advance one's pedagogical understandings.

So now let us look at Ralph 3 years later in 1993 at Time 4 when we find him teaching kindergarten at a private school in Oakland.

RALPH'S 1993 INTERVIEW AND AN OBSERVATION (TIME 4)

In the fall of 1992, after 5 years at Rheem Elementary, Ralph decided to move to a very different kind of school and teach kindergarten. In leaving Rheem, Ralph left behind a comfortable teaching situation, but a stressful year as president of the local teacher's union. However, this change meant joining an independent school where he already knew several of the teachers and families because his stepchildren attended this school. He also felt he would be working with a faculty that embraced a philosophy of education more like his own. It meant leaving behind a very supportive principal at Rheem and joining a school run by a teacher cooperative. In fact, at Ralph's new school, Park Day School, all decisions are made jointly by the teachers who meet twice every week to take care of school business and discuss curriculum needs and student issues, which are then carried out by a director who has overarching responsibility for executing their resolutions.

One of the important values at Park Day School is helping children develop into well-rounded, socially conscious individuals, which is something Ralph agrees with wholeheartedly. Academics are important too, but everyone at Park is concerned with the social development and emotional well-being of the students. For a private school, the population of children attending Park is quite diverse and fairly representative of the student population in California. About 40% of the students at Park are children of color, and 25% of the students receive financial assistance to attend this school. All of these attributes and the chance to work with like-minded faculty appealed to Ralph when he moved there. Finally, Ralph would only have 15 children in his kindergarten class instead of the 28 to 33 third graders he typically taught while in Moraga. All in all, Ralph was very excited about teaching at Park, and in fact would teach there full time for the next 3 years and then part time for 3 more years after that.

Park Day School is a relatively small, independent, and progressive K to 6 school serving about 220 children located in a neighborhood behind a large public high school off a busy commercial street in Oakland, California. The main building at Park was originally built to be an orphanage, and the property is sheltered by trees and dotted with extensive gardens, including vegetables and flowers in raised beds. Because the school recently expanded to two classes per grade level, some of the beautiful grounds have been taken up by classroom buildings. Nevertheless, Park Day School is an oasis in the middle of the city.

When I observed Ralph's kindergarten class during the spring of 1993, I was impressed with the resources available to the children in the classroom and on the grounds of the school where there are trees, flower, and vegetable gardens to tend as well as places to play. Although most kindergarten classrooms I have been in are full of stuff and organized into centers, Ralph's classroom is particularly roomy and well equipped. It is a large, bright rectangular room with lots of windows. I believe that it was once a solarium in the original house. There are two Apple computers set up in one corner of Ralph's room, book shelves full of art supplies including paints and brushes, several easels, an area called the *Kid's Office* with a typewriter, paper, pencils, and other office supplies, a playhouse area with a child-size stove, refrigerator, table, and chairs, more bookshelves full of puzzles and games, and lots of plants on the sills beneath the windows. There is also a cage with a rabbit in it and a terrarium with snails on the windowsill. Books are clustered in several places around the room, and more shelves house school supplies such as crayons, glue sticks, markers, and scissors all stored at a kindergartner's eye level. The walls are covered with children's artwork and other projects including sculptures made from scraps of wood, self-portraits that Ralph told me they drew every month, and other drawings and paintings created by the resident kindergartners. Ralph's desk is in a corner near the computers, and there is a large carpeted area defined on three sides by bookshelves, a piano, and a window seat that served as seating area. Ralph meets with the entire group of 15 children on the rug when they are not dispersed all around the room engaged in different activities.

Ralph has the room set up for several centers that he calls *work jobs*. The five work jobs available for the children to choose from include a listening station with a tape-recorded book and earphones for five children, an area with puzzles of all types, a center for pattern blocks set out on a table, another area with geoboards and rubber bands, and a table with several balance scales on it for a center he calls *Is Heavier Than*.

When the children all gather on the rug, Ralph tells them, "*I am going to explain our five work jobs without using any words and you will choose without any words.*" As he holds up large cards with drawings and words on them, he begins to talk about the five tasks they can choose from. He then places the picture cards in a pocket chart for all to see. Ralph whispers as he describes each task and then calls on children individually by name to select their first work job of the morning. Everyone moves quietly to his or her chosen activity, likely calmed by Ralph's whispering. Only the listening station is limited to five children at a time, and it appears that the favorite choice for many children is the pattern blocks, which they can use in many different ways. When one child looks like she wants to use balance scales, Ralph encourages her to find a partner to work with.

Ralph circulates around the room for a few minutes until everyone is settled with an activity and then moves to the table with the scales. As two girls place different objects on each end of the balance scales, Ralph asks them questions so they can make a prediction and then test their prediction by placing different objects in the containers on each end of the scale. He is asking questions such as, *"Is this wooden cube heavier that this rubber ball?"* *"What do you think?" "How can you find out?" "How about these chips?" "How many chips do you think it will take to balance the wooden block?"*

After 15 minutes, some of the children tell Ralph that they are done with their work job, and Ralph reminds them to check off their names on the list at their chosen center and move on to something else.

More kindergartners come to the table with the balance scales, but Ralph is called away by a group of children who want him to see what they have done with their pattern blocks. Some children stacked the pattern blocks to make small buildings, but several others created patterns with their blocks that were bilaterally symmetrical. As Ralph starts to move back to the balance scales, one boy cries in frustration because another boy had completed a puzzle before he could complete his puzzle. Ralph swiftly diffuses this situation by redirecting the two children to another task. Ralph circulates once around the room and then goes back to the balance scales and begins asking questions of the children working there.

Several children move to the rug to look at books, and others choose new puzzles to take apart and put together. Several children remain at the table with the pattern blocks for a long time. Another child starts to cry, but by the time Ralph gets there the crisis has passed and Ralph is able to go back to asking questions of the children working with the balance scales.

For nearly an hour, the children are engaged with the work jobs that Ralph set out for them for that morning. Some children wander around aimlessly for a few minutes between tasks, but everyone seems to find several things to engage their interest. Ralph uses the checklist at the balance scale table to be sure that all the children have a chance to come and weigh things on the scales, calling over particular children whom he had not worked with yet.

Toward the end of this free-choice, center time, two boys go to one of the computers and start to play a game called *Number Munchers.* Several other children, all boys, go to the computers and soon there are children both using the computers and observing. Several other children begin to play dress-up with the trunk full of clothes and hats in the housekeeping area.

After over an hour, Ralph tells the children to clean up and come to the rug. There is a slight delay before the children begin putting things away and moving over to the rug area where Ralph waits for them to gather.

After talking with the children a little bit about what they learned that morning, Ralph dismisses them to several tables to wait for their snacks, which he set out on paper plates on another table. Ralph decides to ham it up and pretend to be at a restaurant. He uses an old telephone to pretend to call the restaurant to see if their table is ready while the children all listen attentively to his side of the phone conversation. As he continues role-playing, Ralph becomes a waiter and says, *"If your name begins with the letter R, you may come and get your snack.*" He continues to pretend to be their waiter and welcomes them to his restaurant. He calls children to come get their snack if their name begins with an L, and then an S, and so on until everyone is served. He then circulates around the room asking if their food is prepared well and if they need anything from the kitchen. After snack time, the children leave the room for their Spanish class and Ralph and I sit down to talk.

When I return for another observation of Ralph's kindergarten class a few weeks later, the work jobs include writing, listening to a Dr. Seuss book on tape, measuring with dried peas and beans, exploring a gooey substance called *oobleck,* and working with either pattern blocks or geoboards. During the morning center time, I observe only boys at the computer once again and other children in the playhouse, on the floor building with large wooden blocks, and others at tables playing with the oobleck, which changes consistency depending on how it is handled. Ralph tells me that these kindergartners were having free play today because he feels the emotional atmosphere in the room that morning indicates to him that they need to play and are not ready for much structure yet. He also says that he had planned to use the oobleck another day after reading them the Dr. Seuss book about oobleck, but that he pulled it out today because they need something new to work with.

Ralph also tells me that they had parent conferences over the past 2 weeks and that he included the children and asked them to start the conference by showing their parents their portfolios and explaining to them what they had been doing since January. He seems to be very pleased with how productive these parent conferences were in comparison to others he had done in other years without the children present.

After about 45 minutes, Ralph begins to set up paints at one table and get out Easter baskets the children had made earlier from rolled paper bags. When he is ready, Ralph uses a set of chimes to get the children's attention and asks them to *freeze* where they are and watch. He then shows them how to paint their paper bag baskets. In the process, he makes the directions into a brief math lesson by asking the children questions: "*If you make 4 sprays of red and 4 sprays of blue, how many sprays will that be all together?*" "*Can you have only 2 sprays?*" "*How could you make a total of 11 sprays?*"

When 10 children want to paint their baskets all at once and there are only four colors of food coloring in the spray bottles and four dishes of tempura paint on each of two tables, Ralph asks the children, "*How can we solve this problem?*" He asks each child to express his or her ideas, and they finally decide to use two different solutions—one idea at one table and another idea at the other table. Ralph goes over all the rules he expects them to follow about taking turns and for handling the spray bottles before dividing up the children into two groups.

As I observe for another hour, the children are engaged in either painting their baskets or with one of the many the other activities available to them in the classroom. In an aside, Ralph tells me that if this had been October, he would not have known how to handle a day when the children needed something else, such as more play time. He also tells me that he would not have had something like the oobleck ready to pull out when he needed something else to capture their attention.

***

After observing Ralph in the middle of the 1993 spring semester, I wrote in a memo:

> *He seems to be quite unsure or unsettled about things (his teaching, curriculum, etc.) in many ways. But in other ways he brings so much knowledge and experience to this new situation that he is learning and understanding what he sees in 5- and 6-year-olds that are different from 8- and 9-year-olds very quickly. He seems to be reinventing his understandings this year and making adjustments rather swiftly. Examples—the child who says it's not a triangle unless it's turned a certain way; the child who can only seriate three vases but not four when another child can seriate seven vases. These incidents quickly remind him of what he knows about how children develop and this allows him to accept the range (he calls it the spectrum) in his class and also causes him to make sure that his curriculum provides for this range. He quickly understands that it is okay for some kindergartners to look at books while others have memorized parts of the story and yet others are beginning to read on their own, or that some kids will be happy making pictures and designs from the pattern blocks while others can make or copy complex symmetrical patterns and follow sequences that he suggests.*

This is my general impression of what was happening with Ralph more than halfway through his first year teaching kindergarten, but perhaps we should take a closer look at his interview data and compare them to his thinking about behavior, development, learning, and teaching at Time 3.

RALPH'S 1993 INTERVIEW (TIME 4)

During his fourth interview and observation, Ralph articulates a multitude of influences on children's behaviors in the classroom that impact how he sets up the learning environment and what methods he uses to teach kindergarten. Also, it is clear that Ralph's disposition to focus on his students and get feedback from them, and his view of them as his best source of information about what and how to teach, is evident in this list of factors that influence behavior: interest in and willingness to do something, attentional focus and attention span, level of independence, gender, need to explore/experience repeatedly and iteratively (for most children) in both cognitive and social domains (e.g., sharing), level of readiness to do more schoollike things (such as read the pocket chart), imagination and fantasy world, level of independence and ability to function on their own, sense of feeling valuable and important, pride in their work and in what they are doing, social issues and the importance of peers, how much space there is in the room and their sense of space, how much chaos the teacher can tolerate, and how many other adults there are in the room to help out.

At Time 4, just 6 years after Ralph began teaching full time, it is clear that he has an extensive understanding of the factors affecting student behavior. No longer does he focus solely on how family life influences children's behavior or even on how a combination of children's intelligence, experience, interest, and attention influences individual differences in behaviors. In fact, in analyzing the Time 4 interview, I cannot readily separate Ralph's comments about student behavior from his comments about teaching and learning because they are found together in the same responses. This indicates that Ralph's thinking about these three aspects of pedagogy (behavior, learning, and teaching) is tightly coupled in his pedagogical understanding at Time 4. Furthermore, all of these factors influence how he thinks about children's behavior, and about teaching and learning, and how they influence his actions in the classroom.

Ralph's current thinking about behavior, learning, and teaching, grounded in his previous experience with third graders and his current experience with kindergartners, also reinforces his belief that the learning process is more important than specific content largely because the content differs for children depending on their individual needs. In addition, the strong beliefs Ralph expressed in earlier interviews about the importance of providing multiple opportunities for children to learn things in different ways, building in flexibility in the teaching and learning process, and offering lots of opportunities for practice all continue to play out in his practices as a kindergarten teacher.

> *The kids need all that opportunity. And they need a chance to do things over and over and over again, and they need a chance to go where they want. They need to go and spend as much time doing something, and kids won't do certain things, and they shouldn't ever be made to do certain things, et cetera.*

At Time 4, Ralph's understanding of the developmental process and factors that affect the developmental process is also tightly coupled with his thinking about behavior, learning, and teaching. In fact, his understanding of children's development at this time guides his pedagogical choices and provides the foundation and rationale for why he teaches kindergarten the way he does. For example, although Ralph took a little while to adjust to teaching 5- and 6-year-olds at his new school, he was able to apply his understanding of developmental theory fairly readily to the observations he made of his young students. This helped him make sense of kindergartners' behavior fairly quickly, although it caused him to scramble to make adjustments in curriculum and teaching methods.

> *There are all these different avenues, and as a teacher you have to provide as many as you can think of and more. And the reason for that is that what makes sense to one kid doesn't make sense to another kid, and what makes sense to you doesn't make sense to the kids. . . . And, something I very firmly believe, in order for learning to happen and be meaningful, it has to make sense, and the kid has to find a way, or create a way, that makes sense to them.*

As a matter of fact, I believe that his interactions with and observations of his young students while learning to teach kindergartners served as a catalyst for a more elaborate understanding of the factors that impact children's development. Clearly, Ralph's understanding of what develops in children is more elaborate and comprehensive at Time 4 than at Times 2 or 3. For example, in the list of things he talks about developing in children, Ralph includes physical, cognitive, social, and affective factors such as attention, self-control, self-discipline, ego and superego, ability to focus, academic and cognitive factors including broader understanding of concepts, ability to reason about things, specific skills in writing, storytelling, and reading, and specific abilities including the ability to seriate and sequence a series of items, and social factors including social skills, awareness of roles children play in groups, more awareness of the social world, and social relationships.

Compared to Time 2, when Ralph sees the developmental process as one of building new understandings and gaining new perspectives on the world, based on new experiences and new information, and moving from having only personal, egocentric views to gaining broader perspectives. Ralph's current view of the developmental process shows that development does not just happen to children, but is in fact an interaction between children and their social environment mediated by factors such as their mental and physical maturation and their attention and interest in the world, as well as their opportunities to interact in both a physical and social sense with their environment.

RALPH'S TIME 5 INTERVIEW AND AN OBSERVATION (1997)

The next time I saw Ralph, 4 years had passed, instead of the usual 2-year intervals between interviews and observations. This happened because of my own move to North Carolina in the summer of 1993 and being unable to get back to California until 1997. My new position in North Carolina as an assistant professor at the University of North Carolina at Greensboro included many of the same tasks I performed in California, including supervising preservice teachers, just I had done since 1988.

In the meantime, Ralph remained at Park Day School, but after 2 years of teaching kindergartners, he asked for a change and received a fifth-grade class. However, during the 1996–1997 school year, the DTE program invited Ralph to supervise student teachers part time. The DTE program routinely recruited alumni to return as part-time supervisors since 1993. Some graduates from the program took a year or two off from their teaching positions, and a few started to work toward their Ph.D. degrees. Ralph told me that he was not interested in another advanced degree and really was not ready to leave the classroom. Instead he negotiated with Park Day School to job share and teach part time, freeing up 20 hours per week to devote to the DTE program. Because Park had grown in the past few years, this worked out well for both the school and Ralph. They had too many students for one class, but not really enough for two full-time teachers at fifth grade. When I ask Ralph about his professional life over the past 4 years, he says:

> *Kindergarten was terrific, and I certainly learned a great deal. . . . I have the most profound respect for kindergarten teachers because . . . even with 15 kids, that's still the hardest I've ever worked. But I wanted to try the older kids and the fifth-grade position was available, so I took that and very much enjoyed fifth grade. That really hit home right from the beginning. . . . I enjoyed the curriculum, I enjoyed the kids, where they were, and the kinds of discussions we could have. . . . It was just [more] different from third grade than I had anticipated . . . in terms of their sophistication, their knowledge about the world in just two years . . . so I really enjoyed that for 2 years. . . . I left that to supervise student teachers half time. And I did a little curriculum writing for* Creative Publications *and . . . next year I will continue to supervise, and as far as I know I look forward to teaching sixth grade half time.*

At the Time 5 interview, Ralph was supervising student teachers for the DTE program and team teaching at Park, where he is responsible for teaching math to all of the fourth graders 1 day a week. In fact, both lessons that I observe in May 1997 were math lessons. Later on, when we talk, Ralph tells me he felt nervous that I was observing him and that he attributes this to his new role as a supervisor for the DTE program. He tells me he asks some of the same questions of himself that he asks student teachers: "What is your purpose? What are you trying to teach here?" As we talk about this, we both agree that this is a good thing. Teachers benefit from changing roles, and supervising provides the opportunity to observe in many different classrooms. In fact, Ralph stays 3 years with the DTE program as a supervisor and seminar leader.

In both of the math lessons I observe at Time 5, Ralph is teaching probability. In one lesson, his fourth graders gather data at home from five people to test whether they would get the same results reported in a newspaper article. According to the article, when asked to pick a number from 1 to 4, four out of five people would select the number 3. In the other lesson, Ralph has 17 fourth graders create spinners from a set of written directions that they would use later in the lesson to make predictions and then gather data to test their predictions. Many of the features of both of these lessons are familiar because Ralph continues to use several management and teaching techniques I have seen him use before. For example, he asks many students for their input, but only after telling them to first talk over a problem or work it out with a peer or two. He also uses tasks that have some relevance in real life and often embeds practice in the form of a game or some other kind of hands-on activity. He rarely uses commercial materials (except math manipulatives such as dice, coins, pattern blocks, Unifix cubes, playing cards, or Dienes' blocks) and almost always has students construct all necessary materials (spinners, data-gathering sheets, measuring tapes, geometric models, game boards, fraction bars, etc.). In fact, for the second lesson I observe, Ralph turns down another teacher's offer of a set of already created spinners in favor of having his students construct their own. In addition, textbooks are rarely used, except as references, and workbooks are never used. Many of Ralph's ideas for teaching math came from Marilyn Burns' books, *Family Math* activities, children's books, or from other teacher resources he learned about in his teacher education courses (see Appendix F for a list of books recommended by Ralph and the other teachers in this study). Also, assessment is usually built into the lesson, so students know almost immediately whether they are on track. Finally, the tasks selected almost always have more than one solution path, and the lesson usually contains choices for students to make. Variety and student choice are hallmarks of the math lessons I observe in 1997 and of others I have seen over the years. In fact, the following description of an earlier math lesson I observed is representative of Ralph's teaching style because it is authentic, requires students to work together in groups to solve a problem, has more than one solution, and is hands on.

Over several weeks, when I visit Ralph's room to observe a student teacher, I follow one of Ralph's math lessons. The problem Ralph presents is to figure out how many bricks it would take to replace his cement patio that had been damaged in a recent earthquake. To complicate matters, the patio is triangular in shape, and Ralph wants to cut as few bricks as possible because this is difficult to do and bricks are expensive. Each group of students must figure out how to lay the new brick patio using the fewest bricks and making the fewest cuts. He gives them the dimensions of the patio and tapes off the exact size and shape of his ruined patio in two places on the classroom rug. He also gives each group a paper template the size of one brick plus the actual cost of a single brick. Students must calculate the total cost of replacing the patio and present their solution so he can see how the pattern of the bricks would look.

This problem was originally posed on a Monday and the presentations planned for Friday. During class Tuesday, the students try various layouts and discuss possible solutions within their groups of six. On Wednesday, the day I observe, most groups have already used scrap paper to cut out multiple bricks from the template and sketched out several patterns to discuss within their groups. Some groups have made their own paper template of the patio, but others are using the shape Ralph taped on the floor. Some groups are ready to use a calculator to figure out the total cost of the bricks needed for their possible solutions.

Ralph's role throughout the lesson is to ask questions rather than give answers. He also reminds them of the parameters of the problem so they remember to count the number of cut bricks as well as the number of whole bricks in their potential solutions. He does not question when one group totals their costs by hand and another group asks for a calculator.

Although I miss the final presentations, I am able to look at the posters displaying the students' final problem solutions, including all their calculations, the next time I visit Ralph's classroom. Ralph also tells me how awed he is by the cleverness and competence displayed by the children and how dedicated and focused they were as they worked for 4 days to solve this real-life problem. He also tells me that the *winners* are two groups that came up with similar solutions within a few dollars and a few cuts of each other. During another visit a few weeks later, I also see the photos of the finished project displayed next to the students' posters of their solutions to this authentic, real-world problem.

RALPH'S 1997 INTERVIEW (TIME 5)

In analyzing Ralph's interview in 1997, I do not find much to code referring to how he was thinking about children's behavior because he talks mainly about teaching, learning, and development. One of the reasons for this may be that Ralph's focus seems to be on the individuals in his class more than the group. He does not talk about student behavior in the sense of classroom management. Rather he talks about behavior in terms of what helps or hinders student learning. However, he does say that teacher and parent expectations, and the school context, are factors that influence children's behaviors. He also mentions that the children's personalities, individual learning styles, and cultural backgrounds are also factors that influence behavior. In fact, based on his thinking about the school's role in helping children to be responsible, Ralph emphasizes how parental expectations and values influence how he reacts to student behaviors. Furthermore, in the following comments, Ralph talks about how he likes to keep people happy and calm and how he pays attention to the culture and expectations of the parents and the school because these influence his expectations in his classroom:

> *Individuals have really different understandings of what it means to be responsible, and different cultures have very different understandings [of], what responsibility means—what it means to be polite. What my feelings are about what's polite or . . . what's rude . . . has really broadened. Well there was enough diversity to broaden my perspective and question my assumptions. . . . You know I bring my value system to the classroom and I try to be up-front with the kids. . . . My values sort of get played out. But I also try and pick out where the parents are coming from and try to keep them happy. You know, because that's part of my personality, to make people happy and to keep people calm. . . . But it also enables me to kind of pick up that sense of values that are supported in general and where the sense of this group is, so that I'm not going to, not going to misread or force something that's counter to where people are at.*

Yet Ralph's thinking about children's development and the developmental process is quite explicit in this interview. It is also more advanced and certainly more accurately and clearly stated than in his previous interviews, indicating continued growth in this area of his pedagogical understanding. For example, in comparing second graders to fifth and sixth graders, Ralph describes many factors that impact the development of children, who at this age are more socially aware:

> *I think the fifth-grade kids are pretty sophisticated in their thinking. You can get content, and social studies, and science. You can read literature and really talk about things that have perspectives. They have their own personality that is affecting how they're seeing things and how they're approaching their learning. And it's exciting. It's fun. . . . But it's emotional and it's a trickier kind of time from what I have observed from the outside. . . They're older, they're more independent, they're less focused on me and more focused on each other. . . . They become increasingly aware of and concerned with their peers and their social situation and becoming somewhat more independent of their parents. . . .*
>
> *Sixth-graders have more capability and of course more possibilities, and consider other people's perspectives and understand another person's perspective and their own as distinct. And second-graders have one perspective—theirs. I mean that's it, that's their world. They can't even see what the other person thinks.*

Asked about the usefulness of timelines, Ralph uses his thinking about children's development to explain his approach to timelines, which reveals his understanding that development is a movement from concrete toward abstract thinking. Mentioning Piaget's stages of development (preconcrete,

concrete, and formal operations), he says that these are not fixed states, but that people move along a continuum toward higher levels as they develop qualities and characteristics that allow them to represent things in more abstract ways. Ralph also understands how timelines might be understood by young children (as sequences), and how this is quite different from how they might be understood by older children.

There's preconcrete operations, and then there's concrete operations, and then there's formal operations. And, of course it's not like that. It's this long continual movement through things. So kids, as a group, are moving through this state, so they are moving towards formal operations. I certainly wouldn't see fifth graders as formal op, in the stage of formal operations, but they have more of that quality and more of those characteristics, of that thinking, certainly more than third graders do and second graders do. . . . So, they are able to make and see and understand more abstract, other representations. . . . I think that there're a lot of building blocks for that need to come, for kids to understand the passage of time. . . . So I don't know about the timelines . . . with second graders, they've created their lives you know, I don't think it's really about a timeline in terms of understanding relative amounts of time, I think it's more sequencing . . . what comes first, what comes before, what comes way before, what comes after. . . . Yeah, I think it's about sequencing events.

Clearly, Ralph's understanding of the developmental process is more advanced at Time 5 than at Times 3 and 4. Perhaps this is because Ralph's exposure to developmental theory as a supervisor for DTE allowed him to relearn and apply Piaget's theory to his thinking about the relative usefulness of timelines. Perhaps Ralph's original understanding of developmental theory was never washed out by his socialization and years of experience in schools. Maybe his understanding of children's development was always available to influence his thinking and practices. Regardless, his current understanding of development is closely linked with his thinking about what and how children learn and factors that affect the learning process. In fact, in analyzing this interview, it is difficult to separate his understanding of children's development from how he understands learning and teaching at this time.

For example, in talking about the learning process, Ralph understands that learning can and should be physically and mentally active, which is a complex way to think about Piaget's theory as it relates to learning. In other words, although most teachers talk mainly about the importance of providing active, hands-on learning and of children being physically active when manipulating objects in their learning environment, Ralph understands that children can be active learners even when they are not physically manipulating something: "*Kindergartners can be very actively involved when they are listening to a story, and they're not doing anything with their bodies,*" he says, "*and that's true with any grade level.*"

Although Ralph still understands that learning occurs in many different ways, he also understands that people make sense of things in different ways, that children think differently than adults, and that the teacher has to help make learning accessible to children. In these two examples, Ralph's current thinking about development, learning, and teaching are all interwoven.

The same things have to be learned in different ways. It's not just that they can. I mean everyone has to learn them in whatever way makes sense to them. And, what makes sense to me, I've learned, does not make sense to kids. Some kids will see things the way I do, [but not] other kids . . . and you need to be able to explain your thinking, and there needs to be a certain reasonableness to it. Part of my job is to break things down into parts that are accessible to kids, and I also have to make it possible for kids to discover those parts and put them back together themselves. . . . Well, if they had these other experiences and had a chance to kind of sit with them . . . learning kind of starts with what I'm going to be doing . . . in the classroom and they go away and [it] usually percolates in the mind and continues, and whatever goes on in the brain, and the connections are growing or whatever. I think that happens over time and they can sit with it, and other experiences come in and complete the picture . . . that's a time to settle and solidify, and then they can be given the next level.

Ralph's thinking about pedagogy has also advanced in his understanding of why some things are easier to learn than others. Here we see how the role of variables and reversibility, which refer to developmental theory, and of learning styles enter his thinking:

Some things are much more complex. . . . Why is subtraction harder than addition and why is division harder than multiplication? That's my experience, and my general experience of observing other classes and other teachers. Putting things together is easier than taking them apart. . . . And, you know, if there were more variables, the interrelationship of different variables, will make some things hard and some things easy. There are also so many different styles of learning. Some things are easy for some kids and hard for others and vice versa. . . . With fractions, you start with concepts. Again, children need to understand fundamentally the concept of what a fraction is in a large variety of situations and circumstances . . . and then addition and subtraction of fractions are techniques that they can learn . . . but what they are doing is combining and taking apart and putting together fractions and that's the experience they need . . . so that has to come first and then you can teach the skills on top of it.

In addition, although Ralph still thinks that the process of learning is more important than learning specific content, he is clearer now about the kinds of things he hopes his fifth-grade students will learn. Yet as we see next, he is very focused on individual learners in his teaching.

I want them to leave feeling they have accomplished something that is meaningful to them. . . . I want them to know, specifically, a lot. I want the girls to speak up in class. I want them to feel more comfortable voicing their questions and I want all the students to be able to ask questions and to be able just to seek out information that they need, be will-

ing to go in front of a group, you know, question through something or say that they don't understand, and to get the information . . . it's learning to ask the right questions . . . I also want the kids I'm working with to understand what a fraction is. I want them to have improved in terms of their spatial thinking and problem solving and be able to visualize the three-dimensional shape that needs to be made. I'd like them to be able to approach a multiplication problem and be able to solve that problem. There are those specific things depending upon what group I'm working with that kind of stick out.

For Ralph, the individual child, his personality, and what is going on in his life is also important:

Oh you can do this and experiments and formal this and formal that, but it's like wait a minute—remember the kids. . . . You have to pay attention to the kids and all the things they're going through and all the parts of their lives. It's a huge transition and transformation and . . . they have their own personality, which is affecting how they're seeing things and how they're approaching their learning.

He also says there is an appropriate time to give kids information they need, and he does not believe they should have to construct everything, which impacts his choices as a teacher:

But what sixth and second graders can do is very different. And so, I think the teacher, the second-grade teacher sets the boundaries much more specifically, and maybe provides more choices for the kids to work with, and in the sixth grade you let things come from the kids much more and it can be a much more fluid. . . . I think that it can still be productive in that way. [With] second graders, there needs to be more structure from the teacher.

At Time 5, Ralph believes that a teacher "*is like the orchestra leader—playing, getting the instruments to play together. The kids have their music, but it's more like getting the timing so that you can create something together. . . . The teacher is facilitating, the kids are learning.*"

Ralph still generally seems to oppose doing a lot of direct instruction. For example, in discussing how he would teach students what a sentence is, Ralph says he would rather work with individuals based on their own writing and not the whole class because everyone is not at the same place in their ability to understand a sentence and conventional punctuation. In fact, he seems unsure about how he would handle teaching about sentences because he believes it is situational, personal for each child, and quite complex.

He also has the same issue with teaching spelling and questions about when invented spelling is appropriate and when it is not. Teaching spelling is another complex issue for him.

So much depends on the class, . . . and I would think about who wasn't writing in complete sentences and who wasn't writing a lot . . . those are very different kinds of decisions to make . . . with one or two kids, you know, it's a hard thing to handle.

Because Ralph is much more focused on individuals than on the group at this time, he wants to learn as much as possible about his individual students, beginning with their previous teacher.

. . . and getting whatever information that they have. Depending on who the teacher is—taking that information more or less with a grain of salt—they are always good to have input . . . I want to know if the other person thinks there is anything I should be aware of—are there any learning problems? Is the kid receiving any special services? Have there been any serious social or emotional problems that they bring into the classroom? Are there any issues with the parents? How involved are the parents? Are there any suggestions you have? Are there friendships that the kids might have or have they been separated from their friends? . . . But over the course of the first month I'm [also] going to be assessing all the kids for myself. I like to meet the parents . . . and I want for them to tell me about their kid, and I want to see them, and it's good information.

In response to questions about what Ralph feels he was drawing on as he answered the interview questions, he says he seeks information and feedback from other teachers, directly from children, and also from parents. He then uses that feedback to change things as needed:

That comes with familiarity of students and it comes with experience and seeing kids at different grades. Basically starting with student teaching and seeing what kids are doing—talking with other teachers, and going to the previous teacher of the grade you are in and asking what was successful and what might not have been so successful—and looking at published materials . . . [asking] my grade level colleagues . . . "What are you doing? What is your curriculum? When are you teaching this? When are you teaching that?" You get a lot of informal conversation, and then with direct experience in working with the kids . . . and of course, everything is case by case and kid by kid. . . . You get feedback by asking for feedback from the kids. And I get that from journals that I use off and on over the year. Kids write on a daily basis. I ask them specific questions in their journals sometimes and have them respond to that question. I ask kids to evaluate the unit of study that we've done, and tell me which activities they didn't like and why. I have had fifth graders evaluate a test that I gave. Was it too hard? Was it too easy? Was it just right for them? Did they enjoy taking it? Did they hate taking it? What was it like? I'll have them evaluate an in-depth research paper that we write.

To get additional feedback, Ralph regularly sends the students' work home for the parents to see. He:

writes a note on the side of the envelope about what's going on with the kids and [they'll write] about their work back to me—how they're seeing what the kids is doing. I learn things about what the kids are talking about at home or not saying, and problems, with homework.

Remember that Ralph is also in the unique position at this time of being both a part-time teacher at Park Day School and a supervisor of student teachers for the DTE program. Besides learning everything he can about his students from talking with and observing them, consulting with other teachers, and communicating regularly with family members, Ralph is also finding that his new position is influencing how he thinks about pedagogy.

That's a very special part of this particular position because I am working with adults who are passionately involved in the kinds of nuts and bolts of running a classroom, and who are interested in talking about it at great lengths. . . . And I get to do that, and I am forced to explain my positions. I'm forced to articulate what I think. I'm forced to articulate what I see, and in essence I'm forced to think about both in very specific ways [like] How do you handle pencils in your classroom? and much broader. What are the ramifications of such-and-such management system on the development of visual learners? . . . I've had to write 20 pages a week on, over the course of the year, on what I've seen, and what again I think, and why. I have to justify that until it makes sense.

When I ask Ralph what he has learned from teaching several different grade levels over the past 10 years and then working with student teachers, he mentions the influence of the universals of teaching and his own particular teaching experiences, the contextual influences on teaching. He also notes that his perspective has changed, so he is much more aware of the complexity of the teaching and learning process, which seems quite evident in his responses to the interview questions this time.

There are many things that I do know about teaching and tricks that I have—well, not tricks; that's almost a negative word—but a lot of things that I feel that I can do and when I watch student teachers, there are certain things that I can recognize. Particularly over this past year in watching and being in different classrooms and seeing different teachers and watching different kinds of kids. . . . I've come to see how particular my knowledge is to me and the situation that I have been in and that each situation is different, and each group of kids is different, and there is a tremendous amount to learn in order to be able to teach in different kinds of situations. But I think there is something so true about good teaching—that the learners are actively involved, the learners are willing to ask questions and seek information for themselves, and I think the teacher facilitates those kinds of things . . . I've realized that even within the setting I'm familiar with how complex the picture is, that the picture is much more complex than I was aware of before. The more I see the more I see it's bigger than what I had been looking at . . . and what about this and what about that, and why this and why that . . . and what is the context that this is happening in, and is that bad, and what are the values attached to that, and what is my responsibility as a teacher, and what is my goal . . . and I really don't know the answer to all that for myself much less for anyone else in any other circumstances . . .

A lot has to do with looking at the experiences I've had over the past year . . . working and supervising and it's such a privilege, this job is just such a privilege to be able to do this job and sit in the back and observe . . . not a bad role to be in, you know, observing and helping somebody's student teacher, you know . . . and at the same time I'm learning so much and getting the chance to observe so many different styles. I could never be in that many classrooms as a classroom teacher . . . how many places I get to visit, I'm all over the place . . . and I really see now that every classroom and every person is someone I can learn from . . . and that's kind of changed my view of myself . . . a lot and teaching the kids and also teaching the graduate students, which is a whole other thing.

RALPH'S 1999 INTERVIEW (TIME 6)

Another 2 years pass and Ralph is at the end of his third year supervising student teachers for the DTE program. Unfortunately, I cannot observe Ralph in the classroom because he has not taught children this year. During the 1997–1998 school year, he taught sixth-grade science and computers at Park Day School, spending 1½ days a week there and supervising student teachers the rest of the time. This year he has devoted himself full time to his work with the DTE program, assuming responsibility for the weekly seminars in addition to his supervisory role. I am curious to learn how his experiences working with adults during the past 3 years has affected his thinking about pedagogy.

One of the benefits of Ralph's experiences as a teacher and supervisor is the opportunity to compare many different teaching contexts. The 3-year opportunity to observe in many classrooms at many grade levels, added to his own experiences over the past 12 years of teaching third graders, kindergartners, fifth graders, and sixth graders, offers him a perspective that few teachers have. These varied experiences contribute to his pedagogical understanding at this time. For example, responding to my question about the challenges teachers face, Ralph replies:

With any grade . . . there is going to be a broad range of different abilities and different kinds of learners that I will have to accommodate and different backgrounds of kids that I will have to learn about and different kinds of families that I will have to work with— that whole diversity thing. That is true anywhere.

Yet when I ask why he wants to teach younger children rather than the fifth and sixth graders he taught the past few years, Ralph's answer harkens back to some things he mentioned in his first interview on entering the DTE program in 1985:

As kids move through school, expectations [are] raised and there is such a big jump between kindergarten and first grade that second grade is kind of like nothing. I think that one reason that it appeals to me [is] that I get to kind of repair the damage of first grade or kind of smooth things out without having to make that big kind of jump to third or fourth grade; you are making a jump into more academic kinds of work. So, that is one reason that I think it appeals to me. . . . Curriculum-wise, second grade is pretty open and seems like it would be fun and would allow me the freedom to explore and the freedom to do a lot of art. . . . You know, what does this group need? What are these, what does this particular kid need? What do these kids need? How can I design them? That appeals to me. . . . I am more convinced than ever that art is essential for kids, and it is so sad, and it is so easy to include art, and kids love it. We are always stopping kids from doing it, and I mean I understand, I have been in the classroom, I know that there is the pressure, and there are the tests, and I know that there is plenty of material to cover, and I know how much it takes. Getting the art material, and I am sure that it will happen to me again—you can do it, you include it. Art is a natural avenue for kids to focus and for kids to work creatively, for kids to develop relations, for kids to work with their hands, for kids to manifest their mind and their being and the physical world. What more could we want? And to use that medium to address . . . other kinds of learning needs and avenues seems the way to go to me.

Talking about the nature of the teaching process and the kinds of experiences he wants students to have, Ralph reiterates many of the themes that pervaded earlier interviews: relevancy, attention to individuals and their learning styles, multiple experiences and multiple paths for learning, and favoring process and concepts over specific content.

The kinds of experiences that I want my students to have are experiences that are relevant to their previous experiences in some way, and that there is a connection that they can make to what they already know. So, that is one thing. I want experiences that they can engage in visually, orally, and tactilely in as many ways as possible . . . multiple avenues and multiple opportunities for different kinds of learners to engage with the gist or the concept of what is going on in class. I want a variety similar to that. I want a variety of those kinds of experiences around a particular concept. Teaching addition and subtraction in second grade, which I think has to go together. I want there to be 10 different activities on a given day in which the kids can choose from that relate to that, and from that they can get a depth of experience that they can use to create that understanding

Since his 1995 interview, many factors have influenced Ralph's thinking about behavior, development, learning, and teaching as he continued to develop his pedagogical understandings. However, one additional factor, which never came up before, is his perspective on computer technology. Because of Ralph's recent experiences teaching computer classes to sixth graders, he has a fair amount to say about teaching and learning with technology:

I think that it opens up some avenues. In teaching computers with the sixth-graders we did HyperStudio projects, and that is a different way of thinking. . . . Some of the kids were much better at it than I. They picked it up much more quickly than I did, and some of the kids didn't, and that was a beginning step for me. I didn't know quite what to do with that or how to team them up or incorporate curriculum, which would be the best way to go. Those kids could teach it better than I can. Kids can generally teach other kids better than I can, but particularly with something like that and the technology. You know, HyperStudio *is such an accessible format, and it is a different way of presenting information and organizing information and in a way of thinking and for some people it is just like, "Wow, this is great, this so much more moving." So, that is one exciting possibility.*

One of the most interesting aspects of this interview is what Ralph has to say about what he learned working with prospective teachers and how this compared to teaching in the classroom.

Working with adults is different than working with children. Teaching is teaching and there are some things that you teach at any level. There are some commonalities but the whole way of working with adults who have such a greater storehouse of knowledge, who are peers in some ways, rather than an adult–child kind of relationship, and negotiating that. That was very different. . . . I learned a lot about communicating, a lot about writing and talking, and a lot of passion for complex issues, intellectual issues, and emotional issues related to the practice of teaching. I got a lot of practice and experience during that time. I learned over the course of time, gradually, that [the prospective teachers are] adept at how to handle communications with both, groups and individuals, and how to get criticism, when to do that.

They are similar issues that I had with kids—giving criticism and communicating concerns and problems—more [with] the parents than the kids—but directly and honestly communicating straightforwardly [and] sensitively at the same time, but that had been an issue in my teaching before. . . .

I got to look in depth at lessons and what a lesson is and the whole idea of learning objectives and how one assesses those and how you can make them concrete and how they look at different types of lessons. And it caused me to rethink or revisit various basic issues of management and organization and layout of the classroom. I'm constantly looking at those things. . . .

So you know, I had a chance to work in urban schools, which I had not done before, and in individual student placements, but particularly at group placements at Garfield. That was the fifth placement, and I did that last year and this year and got to know the community of the school. I participated in the projects the students were engaged in, and investigated the healthcare in the community. . . . And I feel much more comfortable, certainly at Garfield and in that particular neighborhood, than I did 2 years ago. And I think I am more equipped to work in that kind of setting, so we'll see.

In response to my question about what challenged him during the 3 years he supervised student teachers, Ralph says that it was effective communication, which he believes is one of the most important skills in teaching, especially when dealing with student teachers who are having trouble.

Notice the similarity between Ralph's concern for the preservice teachers he supervised and for individual children in his classes:

> *Criticisms, deliberate criticism to students and balancing between being honest and be-ing mean or destructive, I guess. There was also tension between being aligned with the students who are struggling and the standards of what it takes to be acceptable as a teacher. . . . A myriad of issues can be attached to that. What kind of feedback do I give them? In the first year beginning with the first students, . . . I didn't have enough infor-mation to really judge where this student was at this point in the program or at this point in his or her development. Are they behind where they should be? . . . Is this some-one who is learning more slowly or is [this] someone who really shouldn't be in this pro-fession because they are never going to be happy, and it's not right for the children that are going to be in that class? I felt a certain responsibility and a certain incompetence to make those judgments.*

The importance of good communication in any classroom is one of Ralph's important themes when talking

> *about good teaching or about education. . . . In the classroom, I think that it is real cru-cial. It is about communication, but I think that it is about developing one's thoughts, developing and thinking and being able to talk and being able to listen. Certainly, more than just teaching, but listening. . . . If I want them thinking, it requires communica-tion, requires feedback, interaction and it is a social process.*

I also ask Ralph to talk about what was fun, or easy, or pleasurable during his 3 years working with student teachers. He says he enjoyed the processes of supervising, observing, and analyzing the student teachers' methods and then discussing what went on in the classroom.

> *Oh, a lot of it was a delight. Writing the journals, . . . wasn't always fun because I had nine lengthy journal responses to write each week, and it got tiresome just writing and sitting at the computer. With certain students, I developed a wonderful dialogue and communication. This last semester, all of them were on e-mail, which was new . . . and it was very exciting, the kind of discussion and dialogue that we had. In general, I really appreciated how they wrote and what they thought about and the kinds of issues they gave me to reflect upon and think about. In general I had some things to say because they were talking about a classroom and particular kids, and I felt comfortable in that arena.*
> *I felt comfortable with the observations, and I loved doing the observations and loved talking about the observations. So much of the supervision I did was in those four-to-six sessions each semester. I would take very detailed notes, . . . pretty much a running ac-count of what was done, and then I would analyze that and we would sit down and talk together about what happened and why. The bigger picture is always there within the de-tails, but that was always grounded exactly in what they said and exactly in how kids re-sponded and the timing of things and the outcomes that did and did not take place. It was very interesting to me to look at, and it was pretty fun to talk at that level with peo-*

ple who were as interested in it as I was, and about the same kinds of issues and the same kids, you know, to bring it down to that level of what actually happened in this lesson with those kids and with that student who has been saying this and doing that.

It was also very rewarding with the staff of people that I had to work with. My fellow supervisors dealt with a group of DTE people . . . I feel very fortunate to have a supportive, competent, funny, caring group of people as colleagues.

Curious about how would Ralph would compare the current DTE program to his own experiences as a student in the same program 15 years earlier, I ask him to talk about any changes or differences he saw and whether he thinks there are any stronger or weaker aspects to the program now compared with his experience in 1985–1987.

The most obvious changes have to do with urban education and all the things to do with race, gender, cultural and linguistic minorities, children whose second language is English . . . all of which . . . needs to be there to address the needs of students we have and that we as teachers have. None of that was here when I went through the program, and I think it is tremendously important and has really strengthened the DTE program.

It's a little bigger than when I was there. We were 12, I think, when I was there and now it's a class of 20. Twenty is still pretty small but different . . . I think a lot of things that were strengths are based in the kind of principles of the program, and I think they continue. I really like the small size of the program, the individual attention in terms of the relationship between the supervisor and the students. The principles of development, the conjunction of theory and developing an understanding of child development as a basis of developing teaching practices is very sound. I think the foundation remains just as strong today as when I was there . . .

Finally, I ask Ralph for any other thoughts before launching into the formal clinical interview. Leaving the classroom to experience other things allowed him to develop a broader perspective on education, he says, but he still wants to work with other staff for the benefit of the whole school. He reminisces about his recent 3-year stint supervising at least 15 student teachers from the DTE program who were working at their fifth placement. Most DTE program students take their fifth placement at Garfield Year-Round Elementary School, an urban school in Oakland packed with more than 1,000 children.

It makes me think about teaching as a profession and how many teachers teach when they go into the classroom. For some teachers that seems to be fine and they seem able to thrive with that, but you need to talk about developing that bigger picture, seeing things from other perspectives. I just see this in terms of professional development—I mean all the way through I have seen myself as a teacher. I've not wanted to go away to the university or get a Ph.D. or go into teacher education as my career—that hasn't felt like my roots. It just makes me think about how, what other opportunity could there be for teachers to step outside of their classrooms for a semester or some period of time so they have a chance to have some time out. It is so completely absorbing over the long term. . . .

I have a bigger picture, a broader view than I had 3 years ago. I've seen it from a bit further back, from a different perspective, and I've talked with lots of principals and seen really different kinds of schools, so I have a bigger picture of what education is and from my experience in only two schools really—I don't have that depth of experience in any of the schools, of course, that I was at, but I have a lot of experience in different schools and all different kinds of systems and the way things are set up and run.

What will that mean exactly in terms of what I do in my classroom next year? I don't know. I certainly want to work with other staff members. I'd like to [go] beyond that, make that formal. I see the importance of . . . solidifying the larger structure of the school and how the classroom is connected in some way, which is one of the reasons that I want to go to Garfield—because it is a place where there is potential for that kind of thing to happen. . . . I guess that's the other impact of what I've done over the last 3 years. I want to set something up. I don't want to be a part of an existing structure. . . . Garfield is not limiting, which has its pluses and minuses. There are no limits there and that has lots of possibilities. That's what I want. I don't think I would have wanted that without going through this 3-year education process myself.

He also talks about where his interest in doing art with children and bringing in the arts came from and tells me more about his background before becoming a teacher:

I was a dancer before I came to this and before I came back to graduate school. [I] taught dance and taught theatrical improvisation and I kind of shut that all out because I was going to be a teacher and I was going to be a professional. I had my videotape lesson and my first year of teaching was such a revelation because it was so boring. I was trying to be a good teacher and I couldn't be dramatic because that wasn't professional. I don't know what made me do that. It was just horrible and it was embarrassing, and all of those things, but mostly it was just boring. I said, "I think we can loosen up a little bit here." It was a little bit of that. When I was in Moraga, there was a wonderful math person who did a lot of math and art connections and did all these different kinds of projects, and it was her passion, and I just took everything that I could get and my kids went to town. They just took and would just go with these kinds of projects. They loved it and they would extend it. So as I am reading to the class, they are working on these symmetry projects that may go on for weeks and on these individual projects, and other kids are working on other things. This was very clearly something that I had stumbled on, something very rich.

Then teaching kindergarten . . . was kind of a loosening-up process, and that made it fun. . . . It came about kind of gradually, and I gradually expanded my boundaries and "O.K. let's try this and see how that goes," and by the end of the first year, I found a way that kids could really look, and kids were creating great stuff. I went to workshops and got some of that. So, big paintings and that kind of thing became something that I was more kind comfortable with.

You know, I have done painting on my own. I am not a great artist, but I do paint for my own pleasure from time to time, but again, I was reluctant to bring that in to the school, . . . I mean it is so rare, particularly in the upper grades, to see art. When you do see it, the level of engagement is double from what it otherwise is, when it is done well.

When there is a teacher who has worked on this and knows how to do it and is really working on that. I mean, drama, plays, movement and visual arts.

Finally, Ralph talks about himself as a learner and the obstacles he sees to accomplishing what he wants next year when he goes back to the classroom, hopefully, to teach at Garfield.

I really see myself as a learner going there. I really have a lot to learn. I do have experience and I feel that I do have some things that I can offer, but I have so much to learn and from those kids and the parents and from the other staff, and that's why I want to work there. . . .

There are so many obstacles that it is hard to say. There is a lack of resources, a tremendous lack of resources. It is an urban school. I have to move classrooms every few months. There is no place to set up. No walls, no doors. The kids speak many different languages and they speak languages that I don't know. I may not be able to communicate with the parents. I may not be able to communicate with the child or the student that I have in my class. There are bureaucratic requirements that make no sense and they take a great deal of time . . . and that have no educational value whatsoever. There are no subs. If you are sick, your class gets disbursed and there is no one necessarily to take care of it. The kids are poor and have very limited resources at home. They have no books and are not in an enriched environment.

My final question for Ralph is to think of a metaphor for himself as a teacher. Ralph's reference to *flow* in the metaphor he describes next is interesting, given that Rick also refers to flowing—but the flowing of a river—as a metaphor to describe his teaching at the same point in his career. Furthermore, although these two teachers have similar images in their metaphors, they came to these images very differently, along very different paths, and with quite different teaching experiences. I wonder if a certain level of pedagogical understanding is needed to view the teaching and learning process as one of flow? Ralph answers by saying that he imagines teaching at Garfield as a *reptilian flow*.

I had kind of this reptilian movement, and in the class there was this flow and movement within the class, and it was controlled and smooth and very powerful, and there was this flow—kind of constantly to a movement and aliveness to that. That is not kind of a metaphor for me as a teacher, but I see myself, kind of guiding and containing, I guess and focusing some how this energy.

RALPH'S STORY . . . IN HIS OWN WORDS . . . SUMMER 2000

As Ralph's story comes to a close, he has 10 years of experience teaching elementary-age children. He is contemplating his return to classroom teaching after a 3-year hiatus from full-time teaching to supervise student teachers. How will Ralph apply what he has learned and relearned at the university along with his years of teaching experience in a new context? How will he apply his well-developed understanding of pedagogy—of behavior and development and of teaching and learning—to a new situation? The next part of the story is told by Ralph in response to some questions I asked him to respond to in writing at the end of his first year teaching at Garfield School in Oakland, California:

I work at Garfield Year-Round Elementary in the Oakland Unified School District. Garfield is a large (1,050 students this past year) multilingual, multiethnic urban school. For the past 8 to 10 years, Garfield has been on a year-round, four-track schedule to accommodate the exploding school-age population of East Oakland. For the past 4 years, teachers have rotated rooms to make this schedule work—meaning that all teachers (except kindergarten) move rooms every 3 months of the school year (three different classrooms per year). Next year (due to the influence of new superintendent Dennis Chacones), Garfield will be single track, with a modified traditional year calendar (or so they're saying . . .).

This past year, I taught a third-grade class of 20 students. My class is sheltered, which at Garfield means I have both mainstream English and Limited English Proficient (LEP) students. Last year I had 8 LEP students and 12 native English speakers. Ethnically, last year's group included 11 African-American, 7 Hispanic, and 2 Mien-American students. Among the LEP students, there was a wide range of English ability.

I am struck by how different this classroom is than anything I have worked with before (in Moraga, at Park Day School, or at the University). No wonder it has been such an overwhelming experience.

Perhaps predictably, my sense of what constitutes good teaching and effective curriculum has shifted. My developmental foundation persists (although I think what I mean by developmental *has changed—more on that later). Over the course of this past year, I have become increasingly aware of the pervasive importance of social and cultural contexts of learning. In deciding to teach at Garfield, I very deliberately placed myself outside my own social and cultural framework. Little did I know how profound the disconnect would be and how powerfully it would affect me as a teacher and as a person.*

I entered Room 13 on that first day of school (September 1999) anxious, but with considerable confidence that, although there might be rough spots, I'd be able to work my way through them and create a productive classroom. After all, I had 10 years of classroom experience, had been a successful master teacher, had supervised 3 years worth of student teachers in classrooms not unlike this one, had taught at workshops, and had led seminars. I still recall sitting down after that first day, stunned. And after the first (3-day) week, more stunned. Although I had my first good day the Friday of the second week (with students writing and "publishing" their first pieces of writing—amazing that I can now recall that day so clearly), by the end of the month things were getting worse, not better. Despite all my curriculum, all my developmental understanding, my ability to talk to kids, I floundered. I couldn't maintain control of the class, much less foster learning.

I think that there was not one, or even several, but rather multiple interlocking reasons why this was the case. Most glaringly, I had never REALLY had to discipline chil-

dren before. With one exception, I never physically restrained a child and never sent any child out of the classroom for discipline. I had rarely encountered physical fights (which this past year were a daily occurrence on the yard and, at times, in my classroom). Through excruciating trial and error, by November, I developed some external systems that helped establish a degree of order in the classroom. As one example, I started sending kids "to the office" (having worked this out with the principal and assistant principal) for every (even very minor) physical interaction (the fights stopped completely after a week).

I don't think that poor children need more discipline than middle-class or upper class students. What was happening had more to do with the disconnect between me and my students than with anything else. I understood the discipline system of Moraga at an almost intuitive level; it was what I grew up with myself. At Garfield, on the other hand, I had no clue about the subtext, the motivation, what kids were saying beneath their words, how to be "smart" about handling situations. It's difficult to be "smart" when you don't understand what's going on!

Intertwined with the struggles with student behavior lay issues of learning. Through those first weeks, I was completely at a loss as to how to engage my students meaningfully in learning. Again, there are multiple and many-layered reasons for this: my lack of cultural understanding, my inexperience in teaching beginning reading (over half the class entered reading below first-grade level), the incredible range of abilities, large gaps in skills for many students, two full-inclusion students (one with cerebral palsy, one with mental retardation) and no full-inclusion teacher (a teacher was finally hired after 6 weeks of school), and a number of students with learning, social, and emotional issues. What aspect of reading (or any other academic topic) is important for a third grader whose mother is struggling with substance abuse and has essentially left her in charge of taking care of her younger brother? How can I, as a teacher, create a curriculum that is compelling to her through the anger and confusion she experiences?

What does all this say about my current thinking about teaching practice and curriculum? Now more than ever, I feel that there is no right practice or right curriculum or right approach. Teaching practice must fit the particular and individual needs of students; and it must fit the particular and individual needs of teachers as well. (I have become MUCH less judgmental about what other teachers do as they do their best to teach under difficult circumstances—being there and failing persistently does a lot to create humility!) I continue to believe in a developmental approach to teaching and learning, but I don't see this as the same kind of process I once did. I question the universality of the Piagetian model certainly. What I retain is the conviction that it is UNDERSTANDING, and not just information, that matters—and that all learners construct the framework of their own understanding. I have broadened my thinking as to how many different ways that framework gets built and to the different pressures and needs that shape children's learning. A third-grade student who is struggling to understand her place in the world of East Oakland has very different forces shaping her learning than a third grader in Moraga.

In some ways, I'm now doing what I imagined I would be doing when I graduated from DTE in 1987. There were some intermediate steps that I didn't anticipate. In looking back, I'm grateful for the VARIETY of my experience; teaching in such disparate settings will ultimately make me a better teacher. Not that I consciously set out to do it this way—I've just gone from one step to the next, doing what seems right at the time.

I'll be back at Garfield next year. So far as I know at present, I'll be teaching third grade and teaching in the same room. But I've learned not to count on that (or anything else) in the rapidly changing world of the OUSD.

I will return with bundles of unanswered questions:

I share ethnicity with none of my students. How much will that continue to limit me in knowing them and in knowing how to teach them effectively?

How do I address other issues of race? Why is it that of the six students in my class who are seriously behind, 5 are African American? How do I talk about this and get help so I can teach these students more effectively?

How do I address issues of my own sexual orientation in the school community at Garfield? At present, I'm out with staff/district, bring Jim along to parties and school events, and so on. But I've not brought Jim into my life in the classroom (sharing details with students and families about MY family life). How do I want to go about beginning that process?

Standardized tests have assumed paramount importance at the school (for the district, the state, and some of the parents). Is my disdain for these measures a reflection of an upper class luxury, and should I be doing more to better prepare my students for the testing?

How much time do I allow for art, for hands-on science, for conceptual development as opposed to teaching skills—I had the luxury in Moraga to spend a good portion of my time and energy into more critical and creative pursuits, knowing that the nitty-gritty skills would be covered (at home or elsewhere in the school)—I do NOT have that luxury now.

To what extent do I attempt to address the emotional needs of my students? This past year, I brought in snacks, met with students at lunch, provided modeling clay and board games and choice time and papier-mache. My thinking has been that, by giving them emotional space, they would settle in and could begin learning. To an extent, I still believe this. But I have to seriously question any time spent away from content and skills. Time is too precious, especially when students are already behind and have so much stacked against them.

In addition to these macrolevel questions, I carry many microlevel curricular questions into next year. (How do I carry Writer's Workshop further? How can I create more independent work? How can I use guided reading? What phonics program can I find to help fill in the gaps in a more organized way? How do I involve families more, and how can I actually USE parents in my classroom? What rewards/consequences do I want to establish at the beginning? etc. etc.) I'm only really thinking 1 year at a time right now. I'll see where this might lead. For now, I'm glad I'm back in the classroom. I feel proud, in a new way, to be a teacher.

After cleaning and organizing my classroom, I spent a day observing a second-grade teacher at Garfield. I'd been intrigued by the conversation and bits and pieces that I'd picked up from Mr. Nguyen, and I was anxious to get in to see what was actually going on in his classroom. This was a second-grade Vietnamese bilingual classroom. Being Garfield and being Oakland, two thirds of the students were Vietnamese-American, and one third were African American—a difficult cultural mix to be sure.

I was mesmerized by what I observed. There was cohesion in this classroom—connection between and among students (of both ethnic groups) and between the teacher and students. Out of that, alongside that, Writer's Workshop flourished, writing conferences were held, mental arithmetic went on, students actively LISTENED to one another, and

had that mode to take in information that was sorely lacking for so many in my class-
room (teacher as well as students). It was inspiring—a picture of what can be, indeed,
accomplished with a great deal of hard work. Gives me a (very concrete) goal to keep in
mind.

It will be interesting to see what a second year will bring.

A FINAL OBSERVATION—FALL 2000

Driving through the streets of Oakland, past Highland Hospital and up
Foothill Boulevard to visit Ralph at Garfield Elementary School, I note that
many of the once grand homes in the surrounding neighborhood look run
down and in need a fresh coat of paint. Many of these homes, which originally housed single families, are now multifamily dwellings. One just across
the street from the school is the victim of a recent fire. There are few trees
or shrubs, and there is no grass around any of the houses that surround
Garfield School. This is a neighborhood where many recent immigrants to
California have settled in the past dozen years, displacing most of the African-American working-class families who used to live here. Many neighborhood businesses now have signs in Spanish and Vietnamese.

Garfield School looks cleaner to me than I remember it about 10 years
ago when I first supervised DTE students during their fifth and final field
experience. It seems less chaotic and is certainly less crowded and noisy
than I remember. No longer are over 1,300 students attending Garfield on
a rotating basis all year long in two Spanish-bilingual and two Chinese-
bilingual tracks. Now the school only houses about 950 students on a traditional schedule that starts after Labor Day and ends in June. No longer do
teachers have to change classrooms every 3 months to accommodate multiple tracks and schedules. In fact, Ralph is located in the same classroom,
Room 13 just down from the office near the main entrance to the school,
he was in all last year.

However, the large banner over the entrance just inside Garfield still says
WELCOME in eight languages. I hear two young Spanish-speaking mothers
with babies in strollers chatting just outside the front door and two Mien
grandmothers holding their grandchildren's hands as they wait to cross at
the stoplights on every corner surrounding this large school. In the school's
office, a new student arrives with one parent who speaks little English and a
translator from Social Services. Some of the teachers I see in the halls are
the same ones I remember from years ago, although there are many new
faces too. The principal who greets me as I check in at the school office is
new to me also, although she has been at Garfield for several years.

I note that the school seems better kept than it was a decade ago. There
is less trash on the large, asphalt playground, which I can see outside the

windows in Ralph's classroom. Inside, there are only four clusters of tables and 20 chairs for students. This makes Ralph's classroom seem roomy compared to my memory of Garfield classrooms a decade ago, when there were 30 to 32 students crowded into every room. In fact, this was the case until just a few years ago, when new laws in California mandated class sizes of no more than 20 students in all public kindergarten through third-grade classrooms.

When I arrive to observe Ralph at Garfield, his third graders are in their weekly computer class. We use this time to catch up a bit as I look around the room and help Ralph prepare a morning snack for his students. In addition to the four clusters of tables forming a horseshoe shape in the center of the room, I see there is a large chalkboard on the front wall with a large bookshelf and table on one side of it. An upright piano, overhead projector, more bookshelves, and Ralph's desk are on the other side. Along the top of the chalkboard are a series of commercially produced pictures representing phonetic sounds from the *Open Court* reading program recently mandated in all low-performing schools in the Oakland Unified School District. There is also a poster on the front wall entitled "Room 13 Rules." The rules listed are: 1. Respect others' feelings, bodies, and belongings. 2. Follow adult instruction. 3. Do your best work. 4. Don't say bad words. 5. Don't steal. Also, Ralph has already printed the schedule for the day on the chalkboard.

The entire wall to the left of the chalkboard is filled with windows that look out onto Garfield's large playground. Although it is quiet and shaded at 9 a.m., later in the day Ralph will have to talk over noise of children playing during their lunch recess and close the blinds to cut down on the heat and glare from this western exposure.

Under the windows, Ralph has placed a large area rug and a green sofa to make a place where all the children can gather with him during the day. Behind the sofa is a table with writing materials and bean seeds growing out of clear plastic cups from a recent science lesson. There is also a large round table in the back corner near the windows on which Ralph arranges cups of apple juice, slices of cinnamon bread, and pieces of apple for the students to have when they return from their computer class.

Along the back wall near the door to the hall are coat hooks for the children's jackets and backpacks, storage cabinets, and a low counter with a sink and additional storage for art supplies. One of the storage cabinets holds math manipulatives and math games while the other cabinet houses additional school supplies and a set of textbooks. The doors to these storage cupboards and part of the back wall are covered with student posters representing math story problems. One drawing represents the problem 9 + 3 = ? The accompanying story reads, "Ms. Elaine has 9 apples. Rebecca has 3 apples. How many apples do we have all together?" Another colorful, hand-drawn poster depicts the problem 16 + 8 = ?, and the story reads, "I have 16 cats. I open my door and 8 more cats come inside. How many do I have now?"

The wall opposite the large bank of windows has tables in front of it that hold three different brands of computers and one printer. One of the newer computers is connected to the Internet. There are children's paintings adorning the wall above the computers. These abstract paintings are done with tempura paints and, according to a sign posted, they were made by mixing red, yellow, and blue paint to make secondary colors (green, orange, and purple).

As we wait for the children to come back to the room, Ralph talks to me about the range of achievement levels of the students in his class. He tells me that he has six children who are very capable and who are excellent readers and writers. He also says that he has several children who are emergent readers and writers and who also have a difficult time concentrating and staying on task. There are also about six children who are designated as ELL (English Language Learners). Several of his students are doing first-grade work, and several are able to do fifth-grade work, so Ralph has quite a range in his class. He also tells me this class is very different from the group he had last year, and that he is very pleased to have some high-achieving students this year who can help to set the tone for others in the class.

Ralph also has one child in his class with Down's Syndrome and another child who is identified as EMH (Educable Mentally Handicapped). These two students have an almost full-time assistant who remains in the classroom to work with them during the day. Except for going out periodically for speech therapy or to see the EC (Exceptional Children's) teacher, these students spend their entire day in Ralph's class. Ralph is not responsible for developing curriculum for these two girls, but he includes them in everything he has planned for the class.

Ralph's students are a microcosm of California's current population of children from working poor families. There is one White child in Ralph's class, seven African-American children, six Hispanic, and six Asian, including students whose parents were born in Laos, Cambodia, Vietnam, and China. All these children were born in the Unites States, but many of them are bilingual.

After snack and a morning recess, Ralph begins his day by going over the schedule written on the chalkboard. The first thing on the list is Journal Writing time. The children's journals are already on their desks and they know the routine. Ralph has also written an optional journal topic on the chalkboard: "*Tell me about your weekend. What was the ^{HIGH} point? What was the $_{LOW}$ point? Tell me all.*" Ralph asks one student to read this prompt aloud and then asks two other children what they think he means by HIGH point and LOW point. In response to Ralph's question, one child shares a story about her Karate class and another child shares about her birthday party. Ralph tells them they have 7 minutes to write in their journals, but the time expands to 20 minutes as he circulates around the room collecting permission slips for an upcoming field trip and chatting privately with various students.

I observe that everyone is quiet and writing something in their journal. The EC assistant is working in another room at this time, but the two inclusion students work diligently at writing something in their journals. During this time, another EC teacher comes in the room to work with another student with identified learning disabilities. They move to the green sofa, where the teacher quietly helps the LD student with some phonics work.

At about 10:20 a.m., Ralph chooses four students to sit on the green sofa while the rest of the students sit on the rug. These four students share what they have written in their journal today. As they read aloud, the rest of the class listens attentively. Then Ralph gives verbal directions for their next activity, which is to write a good-bye and thank you letter to the student teacher from the DTE program who has been in the classroom 1½ days a week since the start of school this fall. This is her last week, and Ralph wants the students to write letters and draw pictures that he will bind in a book to give her as a going-away present. The students seem interested and excited to begin this activity.

Before letting them leave the rug, however, Ralph asks the children to share ways that the student teacher, Ms. Wong, has helped them. Nearly every hand goes up, and Ralph calls on many children to share orally. He then reiterates his instructions that they must first write a draft of their letter, have it proofread and corrected by an adult, and then recopy it in their best writing on different paper before they can draw a picture for Ms. Wong. Ralph then dismisses the children one by one to go back to their seats to begin their letters. When all the children are at their seats, Ralph goes to the chalkboard at the front of the room and shows them how they should begin their letters with Dear Ms. Wong.

The children work for the next 45 minutes on this project. At one point, Ralph gives them 5 minutes of silent writing time to encourage them to finish their letter writing. However, another 20 minutes goes by before everyone completes a final copy of their letter and has started on their picture. Those who finish more quickly are encouraged to get a book and read at their desks. Some children use the additional time to make elaborate pictures for Ms. Wong.

After more than 1 hour has passed, Ralph collects their completed letters and pictures and calls everyone over to sit on the rug. He then reads aloud from several new picture books he has checked out from the library, including a new book by one of their favorite authors. Soon it is time for lunch, and Ralph tells them that, because the time he planned for math today was taken up by their writing time, they will have to finish the planned math activities tomorrow.

After the half-hour lunch and recess period, there is a scheduled cool-down time every day when Ralph reads aloud and the students listen from their seats. Many also draw during this time, and several use this time to finish up their pictures for Ms. Wong. Ralph reads from a chapter book by Roald Dahl called *Matilda*. After one chapter, Ralph calls the students by their tables to choose up to four books from the class library, which is housed in the large bookshelf to the left of the chalkboard. He also encourages them to read from the collection of books made by the class and individual students earlier in the year. These are housed in another smaller bookshelf, and several children take them to their seats. The students are to read silently during the next half hour. They are keeping track of the number of minutes they read independently each day, and there are already 122 minutes recorded on the chalkboard. Ralph reads with one boy as they sit together on the rug. The EC assistant helps her charges select some books to look at, but ends up helping the child with Down's Syndrome put a puzzle together at the round table in the back of the classroom when she gets restless.

After a half hour of relatively silent reading time, Ralph suggests that they have time before the next recess to play several rounds of a math-guessing and strategy game called *Hi/Low*. This time the game involves the students guessing a number between 1 and 1000. Ralph decides the target number is 423, which he writes down where the students cannot see it. He then calls on students who raise their hands to make guesses and records them on the board in a T-chart. As they guess, he takes each suggestion but reinforces strategic guesses and scaffolds their progress toward narrowing the range of their guesses in a strategic manner.

H	L
500	105
450	200
430	300
429	400
425	420
	421

In the hour left after the final recess, Ralph has his students finish working on five large murals they are painting together in small groups. These colorful, bulletin-board size murals are a follow-up to a story they read the previous week about a young boy in Panama who painted murals on the walls of the houses in his village. During recess, Ralph sets out blobs of paint in the three primary colors on paper plates, which he calls their *palettes*.

Each group of between three and five students must share a palette and a plastic bucket of water, but the students have their own brush to use and an additional paper plate to use for mixing colors. For the next 45 minutes, Ralph's third-grade students are scattered around the room on their hands and knees surrounding their murals, which are laid out on the floor.

Ralph passes out the materials and then spends the time praising and encouraging their efforts, mediating major and minor disputes within the groups and prodding them to fill in all the white spaces on their murals. The two inclusion students are assigned to groups, but the child with Down's Syndrome quickly ends up with her own paints and paper to use while an adult watches over her. Some of the murals are full of flowers and birds and others have people in them. One mural features a large, colorful rooster, and another mural is covered with particularly intricate flowers and vines. All are colorful. With only 10 minutes left in the school day, Ralph has the students begin to clean up as he moves their murals to the tops of their tables to dry.

Five minutes before the final bell rings, Ralph calls everyone to the rug one last time to explain their homework assignment and to talk with them about their painting experience. He asks them what they liked about painting their murals. He also asks them what was difficult about it. Finally he dismisses them one by one as he hands them their homework. The homework asks them to write where they think the water that comes out of the faucets at school and at home comes from and to name 10 places where you can see water. The homework is to prepare them for a science unit about water that they will be starting this week.

As Ralph talks with the students on the rug at the end of the day, several parents and older siblings wait just inside the door to his classroom. They listen and watch the clock as Ralph finishes and dismisses his students one by one to go home.

*****

AFTERWORD

To update the reader: Ralph is still teaching third graders at Garfield Elementary School. Each year he reports feeling more and more successful about being able to meet the needs of his diverse groups of students.

Chapter 6

The Story of Rick Kleine

Rick is White, married to a former teacher, the father of two daughters, and a teacher. He has taught in the same classroom in the same working-class neighborhood school in Vallejo, California, since 1987. He teaches fourth and fifth graders in a combination class and has been "looping" with half his class for the past several years. Rick is particularly interested in the social, emotional, and ethical lives of his ethnically and linguitically diverse students.

The case study of Rick Kleine presented in this chapter is a synthesis of this teacher's thinking about pedagogy across his 13-year teaching career (1987–2000). In this chapter, I describe how his thinking about teaching and learning developed over time, and how a theoretically cohesive teacher preparation program, such as the DTE program at UC–Berkeley, may have contributed to the development of his thoughts and actions regarding pedagogy. I begin by describing his teaching context and current pedagogical thinking. I also provide a description of his current classroom practices. I discuss influences from his personal life on his thinking as a professional educator because they impact his thoughts and actions as a teacher. I also analyze the nature, sources, and evolution of Rick's praxis and pedagogical beliefs over time, including changes in his personal metaphors for teaching. Finally, I highlight changes in Rick's pedagogical thoughts and actions since he started in the DTE program at UC–Berkeley in 1985.

This case study is structured differently that the three previous cases because I have written about Rick's earlier development in other places

---

This case study appeared in "Lives of Teachers: Update on a Longitudinal Case Study," *Teacher Education Quarterly*, 28, 29–47, 2001.

(Levin & Ammon, 1992, 1996). This chapter compares Rick's development between 1997 (Time 5) and 1999 (Time 6), which corresponds to his 10th through 13th years of full-time teaching. However, like the previous case studies, this one also ends with Rick's own reflections written during the summer of 2000 toward the end of this 13th year in the classroom.

DESCRIPTION OF RICK'S SCHOOL AND CLASSROOM: MAY 1999

Vallejo, California, is about 30 miles north of San Francisco. It is a fast-growing, blue-collar town where a downturn in the local economy and rising unemployment during the 1970s and 1980s led to boarded-up buildings, out-of-business signs, and out-of-work adults. Driving across the bridge over the Carquinez Straits on Interstate 580, you catch your first glimpse of Vallejo to the west. Looking down to the water below, you can see docks that belong to the California Maritime Institute where generations of Merchant Marines were trained. Vallejo was also home to Mare Island Naval Shipyard where many cruisers, battleships, and submarines were built and maintained between 1854 and 1996 when the shipyard was decommissioned.

As you drive through Vallejo, turn west toward now defunct Mare Island, and turn in the direction of Federal Terrace Elementary School, you can see the impact of losing so many jobs on this once viable and vibrant community. Federal housing that surrounds the school, which used to be bustling with military families, is now a ghost town with leaves blowing in the wind off the Bay, but no voices—only echoes of more prosperous times.

Federal Terrace, however, is still the neighborhood school for over 500 students in Grades K to 5. It is 1 of 13 elementary schools in the Vallejo Unified School District. The students who attend Federal Terrace come from mostly blue-collar and low-income *working poor* families. The 31 fourth- and fifth-grade students in Rick Kleine's class represent the ethnic diversity of Vallejo. They are mainly Black, Hispanic, Filipino, Pacific Islander, White, and Asian (Chinese), or a mix of two or more of these ethnic groups. For the most part, both of their parents work outside the home and have a high school education.

Like many California schools, Federal Terrace has several temporary trailers that serve as classrooms plus some space for both paved and grassy playfields. The main building and several wings of the school are all on one level with few interior hallways. Children enter and leave Mr. Kleine's classroom from a single door that opens onto the playground. His room is located at the end of one wing next to the boys' and girls' bathrooms. It is a long walk to the cafeteria and the main office, but Rick does not mind. He is a pretty independent teacher; his focus is on his students, not on school gossip or politics that he might hear if he were more focused on the adults in the school.

Rick came to Federal Terrace in the fall of 1987, having completed one of his student teaching placements in Vallejo at what is fondly known as the *Farm School*. Knowing that he would have support from the principal who first hired him, Elona Meyers, he chose to make the daily 45-minute commute from his home in Berkeley. He never left Federal Terrace, although he has thought about it from time to time. In fact, Rick is in the same classroom in which he started teaching well over a decade ago. Over 350 students have come and gone, but Rick's classroom looks pretty much the same from year to year. The students, however, are not the same when they leave Rick's classroom as when they enter it—but more about that a little later.

The floors of Rick's classroom are wooden, once finished but now scuffed, and the walls are painted a light institutional green. A large bank of windows faces the street on one side, where the empty doors and windows of an abandoned military housing project can be seen across that street. Chairs for 31 students and six large tables are clustered in the main part of the room. Groups of six to eight students sit around each table sharing one basket of school supplies. Their backpacks hang off their chairs, and their notebooks and other materials are scattered on top of and underneath the tables. There is a small alcove for storing coats and school materials near the door to the classroom. Sometimes two or three children will cram themselves into this small space to work on a project or read together. Chalkboards cover two walls and, in turn, are covered with posters with lists on them.

A rather large alcove at one end of the room provides space for three computers and a sink with storage cabinets underneath a paint-stained countertop. Science supplies, art materials, children's half-finished art projects, shoebox-size terrariums, and stacks of textbooks cover these countertops. One large table, piled with student notebooks and journals, sets this alcove apart from the rest of the room. Large posters of all types hang in front of the windows, on the walls, and from the ceiling. They are not commercially made posters with cute pictures and catchy sayings. Everything displayed around the room represents examples of recent student projects: Native-American masks, Venn diagram comparing two pieces of literature, lists of words (nouns, verbs, adjectives, adverbs), lists of mathematics vocabulary from a geometry unit, class procedures and lists of things to do when assignments are completed, student-generated lists of where and when you can see fractions and decimals used outside the classroom, famous people and what they are known for from a social justice book report and research project, a rubric for proofreading student writing, lists of favorite activities during the last 9 weeks, and lots of photos of the students at Vallejo's *Farm School*, which all students in the district visit several times a year. All of these posters are products of student discussions and problem-solving sessions. All are done in Rick's handwriting, and all relate in some way to the academic, social, and ethical life of the students in this classroom.

The room feels vibrant and looks messy, but all the students know what they are supposed to be doing. At each table, students have specific jobs that rotate every month. Over each table, there is a poster made by the students of a state in the United States that they have chosen: North Carolina, Texas, California, Oregon, New York, and Connecticut. One person at each table is the governor in charge of the rest of the citizens at the table. Another student is the treasurer for the state, and there is also an environmental protection officer, a secretary, a technology engineer, and a supply clerk at each table. The treasurer's job is to collect lunch money, money for fieldtrips, or book orders from the citizens of the state. The treasurers take that money to Mr. Kleine so that only 6 or 7 students are at his desk each morning instead of over 30. The governor's job is to maintain order at his or her table, whereas the supply clerk gathers needed materials for any projects, and the secretary collects papers to be turned in among other tasks. Each environmental protection officer is in charge of monitoring the cleanup of the area around his or her table several times a day, and the technology engineer is in charge of the computer schedule and the disks for the group members.

Rick is definitely the CEO of the class, but each student has responsibilities to carry out every day. These table teams are very important groups. Rick arranges them randomly at the beginning of the school year. However, after the first 9 weeks, the students have to decide on their own tablemates according to parameters they decide on, such as equal numbers of boys and girls and a balance of fourth and fifth graders. The task of deciding on new tablemates every 9 weeks is just one of the many problem-solving and decision-making experiences that the students have throughout the year in this room.

In May 1999, I arrive at Rick's classroom about 8:30 a.m. with plans to spend the day observing. I have been in this classroom many times over the past 12 years as both a researcher and to supervise student teachers placed in Rick's classroom through the Developmental Teacher Education (DTE) program at UC–Berkeley. As I look around the room, I make notes—mental ones and extensive notes on paper—about what has changed and what is familiar.

When I arrive, the students are already engaged in playing a card game in pairs. The object of the game is to practice multiplication facts. Students choose two cards from the top of their own deck and multiply to get the total value. As I observe from near Rick's cluttered desk in one corner in the back of the room, one student draws a 9 and a King (9 × 13) and computes his answer (117) on scratch paper while his partner draws an Ace and a Jack

(1 × 11) and computes the total value (11) in his head. The winner, the student with the highest number for each turn, takes all four cards. The game goes on until one of the partners has all the cards from both decks. Rick is playing with one student and also observing the others.

About 20 minutes later, Rick blows the whistle hanging around his neck. He waits for complete quiet before asking the students to sort out their cards, have one person bring up both decks, get out their homework, and wait for the next direction. At Rick's command, "*Carry on,*" the students get busy sorting their cards and gathering up their homework. Less than 2 minutes later, Rick asks the students to pair up and discuss the strategies they used to do last night's homework. For the 14 fourth graders in the room this year, this means discussing how they sequenced information found on a time schedule and how they tallied the total time. For the 17 fifth graders, it means discussing how they lined up the decimal points and did some estimating to check their answers on a practice sheet about adding and subtracting decimals.

After about 7 or 8 minutes, Rick asks the students to find another partner and read each other their drafts of editorials that they also completed for homework. He also asks them to look at one of the charts on the wall in the front of the room that contains a list of criteria for this writing assignment. Rick goes over the items in the list, which the class generated earlier in the week, and he reminds them to rate each other from 1 to 5 on each of these criteria:

___ Neatly written	___ Written so audience can understand it
___ Paragraphs (3)	___ Uses descriptive writing
___ Pro paragraph	___ On the subject—NO BIRDWALKS
___ Con paragraph	___ Opinion paragraph has reasons for opinions
___ Written in student words	___ Factual information, not made up
___ Complete information from article	___ Title, date, name, spelling, punctuation

After 10 minutes, the students appear to be finished with sharing their editorials and doing their peer evaluations, but Rick is still reading some students' editorials. The class gets loud, and Rick asks the secretaries to collect the math homework, the supply clerks to collect the editorials, and the governors to collect the permission slips for their upcoming fieldtrip to the symphony. The treasurers are also asked to collect permission slips and pledge cards for next week's "Jump Rope for Heart" event. This transition takes a long time, but Rick waits quietly without saying a word. One child finally calls out, "*This is not talking time*." Rick responds with a brusque, "*Thank you*," and waits for their complete attention before proceeding.

When the students finally settle down, Rick talks with them about a schoolwide earthquake drill scheduled for later in the morning. After letting the children complain vociferously for a minute, Rick validates their feelings and emotions about earthquakes and earthquake drills and then asks them to practice how they will act during this drill. In between practice sessions, as they try to squeeze their bodies under their tables and stay quiet for at least a minute, Rick asks them to share solutions to conflicts that arise about the lack of space when six to eight children have to crowd together under a table that is no more than 3 × 4 feet. Several times he asks them to "*Give me your best*" and makes them practice four or five times until they get it right—or at least almost right.

All of this takes about 15 minutes, and then it is time to start math. Rick gives the fourth graders directions about their assignment and a new tool to use on the time schedule problem from the night before—a stopwatch. He emphasizes that they are to find a different way to solve the problems and discuss strategies they use with the partner with whom they will share a stopwatch. Later they write down their new strategies in their math journals, which Rick collects and reads after each assignment.

As the fourth graders move to various parts of the room to work with their partners, Rick calls the fifth graders to gather around the overhead projector at the front of the room. He asks them to summarize the data they recorded yesterday during a probability activity involving flipping coins. As Rick asks for ways that they recorded the results of their first 10 trials, he recognizes and praises a student who uses a good strategy to organize his data. On the overhead, Rick develops a chart based on this student's strategy of organizing the data by the number of times he flipped heads in every 10 trials. Rick then models how they might all pool their data and translate them into fractions and decimals. He does the first two examples with them and then asks them to work with their partner to complete the rest of the chart.

# of heads	# of trials out of 10	Fraction N/10	Equivalent fraction N/100	%
0	5	5/10	50/100	50%
1	6	6/10	60/100	60%
2				
3				
4				
5				

At 9:40 a.m., another teacher sticks her head in the door and reminds the class that the earthquake drill is imminent. When the siren goes off, the students are pretty noisy and a few shriek as they dive under the closest table. Rick makes them wait until they are quiet for a full minute before giving them instructions about going outside. A few minutes later, as we walk outside into the bright sunshine, he reminds a small group about showing respect to other people in the school when he finds them talking loudly near one of the portable classrooms that border the playground.

After a 20-minute recess and bathroom break, the students return to the classroom and go back to work on their math assignments. Later at PE time, Rick will ask everyone to run three laps around the grassy playground area near the ball diamond. He will remind them to pace themselves and not cut corners. Rick will walk the same path with several of them and talk with individual children while encouraging others to keep going. Rick later tells me that this break is intended to get them ready to concentrate for the rest of the morning and to shake off the emotions generated by the earthquake drill.

Later that morning during science, Rick gives directions about what needs to be accomplished with regard to the plant experiments they are in the midst of doing with their terrariums. Before dismissing them to make observations and record them in their science notebooks, Rick asks students to repeat his instructions one at a time. He also asks them to discuss how they might solve the problem of having limited space and only one sink. The students have several ideas, but there is no agreement. Instead of dismissing them, Rick takes the time to process this problem and encourage them to see patterns in this discussion compared to previous discussions when they have tried to solve other problems. Some of the students mention that they have been working on listening to each other's ideas without finding immediate fault in them. After a 10-minute discussion, he tells the students to "*Carry on*," and they begin their assigned tasks: observing any changes in their terrariums, measuring their plants with handmade paper measuring tapes they made earlier, and recording their observations and measurements in their notebooks. As students finish their journal entries, they take them to Rick. After he reads their entries and asks them about their observations, most of the students get out a weaving project they have been working on for about a week.

Sometime during the half hour devoted to science, Rick talks privately with Antonio, tells him that he will need to go home today if he is going to hurt someone, validates his feelings as Antonio shares what Desmond said to him, and rubs his back. Rick then listens to Desmond's side of the conflict and asks the boys to talk together until they can decide what they are going to do about their conflict. Rick then talks to Tyler about not bothering other children, even if he is not interested in working on his weaving. He also talks with Tyler about quitting too easily when things get hard. He then moves on to talk to three other children who appear to not be using their time productively.

At 11:30, he asks everyone to clean up and get ready for PE. After their three laps, he calls them together to work on the same challenge game I observed him lead several years earlier with a different group of students. This challenge requires the students to organize themselves in such a way that the entire class can get through a turning rope in a sequence that starts off with one student, then two, then three students, then a group for four, and then five students, and so on until all of the class has made it through with no hesitation and no gaps. This class has been working on this challenge for about 3 days. Before they begin, Rick talks with them about what a class that is working together and being fair to each other would look like, sound like, and act like as they solved this challenge. He lets them know that this is a difficult challenge and asks them to experiment for 10 minutes with solving this problem. He also invites those who are not willing to try to stand aside. One boy takes the lead and suggests an idea, which they try. They almost make it, but then things fall apart and there is a lot of squabbling among the students. Some wander off. Rick says nothing and just keeps turning the rope as they try another student's idea. After nearly 40 minutes outside and no luck in meeting this rope challenge, Rick sends them inside for silent reading time before lunch.

The last time I observed this activity, which Rick uses to help prepare the class to work together during their end-of-year camping trip, the students were a bit more successful at listening to each other's ideas and trying them out. When I talk with Rick about this later in the day, he tells me that this class has only just begun to try to solve this challenge and the other group had worked on it longer. He also tells me that he does not interfere as much or direct them about how to solve the challenge. He also does not settle their conflicts because he has done this often enough that he knows they will eventually find a solution and learn to work together. Instead he says he has learned to trust the process and understands that it takes more than a few days.

Later on after lunch, Rick gets out his guitar and sings with the students. By this time of year, they have a whole repertoire of songs, and every student is enthusiastically involved. After playing and singing five or six requests, Rick talks with the class about which songs they want to sing for a school assembly next week. They discuss what criteria they should use to select songs appropriate for children of all ages who will attend the assembly. Nothing is decided before it is time for Reader's and Writer's Workshop, which goes on for the next hour and concludes the academics for the day.

RICK'S TEACHING CONTEXT

Rick continues to teach about 30 to 32 fourth- and fifth-grade students each year in the same classroom at the same school he began teaching in after his graduation from the DTE program in 1987. The school has been on a year-round teaching schedule (14 weeks on, 5 weeks off) for about 8 years. Rick has never particularly liked this schedule because he feels that he has to start school four times a year and thinks that he and the students lose their momentum at the breaks. They then have to spend time getting back into the routines that were flowing so well before the break (Clinical interview, Time 4, May 1993).

Recently, Rick has been able to *loop* with his fourth-grade students so that he has half his class for 2 years. For Rick, this opportunity to work with students over a longer period of time is one of several factors that keeps him from changing schools or school districts. He says it helps him feel like he can make a difference in his students' lives. He feels that looping gives him more freedom to help his students develop into the kind of people he wants them to become, and it also gives them time to get used to him and the expectations he has for them:

> *I have a good situation right now with the looping. I'd like to see that out. I need more practice at that. I want to see what they can—I want to push that and see what it can do. . . . The reason I want 4-5 now is because of this looping thing. It's what I've wanted all along. And I finally got it and I'm happy with it . . . and in the looping situation where half the class is already comfortable here and knows me real well, I can work on how to integrate them quickly and make them empowered to speak and to take leadership. . . . The wonderful thing about the looping thing is that I get two years with them, so I don't feel any pressure. If we spend more time on something that feels real important or they're real invested in, I've got a whole year to make up the time. I'll figure out some way to get all that other stuff done. You know, if we don't study the Gold Rush we'll do it next year. Who cares? I love it. It's so free. It's incredibly freeing. So we've spend more time on certain projects because I don't feel like I have to finish it by the end of the year.* (Clinical interview, Time 6, May 1999)

In his teaching context, Rick also continues to value his colleagues and especially the ongoing support of his principal, Elona Meyers, who he considers to be exemplary (Levin & Ammon, 1996). Rick's principal continues to engage him in discussions of educational methods and theories, and she challenges him to grow as a teacher:

> *I have a principal who understands what I do and values what I do. I'm not sure I could do what I do just anywhere. . . . Not everyone at this school teaches the way I would like them to, but I believe that everybody, every teacher at this school truly cares about kids and is trying to do the right thing for kids. . . . I need to be around people like that.* (Open-ended interview, Time 6, May 1999)
>
> *My principal's great about bringing in whatever's new—it used to be new to me but now I know it about the same time she does, so it's—she's become less of a resource in terms of bringing something new to me, but still the same kind of resource in terms of being up on it. So, when I talk about it with her we're on the same page. I'm not teaching it*

to her, we're learning it together . . . and that's important. (Clinical interview, Time 6, May 1999)

Another important aspect of Rick's teaching context is that he feels part of a community at his school. For example, each Monday at lunchtime, Rick regularly joins several of the teachers at his school to share and talk about their triumphs and tribulations. For Rick, this is an opportunity to talk about teaching, share perspectives, and problem solve with his peers. This is similar to the kinds of experiences he tries to establish for his fourth- and fifth-grade students. He believes strongly that his students should also work in groups, learn from their peers, and be engaged in activities that allow them to understand each other's perspectives and see how others might solve a problem.

I want to be in this really dynamic environment where people are thinking about the same kind of things that I am and they are working with their kids and when I get them they have already had a few years of it and I can take them someplace new with that, they have some background in them. I have a lot of energy for that. What we are doing on these Mondays is a part of that. It is satisfying something for me. I didn't think it would but it really surprised me. (Clinical interview, Time 5, May 1997)

In recent years, Rick has also engaged in several professional development opportunities with other teachers at his school. He feels these are helping him stay fresh and open to sharing and exploring ideas to see how they fit with his philosophy. For example, since 1997, his school's affiliation with the Developmental Study Center (DSC) has been a good match for Rick's goals for his students:

I guess the biggest thing that's changed is that our school got a grant to work with the Developmental Study Center, so they came out here. And I've been incorporating a lot of what happens in Developmental Study Center and a lot of the reading, that along with the cooperative adventures stuff that I've always done . . . and that's probably the biggest change. (Open-ended interview, Time 6, May 1999)

This is the other thing that the DSC helped me do. It helped me to frame what I do. I'm trying to create academically and socially and ethically responsible kids. And it makes—what I do is I look at everything I teach and I think about "Does it meet all three of those criteria?" If it doesn't then I have to stop doing it and I have to do something else. (Clinical Interview, Time 6, May 1999)

In summary, Rick's teaching context remains very stable in that he has taught in the same school for many years. Although he does not relish the year-round schedule at this school, he feels that he has an ideal situation because he is able to loop with his students as they move from fourth to fifth grade, which allows him to work with his students for 2 years. Furthermore, he continues to have the support of a principal whom he admires, as well as teaching colleagues with whom he feels comfortable sharing and problem solving on a weekly basis. He also continues to engage in schoolwide professional development opportunities that engage and challenge him. These professional influences on Rick's thinking, along with the personal and family influences in his life described next, influence Rick's current pedagogical thinking about children's behavior, development, learning, and teaching.

RICK'S PERSONAL LIFE: FAMILY LIFE AND OTHER INFLUENCES

Although Rick does not like the choppiness of the year-round schedule at his school site, he does like having time during the year to volunteer in schools that his daughters attend in another district. In fact, comparing his daughters' classroom curriculum and activities and their achievement with his own classroom practices and his students' achievement has provided him with insights about his own students' needs.

> *My own kids . . . when you look at your own kids going through and you see what is missing from their school. . . . It has made me look really hard at what I am doing. How would a parent look at what's going on in here? Am I communicating well with the parents? Do they understand? Do they care? I think they are just happy that their kids are happy.* (Open-ended interview, Time 6, May 1999)

Besides enjoying the opportunity to talk with his colleagues and educators from the Developmental Study Center about teaching, Rick especially loves being able to discuss teaching and educational ideas with his wife, Julie, who returned to the Graduate School of Education at UC–Berkeley for a Ph.D. in 1998. Julie was also a classroom teacher for many years, and Rick values her opinion.

> *My wife—she's a resource just because she understands all the stuff and we can talk things over. She's a teacher, she knows about this stuff. We can collaborate that way and talk through things that we're in flux about. But she's also a resource for me because she reads so much educational material that I can't get to.* (Open-ended interview, Time 6, May 1999)

From Rick's point of view, his wife's experiences are a big influence on his development as a teacher because her own learning impacts his learning, especially as he tries to apply what he is reading and discussing with her to his own classroom praxis:

I guess the other big influence that's happening is Julie going back to school. She's teaching me all kinds of things, keeping me up on all the literature. . . . There's just too much to read. I can't read that fast. She's good at it, but I pick up snippets and stuff and I let her give me the Cliff Notes version of stuff so I'm learning and relearning a lot of what I know and applying it to what I do. It's nice. It's nice to hear those theorists' names again and hear what they're talking about and thinking about how that fits with what I'm doing and whether I'm really putting that into practice or whether it's just ideals. And then trying, I guess, the big, the struggle is always to think about those things and how do you put that into practice with kids. . . . So that's it's a challenge; it's fun. (Open-ended interview, Time 6, May 1999)

From Rick's perspective, his interactions with his wife greatly influence his thinking because he reads or rereads and discusses educational theory and research with her. This appears to influence his thinking in two ways: First, Rick sees these conversations as opportunities to think more about things that he is in flux about. Second, Rick always tries to use his readings and discussions with his wife as opportunities to think about and solve problems in his classroom, and especially to help him understand individual students in his class.

And then, just books. Books, books, always books. I'll get one author and then that author will lead me to some other author. Just some new take always on how to present this, how to think about it, how to frame it, make it easier for kids, or make it easier for me to understand and make it part of a life. (Clinical interview, Time 6, May 1999)

With regard to the influence of the books he reads, Rick talked about reading William Glasser's work on control theory at Time 5 in 1997 (during his 10th year of teaching) and how this had an influence on his thinking about children's need for fun and freedom. At that time, he said that Glasser's theories helped him shift away from feeling that it was his job to control his students. Reading and discussing Glasser at that time appeared to be a catalyst for helping him enact his understanding that students need to develop internal mechanisms for controlling and accepting responsibility for their own behaviors. In the same way, reading Howard Gardner's theories about multiple intelligences and learning more about learning styles also provided Rick with the impetus to change his curriculum so that every student could find ways to be successful in their learning. Other authors such as Alfie Kohn (specifically his 1993 book, *Punished by Rewards*) and James Comer (writing about involving parents and the community in schools) also influenced Rick's thinking about his students and his teaching context.

I think the biggest change for me, about 2 years ago I read Punished by Rewards, and that radically changed what I do. Not because I was using a really strict behavioral re-

wards system like that, but there were remnants, large remnants, of do this—do this and you'll get something—structure about what went on in here. Which is not to say that there aren't remnants of it still. But I'd say that's the biggest change. I've tried to work really hard to eliminate those things and to have negotiation and thinking about those basic needs without control theory, and thinking about freedom and fun and there are needs for those things. (Open-ended interview, Time 5, May 1997)

In summary, from Rick's perspective, the things that changed personally for him between the Time 4 interviews and observations in 1993 and the Time 6 interview in 1999 included his wife going to graduate school, having ongoing opportunities to share and discuss educational issues with her, and also discussing the books he reads with her and other professionals.

CONTEMPLATING CHANGES

Nevertheless, as many teachers do around their sixth or seventh year of their careers, Rick began thinking about whether he wanted to remain in teaching and stay at his present school. At Time 5 in 1997, during his 10th year of teaching, Rick reflected back on his thoughts about this issue.

I think the biggest change personally has been what I was talking to you before about feeling that everything was passing me by and that there was all that information out there that I'm not accessing or privy to. People are learning things I don't know, which drives me insane. I'm a hunter-gatherer and Julie is just learning all these new things and trying out all these new things. She was filling out her resume this weekend—it has a million things on there—so I've been dealing with that and trying to think through—Do I really want to go off and do a bunch of things? And the answer is NO. I really like teaching, I'm really happy teaching. Do I need to push myself to try some different things? YES, probably, and I think for me that is the answer. It's not so much that I need to re-map my whole life. I need to branch out a little, and so I'm putting myself on some committees. When I first started, I was on every committee possible and then about midway, my 6th year, I said I need to concentrate on my classroom. And now I have been hibernating too long and so I'm trying to get myself out again and get back on the committees and when people offer me things I'm going to say yes instead of no. (Open-ended interview, Time 5, May 1997)

When I interviewed Rick at Time 6 in 1999, toward the end of his 12th year of teaching, he had considered and dismissed the idea of leaving his school and district for another teaching position closer to home. Although he often felt that his daily commute interfered with having more time for his family, Rick decided to stay where he was for several reasons: his principal, having established a reputation at his school, and because he was able to do the things he wanted and needed to do in his teaching, such as looping with his students so that he could work with them for 2 years.

I started thinking about what I have here and . . . I thought about it and I guess what turned me around was that—you know. I have a certain amount of reputation here that's nice. I don't have to explain myself here. I have a principal who understands what I do and values what I do. I'm not sure I could do what I do just anywhere. And I feel like I'm at a school . . . not everyone at this school teaches the way I would like them to, but I believe that everybody, every teacher at this school truly cares about kids and is trying to do the right thing for kids. . . .

    I'm not here for life, I don't think. I don't know. But I realize that—you know my father always used to say, "Never make a change for the worse." I started thinking that this might be one of those times. I might be changing just for change's sake and I don't know if I need to do that. I have a good situation right now with the looping too, I'd like to see that out. . . . (Open-ended interview, Time 6, May 1999)

EXAMPLE OF RICK'S CURRENT PRAXIS

Based on observations of Rick's teaching at Time 5 and Time 6, during his 10th and 12th years of teaching, it became clear that his thoughts and actions are highly coordinated. That is, what he talks about in his interviews and what he does in the classroom are very congruent. His stated goal is to help his students develop into academically, socially, and ethically responsible people. Toward this end, Rick designs learning activities to meet this goal. For example, he uses Literature Circles and Writer's Workshop as structures for teaching reading and writing to his fourth and fifth graders.

When I observed in May 1999, Rick's students had already selected chapter books they wanted to read from about eight class sets available to them. Earlier, Rick previewed each of these books for the students and allowed them to make their own choices. They were already well into reading their self-selected novels during this particular observation. After lunch, the students spread out around the room to read either alone or in pairs and then regrouped to discuss their reading in their small Literature Circles. The discussion leader for the day posed a question from a series of generic questions Rick had brainstormed with them earlier. After talking with those who were reading the same novel, Rick asked them to meet with a student from a different group to talk about their respective books.

Following this, the students each wrote in their literature journal about today's reading and small-group discussion. When they finished recording their most recent responses to the novel and the discussion with their peers, they began to work on their writing. The afternoon routine of Reader's Workshop flowing into Writer's Workshop lasted for over an hour. During this time, Rick met with each literature group briefly to talk with them about their book. He made sure that each student told him something about their reading or the group's discussion today. A parent volunteer arrived in time to work with several of the Literature Circle groups and stayed to help conference with the students about their writing.

For over an hour, these fourth and fifth graders worked with their Literature Circle groups, met with Rick to talk about their book, and then worked independently or sometimes with a peer on their writing. The shift from reading to writing was very subtle because the students were working at different paces in both areas. They were also self-directed and clearly knew what they were supposed to be doing.

Of course, Rick monitored the whole group, but his focus was on talking with small groups of students about their reading and then talking with individuals about their writing. Rick did not solve any problems that arose for the students or tell them how to do something. Instead I observed him asking questions of the literature groups and individual students. However, he did remind both individuals and the whole class at times of his expectations and their current responsibilities.

Observing how Rick set up and facilitated reading and writing in his classroom matched what he talked about in his interview at the end of the day:

> What I wanted the afternoon to be is really Language Workshop. We call it Writer's Workshop rather than Language Workshop just for them because it's too confusing. They need the separation in language, but basically what I want them doing all afternoon is reading and writing, making choices about that, and learning how to do what adults do, which is book "talk" and write "talk." And so that's what the whole process is. The idea is that they choose a book . . . they choose a group—they have to choose a mixed group. For them mixed means 4th and 5th grade mixed and boy and girl mixed. They decided on that. That is what mixed was going to mean. They first choose a group. They then together choose a book that they all agree to read. They find good places to read. They sit down and they read. They figure out how to take turns. They figure out how much each person's going to read before the next person reads.
>
> And then when they're finished, I stop them at a set time . . . and their job is to pick somebody to summarize each day. Somebody different every day. . . . And everybody else's job is to add on anything that they missed-anything important. . . . We've talked a lot about what minor details are and what major details are. And then after they've finished the summary, then they're supposed to choose a discussion question—something a little more meaty to discuss. What are the characters like in this story? How are these characters similar to stories they've read—the characters in other stories they've read? How is this book similar to another book that they might have read? If you were a character facing the decision that the character is in the book, how would you have handled it? There's a list [of discussion questions] and we've gone through them all earlier. First I just let them go through every single one of them in order. Then I started giving them 4 or 5 to choose from each day and doing a different 4 or 5. Now they probably need to do that again. They've forgotten since we've gone on break. They've forgotten all the options they have, but anyway, they have the list someplace, too.
>
> Then, they come and tell me when their group is finished with that and they go on with their writing project. They have a notebook and they are working on some kind of

project. Some of them are taking off on something that they're reading and they're writing response is extending the story or they're rewriting the story from a different point of view. Others of them are working on different kinds of projects from comic book writing to . . . a bunch of kids now are really into horror stories, which is really great. I hope they keep it up because writing a horror story is a great way to talk about suspense and dialogue and drama in writing—you have to be descriptive to write horror or it's not horrifying. There's nothing horrifying with "the guy walked in and stabbed him with a knife three times." So I'm hoping they stick with that. . . . (Clinical interview, Time 6, May 1999)

In asking Rick to elaborate on what has been going on with his teaching of reading and writing in the time since my last observation, Rick described changes in his praxis in this way:

I think the big difference that's changed in the last few years for me is that I've really started to—I really wanted to know more about what each kid could do and where their thought processes were going and why they were writing the kinds of things they were writing. And how to get them from one place to the next—to move them further along and to be more individualized about that. So I've really made an effort to conference with them individually much more often both in reading and writing, and when they come to me I'm asking them about what they decided to discuss. I don't really want to hear the summary. The summary is kind of inconsequential to me. . . . So I'm looking for what kind of things they're discussing. I want to hear from each person about what their discussion was, what they thought about it, what was their idea. I want to impress upon them that I'm expecting each person to be involved, be part of that group. That's the part that's really much better now. When they have discussions, 90% of them are really involved in that discussion. They know they are supposed to and they get into it and they do it so I'm happy about that. So it's just I want to make sure that I have—the thing for me now is that I want to make sure that I touch base with every single kid in reading and writing every day. (Clinical interview, Time 6, May 1999)

From this example of Rick's classroom practice, it is clear that his pedagogical actions in the classroom are congruent with his expressed goal that everything he does should have academic, social, and ethical value for his students or it is not worth doing. It is also clear that he has shifted the responsibility of learning to his students by establishing situations where they are responsible for making choices, working together with their peers, solving problems in their groups, and learning in a social context.

RICK'S CURRENT PEDAGOGICAL BELIEFS

Every time I observe and interview Rick, I ask him what goals he has as a teacher and what he most wants to accomplish, which is one of the clinical interview questions. Most recently, in May 1999, Rick responds clearly and succinctly: "*Academically, socially and ethically responsible kids. Kids who know how to win in any contest*" (Clinical interview, Time 6, May 1999).

In response to my question about how he sees his students as being different after being with him, Rick states:

> *I guess the general kind of lens that I'm looking for is a sense of self-evaluation. The ability to value giving your personal best is very important to me. It's one I'd like to pass on to them. So we spend a lot of time talking about that. What your best looks like. . . . They self assess a lot. I ask them—I cause them to do it a lot. Through portfolios and through individual assignments and through—and not just on content, but everything—you know we did it outside, too. You know we talked about getting them to visualize. That skill of being able to visualize and see the possibility of something different in order to get beyond the concrete, the factual—and see how it could be different.* (Clinical interview, Time 6, May 1999)

He also describes the teacher's role in the learning process in the following way:

> *I would describe my role as the . . . definitely that facilitator model. I see myself not so much as teaching content, but teaching them how to learn, how to access things. And so I spend a lot of time working with them, thinking about how to prepare themselves, how to have the right tools available, how to—kind of clueing them in on the social customs, and the educational customs, and academic customs, and ethical customs of a society. And then how to research—how do people who are good at math go about the business of problem solving? . . . My role also is to give them space. Let them struggle. Make them feel comfortable struggling. Create an environment where struggling is valued, where effort—pain staking effort is valued. And an understanding of the value of practice and the value of mistakes as information . . . in a place where they're supported and have people collaborate with them.* (Clinical interview, Time 6, May 1999)

CHANGES IN RICK'S PEDAGOGICAL BELIEFS OVER TIME

Although these responses appear similar to the answers Rick has given to these same questions over time, especially seeing himself as a facilitator and guide of student learning, there are qualitative changes evident in his thinking. For example, at Time 2 in 1987, when Rick was about to graduate from the DTE program at UC–Berkeley, he stated that he wanted to be a facilitator and set up a learning environment and experiences for his students and then guide them through their interactions. At that time, Rick's overall pedagogical understanding was coded as Level 3 in the Ammon and Hutcheson Model of Pedagogical Thinking because he was not quite able to think about the importance of teachers knowing what they want their students to get out of particular learning experiences, just that they want to provide such an environment (see Appendix A). At that time, setting up learning opportunities seemed to be enough for Rick.

By Time 3 in 1990, after 3 years of teaching, Rick had a much better sense of not only what he wanted his students to learn from his lessons, but also how he was going to begin to help them think like a mathematician or a social scientist. He still expected to be a facilitator and guide who would be there to ask questions at the right time, and he believed in promoting disequilibrium, challenging students' thinking, and encouraging risk-taking (Levin & Ammon, 1992). Hence, although Rick still believed in the value of earlier thinking about providing a hands-on, active learning environment, and he continued to believe that his role as the teacher was to guide and facilitate learning, his pedagogical understandings were becoming less global and more differentiated. However, as developmental stage models predict (Kohlberg & Armon, 1984), Rick did not completely abandon earlier ways of thinking. Rather, he included them in his more advanced schema of pedagogy as it developed. In fact, his idea that his role should be one of a facilitator and guide became a logical necessity. However, what continued to develop over time—with more experience and thoughtful reflection on his role as a teacher—was Rick's understanding of how he could facilitate learning and a more purposeful approach to setting up the learning environment for his students.

By Time 4 in 1993, when Rick had been teaching the same age students in the same school for 6 years, his understanding of pedagogy continued to advance (Levin & Ammon, 1996). At this time, he still felt the teacher should guide and facilitate learning, but he saw that this should happen in both social and academic domains. He was also beginning to encourage his students to think about their own thinking and learning (metacognitive thinking) in much the same way he was thinking metacognitively about his praxis. At Time 4, Rick saw that his role as a teacher still included asking challenging questions, offering choices to students, and encouraging independence, but he now saw that these things had to be done in both the social and academic worlds of his students. After 6 years of teaching, he understood that learning is interconnected with everything social and academic as well as the child's development, which is a Level 5 way of thinking about pedagogy according to the Ammon and Hutcheson model. At this time, he also understood that it is the students who have to resolve their disequilibrium, not the teacher, and that when students experience disequilibrium they often have to reorganize everything they know into a new way of thinking about things. This kind of thinking represents many aspects of Level 5 thinking in Ammon and Hutcheson's model, and Rick's thinking about pedagogy was becoming more integrated within and across domains—also a Level 5 way of thinking.

By Time 5 in 1997 and Time 6 in 1999, when Rick had been teaching fourth and fifth graders for 10 and 12 years, respectively, he continued to see the teacher's role as that of facilitator and guide. However, by his 10th year of teaching (1997), Rick also believed that his job included setting parameters or boundaries for the learning activities and then guiding students choices within those purposeful boundaries. He could no longer imagine just setting out materials to explore or designing learning activities without specific academic and social purposes in mind. For example, he routinely and explicitly integrated academic lessons (such as language arts) with developing students' skills (such as listening) while also encouraging the social needs of students this age (such as developing empathy and perspective-taking while learning to listen to others as they worked in groups). By his 10th year, he also began to embrace and use the concepts of learning styles and multiple intelligences as means to provide various access points to learning opportunities for his diverse students and as ways to meet their individual needs.

At Time 5, after 10 years of teaching, Rick's actions and classroom practices were in sync with his level of pedagogical understanding of teaching, learning, behavior, and development. In fact, the examples he provided in his interviews to explain his thinking and the lessons I observed were very tightly coupled. Everything about his praxis was integrated with his pedagogical understanding, which is an excellent example of Level 5 understanding in the Ammon and Hutcheson model. However, at Time 5 in 1997, Rick still felt that he should be in charge of making this all happen for his students. He was not content to provide catalysts for helping his students learn. Rather, he felt he had to control this and make it happen. He felt that he was not only the facilitator and guide for learning, but also the director.

ADVANCES IN RICK'S PEDAGOGICAL THINKING: IS THERE A LEVEL 6?

After observing Rick for the sixth time in 1999, which was near the end of his 12th year of teaching in the same context, I began to wonder if there was an even more advanced or sophisticated way to think about pedagogy than described as Level 5 in the Ammon and Hutcheson model. I wondered if there could be a sixth level and what a Level 6 way of thinking about pedagogy would look like. However, I was doubtful that I could describe it given limitations in my own development as a teacher, teacher educator, and researcher. However, after reanalyzing his interviews over time from 1985 to 1999, charting and comparing his responses side by side in tables, and connecting them to my observations in his classroom, I believe (based on Rick's thoughts and actions) that there may be a Level 6 way to understand pedagogy that is qualitatively different from Level 5.

Based on Rick's interview and observation data, I suggest that the following features may be hallmarks of Level 6 understanding of pedagogy:

- The goal of instruction is for students to attain the attitudes, skills, and
self-awareness to be responsible for their own learning, although understanding that if students do not have a passion or a need for learning they
may not be ready for this.
- To obtain these learning objectives, students must learn to be responsible for their own learning and behavior both individually and within their
groups; they must be allowed to select their own groups, make their own
rules within their groups, and resolve their own conflicts; they must become
aware of their own learning styles; and they must also begin to think
metacognitively about their learning.
- Teachers teach by having academic, social, and ethical purposes for all
learning activities. They must know each student's thought processes well
enough to differentiate instruction for every child when needed. They must
touch base with every child every day about their learning, and they must
regularly and consciously use problems and conflicts to model, discuss, and
think metacognitively with the students about possible resolutions.

If these are hallmarks of Level 6 thinking, then the teacher is still a facilitator and guide, but no longer feels the need to control the outcomes of instruction or determine the outcome of any problem solving. Rather, the
teacher's role is to set up a learning environment that allows students to
learn how to make good choices, understand the consequences of their actions and decisions, resolve conflicts, and take risks. Furthermore, the
teacher must do all this in a thoughtful and conscious way that includes
consideration of the social, academic, and ethical dimensions of the problems to be solved or material to be learned.

CHANGES IN RICK'S METAPHORS

In addition, comparing Rick's metaphors for teaching across time is telling
and represents another way to show how his thinking about pedagogy has
changed and developed over time. His current image for his teaching may
also provide a good metaphor for Level 6 thinking.

In the beginning, Rick told me that his metaphor for teaching and learning had to do with growing: "*It used to be the plant metaphor. That's always a
good one for me. . . . I used the plant one for a long time.*" When I asked Rick
about a metaphor for his teaching in 1997, at the end of 10 years of teaching, his response was the same as it had been in 1993 after 6 years of teaching. His metaphor was still the *Monkey's fist,* which represents a complex

knot of rope that Rick wears daily around his neck. The three strands of the rope are symbols for trust, risk, and cooperation. One of the concepts behind the Monkey's fist is that you cannot achieve or learn without making mistakes and taking challenges, and that you cannot really do these things without trust, risk, and collaboration.

Rick's students have the opportunity to earn the Monkey's fist necklace during or after their annual year-end camping trip, although not everyone earns it their first year with him, and some never earn it. For Rick and his students, the Monkey's fist represents that they have (a) pushed themselves to try something that is difficult for them personally; (b) made a good, conscious decision to take risks; and (c) learned something about themselves as a result. Rick explains the Monkey's fist this way:

> When I talk to them about the Monkey's fist, I talk to them about the marble that is inside. For me it symbolizes the challenge that I work on for myself and that I choose for myself every year. And I talk about what it is and how my wearing it doesn't say that I conquered it. It's not a trophy but it is something that reminds me. It's there and it tells me that this is the thing that you said you were going to try to do, and that I screw up all the time, but it reminds me that I need to keep putting effort into that problem and it's not something I'm going to overcome—it's just always going to be there. (Clinical interview probe, Time 5, May 1997)

In 1999, toward the end of his 12th year of teaching, Rick's metaphor had changed. This surprised me at the time, but in thinking about Rick's newest metaphor for his teaching—that of a *flowing river*—I believe it is appropriate and captures a new quality to his thinking about pedagogy, especially about teaching and learning.

> There's something about water now that's been grabbing me lately. Something about being on a river. And how rivers deal with obstacles . . . sometimes they're powerful enough to push through them and sometimes they don't need to be that powerful; they can just go around or under and I guess—that's important for me now because of the flexibility that that allows for. There are some times that I have to just be determined and plow through something and other times, that's just beating your head against the wall and there's other ways to be creative about it. (Clinical interview probe, Time 6, May 1999)

According to Csikszentmihalyi (1975), flow is, "the holistic sensation that people feel with total involvement" (p. 36). The person in a state of flow "experiences a unified flowing from one moment to the next, in which he is in control of his actions, and in which there is little distinction between self and environment, between stimulus and responses, or between past, present, and future" (p. 36). In Rick's case, I believe this captures the essence of his total immersion in his teaching, his attunement to his students' individual needs, and his conscious striving to meet those needs at every moment of the day. It also matches his goals for his students as they work to become a cohesive unit able to solve their own problems and understanding of the needs of others in the group and not just their own. Being in a state of flow means that you are working in harmony with others and looking after the good of the whole and not just the parts, which is certainly a stated goal that Rick has for his students. Perhaps a Level 6 understanding of pedagogy represents flow as well.

The concept of flow can be traced back to the eastern philosophy of Tao, which urges harmony and the natural order of things. Taoists believe that there is a natural order of things in life and that change, like a flowing river, is perpetual. Taoists also believe that we can best facilitate flow by unblocking it and removing obstacles from its way, which aptly captures Rick's current efforts as a facilitator and guide in his classroom as discussed earlier.

SUMMARY OF CHANGES IN RICK'S PEDAGOGICAL
BELIEFS AND PRAXIS

Influences on the nature, sources, and evolution of Rick's praxis and his pedagogical beliefs appear to be both professional and personal. Personally, the development of Rick's thinking about pedagogy over the past several years has been influenced by seeing his own children develop and learn, especially as he compares their experiences after observing and volunteering in their classrooms with his own students' experiences and development. Rick's personal life also overlaps with his professional life. This is partly because he is married to another educator with whom he shares professional interests, but also because he has opportunities for ongoing dialogue with her about issues and theories of teaching and learning. Reading and discussing books about education, which Rick does regularly, is also a place where Rick's personal and professional lives overlap because he often discusses ideas he is reading and thinking about with his wife, his principal, friends, and sometimes his colleagues.

Professionally, Rick's thinking about pedagogy continues to develop in a school climate where he has colleagues he values, ongoing professional development opportunities that he can connect to, and a principal who supports and challenges him to continue thinking about pedagogical issues. At Time 5 in 1997, Rick described some of these influences this way:

I'm at the point where these Monday meetings are good for me because I'm trying to explain what I'm doing to somebody else and I'm really having to process it so much more deeply and catching myself in ways that I wouldn't if I was just doing it. The process of talking about it has really helped me. I am hoping this Developmental Studies Center project goes through and that will be a great source of change for me for sure. Some of the people in that group are also readers of educational literature and we've been tossing around titles to read. (Clinical interview, Time 5, May 1997)

Two years later, at Time 6 in 1999, Rick described what happened in his class as a result of his professional development experiences with the Developmental Study Center:

I've been incorporating a lot of what happens in Developmental Study Center and a lot of the reading, along with the cooperative adventures stuff that I've always done. . . . It was only a year but, you know, it was enough for me. I went on and I read a bunch of stuff and found all these really good books about it and I got what I needed from it . . . it wasn't so much an eye-opening thing. It wasn't something I didn't know, but it put . . . into terms these ideas about "fairness" and "kindness" and "caring" and "responsibility." Being able to put it into those kinds terms for kids is really important. I was always talking about those kinds of things. I was always talking about these kinds of values all the time. But labeling them for kids and having that be a consistent part of what we talk about has made a huge difference. It's just so much, it's just being taught better. You know, it's the difference between teaching something for the first time and then going back to it and fixing all the problems, working out the kinks. It just feels smooth, it feels easy. (Open-ended interview, Time 6, May 1999)

For Rick, opportunities to read and discuss books at both home and school, followed by his own efforts to test out his thoughts in his classroom, have influenced the development of his praxis and impacted his thoughts and actions. "*I sit at home and I think, 'OK, is this going to meet their needs academically, socially, ethically?' If it doesn't, then I change it*" (Open-ended interview, Time 6, May 1999).

IS RICK'S PEDAGOGICAL DEVELOPMENT UNIQUE?

Many of the factors—personal or professional—that might impact a teacher's development, especially a teacher's understanding of pedagogy, may not be the same as those that have influenced Rick's thoughts and actions. Other educators, even career teachers like Rick with many years of experience working with the same age group of students in a stable and supportive context, might not continue to develop their pedagogical understanding. For example, not all teachers continue to read and think about educational theory and research beyond their formal training. Not all teachers have personal relationships with other educators beyond their colleagues at school or have the opportunity to visit other schools and classrooms to observe and work with children in different contexts. Not all teachers even identify their sense of self as a teacher (Nias, 1989a). Not all teachers work in supportive places, experience effective professional development, or have quality principals who nurture their growth. Furthermore, there seem to be personal, internal factors that are necessary for continued growth as a teacher.

For Rick, a combination of many factors, personal and professional, have influenced his development as a teacher and pedagogue. Rick is a consummate professional who sees teaching as a career and profession, not just a job. He continues to develop and work toward enacting the vision he has for his students. Not every educator has a vision, much less the same highly sophisticated understanding of what children can be and do that Rick has as part of his vision. Many teachers espouse the belief that "all children can learn," but few people work hard at making this come true. Furthermore, the belief that all children can learn is a rather global, generalized view, which Rick has actualized in a more complex and sophisticated way, as he states his goal that: "*I'm trying to create academically and socially and ethically responsible kids. And it makes—what I do is I look at everything I teach and I think about, 'Does it meet all three of those criteria?' If it doesn't, then I have to stop doing it and I have to do something else*" (Clinical Interview, Time 6, May 1999).

LOOKING AHEAD

When I asked Rick at Time 6 in 1999 about his goals and future plans, he articulated a desire to continue working on areas he feels he has not yet addressed. He talked about two things: parents and racism. We had the following interchange, which captures a lot about how Rick thinks about and deals with his own challenges as a teacher:

> *I guess I just want to refine all these things. I guess lately—this is very recently—just before our break in April we had a district-wide workshop and we had this guy come in and talk to us about racism. It affected me pretty heavily. I started thinking about who the kids are in my class who get in trouble a lot. He talked a lot about how it feels for him as an African-American man, feeling that wherever he goes he's always in the minority and how rarely he's in a situation where he sees people who look like him, who have the same kind of cultural background as him, and where he feels comfortable immediately upon entering the room. And I started thinking a lot about how it must be for a lot of these kids who come in here.*
>
> *I have this style of running the classroom. For the kids who also share that style, it's great. It's no problem. For any kid who comes in this classroom who doesn't share that style, it's a different way of doing of things. They're always walking in here having to shift gears in order to be successful. So I think that's the other thing that I'm really going to start giving some thought to is how to . . . I can't change my style but I can—I think what I can do is I can get enough—make things so—how can I say this—I think I can give enough power away, enough control away to change what the room looks like, to*

change how kids perceive what's happening in the room—to make it more accessible to different styles. It's still in the thinking stage. But I know I have to do something about that.

He sort of challenged everybody in the room, that if you weren't willing to do something about it, then you might as well not listen to the rest of what he was going to say, because it wasn't going to matter. It wouldn't matter how disturbing any of the statistics he gave were going to be. It wasn't going to matter that 75% of people of color—kids of color—are going to fail. None of that stuff's going to matter. You've got to first be willing, you know. So I sat there and I though well, am I—I've got to be willing. So now, I have to do something about it. . . . So that struck a chord with me. He spoke to me like I would speak to my kids, so that worked.

But it's—the other thing he said—it was good 'cause he got up there and he didn't try to give everybody answers. He didn't have any answers. What he said was, "If you're serious about this you gotta go find answers," and I started thinking about that. For me, that means I need to go read about this. I need to go find somebody who's done something about this and find out how they do it and whether they do it well. Whether it's going to work, I have to try it. And then I have to see if it works for me. And then I have to go talk with some more people. And then I have to get in touch with these people's parents. I have to find out where they do come from and I have to find out what does work for them at home. And then I have to try and make what happens in here look something like that and all while still doing right for the kids that it works for now. And so I don't know when that's going to happen, but I know about it. It has to sit with me for awhile. I have to think it through. Starting next year, I'll do something about it. It'll not be the right thing but it'll be something and then we'll go from there. (Clinical interview probe, Time 6, May 1999)

RICK'S STORY . . . IN HIS OWN WORDS
. . . SUMMER 2000

Throughout this longitudinal study, I interviewed and observed Rick regularly every few years. I tried to describe his development as a teacher, particularly his understanding of pedagogy, teaching and learning, and behavior and development across time (Levin & Ammon, 1992, 1996). Recently, I asked Rick to respond to some questions in writing as another way to try to capture his story. Here are Rick's words, written during the summer of 2000 toward the end of his 13th year of teaching fourth and fifth graders in Vallejo, California:

I am currently teaching a looping 4th/5th-grade clustered GATE class of 32 students in Vallejo, California. The population of the school is multiethnic, with about a third African American, a third European American, and the rest a mix of Asian Americans. I've been teaching at Federal Terrace Elementary for 13 years with the same principal, Elona Meyer. As for my students, each year is so different. This last year I had a preponderance of GATE (Gifted and Talented) students, with about a third of the kids slightly below or below grade level. Every kid in my class could read, which is unusual for our school and my class. I usually have a solid third of the class that is Chapter 1, including two or three kids who qualify for resource. I don't usually let them go with the parent's permission because what they do in resource is a lot of drills with math or reading that seem counterproductive to what I'm trying to give them in class. I therefore work out an intervention plan that happens as part of the normal day. The other unusual thing about this past year was the diversity of the class, which was not very. The fourth-grade group I got is almost entirely White, and these will comprise my fifth grade this coming year. I normally have a much more diverse class, although it does not fully reflect the diversity of our school.

Currently, my thinking about my teaching practices centers around the idea of meeting the social, ethical, and academic needs of children within the context of the variety of the developmental range of the class and the differing learning styles and cultures of individuals and groups within the class community. As a teacher, I believe it is my job to empower students to learn how to learn, how to build and engage in effective social relationships, how to question and process information, how to create connections between what they know and what they wish to know, and how to make productive decisions regarding all of the above. I believe strongly in constructivist theory, which in practice allows me to facilitate the integration of learning through varying levels of questioning and challenges that cause the disequilibrium necessary for growth. We value mistakes as information, build a community of learning and support through consistent interaction in different sized groups, explicit teaching of conflict-resolution strategies and the art of negotiation, and dedicated time to sharing all of our personal lives and reflecting on our strengths and weaknesses as whole people (as opposed to simply students and a teacher). The curriculum must meet all of these needs to have a place in my classroom and is frequently altered so that it can be done cooperatively, actively, and with a spirit of "our success is my success" and vice versa. All subjects are taught within the context of personally challenging each learner, and lesson objectives are broad enough to allow access to everyone and an appropriate level of difficulty for each access point so as to promote optimal development for each student. Furthermore, there is an effort made to be sensitive to the different learning styles within the classroom so that concepts and projects can be approached from visual, auditory, tactile, or other modalities.

I came to this style of teaching from a meandering road of personal and professional influences. I began in education working at a school for autistic children in San Diego while studying behavioral psychology at UCSD. The school's teaching philosophy was heavily entrenched in Skinnerian operant learning. With that practical background coupled with classes stressing this method in college, I began my teaching credential program at Cal as a staunch behaviorist. Almost immediately, the tenets of the Developmental Teacher Education (DTE) program began to reverse my ideas of both teaching and classroom management. While I had read a great deal of Piaget during my undergraduate years, it was outside of my practice and so was submerged in my subconscious mind waiting to be awakened by the excitement of this way of thinking about children that was presented in DTE. I struggled greatly as a student teacher trying hard to make the change in practice while often relying on simplistic behavioral tricks to manage students rather than teach them. Throughout the 2 years of the program, my gift as a teacher was the ability to form relationships with the children (i.e., know them personally, which I realized was the key to teaching them). However, I knew very little about curriculum (how to deliver it effectively, how to integrate it into the classroom culture, etc.). This is what I've been working on for the past 13 years.

My first influence postcollege was my principal, Elona Meyer, who encouraged me to go to every workshop possible, which thankfully I did. One of the most important was getting to see and listen to Donald Graves while reading his definitive book on Writers' Workshop. This became the basis for all my teaching. When I saw students working on different projects, learning daily about the beauty of language and the excitement of expressing themselves, making decisions about their own learning, and learning how to work together and support each other's growth as writers within the context of an actual writing community, I knew that everything else I taught had to somehow be like that.

Next came Dave Nettell, a former teacher/park ranger who operated a company called Cooperative Adventures. He began doing workshops for teachers that helped them build classroom communities where students felt safe to take physical and emotional risks while learning how to work together cooperatively. He also led camping trips wherein students would engage in group challenges that tested them individually and cooperatively while helping them to emotionally and intellectually metacognate through their difficulties and accomplishments. I have taken my class camping with Dave now for 9 years, each time learning more about how to support my students' efforts to build deeply satisfying relationships that result in better learning opportunities. He has also turned me on to many different authors who have influenced me as well—most notably, Alfie Kohn.

Alfie Kohn's books on the evils of competition and behavioral teaching have led me to refine my classroom into what I described earlier. Both his writings and those out of the Developmental Studies Center here in Oakland, California, which stress the social and ethical development of children as well as the academic, have provided me with an essential frame within which to judge the merits of my teaching. Will this lesson promote their ethical development or will it cause them to compete with each other? What happens to those who finish first or last? How do we treat each other in a group project? How do we divide up the work fairly? How do we make decisions about procedures in the classroom? Any question that arises can be answered through the lens of this frame.

Finally, but not chronologically, has been the influence of my wife and children. Julie, my wife, is also an educator, first with elementary children, then adults in a teacher education context, and now a Ph.D. student at Cal studying teacher education. She has been my sounding board, my avenue into new opportunities for learning, my link to recent research findings, and my defender against the pressures of the back to basics militia. My children have been the humbling and perspective-taking influence I needed to help me better understand the rigors of the parents of my classroom and their need to be involved in productive ways in their children's school lives. They have helped me open up the doors of my classroom to parents and bring them more into the community.

While I believe the foregoing is constantly in need of refining and my relationship with Dave and the DTE program, which supplies me with student teachers who cause me to reflect on what to do continuously, there is a more pressing issue on my mind now that is leading me away from further teaching development and into the political arena. The current climate of high-stakes testing, performance incentives in education, voucher initiatives, and public school bashing that exists in California weighs heavily on my mind. The intense pressure is being felt at every level in our district, and I see the results. Teachers who used to teach the love of literature now spend countless hours drilling phonics and sight words. Daily oral language lessons consume an hour of the day, and the

*gains we have made as a school to commit to schoolwide community-building efforts are
fading away as more and more teachers feel compelled to start practice testing months in
advance or are busily scoring individual assessment data and recording it in compli-
cated matrices. Student morale is eroding, excitement for learning is dying, and the message of "learn this now or you're stupid" is loudly heard throughout the school. As a result, I am very focused now on fighting this trend in my community, Vallejo, and the
state, and I can see that that is the direction my teaching is heading.*

*The only thing I can think of that I have not covered is that I have been fortunate to
know older teachers who were still dynamic in their later years. I have known plenty who
regard the job as just a job and complain constantly about anything, but some still love
teaching, still love children, still crave learning more about their craft, still view what
they do as all important. That is who I want to be, and it is a vision of this constantly
developing and growing teacher that I keep as my model.*

*   *   *

AFTERWORD

To update the reader: Rick continues to teach fourth and fifth graders at
the same school in Vallejo, California. He also continues to work toward
helping his students develop into academically, socially, and ethically responsible people.

Part III

ANALYSIS

Chapter 7

Answering the "So What?" Question: What Do These Case Studies Tell Us?

Whenever I engage in research or work with graduate students or talk with other educational researchers, I always ask these questions either explicitly or implicitly: "*So what? So what is the point of this research? So what can we learn from this study?*" In fact, I believe the "So What?" question is very important to ask during the planning, analysis, interpretation, and dissemination stages of every research study. In keeping with my beliefs, I must ask myself these same questions: So what do these teachers' stories have to tell us about teacher development, especially about the development of teachers' thinking in the pedagogical domain? The answer to this question rests with what case studies of these four teachers have to say with regard to these five questions:

- When teachers face the reality of classroom life and become socialized into the profession and school culture, do they lose what they learned during a teacher preparation program?
- How do teachers' pedagogical understandings grow and change over time?
- What influences teachers' thinking about pedagogy? What personal and professional influences in teachers' lives influence their understanding of teaching and learning throughout their careers?
- What do other theories of teacher development have to say about teachers' lives?
- What lessons can be learned from longitudinal case studies of teachers' thinking about pedagogy?

In this chapter, I offer my answers to each of these questions based on a cross-case analysis of the four case studies presented in this book. Obviously my answers are not the only possible answers to these questions, so I challenge you as the reader to think about what makes sense to you based on their stories and given your experiences with teachers in your context. I also invite you to think about what I might have missed or misinterpreted in the case studies presented in this book. I hope that as you read this chapter, you think about how you can apply what you understand about the development of teachers' pedagogical thinking based on the case studies of these teachers. Perhaps the lives of the teachers in this book will have some additional value if you can use what you learn from them in your own teaching and in mentoring other teachers.

To reiterate, this longitudinal study of the personal and professional lives of four educators was undertaken to understand the complex nature of teachers' pedagogical understandings as they develop and to uncover influences on teachers' pedagogical thinking over time. These influences include (a) teachers' prior beliefs and personal values; (b) professional experiences as teachers (e.g., their formal teacher preparation, various ongoing professional development opportunities, and day-to-day classroom experiences with students); (c) the contexts in which they find themselves teaching (e.g., supportive or nonsupportive colleagues and administrators, changing school and political climates); (d) their personal relationships both in and out of school (e.g., the influence of friends, mentors, colleagues, and family); and (e) other life circumstances (e.g., children, health, and changing educational policy climate). What also emerged from this study are three important themes that shape the development of teachers' thinking in the pedagogical domain: (a) The importance of a support system, (b) the necessity for ongoing professional development, and (c) a propensity for reflection and metacognitive thinking. These three factors are so essential for teacher development in the pedagogical domain that I believe teacher education programs must find more and better ways to foster support for teachers, offer them continuous professional development and other opportunities to learn, and cultivate their ability to reflect and think metacognitively about their pedagogy.

This chapter is organized around the five main research questions that guided this study. In answering each question, I looked across all four cases for evidence to support my claims based on the longitudinal data that comprise the foundation for each case. In this final chapter, I also describe several other models of teacher development. I conclude with recommendations for ways that teacher education programs can support preservice teachers so they are likely to continue developing their understandings about pedagogy as they graduate and move into the real world of today's classrooms.

DO TEACHERS LOSE WHAT THEY LEARNED DURING A TEACHER PREPARATION PROGRAM?

The simple answer to this question is that "it depends." Whether teachers lose what they learn during their teacher preparation program, whether teacher education *washes out* as some researchers have written (Lortie, 1975; Veenman, 1984; Zeichner & Liston, 1987; Zeichner & Tabachnik, 1981; Zeichner, Tabachnik, & Densmore, 1987), depends on several factors. Among these factors are (a) the nature of individual teachers and their propensity to learn and apply what they learn as teachers, (b) the focus and structure of the teacher education programs they attended, and (c) the nature of the various contexts in which teachers find themselves throughout their careers. I do not answer "it depends" to the washout question to equivocate. Rather, my response to this question captures much of the complexity of the teaching–learning situation for preservice teachers learning to teach in vastly different teacher preparation programs and then applying their knowledge, skills, and dispositions to teaching–learning situations in the unique contexts in which they find themselves during the induction years and beyond. However, I do answer the washout question with an unequivocal "NO" for the teachers who are the focus of this longitudinal research. The teachers in this study did *not* lose what they learned in their teacher education program. In fact, I believe what they learned in their teacher education program about children's development and learning, and about teaching, is still foundational in their thinking about these topics today. To support this claim, I present evidence from across the cases in this study and offer my reasons for making this claim.

Evidence Countering the Washout Effect

Throughout the interviews and observations on which this book is based, these educators articulated their understanding and application of the developmental-constructivist theory they learned as preservice teachers in the DTE program. Sometimes their current level of understanding and applying developmental-constructivist theory to their practice was implied in their interview responses, but often is was stated explicitly. In fact, they talked about Piaget and developmental-constructivist theory in every interview, although none of the clinical interview or open-ended questions ever asked directly about theories or theorists (see Appendix B). Instead, their responses and actions revealed that their understanding of theory is foundational to their thinking. Even in their most recent reflective writing, which was undertaken 15 years after entering the DTE program, these educators refer to developmental and constructivist theory. For example, Julie wrote that, "*Children need to explore materials and concepts on their own to capital-*

ize on the brain's desire to make sense of the world," which sounds like something Piaget could have written. Sandy wrote about how her understanding of children's development always underlies her thinking and planning:

> *. . . I am still very committed to developmental education and believe that instruction should match the individual learning styles and the development of the student. Being a teacher is fascinating work. I love to watch the children grow and develop during the school year. Since they come from such different backgrounds and experiences, I know that no two children are the same. Therefore, I try to understand where each child is developmentally and use that knowledge to guide our work together for the rest of the year.*

Ralph's understanding of developmental-constructivist theory has also evolved and broadened due to his experiences in several different teaching contexts. As he notes, he now questions whether Piaget's model of cognitive development applies in all cultural contexts, but he still believes in the basic tenets of developmental-constructivist theory as posited by Piaget and other constructivists.

> *I continue to believe in a developmental approach to teaching and learning—but I don't see this as the same kind of process I once did. I question the universality of the Piagetian model certainly. What I retain is the conviction that it is UNDERSTANDING, and not just information, that matters—and that all learners construct the framework of their own understanding. I have broadened my thinking as to how many different ways that framework gets built, and to the different pressures and needs that shape children's learning.*

Rick also expresses his current understanding of developmental-constructivist theory as he applies it in his classroom in a coherent and integrated manner. Rick's application of Piagetian theory to his curriculum is complex and sophisticated, as can be seen in this excerpt from his recent reflective writing during the summer of 2000.

> *Currently, my thinking about my teaching practices centers around the idea of meeting the social, ethical, and academic needs of children within the context of the variety of the developmental range of the class and the differing learning styles and cultures of individuals and groups within the class community. As a teacher, I believe it is my job to empower students to learn how to learn, how to build and engage in effective social relationships, how to question and process information, how to create connections between what they know and what they wish to know, and how to make productive decisions regarding all of the above. I believe strongly in constructivist theory, which in practice allows me to facilitate the integration of learning through varying levels of questioning and challenges that cause the disequilibrium necessary for growth. We value mistakes as information, build a community of learning and support through consistent interaction in different sized groups, explicit teaching of conflict resolution strategies and the art of negotiation, and dedicated time to sharing all of our personal lives and reflecting on our*

strengths and weaknesses as whole people (as opposed to simply students and a teacher). The curriculum must meet all of these needs in order to have a place in my classroom and is frequently altered so that it can be done cooperatively, actively, and with a spirit of "our success is my success" and vice versa.

These excerpts show that what these teachers learned about children's behavior and development and about teaching and learning in the DTE program did not wash out. Rather, it is still foundational to their pedagogical understanding today. Of course, each of these people understands and applies developmental-constructivist theory in different ways because they are different people with different understandings and developmental trajectories of their own. So, the question of whether teachers lose what they learned during their teacher preparation program when they face the reality of classroom life and become socialized into the profession and school culture is answered with an unequivocal "NO" for these teachers as it may be for many teachers from other teacher education programs. However, the question of how and why their understandings did not wash out needs a fuller explanation.

Nature of the Teachers. Beginning with the character of the four people in this study, I believe they all have a desire to learn and apply what they learn to their lives as educators. They all entered the DTE program predisposed to learn what was offered to them over the 2 years they spent at UC–Berkeley. This is evidenced by the fact that they chose a rigorous, theoretically coherent, 2-year postbaccalaureate program leading to a master's degree at a major research university for their own preparation to teach. They could have chosen many other routes to obtain teaching credentials, but they did not. They were interested in understanding *why* children behave and learn as they do, which was a good fit for what the DTE program had to offer them. Although some people enter their teacher education programs believing they already know a lot about children and teaching, these four people believed they had a lot to learn about teaching and learning and about behavior and development. They were open to learning how to teach and desirous of understanding the *why* behind what they were observing as they learned to teach.

Nature of Preservice Teacher Preparation. In fact, they did learn why and how children develop and learn from the perspective of developmental-constructivist theory, mainly from the perspective of Piaget. They accomplished this mostly by thinking about how the theories they were learning in their foundations and methods courses applied to what they were seeing and learning in their field experiences. However, one unique advantage of their attending the DTE program was that they learned more about Piaget's theories of cognitive, social, and moral development than most students who major in education psychology or child development. Not only did they learn the theory in detail, but they also learned how Piaget's theories can be applied to teaching and learning in school settings. During their teacher education program, they (a) read and discussed many primary sources (albeit translated into English) as well as secondary sources, (b) conducted many Piagetian experiments with children, (c) learned to use school subjects and readily available school materials to create additional Piagetian-like assessment tasks, (d) viewed and analyzed videotapes of others conducting Piagetian tasks, and (e) practiced asking the kinds of questions (known as *clinical interview questions*) that are designed to get at how students think about and understand various concepts. They also learned about children's thinking in the social and moral domains from the perspectives of Piaget and Kohlberg, and about the application of this kind of thinking to classroom practices, including cooperative learning and classroom management. Furthermore, they were exposed to applications of these theories throughout their 2-year program, rather than in just one or two courses, which is typical of most teacher education programs. In the first year of the DTE program, they explored Piaget's theories as they learned about the students and the content they would teach, and then they revisited these ideas again at a deeper level in the second year when they worked to apply Piaget's ideas to the curriculum and to more students in their classrooms.

In addition, the kind of teaching they were exposed to in their methods classes included inquiry-based, hands-on methods designed to encourage students to act like young scientists and explore and inquire about their world before didactic instruction begins or algorithms are presented. This was the focus of their methods classes about teaching science, math, social studies, and the reading and language arts curriculum. They also tried out this kind of active instruction in their field placements, which they participated in concurrently with their theoretical and methods coursework throughout their program. More information about the structure and curriculum of the DTE program is located in Appendix D, which describes the sequence of experiences and coursework, and in Appendix C, which describes the kinds of developmentally appropriate practices stressed throughout the DTE program.

Nature of the Teaching Context. Finally, these teachers were able to observe and practice what they learned in classroom settings that matched and modeled what they were learning in their theory and methods classes. Field experiences were carefully selected so that DTE students could see and try out developmentally appropriate and constructivist teaching methods at several different grade levels. Master teachers (as the DTE program calls its *cooperating teachers*) were carefully selected because their teaching philosophy and practices closely matched the developmental and constructivist philosophy of the DTE program. In addition, every DTE student was placed in the classroom of at least one DTE graduate so they were sure to see in action the kinds of things they were learning about in their coursework, and so that they would have a master teacher who could talk with them from the same perspective they were learning in their university courses. This careful attention to the selection of teaching contexts was extremely important in helping DTE students move beyond just learning about developmental constructivist theory to actually being able to see it applied with real students in real classrooms, and to try out developmental constructivist theory and practice in supportive contexts.

Furthermore, the teaching contexts that Julie, Sandy, Ralph, and Rick found themselves in after leaving the DTE program were more or less a match for what they had learned about how children develop and learn. Unfortunately, Julie felt little support in her school and was frustrated by the demands of having to develop so much of the curriculum on her own. It was not until her last year of teaching that Julie had a few colleagues to team with and talk to about teaching. Sandy always worked with DTE grads at the two public schools she taught in for 10 years and is currently teaching in a private school that is a very good philosophical match to the DTE program. In fact, Wilson School in San Leandro where Sandy taught for many years regularly hires DTE graduates and has hosted many DTE student teachers over the years due to supportive administrators and a compatible staff who understand and regularly use developmentally appropriate constructivist teaching practices. Ralph found himself in a rather traditional school at first, but he had a few colleagues and an administrator who supported his efforts to teach the ways he learned in the DTE program. Later he moved to a private school that was also an excellent match philosophically to the DTE program and where he had many colleagues who understood and applied developmentally appropriate teaching practices. Rick has remained in the same school since 1987 largely because he has a knowledgeable and supportive principal, as well as enough colleagues and other mentors who value what he does and support him in his continued efforts to teach in developmentally appropriate ways.

All four of these teachers also had student teachers from the DTE program placed in their classrooms over the years. Taking on the role of mentoring a prospective teacher provided them opportunities to articulate, model, and answer questions about why and how they teach as they do. This role also put them in a position of having to reflect on their teaching goals and practices, which often served as a catalyst for metacognitive thinking about their students' learning and their own teaching (Levin & Ammon, 1992).

Factors That Promote the Development of Reflective Teaching.   Zeichner and
Liston (1987) described several factors they believe impede the development of reflective teaching. Among these factors are apprenticeship models of teacher education with limited field experiences for student teachers
and the *ideological eclecticism* and *structural fragmentation* of most teacher education programs, which are still all too common in many teacher education
programs. These factors can easily limit the realization of program goals
and likely contribute to an apparent wash out effect for some students in
some programs. The structure and focus of the DTE program, however, appears to circumvent many of the factors that Zeichner and Liston (1987)
claimed can prevent teacher reflection and hence interfere with teacher
development. In fact, several components of the DTE program appear to
foster the continued development of teacher:

- The DTE program is a 2-year program of ongoing theory and methods
coursework taken concurrently with five progressively more involved student teaching placements. With five master teachers to compare, the structure of the DTE program counteracts the apprenticeship model of teacher
education by encouraging prospective teachers to construct their own understandings of what good teaching looks like. Furthermore, with the extended 2-year time frame, DTE preservice teachers are able to consolidate
what they learn in the first year of the program based on additional coursework and field experiences taken during the second year. By reflecting on
what they learn at the university and in the schools, they are able to develop
deep understandings about how children learn, behave, and develop.

- Problem solving through reflection is a *habit of mind* cultivated in the
DTE program. DTE students write dialogue journals regularly throughout
their 2-year program. DTE supervisors respond in writing to these journals
and maintain an ongoing dialogue through these journals, and in person,
with the goal of helping the preservice teachers make sense of their observations and experiences as they learn to teach. This practice conveys to
DTE students that ongoing reflection is an integral and necessary part of a
teacher's development.

- A thorough grounding in developmental-constructivist theories, especially Piagetian theory, for all DTE students offers a foundation for testing
out their own ideas and making sense of their observations and experiences
in the field. With this knowledge base, they have a foundation against which
to examine their own developing conceptions of teaching, learning, behavior, and development. These three practices in the DTE program—extensive fieldwork, in-depth study of developmental constructivist theory and
methods, and ongoing reflective writing—work together to provide both a
foundation and vision for what effective teaching can be from a develop-
ment-constructivist perspective.

- The small size of each DTE cohort group, and of the DTE program faculty, also mitigates against the *structural fragmentation* and *ideological eclecticism* decried by Zeichner and Liston (1987). All facets of the DTE program are guided by a shared theoretical perspective, which underlies the theory, foundations, and methods courses. The program faculty all share a fairly cohesive philosophy, and the small numbers allow for individual attention to each prospective teacher's development.

- One aspect of that shared philosophy is that learning to teach is an ongoing process. DTE students develop a metalevel understanding that the program can provide them with some tools and a cohesive theory from which they can operate as beginning teachers, but that figuring out what and how to teach is something they will continue developing throughout the course of their careers. The result is that most DTE teachers see themselves as developing teachers in much the same way as they understand their children as developing learners.

- Finally, there is the fact that the DTE program makes a concerted effort to stay in touch with its graduates and asks them to serve as master teachers for new groups of prospective teachers. This mentoring experience offers program graduates opportunities to articulate, model, and answer questions about why they do what they do in their classroom and opportunities to articulate their teaching philosophy and practices. Such opportunities offer additional chances for further reflection and metacognitive thinking, hence opportunities for continued development of their pedagogical thinking. In addition, in recent years, the DTE program has hired program graduates to serve as supervisors for 1 to 3 years, either full time or part time, if they continue to teach part time.

Although not all DTE graduates have student teachers every semester or get the opportunity to return to the university to be a DTE supervisor, each of the teachers in this study has had multiple opportunities to serve as a master teacher since their graduation from the DTE program in 1987. Ralph served as a DTE supervisor for 3 years. Programs that maintain connections with their graduates and employ them as supervising teachers have the opportunity to pass on their program philosophy and continue to influence their thinking. However, it still takes a desire to continue learning as a teacher, the foundation of a theoretically coherent rather than a structurally–fragmented teacher education program, and supportive teaching contexts throughout a teacher's career to prevent the wash out effect.

As Sandy said at Time 5 in 1997:

> *DTE teachers are really different than those who come from elsewhere, and I think that I wouldn't be the teacher that I am without DTE. It just made me more aware of developmental education and how children develop and [how] everyone develops at their own*

rate, and goes through stages. I would hope that most credential programs study Piaget, but we did it in such depth. I do have to say that what we did then I did not appreciate and I don't think I got it. I wasn't ready to hear a lot of what Paul [Ammon, the codirector of the DTE program] or even Allen [Black, also a codirector of the DTE program] said, because I was coming from a really technical background in economics, math, and psychology and children were really foreign to me. I think that the people that go through the program now are a lot more experienced, and so they are ready to receive that information and probably got a lot more out of it than I did. But I think it set up that bug in my head that this is the way that they learn and laid the foundation so that everything that I learned or heard had to jibe with that or else I didn't use it or it didn't make sense to that theory. I think that a lot people when they come into teaching, they don't know how children learn, they don't have an understanding or a philosophy of how kids learn, they just do things without thinking about why and what it means for the kid.

HOW DOES THE PEDAGOGICAL UNDERSTANDING OF TEACHERS GROW AND CHANGE OVER TIME?

The previous response to the washout question focused on theoretical and structural influences on the development of teachers' thinking. I now turn to a process question that asks *how* teachers' understandings can grow and change over time, assuming that structural supports are in place as described before. The question of *how* these four teachers' understandings about pedagogy developed over time has been of great interest to me throughout this longitudinal study. My own thinking is influenced by developmental-constructivist theories of learning offered by Piaget (1952, 1963, 1972) and Vygotsky (1986) as well as by the data collected during this study. That is, I believe that the pedagogical understandings of these teachers developed on two levels simultaneously—on an inner level and also on a social level. By *inner level*, I mean that my data show that these teachers' pedagogical understandings changed and developed into more complex ways of thinking when they had to solve problems or when they confronted dilemmas in their practice. This happens when things are not going the way teachers imagine they should in the classroom or when there is a mismatch between a teacher's image of teaching and learning and the reality they observe in the classroom. For example, when students are not behaving as expected, when students are not learning what the teacher believes they are capable of learning, or when a lesson does not meet the needs of many of the students in the class, the teachers in this study see a problem to be solved.

These kinds of experiences happen to teachers every day. Some teachers ignore a failed lesson and move onto the next lesson. Some teachers ignore misbehavior or a student who is not learning as expected until they can figure out what to do about it. Some teachers even think that some students cannot learn, are not motivated to learn, don't behave appropriately at school, or cannot learn because of their home life.

One of the unique things about the four teachers in this book, unlike many teachers I have know in my 13 years as a teacher educator, is that they do not blame their students. When something is not working in their teaching, when a student is not learning or behaving as expected, or when their interactions with students are not productive, they believe they are the ones who need to make changes. After all, they are the professionals. They confront the typical problems and dilemmas of teaching and learning as puzzles or problems to be solved, not as problems. They do not believe that it is the students who have the problem. Instead, they understand that they need to change their approach or instructional methods to meet the needs of their students. They struggle with what they know and what they need to know to solve the problem at hand. Much of this struggle takes place as internal dialogue about the problem—as reflection and metacognitive thinking about their teaching practice and about how children learn. Piaget would describe this as *self-regulation.*

In a way similar to Piaget's notions of disequilibrium, these teachers enter a state of cognitive conflict (and sometimes moral and ethical conflict too) or disequilibrium when they have a problem to solve. They struggle within themselves and with the limitations of their current understanding of the students or the curriculum until they find a solution to the problem at hand. Sometimes they seek help from outside sources, such as talking with other teachers, reading books, or attending workshops. Sometimes they get more insights from talking with the students, with family members, or others with more knowledge than they do about particular students, instructional strategies, or curriculum. Once they have some new input from outside sources, they can assimilate it to their current ways of understanding, ignore it altogether, or transform the way they understand the problem by changing or accommodating their way of thinking about the problem at hand. This often happens internally through self-talk or inner dialogue, although sometimes it may look like an intuitive leap in understanding. It also happens when they try something and consciously evaluate the results by reflecting on them. Both metacognitive thinking and self-regulation are involved in this process.

Sometimes the teachers in this study are able to solve the problem at hand through dialogue with others. Perhaps they consult with another teacher who has taught their children or the curriculum. They particularly benefit from consulting with other DTE graduates and student teachers from the DTE program, who think about the problems of practice in similar ways because they have the same theoretical perspectives and similar images of the way things should operate in the classroom from a developmental-constructivist orientation. In conjunction with their own inner dialogue about the problem at hand, sometimes the opportunity for dialogue with colleagues and supportive family and friends outside of education assists them in thinking about how to solve the problem. Thus, the pedagogical understandings of the teachers in this study often develop simultaneously on an inner level and a social level as they seek to resolve pedagogical problems. Some examples of how this works for the teachers in this book follow.

At the time of her graduation from the DTE program in 1987, Julie believed that her skill in observing and analyzing her students and her predilection for being reflective are two major factors that explain how her thinking has changed in response to classroom situations.

> *Probably the ability to evaluate what's going on in my classroom, and evaluate myself, how I'm feeling about what's going on, and the ability to analyze. If the kids weren't responding to this, could it be that I didn't present it in the right way, or they're not ready for it—just the ability to analyze the learning situations and what I'm doing. The ability to look at myself and see what I might change, and all that kind of thing, through just thinking about what's going on in the classroom, observing things in the classroom. (Time 2, Clinical interview, 1987)*

After 3 years in the classroom, Julie describes how her experience teaching students, the reading she has done, and her background in developmental theory are additional factors that, combined with her reflective nature, explain how she thinks about and solves problems in her teaching.

> *Experience in the classroom definitely . . . and then also the things that I learned during DTE, different parts of the program, like the developmental theory, Piaget's theory. . . . Things I've read and my own pulling together of the information and making sense of it. Things that I've learned, theories I've learned, and things that I've done in the classroom—it all fits together.*
>
> *I think I'm a real reflective or introspective person, so that's something that helps. Sometimes it hurts too, but it helps me process things and think about what's going on and how come that didn't work, what can I do next time. So having that inner dialogue with myself helps too. . . . (Time 3, Clinical interview, 1990)*

Again in 1997, Julie reiterates her predilection for reflecting on her experiences, as well as how several external factors (reading professional literature, attending staff development opportunities, and talking with other teachers) influenced her own development as an educator and explain how she understands pedagogy at this time.

> *I think other teachers are a great resource. And then I've always enjoyed reading professional material, journals and things, "Mathematics Teacher" or "Teaching Children Mathematics" magazines that are put out by various professional organizations. I've always enjoyed going to staff development opportunities. So those are all great resources*

and I think that that's probably something that really kept me motivated and learning new things was trying other things and exposing myself to new ideas and talking with other teachers and continually trying new things. . . . And I just think that I've had time to reflect over the years and I think I'm still making connections with things that I learned. You almost forget at some point where you learned something but I think the connections still are being made to experience that I had due to teaching or whatever and still sort of putting things together and realizing things. (Time 5, Clinical Interview, 1997)

For Sandy, similar factors were at work when she confronted problems in her teaching over the years: observing her students, thinking about her teaching, taking courses, talking with other teachers, and being willing to change. For example, at Time 2 in 1987, when she was graduating from the DTE program, Sandy explained that one of the ways she knew what and how to teach was by observing others:

Seeing how they teach a certain subject or how they deal with a certain problem, courses that you can take to learn about content. But I think friends and teachers [mainly]. Especially people from this program, since we've had the same background and lot of us are staying in the same area. I would see them as being a real resource. (Time 2, Clinical interview, 1987)

At time 4 in 1993, Sandy said the same things influenced her thinking: her experience, attending workshops, reading educational books, talking with other teachers, and her training in the DTE program, which she elaborated on:

The terminology gets lost sometimes, but I have to say also that it's easy to get caught up in the everyday stuff, all the everyday worries that we have to think about, and to forget about the developmental stuff. I was thinking about this the other day because I think one of the reasons why . . . , it's made me think, maybe, more developmentally is because I've had student teachers. I hadn't had a student teacher in a year and a half, and it was easy [to forget]. I felt like when I talked to Carli [her current student teacher from the DTE program] that she was bringing me back to thinking about some of these issues that I tended to lose track of over the last year and a half. [But also,] I still have a basic philosophy that I develop about education, in which I assume a lot of the terminology and jargon and stuff. . . . (Time 4, Clinical interview, 1993)

Sandy also mentions some of these same influences on her thinking at Time 5 in 1997, when she came back to teaching after taking 2 years off to stay at home with her children:

In some ways I think that I know a lot more now than I did 2 years ago or when I graduated. A lot of it is inside, and being able to articulate it is difficult. I read a lot, and what I read makes sense at the moment, but it's difficult to be articulate. We were talking about having a community where I could talk about these ideas or having a student teacher—I feel like I was more thoughtful and more articulate about it then. Yeah, I have learned a lot and yet I feel in some ways I have regressed a little bit in not having an opportunity to discuss my teaching with others. (Time 5, Clinical interview, 1997)

Ralph also understood that teaching and learning involved problem solving very early on. At Time 1, when he first entered the DTE program, he remarked that learning is like "*solving a puzzle or problem or dilemma, a quality of opening . . . a way out of a particularly stuck place . . . understanding something that was a mystery . . . a tension that is resolved.*" In a later interview at Time 5, he elaborated on these same notions and described in detail how he goes about solving his puzzles, problems, and dilemmas by observing, seeking feedback, and talking with his students and other teachers.

That comes with familiarity of students and it comes with experience and seeing kids at different grades. Basically starting with student teaching and seeing what kids are do-ing—talking with other teachers, and going to the previous teacher of the grade you are in and asking what was successful and what might not have been so successful—and look-ing at published materials . . . [asking] my grade level colleagues . . . "What are you do-ing? What is your curriculum? When are you teaching this? When are you teaching that?" You get a lot of informal conversation, and then with direct experience in working with the kids . . . and of course, everything is case-by-case and kid-by-kid. . . . You get feed-back by asking for feedback from the kids. . . . (Time 5, Clinical interview, 1997)

Ralph also talked about the value of interacting with others and ex-plained the process of how he dealt with his own understandings about pedagogical issues in his role as a DTE supervisor in 1997. Here he explain how he justifies his thinking both to himself and to the preservice teachers he dialogued with every week, both in his written responses to their weekly journals and in conversations with them.

And I get to do that, and I am forced to explain my positions. I'm forced to articulate what I think. I'm forced to articulate what I see, and in essence I'm forced to think about both in very specific ways [like] How do you handle pencils in your classroom? and much broader. What are the ramifications of such-and-such management system on the development of visual learners? . . . I've had to write 20 pages a week on, over the course of the year, on what I've seen, and what I think, and why. I have to justify that until it makes sense. (Time 5, Open-ended interview, 1997)

Rick also reflected throughout his career about how he solves the prob-lems and dilemmas that arise for him in his classroom, but he summarizes it best in the writing he completed for this book during the summer of 2000:

I believe strongly in constructivist theory, which in practice allows me to facilitate the in-tegration of learning through varying levels of questioning and challenges that cause the disequilibrium necessary for growth. We value mistakes as information, build a community of learning and support through consistent interaction in different sized groups, explicit teaching of conflict resolution strategies and the art of negotiation, and dedicated time to sharing all of our personal lives and reflecting on our strengths and weaknesses as whole people (as opposed to simply students and a teacher). The curriculum must meet all of these needs in order to have a place in my classroom and is frequently altered so that it can be done cooperatively, actively, and with a spirit of "our success is my success" and vice versa.

Rick also talked at Time 6 about how he approached a personal challenge he wanted to take on in this explanation of how he plans to tackle the issue of racism in his classroom following a talk he heard about racism in schools:

But it's—the other thing he said—it was good 'cause he got up there and he didn't try to give everybody answers. He didn't have any answers. What he said was, "If you're serious about this you gotta go find answers," and I started thinking about that. For me, that means I need to go read about this. I need to go find somebody who's done something about this and find out how they do it and whether they do it well. Whether it's going to work, I have to try it. And then I have to see if it works for me. And then I have to go talk with some more people. And then I have to get in touch with these people's parents. I have to find out where they do come from and I have to find out what does work for them at home. And then I have to try and make what happens in here look something like that and all the while still doing right for the kids that it works for now. And so I don't know when that's going to happen, but I know about it. It has to sit with me for awhile. I have to think it through.

So for Rick and the other teachers, solving cognitive conflicts and resolving any disequilibrium they feel proceeds on internal and external planes. It involves thinking, reflecting, and the ability to think metacognitively about the problems at hand, but it also occurs with external supports such as conversing with others, reading, and attending workshops to gather information on which to reflect. This is the process of *how* the teachers' pedagogical thinking in this study developed over time.

WHAT PERSONAL AND PROFESSIONAL INFLUENCES IN THE LIVES OF TEACHERS IMPACT THEIR PEDAGOGICAL UNDERSTANDINGS THROUGHOUT THEIR CAREERS?

The words these teachers use to explain *how* teachers' thinking about pedagogy develops over time certainly apply to this question as well. However, the focus of this question is on *what* personal and professional influences in their lives have impacted these teachers' pedagogical understandings over time. In their written reflections and throughout the data collected over the past 15 years, five themes appear to have influenced their thoughts and actions as educators: (a) prior beliefs and personal values; (b) professional experiences as teachers (e.g., their formal teacher preparation, various professional development opportunities, and day-to-day classroom experiences with students); (c) the contexts in which they find themselves teaching (e.g., supportive or nonsupportive colleagues and administrators, changing school and political climates); (d) their personal relationships both in and out of school (e.g., the influence of friends, mentors, colleagues, and family); and (e) other life circumstances (e.g., children, health, and changing educational policy climate). These factors have all interacted over time to influence the development of their understanding of learning, teaching, behavior, and development and lead to their current thinking about pedagogy. For all four teachers, their predispositions to reflect on their practice; converse with other educators about their students, curriculum matters, and their teaching; and continue professional development through readings or attending workshops and conferences have influenced their thinking. However, each person also experienced other things in their personal and professional lives that influenced the development of their thinking.

For Julie, the opportunity to develop curriculum in the area of mathematics took her in a different direction professionally. For Sandy, her early interest in emergent literacy influenced her professional life for over 10 years, and the birth of her two daughters also influenced her career as a teacher because it led her to job sharing, part-time work as a reading specialist, and finally teaching in the private school her daughters attend. For Ralph, his personal life as a gay man influenced the path of his professional career as he sought compatible teaching contexts with people who valued diversity and thought about teaching and learning in the same way he did. His time as a DTE supervisor also influenced his professional life as he sought the opportunity to teach in a diverse and large urban school so that he could "walk the walk" and not just "talk the talk" about what it takes to teach in such a setting. Rick, like the others, also benefited greatly from timely professional development experiences, his own reading, and his interactions with other teachers. In addition, Rick's personal and professional lives are tightly coupled, and the opportunities he has had to read and discuss education-related issues with his wife, also an educator, and his principal have been influential for him. The connections Rick makes between thinking about the kind of education his own children are getting and what he offers his students are also important factors as he works to provide the best learning experiences possible for the students in his classes. For Rick and the other three teachers highlighted in this study, continual reflection on their practice and teaching goals also influences the development of their pedagogical understandings. In fact, the following words offer rich information about the influence of their personal and professional lives on their development, especially on the development of their pedagogical thinking.

In retrospect, Julie's metaphor expressed at Time 3 in 1990 reveals her surprise at the demands of teaching and foreshadows some of the reasons she ended up leaving the classroom after 5 years.

Teaching has just been incredibly, I don't know what I ever thought it was going to be, but it's more. . . . I compare it to being on a roller coaster. You're like up in the air, then you're down at the bottom, and you're up in the air. It's just so many different things. It just pulls so much from you. You're like an actor. You have to be dramatic. You have to be patient. You're like an actor. You're just so many different things, it's just mind boggling sometimes. I guess I didn't realize that teaching was going to be such a varied, have such varied demands, I guess.

Three years later, Julie was in a new position and reflected on some of the reasons she left teaching for a job with a large publishing company.

I would say probably off and on in my fifth year, probably end of December or January. . . . I had these intense periods of frustration. It just seemed like I wasn't happy with the job I was doing. It felt like I was just kind of cruising. I had lost my enthusiasm. And I heard myself saying things to the kids that I . . . didn't want to be, I didn't like the way I sounded. And I just thought I've got to take a break. I had a couple kids that . . . took a lot of my energy, and . . . I would just get so mad at these kids and then, inside of myself I was just saying these horrible things and I thought, you know, this isn't right. I'm not having a good time right now, and they probably aren't either, so I should take a break.

At Time 6 in 1999, Julie also reflected on the reasons she left teaching, and they included both personal reasons (frustration, high personal expectations, feeling pressured and stressed, lack of confidence, headaches) and professional reasons (pace of teaching, teaching context, lack of a set curriculum, pressures from her students' parents, large class sizes).

One feeling that I had was that I could never accomplish everything. I remember this and I wonder if it would be different in a different setting. But, I remember when I was in [East Bay] that we really weren't using the new textbooks and we were pretty much creating a lot of our own curriculum and the district was pretty lose about the expectations were, so I felt a huge burden to figure out what to do with these kids and how to do it. It was kind of up to me to connect with other teachers to figure it out . . . but that was a huge thing for me. Having to plan a curriculum was so big.

I felt pressure from the parents in my classroom. I don't know, I just felt a lot of pressure about their expectations. They always wondered about homework and especially in the beginning they didn't like having a new teacher looking after their child. Writing me long notes about things—I didn't like that.

I didn't feel confident enough. I think towards the end I did, but that was hard and I didn't like the pace of the classroom, just the unending—all the decision making that happened. Having to deal with all the different kids. I felt like, I think that was a stress for me. I remember just being annoyed and having a headache everyday when I got home. Now I look back and wonder. Maybe that just wasn't the right place for me. I wonder what it would have been like at a different school or at a different grade level. What would I do better in? Would I be better at getting the classroom in the right climate for my style or whatever? That was really something—the annoyance, and the kids and everything. . . . The class size too, that would make a difference.

For Sandy, personal and professional influences on her development as a teacher are intertwined because of trying to juggle being a mother with being a teacher. In her effort to make time for family, Sandy job shared and worked part time for many years, which influenced her professional development. At Time 4 in 1993, she talked about her struggles trying to balance her life in the classroom and at home:

It makes it harder. There are a lot of things going on. Part of it is that I have a baby, so I don't have as much time at home in the afternoons, and evenings, and on weekends to spend planning for school. The other part is teaching part-time and job sharing. . . . I'm not completely free to do what I want to with the curriculum, and so I'm kind of tied down that way. . . . Right now I'm thinking of possibly taking a leave next year and doing something related, but I don't want to give up everything that I've done the last seven or eight years [since] DTE. And I'd like to do something related to teaching, . . . work in a preschool or go back and take some more classes, or do something somewhere else that's related to teaching, because I've got all this stuff at home, and I don't want to give it up, and I want it to be used . . . I like being with the baby, but I don't know if I could be there full time. So that's the other thing . . . part of me doesn't want to get out of teaching because I think it would be hard to go back into teaching once I leave, because I think that the classroom dynamics are changing so fast.

In that same interview, I asked Sandy about whether she would like to teach in a private school where the class sizes are smaller. Ironically, this conversation foreshadowed what Sandy eventually ended up doing after 10 years in public schools. However, at the time, she was not thinking about teaching anywhere else, although she was feeling the pressures of teaching in the public school system.

That goes against my philosophy . . . and all my training from DTE to work in public schools. We're going through this dilemma now that Hannah's a year old. What are we going to do when she gets to be school age? Are we going to send her to private school or to a public school? . . . My husband is pretty frustrated with the whole process . . . [and] I think if she were going to school next year we'd be sending her to a private school. . . . I believe in public education, but I also think that there have been a lot of changes and a lot more demands put on the teacher that make it more difficult for the teachers to teach.

The money's not there, so the class sizes have gotten bigger. The support for the teachers has gone out the window. You don't get the psychological help that you need for the kids, and the support from the parents isn't there, and you're getting a lot more non-English speaking kids, like I said before, in your classroom. And you're not getting help for that, and then we've got some kids in there that need a lot of psychological help and the special programs aren't there to take them into the special day class or the emotionally disturbed class. Those programs aren't there, so everything's being done by the teacher. . . . So there're just a lot of demands being put on us, the public school system, and the teachers can't deal with it by themselves. Or like, I shouldn't say they can't, just that it's very demanding, and it's hard to meet everybody's needs.

In 1993, Sandy also elaborated on the conflicts related to job sharing and balancing having a baby at home and her teaching.

I wouldn't job share if I didn't have the choice. . . . That's why I'm thinking of taking a leave. I'm thinking that there's something else that I could do. I would really love to be teaching full time if I . . . felt like I could do a good job and yet not take away from my being a mom. But I can't. So, I have to give that up.

It's frustrating, that part of it, not being able to do what I want to do because I'm job sharing. That's frustrating, and not being able to plan, . . . even if I did have my own classroom, which I could do, then I wouldn't be able to plan for it like I wanted to do, because I have a baby at home. So, there's all these things going on, and . . . It's hard to know, which one is weighing more heavily.

Sandy almost left teaching permanently, but after taking 2 years off to stay home when her second child was born in 1994, she did return to the same school to teach several days a week as a Title I teacher and then as a Reading Recovery teacher. She was job sharing during this time, but in reality she was splitting a full-time position with another teacher and they worked with different groups of students in both pull-out and push-in situations.

The thing that has been good is that I have been able to work part time, but I haven't had to split my time with someone else and coordinate, because that kind of wore on me. Next year the teachers are saying we need somebody to work with the kids and them, so they want more time, and they want to look out for the kids so they're talking about pull-out again and working with the kids, not the teachers, and probably more a full-time position, 80% or 100%, and I don't want to work that much yet, so . . . I'm in flux again.

I'm willing to work up to 80% but that's my limit. If they want more I'll have to share with somebody, which will then get me back to that same situation. On the one hand I'm pretty independent, and I like to do my own thing, and [although] I see the value of working with other people, . . . it's just how much time that takes and whether I am on the same wavelength. Because if I'm working [with] somebody who doesn't do things the same way I do or think the same way I do, then it's difficult . . . so . . . I'm kind of waiting to see what's going to happen next year.

Sandy's personal life as a parent of two daughters also influenced her thinking about how children learn and beliefs about their behavior and development. At Time 5 in 1997, she said, "*Seeing just how they develop is fascinating, how they grow and change and make sense of their world and starting to read and write and watching it develop and talking.*" Being a parent also changed how she thought the nature versus nurture question: "*They are who they are because of who they are and not entirely their family.*" She also developed more empathy for the perspective of her students' parents.

> *You look at kids as your students, not as somebody's children, so that now that I have my own children I think well, gosh I really want their teacher to know this and that about them. It's not that I didn't think about it, but when you have so many kids, it's really hard to think about each child when you have the whole class, and what you can do for the class. Of course there were individual children that would stick out and you would worry, but as a teacher you worried more about the group and not the individual child, so [having a child] just made me more aware of these kids as people. . . . It sort of makes me appreciate the parents' point of view, which I didn't have that perspective.*

Being a parent changed her perspective, which caused some of her pedagogical beliefs and practices to change.

> *I never used to like sharing because I always thought that it would be something that they brought from home, and it would be materialistic and . . . [I] thought it took time away from academics. Being a parent, you realize how important it is for kids to bring something to share. My daughter always wants to bring something to school, a toy or whatever. And I never wanted toys in my classroom, but I think that it's made me realize that they need something to help them bridge that gap from home to school. . . . I read an article about this recently, it was just [about] how sharing is a good thing because it does bridge that gap for the younger kids. But then for the older kids, it doesn't have to be something from home, but something about them or something that they have done at school, and it could be academic or not.*

At Time 6 in 1999, Sandy was still job sharing, but with a new partner, and she was still finding it challenging to balance home and school life.

> *Well, I taught second grade for 3 years and then I went to first grade, and I taught first grade for 3 years, and then I took 2 years off, and then I did Title 1 for 3 years. But that was mostly language arts, and I was working with different age groups, and mostly it was in intervention, . . . helping the second graders who weren't reading yet, or going into classrooms and helping the kids who were struggling readers in those classrooms, and helping teachers set up some kind of program that was able to meet their needs. . . . So this has been a real learning experience for me . . . I worked with fourth graders during the last two years, but my whole focus at the beginning of my teaching career was all in primary grades and developing literacy. My training was . . . emergent literacy, and so in working with older kids and teaching fourth grade, I have learned a lot and I am still learning.*
>
> *Everything that I did in second and first grade I threw out, partly because I have learned a lot more since I was in the classroom last time, and partly because I was start-*

ing with a new partner. We just threw everything out and started from scratch. Being at a different grade level I feel like I am just starting anew. So it has been quite a learning experience for me, and the other thing is that I don't have the time to devote to thinking about teaching and planning as I did when I was first starting out. Now I have kids at home. Back then my weekends were wide open and my evenings were wide open, so it is very different.

The benefits of Sandy's varied teaching experiences since she started teaching in 1987 seemed to pay off, however, in an increased sense of efficacy, which now permeates her professional life.

Because I have moved around so much, now I feel like that at any age group, I could teach them and learn something from them, and each group has their own special need, and not just need, but an area that I could get interested in—so like, say fourth and fifth grade, the literature is really rich and the social studies curriculum is really rich. But in the primary grades, like first grade, teaching them how to read and write is really exciting too. . . .

Nevertheless, Sandy still felt she was not able to be the kind of teacher she envisioned for herself because she also wanted to be a good parent—a paradox that many teachers face.

I guess my obstacles would be that I can't be the kind of teacher that I want to be. I can't put out that much effort and have a family too. So I work part time and then I get frustrated as a teacher because I am not doing what I want to do and I don't have the systems in place, I don't have the time to plan or to think or research, or whatever it is that I need to do to be the kind of teacher that I want to be. I know that is an opportunity cost for me and that I have to sacrifice who I am as a teacher so that I can be a half-decent or good-enough parent and that once I get beyond the child rearing age I can then focus more on teaching, but also have a life.

One final note about Sandy is that she did leave public school teaching in 1999 to teach at the private school her daughters attend in Berkeley. This school is not only more convenient for her as a parent, but also is an excellent match philosophically with what she learned in the DTE program and still believes about teaching, so the personal and professional factors in her life are now more closely aligned. The only drawback is that this school is a cooperative and so every teacher has many additional duties to fulfill. However, as Sandy wrote during the summer of 2000, she still thinks about trying something that would be more compatible with her family life.

[When I think about the future] I would really like a 9–5 job, with a 5-day workweek!! I'm still trying to decide if classroom teaching part time works for me (you'd think I'd know after 5 years and four different teaching partners!) and if working as part of the collective is where I want to put my extra energy, since it takes away from my teaching.

Thoughts of grad school enter my head once in a while as I would like to learn more about literacy, as do ideas of working in a children's bookstore where I can read books I love all day long! I would then have evenings free to quilt.

Being a parent has changed my life as a teacher. On a very concrete level, it's affected how much I teach and how much time I'm able to give it. I can also live like Piaget and test my theories and understandings about child development on my children. But mostly, parenting has challenged me to find balance in my life—to make time for my family, hobbies, and exercise, because teaching itself can be a 24-hour job. . . .

Although Ralph had plenty of personal factors that likely influenced his thinking during this study, including similar issues about juggling family life with teaching school, he did not discuss them with me during the clinical interviews. In fact, it was not until the 1997 interview, when I first began to ask open-ended questions preceding the clinical interview questions, that I even knew Ralph had stepchildren he was raising with his partner, Jim. However, during the summer of 2000, following his first year at Garfield School, Ralph wrote about the many questions and few answers he had after a challenging year in a teaching context that was different from any of his other teaching positions. Some of his questions relate to his personal life and the differences between Ralph and his students (e.g., ethnicity, social class, and lifestyle), and some of them relate to professional issues that are influenced by his personal beliefs (e.g., standardized testing, value of arts in education, skill development vs. concept development):

I will return with bundles of unanswered questions:

I share ethnicity with none of my students. How much will that continue to limit me in knowing them and in knowing how to teach them effectively?

How do I address other issues of race? Why is it that of the six students in my class who are seriously "behind," five of those are African American? How do I talk about this and get help so I can teach these students more effectively?

How do I address issues of my own sexual orientation in the school community at Garfield? At present, I'm "out" with staff/district, bring Jim along to parties and school events, etc. But I've not brought Jim into my life in the classroom (sharing details with students and families about MY family life). How do I want to go about beginning that process?

Standardized tests have assumed paramount importance at the school (for the district, the state, and some of the parents). Is my disdain for these measures a reflection of an upper class luxury—and should I be doing more to better prepare my students for the testing?

How much time do I allow for art, for hands on science, for "conceptual development" as opposed to teaching skills—I had the luxury in Moraga to spend a good portion of my time and energy into more critical and creative pursuits, knowing that the nitty-gritty skills would be covered (at home or elsewhere in the school)—I do NOT have that luxury now.

To what extent do I attempt to address the emotional needs of my students? This past year I brought in snacks, met with students at lunch, provided modeling clay and board games and choice time and papier-mache. My thinking has been that by giving them "emotional space" they would settle in and could begin learning. To an extent, I still believe this. But I have to seriously question any time spent away from content and skills. Time is too precious, especially when students are already "behind" and have so much stacked against them.

In addition to these macro-level questions, I carry many micro level curricular questions into next year. (How do I carry Writer's Workshop further? How can I create more independent work? How can I use guided reading? What phonics program can I find to help fill in the gaps in a more organized way? How do I involve families more, and how can I actually USE parents in my classroom? What rewards/consequences do I want to establish at the beginning? etc. etc.) I'm only really thinking 1 year at a time right now. I'll see where this might lead. For now, I'm glad I'm back in the classroom. I feel proud, in a new way, to be a teacher.

Even after nearly 10 years of teaching and 3 years as a DTE supervisor, it is obvious that personal and professional issues are interrelated and continue to influence Ralph's thinking about pedagogy. In this case, a new teaching context triggered many of these questions, but some are personal issues as a gay man that he has dealt with throughout his career. Fortunately, Ralph is able to articulate many of the questions and issues he is grappling with and therefore should be able to think about them metacognitively and will self-monitor his progress toward resolving them. For teachers who are unable to articulate the questions, problems, or dilemmas they need to address, it is less likely that they will be able to resolve the cognitive conflicts they experience related to their personal and professional lives. Ralph's ability to reflect and previous experience with solving earlier problems will very likely help him continue to think about and find ways to answer these questions satisfactorily. In fact, my observation of Ralph at Garfield during his second year there, and subsequent conversations with him, indicate that he has begun to resolve many of his pedagogical questions successfully.

The personal and professional influences on Rick's pedagogical thinking were highlighted in his case study in the previous chapter, but are reiterated here. For example, as Rick says at Time 6 in 1999, he is both supported and challenged by his principal, with whom he often discusses educational theory and policy:

I have a principal who understands what I do and values what I do. I'm not sure I could do what I do just anywhere. . . . Not everyone at this school teaches the way I would like them to, but I believe that everybody, every teacher at this school truly cares about kids and is trying to do the right thing for kids. . . . I need to be around people like that.

Rick's colleagues are also an important professional influence because they offer him the opportunity to talk about teaching, share perspectives, and problem solve. He especially enjoyed several years of Monday meetings during lunch when interested teachers would get together to discuss their students and teaching in a supportive, problem-solving environment.

> *I want to be in this really dynamic environment where people are thinking about the same kind of things that I am and they are working with their kids and when I get them they have already had a few years of it and I can take them someplace new with that, they have some background in them. I have a lot of energy for that. What we are doing on these Mondays is a part of that. It is satisfying something for me. I didn't think it would but it really surprised me.*

However, Rick's personal life also influences his professional life in at least two ways. First, Rick volunteers in his daughters schools when he was on breaks from his year-round schedule, which caused his to think about and compare their classrooms to his own.

> *My own kids . . . when you look at your own kids going through and you see what is missing from their school. . . . It has made me look really hard at what I am doing. How would a parent look at what's going on in here? Am I communicating well with the parents? Do they understand? Do they care? I think they are just happy that their kids are happy.*

Second, Rick and his wife, a classroom teacher for many years and now a graduate student and teacher educator, regularly read and talk about educational issues at home. She also serves as a sounding board for him as he tries to work out problems in his classroom.

> *My wife—she's a resource just because she understands all the stuff and we can talk things over. She's a teacher, she knows about this stuff. We can collaborate that way and talk through things that we're in flux about. But she's also a resource for me because she reads so much educational material that I can't get to. . . .*

From Rick's perspective, his interactions with his wife and family, as well as with his principal and colleagues, have influenced his thinking about teaching and learning over the years. Like Sandy, Rick also reads a lot of educational theory and research articles for pleasure, as well as for input in finding ways to improve his teaching.

> *And then, just books. Books, books, always books. I'll get one author and then that author will lead me to some other author. Just some new take always on how to present this, how to think about it, how to frame it, make it easier for kids, or make it easier for me to understand and make it part of a life.*

These examples of the personal and professional factors that influence the thinking of the teachers in this book seem rather obvious in retrospect, but teacher educators, myself included, often do not acknowledge their impact on teacher development. We especially do not enough pay attention to the influence of teachers' personal relationships both in and out of school, such as the influence of friends, mentors, colleagues, and family, or the influence of other life circumstances on teacher development, such as children, health, and changing educational policy climate. Perhaps this is because we have little control over these factors, just as we have little control over teachers' prior beliefs and the teaching contexts they work in beyond student teaching. However, we can and must acknowledge these influences, and we must make an effort to incorporate them into our teacher education curriculum. This is one of the many lessons I have learned from conducting this research.

Although the Ammon and Hutcheson Model of Pedagogical Development is foundational to this study, there have been many other theories of teacher development suggested over the years. What follows is my response to the question of how other theories of teacher development describe the lives of teacher.

WHAT DO OTHER THEORIES OF TEACHER DEVELOPMENT HAVE TO SAY ABOUT THE LIVES OF TEACHERS?

In addition to the Ammon and Hutcheson Model of Pedagogical Development, several models and theories of teacher development have been posited over the past three decades. Although none of these studies focuses solely on the development of teachers' thinking about pedagogy as the longitudinal case studies presented in this book do, all of them address teachers' thinking, teachers' lives and careers, and teacher development in some way. Although most of the research on teacher development focuses mainly on teachers' early development, especially on their preservice and induction years (e.g., Fuller, Hollingsworth, Kagan, Ryan, Sprinthall), other work addresses teacher development across the span of teachers' careers (e.g., Berliner, Bullough, Huberman, Nias). Although no one theory or model captures the complexity of the development of teachers' thinking or addresses all domains involved in teachers' thinking about the teaching–learning process, each offers heuristic value to help us think about ways to better understand and support teachers as they develop during their preservice and student teaching experiences and throughout their careers in the field. It is with this heuristic value in mind that I summarize and comment on nine other studies of teacher development that have been published during the last three decades.

In response to the question of what do other theories of teacher development have to say about the lives of teachers, I describe these studies in chronological order. I begin with Frances Fuller's seminal work on teacher concerns (Fuller, 1969; Fuller & Brown, 1975), include the theoretical and empirical efforts of Norman Sprinthall and his colleagues to apply cognitive-developmental theory to teacher education (Glassberg, 1979; Sprinthall & Thies-Sprinthall, 1980, 1983; Thies-Sprinthall & Sprinthall, 1984), Kevin Ryan's (1986, 1992) description of stages of teacher development through the induction years, the work of David Berliner (1988) and his colleagues on the development of teacher expertise (Berliner, 1986; Carter, Cushing, Sabers, Stein, & Berliner, 1988; Carter, Sabers, Cushing, Pinnegar, & Berliner, 1987; Sabers, Cushing, & Berliner, 1991), the research of Sandra Hollingsworth and her colleagues' (Hollingsworth 1989, 1994; Lidstone & Hollingsworth, 1992) longitudinal study of the learning to teach process, and Donna Kagan's (1992) review of the evolution of teachers' professional growth in the early years of teachers' lives. I also briefly describe Jennifer Nias' (1989a, 1989b) study of primary teachers' sense of self as teacher and Martin Huberman's (1989) work on the life cycle of teachers because both of these take a longitudinal look at teachers lives and careers. Nias' longitudinal study looks at British primary teachers' individual sense of self as teacher 10 years into their careers, and Hubermans's cross-sectional study of secondary teachers focuses on the professional life cycle of teachers. Unfortunately, none of this research includes in-depth case studies that describe the development of individual teachers' thinking in detail. Rather, they are based on interviews with many teachers. Therefore, I also discuss the work of Robert Bullough and his colleagues (Bullough, 1989, Bullough & Baughman, 1997; Bullough & Knowles, 1991; Bullough, Knowles, & Crow, 1991), including his longitudinal study of Kerrie because of the length and depth of this single case study (Bullough, 1989, Bullough & Baughman, 1997).

It should be noted that these studies and models represent different theoretical perspectives and describe different aspects of teacher development than the developmental-constructivist model of teachers' thinking about pedagogy, which is foundational to this book. For example, Fuller's model takes a counseling and psychological perspective and focuses on the concerns of beginning teachers. Sprinthall's work was based on the application of cognitive-developmental constructs, including moral, ego, and conceptual development as these apply to teacher education. Berliner's model was based on schema theory and information processing; it focuses on teachers' cognitions about classroom practices as exemplified by teachers who range from novices to experts. Kagan's work validates and elaborates on the Fuller and Berliner models to describe some of the mechanisms that occur as teachers develop and grow as professionals. Hollingsworth's study (Hollingsworth, 1989; Lidstone & Hollingsworth, 1992) started out using cognitive psychology and information processing as its theoretical framework, but at the end of this 6-year study, Hollingsworth interpreted her findings from a feminist perspective (Hollingsworth, 1994). Nias' theoretical perspective is based on psychological, philosophical, and sociological theories, including symbolic interactionism and Freudian and Kahoutian notions of self. Huberman's study is grounded in psychological and sociological perspectives. Nevertheless, each of these models allows us to look at the development of teachers' thinking from different perspectives, which should provide additional insight into the lives of the teachers in this study.

Fuller's Model of Teacher Concerns

Frances Fuller's (1969) original model described three stages of teacher concerns. Fuller and Brown (1975) later modified this model to include four stages: fantasy, survival, mastery or craft, and impact. These stages describe the focus of teachers' concerns, which begin during the fantasy stage, with preservice teachers being concerned about how their cooperating teachers and students will perceive and judge them. This first stage is followed by the survival stage, when preservice teachers' concerns focus on how well they will be able to handle a class, and then by concerns about how they will be able to teach the curriculum during the mastery stage. The last stage of concerns described by Fuller and Brown focuses on how well all students' needs will be met during the impact stage.

Shifts in the focus of concerns of preservice teachers from self to students, which Fuller and Brown's (1975) model describes, is one that most teacher educators observe repeatedly in most of their beginning teachers. However, the amount of time that preservice and induction-year teachers spend in each of these stages varies greatly. Furthermore, whether these stages constitute an invariant sequence in the concerns of beginning teachers is disputed (Kagan, 1992). Nevertheless, this model is useful to consider when looking at the development of beginning teachers, especially when trying to understand where their focus and concerns lie.

Sprinthall's Cognitive-Developmental Framework for Teacher Development

In the early 1980s, Norman Sprinthall and his colleagues applied the cognitive and developmental psychology-based theories of Hunt (1974), Kohlberg (1969), Loevinger (1976), Perry (1970), and Piaget (1963, 1972) to understanding adult learning and development in general, and to their own theoretical framework for teacher education in particular (Sprinthall & Thies-Sprinthall, 1980, 1983; Thies-Sprinthall & Sprinthall, 1984). These papers reviewed and applied the current research (at the time) on cognitive, moral, and ego adult development to teacher education by suggesting that instruction should begin with teachers' current levels of cognitive complexity and proceed with the goal of helping teachers move ahead to the next highest level of development in each of these domains. They also proposed a cognitive-developmental framework for teacher education based on matching instruction and field experiences to teachers' levels of cognitive development and conceptual complexity. Part of Sprinthall and Thies-Sprinthall's proposed framework for teacher education included creating optimal mismatches and cognitive dissonance that would provoke disequilibrium in teachers, hence the possibility of promoting developmental growth toward more complex ways of thinking and teaching. Their assumption was that teachers with higher levels of cognitive, moral, and ego development and cognitive complexity are better suited to meet their students' varying needs. They suggested that such teachers are more flexible in their instructional strategies, use higher order and more complex thinking strategies with their students, and are better able to tolerate ambiguity (Glassberg & Sprinthall, 1980; Sprinthall & Thies-Sprinthall, 1980, 1983; Thies-Sprinthall & Sprinthall, 1984).

Unlike most of the thinking about adult development at the time, these educators believed that the thinking and conceptual levels of adults can be developed. They also believed that teacher education was in desperate need of "coherent theory and practice to promote teacher development" (Glassberg, 1979, p. 2). Agreeing with others at the time who called teacher education atheoretical, Thies-Sprinthall and Sprinthall (1984) posited six assumptions for their framework, which are based in cognitive-developmental theory:

(1) All humans process experience through cognitive structures . . .

(2) These cognitive structures are organized into a hierarchy of stages, a sequence from less complexity to more complexity.

(3) Growth occurs first within a particular stage and then only to the next stage in the sequence. This latter change is a qualitative shift, a major quantum leap to a significantly more complex system of processing experience.

(4) Growth is neither automatic nor unilateral, but occurs only with appropriate interaction between the human and the environment.

(5) Behavior can be determined and predicted by an individual's particular stage of development. Predictions, however, are not exact.

(6) The stages themselves are conceptualized as a series of partially independent domains. A domain is a major content-structure area of human activity. . . . (p. 39)

Thies-Sprinthall and Sprinthall (1984) suggested the following ways to promote increasing levels of cognitive development for teachers: (a) significant role-taking experiences, (b) roles that are sufficiently matched to the cognitive complexity of the teacher, (c) careful and continuous guided reflection with feedback, (d) a balance between real experience and discussion and reflection on teaching, (e) continuous use of the previous techniques including peer teaching and tutoring, (f) personal support and challenge by a leader who would also provide modeling and create some dissonance, and (g) assessment of cognitive, moral, and ego development using several measures.

Sprinthall and Thies-Sprinthall (1983) also compared developmental stages across different domains relevant to teacher development studied by the major theorists of human growth and development. This work provides a theoretical framework for teacher development that has similar theoretical underpinnings to the Ammon and Hutcheson Model of Pedagogical Development, although it address teachers' cognitive development in general, rather than in the pedagogical domain specifically.

The work of Sprinthall and his colleagues (Glassberg, 1979; Glassberg & Sprinthall, 1980; Sprinthall, Reiman, & Thies-Sprinthall, 1996; Sprinthall & Thies-Sprinthall, 1980, 1983; Thies-Sprinthall & Sprinthall, 1984) is especially useful for thinking about how teachers' cognitive development can be fostered and for understanding how cognitive, ego, and moral development interact.

Ryan's Model of Beginning Teacher Development

In 1986, Kevin Ryan described four developmental stages that new teachers go through as they begin teaching and throughout their induction years. Using similar terms and a sequence much like the one posited by Fuller (1969), Ryan described four stages: fantasy, reality, master of craft, and impact. The fantasy stage, which begins when prospective teachers first begin to think about themselves as teachers and what their life might be like as a teacher, usually extends to the time teachers begin their first teaching position. Ryan also wrote about *dark* fantasies that teachers have when they get closer to having their own classrooms and begin to have anxieties about managing a classroom on their own. According to Ryan (1986),

> Whether the fantasies are pleasant or anxious, preservice teachers often do not think about their future careers in a careful, analytical manner. One reason why preservice teachers find education courses irrelevant is that these courses often have little to do with what is going on in their fantasy lives. (p. 11)

From Ryan's perspective, the reality stage sets in during or shortly after the excitement of the initial weeks of teaching, when beginning teachers find themselves continuously adjusting and readjusting their plans and ideas about students, and they are trying to solve a multitude of problems they encounter. Ryan (1986) wrote that the survival stage for many teachers often extends through their first year in the classroom and is one of the biggest challenges in their personal and professional lives. In talking about the survival stage, Ryan stated that it ". . . can have far-reaching and complex effects depending on the individual teacher. It can affect the way in which the teacher will view teaching in the future" (p. 14).

Having survived the reality stage, confronted problems, and succeeded or not as the case may be, Ryan's next stage is the mastery of craft. For some beginning teachers, this stage may begin as early as February of the first year, but for others it may take much longer. In this stage, the beginning teacher gradually masters the six most common problems that beginning teachers have to deal with: shock of the familiar, students, parents, administrators, fellow teachers, and instruction.

Ryan's final stage of beginning teachers' development is the impact stage, when teachers begin to resolve and master all the problems described earlier so they can focus on their students' learning.

Like Fuller and Brown's model of teacher concerns, Ryan's model is useful for looking at what teachers are focused on in the early years of their development. However, neither Ryan's nor Fuller and Brown's model addresses teacher development after the induction years or discusses mechanism for helping teachers change their focus to the next level.

Berliner's Model of the Development of Teacher Expertise

David Berliner's studies of teacher expertise (Berliner, 1986; Carter, Cushing, Sabers, Stein, & Berliner, 1988; Carter, Sabers, Cushing, Pinnegar, & Berliner, 1987) represent an information-processing view of teacher cognition. His 1988 paper focuses on the implications of these studies of pedagogical expertise for teacher education and evaluation. In this research, Berliner highlighted the role of experience in teachers' understanding of pedagogical thinking, skills, and attitudes as they develop from novices to experts. He described five stages of development, each of which is characterized by distinct views of pedagogy: novices, advanced beginner, competent, proficient, and expert (Fig. 7.1).

At the novice stage, which Berliner said corresponds to student teachers and many first-year teachers, the novice teacher is learning context-free rules and labels through real-world experience. At the advanced beginner stage, which often corresponds to the second and third years of teaching in Berliner's model, the teacher is developing episodic and strategic knowledge, and context is beginning to influence the teacher's behaviors. However, advanced beginners still have difficulty knowing when to break or follow rules and established procedures. The competent stage for many

Stage 1: Novice. At the novice stage, which corresponds to student teachers and many first-year teachers, learning about commonplace tasks surrounding teaching, context-free rules (such as "Don't smile until Christmas"), and the multitude of labels used by teachers takes place through real-world experience, and only minimal skill is expected.

Stage 2: Advanced Beginner. At the advanced beginner stage, which often corresponds to the second and third years of teaching, the teacher is developing episodic and strategic knowledge and context is beginning to influence the teacher's behaviors. However, advanced beginners still have difficulty knowing when to break or follow rules and established procedures, and may not have a sense of what is most important.

Stage 3: Competent. The competent stage for many teachers may develop as early as the third or fourth years of teaching, when teachers are able to make conscious choices and set priorities and plans based on rational goals. Competent teachers are able to distinguish between what is and is not important in the classroom and do not usually make timing or targeting errors. They also feel more personally in control of classroom events and their curriculum.

Stage 4: Proficient. The proficient teacher emerges in the fifth year for a modest number of teachers when their intuition and know-how have developed. Proficient teachers recognize similarities in situations they have used before and can predict events. They are also analytical and deliberate in their decision making.

Stage 5: Expert. Expert teachers are characterized by fluidity and flexibility in their thoughts and actions. In fact they have developed to the point where they do not need to think deliberately or be consciously analytic anymore because they have achieved mastery and flow of their pedagogical practices, unless a problem develops. In this case, expert teachers are quickly able to recognize a problem and deliberately analyze it.

FIG. 7.1.   Berliner's (1988) model of pedagogical expertise.

teachers may develop in the second or third year of teaching, when teachers are able to make conscious choices and set priorities and plans based on rational goals. Competent teachers are able to distinguish between what is and is not important in the classroom and do not usually make timing or targeting errors. They also feel more personally in control of classroom events and their curriculum. Berliner says that the proficient teacher begins to emerge in the fifth year, when their intuition and know-how have developed. Proficient teachers recognize similarities in situations they have experienced before and can predict events. They are also analytical and deliberate in their decision making. Finally, according to Berliner's model, expert teachers are characterized by fluidity and flexibility in their thoughts and actions. Expert teachers have developed to the point where they do not need to think deliberately or be consciously analytic anymore because they have achieved mastery and flow of their pedagogical practices—unless a problem develops. In this case, expert teachers are quickly able to recognize a problem and deliberately analyze it.

I agree with Berliner that this model of teacher expertise development has heuristic value for how we might think about educating and evaluating teachers. That is, this model and the others described before, including the Ammon and Hutcheson Model of Pedagogical Development that undergirds the analysis of the teachers in this book, provide us with alternative ways to think about teacher development. Although Berliner's work uses schema theory and includes a lot of behavioristic language, it offers another way to describe the development of teachers' pedagogical thoughts and actions across their careers.

Nias' Model of the Development of Teachers' Sense of Self

Nias' (1989a) longitudinal study of British primary teachers focused on understanding the ways teachers' conceptions of their careers change from the beginning to the midpoint of their careers and how they define and derive their sense of self as teachers. Nias also addressed teachers' satisfactions and dissatisfactions with their work and what it means to feel like a teacher. As mentioned earlier, Nias used psychological, philosophical, and sociological theories, including symbolic interactionism and Freudian and Kahoutian notions of self, to explain the influences on and the developing nature of teachers' sense of self as teacher. This study was based on semistructured interviews with 99 beginning teachers conducted in 1975 to 1977 and follow-up interviews with 51 of these teachers 10 years later at the midpoint of their teaching careers. In her book, Nias (1989a) described teacher development as who a person becomes as a teacher and the importance of the affective, cognitive, and practical tasks of teaching. Nias said these cannot be separated from teachers' sense of self because they are central to the work of teachers. The role of the school context is also a major theme in Nias' study.

Nias' study provides a long-term view of how teachers' conceptions of their work change from the beginning to the midpoint of their careers, which matches the time frame of the longitudinal study in this book. Her study highlights different ways that career teachers view and identify themselves as teachers and the sources of their identity development, using multiple examples from the extended interviews she conducted (Nias 1989a, 1989b). Although there are no in-depth case studies of individual teachers in Nias' work, she does address the importance of teachers' roles in both their personal and professional lives as these influence their sense of self.

The results of Nias' (1989a) study relate to this study at Time 5 in 1997, which was the 10th year of teaching for Sandy, Rick, and Ralph. Unlike the teachers in this study, a good portion of the teachers in Nias' study did not see themselves as career teachers, were frustrated at their lack of vertical promotion and increasing responsibilities, or even took on extensive out-side interests to offset boredom, which Nias called *parallel careers*. Sandy's case is similar to many of the married female teachers in Nias' (1989b) study because they also found ways through part-time and flexible roles to continue their personal and professional growth and to have an influence on others. Similar to some of Nias' midcareer teachers, Rick also expressed some potential career dissatisfaction at Time 5 after 10 years in the class-room, when he resolved to remain at his school but to get more involved in school committees again.

Huberman's Model of the Professional Life Cycle of Teachers

Martin Huberman's (1989) longitudinal study of teachers' professional lives was based on cross-sectional data gathered from self-reports of 160 mostly male secondary teachers in Switzerland in the 1980s. The goal of these studies was to describe the evolution of the professional life cycle of teachers throughout the span of their careers as a heuristic for understand-ing the influence of both psychological and sociological factors on the life cycle of teachers. Huberman's purpose was also to describe possible stages or periods in the professional life cycle of teachers' careers, which he be-lieved have heuristic rather than prescriptive value. Huberman did not fo-cus on teachers' pedagogical understandings, but his work provides an-other useful perspective on teacher development and includes descriptions of what teachers focus on at various stages of their careers. A summary of each of these stages follows (Fig. 7.2).

The first stage in Huberman's study, the career entry stage, is character-ized by themes of survival, discovery, and exploration.

> The "survival" aspect renders what is commonly called the "reality shock" of the initial year—the initial confrontation with the same complexity of profes-sional work that most experienced members of the profession deal with—and its attendant dilemmas, continuous trial and error, preoccupation with one-self and one's sense of adequacy, wide discrepancies between instructional goals and what one is actually able to do in the classroom, inappropriate in-structional materials, wide swings from permissiveness to excessive strictness, concerns with discipline and management that eat away at instructional time, recalcitrant pupils, and the like. On the other hand, the "discovery" theme

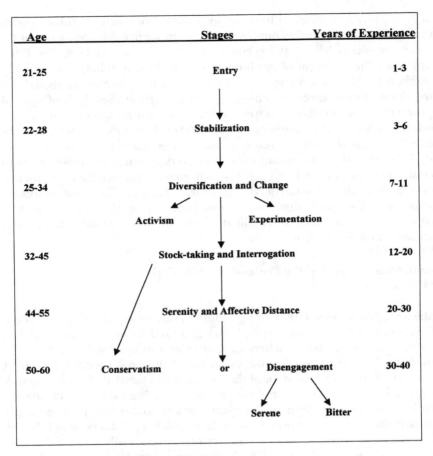

FIG. 7.2.   Huberman's (1989) model of the professional life cycle of teachers.

renders the initial enthusiasm of teaching, the sharp learning curve, the headiness of having one's own pupils, one's classroom, one's program; the pride of collegiality and of "place" within a profession. (Huberman, 1989, p. 349)

Huberman said that the survival and discovery stages often occur in parallel during the entry stage, with the excitement and challenge of the discovery stage serving to pull beginning teachers through the survival stage. The exploration theme also has to do with discovery and experimentation in the classroom as new teachers enter their careers.

The second stage in Huberman's model, the stabilization stage, is characterized by personal commitment, becoming responsible, earning tenure, independence, liberation, emancipation, growing sense of instructional mastery, and greater confidence. Huberman reported that many teachers perceive this stage positively and describe it as a period of commitment to the choice of teaching as a career, as having a more assertive sense of professional autonomy, and as a time for developing instructional mastery.

> Generally speaking, there is the juncture of a personal commitment (the decision to make a career of teaching) and an administrative act (the granting of tenure). One is now a teacher, both in one's own eyes and in the eyes of others—not necessarily forever, but for a good block of time. . . . Virtually all empirical studies associate the period of 3–5 years into the career with a growing sense of instructional "mastery." . . . With greater ease in more complex or unexpected classroom situations, teachers describe themselves as consolidating, then refining a basic instructional repertoire on which they can, finally, rely on. (Huberman, 1989, p. 350)

According to Huberman, these first two stages are fairly ubiquitous in studies of teachers' careers, but the paths individuals take beyond the first 6 or 7 years in the career cycle are quite divergent.

Huberman called the next stage the *diversification and change stage* because the teacher's career can go in two directions: activism or experimentation. According to Huberman, reasons for seeking diversification and change range from a desire to make use of one's sense of instructional mastery by seeking stimulation, new ideas, and challenges to a fear of stagnation. However, the fear of stagnation was stronger for teachers with 11 to 19 years of experience, whereas those with less than 10 years of experience were more likely to seek diversification and variation from established routines. Experimentation and diversification are characterized by

> . . . the consolidation of an instructional repertoire [that] leads naturally to attempts to increase one's effectiveness in the classroom. There then follow a series of modest, largely private experiences, during which one experiments with new materials, different pupil groupings, new assignments, different combinations of lesson and exercises. In a sense, these attempts compensate for the uncertainties of the first years of teaching. . . . (Huberman, 1989, p. 351)

However, a fairly large subset of Huberman's sample (35%–40% of the 160 teachers he interviewed) appeared to seek a more activist role, which he described in this way:

> *Having "stabilized" one's classroom, one takes aim on the aberrant practices or inadequate resources within the system by joining or mobilizing groups of peers, signing on for reform, lobbying or joining key commissions.* (Huberman, 1989, p. 351)

However, the motives for such activism were not clear and in some cases appeared related to a desire for career advancement.

Stock-taking and interrogation are themes during the midcareer of a teacher's career cycle (12–20 years of experience), especially for men ages 32 to 45. This may be a time of increased vulnerability and reflectiveness, possibly precipitated by a psychological crisis, an unsatisfactory structural change in the teaching context such as a new principal, or family changes. In some cases, this stage follows a period of unsatisfactory attempts at diversification or a *midlife crisis* that causes teachers to rethink their original desire to spend their lives as teachers and a nagging desire to try another profession before it is too late.

The next stage, which Huberman called the *serenity and affective distance stage* in a teacher's career cycle, begins sometime between 44 and 55 years of age, or with 20 to 30 years of experience and often following an active period of self-doubt. Huberman described this phase as a time of reflection and self-acceptance when a teacher's level of ambition and investment in career decreases. However, he also said these themes are balanced by confidence, effectiveness, and serenity, and sometimes by increased distance from pupils due to increasing generational differences.

The last stage of a teacher's life cycle may be marked by *conservatism,* and negativism often marks this stage for many teachers ages 50 to 60 years. Teachers at this stage of the career cycle are often more prudent and quite skeptical of reform, less tolerant of younger teachers and pupils, and generally more dogmatic and rigid in their thoughts and actions. In Huberman's (1989) study, one group of highly conservative teachers bypassed the serenity stage and moved straight to a self-questioning, dissatisfied stage at midcareer into a final disengagement phase.

Disengagement, which can be either serene or bitter, is the end stage in Huberman's scheme of the professional life cycle of teachers with 30 or more years of experience. This period is marked by gradual internalization and withdrawal, in a generally positive way with few regrets, as veteran teachers spend more time on their interests outside of school. Such disengagement sometimes begins in the serenity stage and continues through the conservative phase, when teachers feel marginalized because they disagree with changing school policies and practices. For others, however, this period is bitter and more extreme.

In all cases, however, there was a disinvestment in concerns outside the classroom. Seniority had brought for them a convenient schedule, favorable class assignments, freedom from unwanted intrusions, and their goal was both to preserve these privileges and to fend off solicitations to increase their level of investment. (Huberman, 1989, p. 355)

Huberman's career stages are useful in thinking about the teachers in this study, especially the three who are still teaching: Sandy, Ralph, and

Rick. The career entry stage (Years 1–3) for all of these teachers can be characterized quite well by the survival, discovery, and exploration themes that Huberman (1989) described. Huberman said that the survival and discovery stages often occur in parallel, with the excitement and challenge of the discovery stage serving to pull beginning teachers through the survival stage, which I think is quite true of these teachers. However, it is unlikely that Julie reached the stabilization stage (Years 3–6) before she left the classroom for other opportunities. Nevertheless, after 13 years of teaching, Sandy, Ralph, and Rick appear to currently be in the diversification and change stage, which Huberman said can take two directions. My data indicate that their careers currently fit best with Huberman's experimentation mode, which he described as coming from a desire to make use of one's sense of instructional mastery by seeking stimulation, new ideas, and challenges due to fear of stagnation. However, rather than experimenting in the sense of tinkering with new materials and lessons, these teachers appear to be refining their pedagogical practices as they come closer and closer to achieving personal teaching goals and enacting their vision of teaching from a developmental-constructivist perspective. Rick also seems to be thinking about taking on the more activist role that Huberman talked about as another aspect of the midcareer, diversification, and change stage. Finally, Huberman described the stock-taking and interrogation stage (Years 12–20) as a time of increased vulnerability and reflectiveness, during which change may be precipitated by personal or professional dissatisfaction or crisis. How these teachers will deal this next phase in the life cycle of their careers is unknown at this time.

Kagan's View of Teacher Development

Donna Kagan's (1992) work, based on a review of over 40 empirical research studies in the learning-to-teach literature between 1987 and 1990, yields a model of teachers' professional growth that she constructed from the patterns of findings she discerned in the studies she selected to review. Kagan concluded from her analysis that the Fuller and Berliner models can be integrated and elaborated on. Kagan's model for teacher development suggests that novice teachers' primary task is to acquire knowledge of students while the novice acquires knowledge of self. Another task of the novice teacher is to form standardized routines for procedures that integrate classroom management and instruction. Kagan suggested that the resolution of these two tasks allows novice teachers to focus on their students' learning. Figure 7.3 represents my own interpretation of Kagan's model of preservice teacher development, including the tasks she suggests for novice teachers and needed changes she suggests for preservice teacher education (Kagan, 1992).

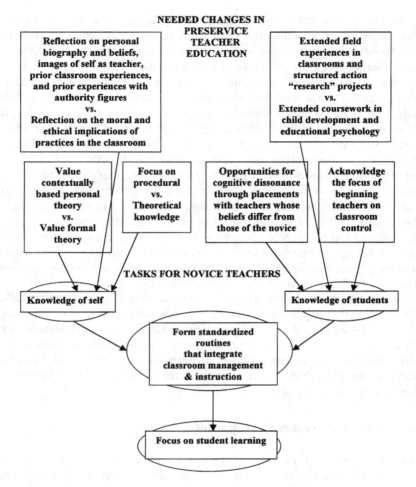

FIG. 7.3.   Kagan's (1992) model of preservice and beginning teacher development: Factors affecting professional growth.

Based on her review of learning to teach studies, Kagan (1992) inferred and suggested several changes in preservice teacher education to promote beginning teachers' professional growth. Among these are (a) a focus on procedural over theoretical knowledge; (b) self-reflection on personal biography and beliefs, images of self as teacher, prior classroom experiences, and prior experiences with authority figures over reflection on the moral and ethical implications of practices in the classroom; (c) extended field experiences in classrooms and structured action research projects over extended coursework in child development and educational psychology; (d) opportunities for cognitive dissonance through placements with teachers whose beliefs differ from those of the novice; (e) acknowledgment of the focus of beginning teachers on classroom control; (f) acknowledgment that some preservice teachers may not be ready to handle a classroom successfully and should be counseled out of the preservice program; and (g) valuing contextually based personal theory over formal theory.

Kagan's work has been criticized for leaving out several major studies of professional growth among preservice teachers (Grossman, 1992) and not distinguishing between teacher beliefs and teachers' pedagogical practices (P. Ammon, personal communication, September 25, 1992). Her suggestions for how to promote teacher development also differ in substantive ways from the recommendations of other models (Black & Ammon, 1989, 1992; Levin & Ammon, 1992; Ryan, 1986). Nevertheless, Kagan's work offers another way to look at the factors that influence the development of teachers' thinking.

Hollingsworth's View of the Process of Learning to Teach

Sandra Hollingsworth and her colleagues (Hollingsworth, 1989, 1994; Lidstone & Hollingsworth, 1992) conducted a 6-year longitudinal study of the learning to teach process, beginning in 1987 with a group of 14 preservice teachers from another teacher education program at UC–Berkeley. Although some of the research goals in Hollingsworth's "Learning to Teach Reading" project were similar to those that guided this study, her research was theoretically grounded in cognitive psychology and information processing. Specifically, Hollingsworth was interested in understanding the process of cognitive change, "the nature of the intellectual growth and identity maintenance while learning to teach" (Hollingsworth, 1989, p. 161), and in determining how teacher education can support preservice teachers as they learn to become good teachers of reading in urban schools. However, as her 6-year longitudinal study progressed, Hollingsworth embraced feminist theoretical perspectives (Harding, 1987) as she began to see her work with 4 of her original 14 teachers as mostly about how collaboration and conversational processes influenced the process of learning to teach (Hollingsworth, 1994, p. 7).

Although the program goals and philosophy of the postbaccalaureate teacher education program at UC–Berkeley that Hollingsworth studied were somewhat different than those of the DTE program, her participating teachers took some of the same courses, including child development courses based on the developmental-constructivist theories of Piaget and Vygotsky. Similar to several earlier studies described before, Hollingsworth (1989) and her colleagues (Lidstone & Hollingsworth, 1992) found that the preprogram or prior beliefs of preservice teachers were a strong influence on how they understood and enacted the content learned in their teacher education classes and how they applied it to teaching opportunities in urban classrooms. Essentially, teachers' prior beliefs served as a filter for the knowledge about teaching and classrooms that they acquired as preservice teachers. Lidstone and Hollingsworth (1992) also found that the preservice teachers in their study needed to get classroom management under control before they were able to develop and effectively deliver subject-specific content and pedagogy and before they could begin to focus on children's learning in the classroom. Hollingsworth (1989) also noted that preservice teachers needed to be motivated by an interest in students as individuals and a developing interest in subject pedagogy (in this case, on teaching reading) that comes from their teacher education courses. This had to be in place for teachers to change their understanding of how reading can be taught effectively in urban schools, hence for growth in their pedagogical knowledge. She also found that support factors were necessary for changes in pedagogical and content knowledge to occur. These included permission and encouragement from cooperating teachers to experiment with new methods of teaching reading, expectations from the teacher education program that such experimentation was important, and support from the university supervisors as student teachers experimented with new pedagogical practices for teaching reading and writing.

As a result of analyzing changes in the beliefs, cognitions, and practices of eight of the original teachers in this study, Lidstone and Hollingsworth (1992) offered a model of how teachers' thinking changes and what influences those changes. This model of cognitive and behavioral changes in learning to teach, the *Model of Complexity Reduction*, described shifts and patterns in learning to teach after 4 years in the classroom. It was based on interviews and classroom observations of eight teachers. How cognitive changes occur in this model was summarized by Lidstone and Hollingsworth (1992) in the following way:

> Because learning to teach is extremely complicated and the nature of attentional capacity is selective (Bransford, 1979), new teachers seem to actively attend to only a few concepts and skills at a time As they learn basic conceptual routines and are able to put them on "automatic pilot" (being free of having to devote conscious attention to them), they can concentrate on more advanced concepts and pedagogical practices. Thus, the overall complexity of teaching is gradually reduced to manageable proportions as the teacher develops over time. (pp. 40–41)

The *Model of Complexity Reduction* (Lidstone & Hollingsworth, 1992) focused on three factors that affect the learning to teach process: the role of prior beliefs in learning to teach, three areas of cognitive attention for teachers (classroom management/organization, knowledge of subject/pedagogy, and student learning from academic tasks), and three levels of cognitive understanding (rote, routine, and comprehensive). Although, Lidstone and Hollingsworth (1992) described two patterns through their model that teachers follow while learning to teach, essentially a teacher's ability to focus on student learning from academic tasks requires that the teacher integrate both classroom management and organization and knowledge of subject matter and pedaogy at least at a routine level.

> This integration usually develops after the beginning teacher has routinized management and subject/pedagogy knowledge separately, although some teachers never integrate the two. Skilled teachers know that management problems do not usually occur in isolation from the lesson being taught. If the subject matter or pedagogy is too easy or too difficult, and/or it the task does not require at least some active construction of knowledge on the part of the learner, behavioral problems will most likely develop. (Lidstone & Hollingsworth, 1992, p. 43)

In this model, prior beliefs affect how deeply teachers are able to master specific skills and concepts. In other words, beliefs affect the level of cognitive processing and behavior of the teacher so that their focus on classroom management, subject matter and pedagogy, and students learning from academic tasks can be at a rote, routine, or comprehensive level, which in turn affects their understanding of classroom management, subject matter and pedagogy, and students learning from academic tasks and how well this knowledge is integrated with their beliefs.

Lidstone and Hollingsworth (1992) concluded their study with a call for support from university supervisors, university instructors, cooperating teachers, principals, other teachers, staff developers, and researchers:

> All beginning teachers need: (1) Support in seeing other perspectives, possibly opportunities to observe in other classrooms, from participating in collaborative groups made up of both types of teachers . . . , or in doing action research projects collaboratively with other teachers; (2) Support from an induction program where other beginning teachers are struggling with similar problems; (3) Support people who have some sense of their particular beginning teachers' beliefs, background knowledge, and biography, and who consider these important variables in teacher education; (4) Support people who have a schema of teacher change, such as the Model of Complexity Reduction (Hollingsworth, 1989) or the Ammon and Hutcheson Model (1989), so that they have in mind the range of beginning teachers' understanding of learning to teach. (p. 56)

The model proposed by Hollingsworth and her colleagues (Hollingsworth, 1989, 1994; Lidstone & Hollingsworth, 1992) is somewhat similar to the description Kagan (1992) gave about the important tasks of novice teachers: acquire knowledge of students while the novice acquires knowledge of self, and form standardized routines for procedures that integrate classroom management and instruction. Perhaps this is due to the use of cognitive information-processing theories by both Kagan and Hollingsworth as they thought about and studied teacher development in the early 1990s. At any rate, the perspectives of both Kagan and Hollingsworth about teacher development are interesting to consider, and the suggestions of how to support teacher development are quite similar to those found as a result of this study.

Robert Bullough's Longitudinal Case Study of Kerrie

Robert Bullough and his colleagues (Bullough & Knowles, 1991; Bullough, Knowles, & Crow, 1991) have written several case studies of first-year teachers in an effort to help beginning teachers think about themselves as developing professionals and elucidate factors that influence beginning teachers' development to help their teacher education programs to better prepare and support developing teachers. In the process of developing and analyzing year-long case studies of six first-year teachers, Bullough, Knowles, and Crow (1991) discovered that teachers' metaphors are powerful predictors of how well beginning teachers may or may not adjust to teaching as a profession. Essentially, when beginning teachers' metaphors are a good match for their teaching context, they usually make a good adjustment to the teaching profession. However, in cases where their metaphors and beliefs about teaching are not a good match, beginning teachers will likely struggle during the induction years unless they are able to adjust their views. Although this is an oversimplification of the extensive work of Bullough and his colleagues in supporting teacher development, as well as of the power and limitations of metaphors, they described their use of metaphors in this way: "Emerging as a teacher is, therefore, a quest for compelling and fitting metaphors that represent who beginning teachers imagine themselves to be as teachers" (Bullough, Knowles & Crow, 1991, p. 8).

Robert Bullough also conducted an in-depth, longitudinal case study of one teacher's development during her first year in the classroom (Bullough, 1989) and the follow-up book that looks at Kerrie's life and career as a teacher across 8 years (Bullough & Baughman, 1997). The depth and breadth of this case study and the inclusion of Kerrie as co-author of the follow-up book is noteworthy for its authenticity, attention to the role of context, and detailed analysis of the influences on her life as a teacher. The juxtaposition of the commonalities and uniqueness of Kerrie's story are helpful because they invite readers to compare and make sense of Kerrie's experiences in light of their own experiences. As we read details of how Kerrie coped with the typical problems that most first-year teachers face, we are able to think about how we faced similar issues or helped others face them. Furthermore, by reading about Kerrie 8 years later, we are not only able to see changes in Kerrie's life, her thinking, and her practice, but we are also able see how changes in her teaching context affected her and how being the subject of a longitudinal study influenced her as well. In her case, Kerrie felt that she benefited from being able to talk about her teaching on a regular basis with someone interested in listening, and that such talking (and the anticipation of it) influenced her thinking by encouraging her to reflect on herself and her teaching. As Kerrie reported, "Every time I talk to you . . . it's just a catalyst because it makes me think about what I'm doing. It's not necessarily you, it's me thinking about me" (Bullough, 1979, p. 139). In these books, Bullough (1979) and Bullough and Baughman (1987) illuminated the complexity of one teacher's development over time.

This book provides four more in-depth case studies and adds to the teacher development literature by offering a look at these teachers' personal and professional lives, with a special focus on the development of their pedagogical understandings over a 12-year period.

Usefulness of Various Models of Teacher Development

Although the preceding summary of research on teacher development covering the past 30 years is not exhaustive, it does represent attempts to offer research-based models of teacher develop, describe changes in teacher development and how they might occur, and apply various theoretical perspectives to understanding teacher development. Despite any epistemological differences that readers may have with any of these studies or models, and considering the methodological problems with stage theories that may overemphasize quasibiological variables and underemphasize the influence of social conditions and individual differences, I agree with Berliner (1988) and Huberman (1989) that their heuristic value should be honored. Consideration of how each phase in a teacher's career might lay the groundwork for the next phase, and also perhaps limit the range of possibilities for what happens next (Huberman, 1989), helps us think about the variables that might influence the lives and careers of teachers. Furthermore, I also agree with Huberman (1989) that we should not view psychological or developmental stage models as deterministic or insensitive to individual differences. More likely, as Huberman stated, adult development is dialectical, and the goal is to describe and understand the contribution of personal and professional influences on the development of teachers over time.

Furthermore, what Glassberg wrote in 1979—"A major source of difficulty in teacher education has been the lack of coherent theory and practice to promote teacher development." (p. 2)—still seemed to be true in the year 2000. We still do not have comprehensive or agreed on theories of teacher development that can help guide us in supporting teachers' development. Instead, we have several models that address different aspects of teacher development from different theoretical perspectives. However, we now have various sets of state and national standards—both generic and discipline-based standards that direct teacher education curriculum. Unfortunately, most of these standards are not explicitly grounded in a specific theoretical framework and do not often address how we might help teachers meet these standards. In other words, we have standards and goals for teacher education, but no agreed on theory that would help us understand why and how teachers develop as they do so that we can support them in their development. We need to build on the research and models of teacher development described earlier so that we can promote teachers' development in ways that are theoretically coherent and empirically tested. We also need to apply the lessons learned from each of these studies to help teachers continue to grow and develop.

WHAT LESSONS CAN BE LEARNED FROM LONGITUDINAL CASE STUDIES OF TEACHERS' THINKING?

Based on my analysis of the data collected during this longitudinal study, I believe three major factors were influential in the development of these four teachers' pedagogical understandings throughout their careers. These are three lessons I learned from this study, and I believe they are important ones for educators to consider when thinking about how we can offer scaffolding that promotes teacher development:

- First, teachers need ongoing support in order to continue to develop their pedagogical understandings and to remain in the classroom.
- Second, teachers need opportunities that encourage and allow them to continue to be learners if they are going to develop their pedagogical understandings. Ultimately, teachers need to be learners to continue to develop their pedagogical understandings over time.
- Third, teachers need to be reflective if they are to continue to develop. They also need to develop the ability to think metacognitively about teaching and learning, and about behavior and development.

Based on this study, these three elements appear to be fundamental in influencing the development of pedagogical understanding over time: support system, opportunities for ongoing professional development, and propensity for reflection and metacognitive thinking. In fact, based on this study, I would go so far as to say that the lack of any one of these three factors could be detrimental to the development of a teacher's pedagogical understanding, although this is an empirical question that needs further assessment beyond these four cases. I also believe that these three factors lead directly to a major lesson that can be learned from this study: We can and should provide the foundation for these factors (support, professional development, reflection, and metacognitive thinking) during initial teacher preparation and continue to support them throughout a teacher's career by the kinds of policy initiatives that we generate at school, district, and state levels. What follows is a more thorough explanation of the three elements that were major influences on the development of teachers' pedagogical understandings during this longitudinal study.

1. Having a Support System Influences Teachers' Pedagogical Development. Teachers can continue to develop their thinking about pedagogy when they interact with others to get needed support. This includes support from family, friends, colleagues, or mentors. Support is something that these teachers experienced during their careers, especially Sandy, Ralph, and Rick. However, I do not mean that support is just having the encouragement of people in their personal lives who are supportive of what they do because all of these teachers have family members who support their career choice. Rather, what Sandy, Ralph, and Rick have are multiple forms of support in their personal and professional lives from people who they can talk with about their teaching. For example, Rick has strong support in both areas from his wife, principal, other teachers, best friend from childhood, mentor Dave, and student teachers. In fact, he engages regularly with these people in conversations about his teaching, his students, things he is trying to learn more about, and works they have read together, including books about educational theory. Ralph has his partner, teachers at the various schools where he has worked, student teachers over the years, and, more recently, his students and colleagues in the DTE program. All of these people engage with him as he reflects on his teaching and tries to understand what his students are thinking and how they are learning from his lessons. Sandy has several colleagues and teaching partners, including other teachers who also graduated from the DTE program, her principal for many years, and student teachers over the years whom she talks with about teaching ideas. She has also participated in several formal and informal teacher collaboratives where the focus was on discussing curriculum and pedagogy. In contrast, Julie felt she had little support during her 5 years in the classroom. She did not feel supported by her three principals or her colleagues early on. In fact, it was not until her last year in the classroom that she found teachers in her school who regularly engaged with her in curriculum development or problem solving. Julie did have a few student teachers from the DTE program, but she did not feel enough support at her school, nor did

she have support at home because she was single at the time. Unfortunately, Julie apparently lacked the support she needed to remain in the
classroom, although it should be noted that lack of support is only one of
the reasons that Julie left teaching after just 5 years.

By *connections* I mean maintaining connections with colleagues, as well as
having other professional connections. For the teachers in this study, this
included staying connected to the DTE program over the years by mentoring student teachers in their classrooms or, in Ralph's case, serving as a
supervisor for the DTE program for 3 years. For example, Sandy talked
about the importance of support at Time 4 in 1993:

> *Having people available to talk to, a support group, is great. I think I had a lot of ideas*
> *when I was first teaching but I was by myself and nobody was doing what I was doing.*
> *Then I moved from Washington to here. I feel there is a lot more support. I have a lot*
> *more friends and people that think the same way whom I can to talk to. Yes, there's an-*
> *other woman here, this is her first year here, and there is another teacher here who went*
> *through the California Literacy Project last summer. There's Tracy [another DTE grad]*
> *and Cindy [the Vice Principal], and without Jim's support [the Principal] from the very*
> *beginning, it would have been impossible—just their confidence that we are going to do*
> *the best for the kids, even though they don't always understand what you're doing.*

Every one of these four teachers stayed connected with the DTE program by having student teachers regularly in their classrooms. Rick took
student teachers during a particular placement most every fall semester.
This was a time when the student teacher would be there all semester and
when he felt they were experienced enough to benefit from what he was doing in his room. He had eight student teachers in the years between 1987
and 1999. Both Sandy and Ralph took student teachers from the DTE program any time they were asked, often in both the fall and spring semesters.
Sandy mentored eight student teachers during the 10 years she taught in
the public schools. In addition to the 15 student teachers he mentored between 1987 and 1995, Ralph also observed and coached another 40 student
teachers during his 3 years as a supervisor in the DTE program. Julie had
four student teachers during her 5 years at Marin School, taking her first
one during her second year teaching there.

Although it may seem unusual for a beginning teacher who is still struggling to become proficient and comfortable with her own teaching, it is the
policy of the DTE program to place their student teachers with as many program graduates as possible. The goal is for the preservice teachers to see in
practice what the DTE program is advocating in their courses at the university. The DTE program faculty have no qualms about using beginning
teachers who are graduates of their program as cooperating teachers. They
feel that they are well able to articulate their thinking and believe that the
questions student teachers ask, and the ensuing conversations, are helpful

in pushing both the preservice teachers and the slightly more experienced (but still beginning) teachers to continue to think about why they teach the way they do. They also feel that the pedagogical thoughts and actions of recent program graduates are not yet automatized, hence they are readily available for both teachers to continue to examine. Serving as master teachers, which is what the DTE program calls all their cooperating teachers, therefore offers a form of support for their program graduates.

As Sandy reported at Time 3 in 1990 and then at Time 4 in 1993, having student teachers from the DTE program makes you accountable for your thoughts and actions, but also provides help for the students in the class.

> So I have student teachers from DTE . . . The teachers just talk to us about how much work it is, and how the kids need to spend their time with just us, but I think it is important for the kids to have another teacher in the room to interact with and to help them. For me, a student teacher is better than an aide because, coming from the DTE program, they already share the same philosophy that I have. (Time 3, additional interview, 1990)
>
> It makes you think about what you did and why you did it. And they also ask you questions about what you're doing . . . in class, or why are you doing this. And you have to be more responsible for what you're doing. (Time 4, Clinical interview probe, 1993)

2. Ongoing Professional Development Influences Teachers' Pedagogical Development.   Teachers can continue to be learners and develop their pedagogical understandings by engaging in ongoing professional development opportunities. A clear influence on the pedagogical development of the teachers in this study came through maintaining ongoing professional connections and engaging in opportunities for professional development. While this included staying connected to the DTE program over the years, maintaining professional connections that offer both professional development and support also means keeping connected professionally to various organizations for teachers, such as the Bay Area Writing Project (Julie, Ralph, Rick, and Sandy), the California Reading and Literacy Project (Sandy), or the Developmental Studies Center (Rick). Professional development and support also occurs through regularly attending conferences such as the one sponsored annually by the California Math Council at Asilomar (Julie, Ralph, Rick, and Sandy) or by attending CUE (California Computer Using Educators) conferences (Ralph, Sandy). Support and ongoing professional development, opportunities to interact with colleagues at conferences or workshops, and time to learn about current best practices are vital forms of professional development and support, which all four of these teachers have had throughout their careers.

Although there was no specific question in the clinical interview protocol that asked about professional development opportunities, each of these teachers referred to learning opportunities they had from time to time during their interviews. They also described some of their professional development activities in response to a question I asked about what they see as their greatest resources or sources of information in their own development as teachers. Toward the end of this study, they provided me with a list of the professional development opportunities they had engaged in over the years that they felt were especially influential. Appendix E is a list of the professional development experiences recommended by these teachers, and Appendix F is a list of books that these teachers found particularly influential and valuable to their ongoing development over the years.

As Julie mentioned at Time 6, in thinking back about the resources she was drawing on to answer my questions and the sources of information she relies on,

> *And then I've always enjoyed reading professional material, journals and things, "Mathematics Teacher" or whatever, "Teaching Children Mathematics" magazines that are put out by various professional organizations. I've always enjoyed going to staff development opportunities so those are all great resources and I think that that's probably something that really kept me motivated and learning new things was trying other things and exposing myself to new ideas and talking with other teachers and continually trying new things. . . .*

Julie was also an active member of the California Math Council and the Bay Area Writing Project during her tenure as a classroom teacher. She also mentioned using several books to help her develop her math curriculum while she was teaching: Mary Baratta-Lorton's *Math Their Way, Family Math* from the Lawrence Hall of Science, Kathy Richardson's *Number Concepts,* and Marilyn Burns' *Math Solutions.* She also participated in a math leadership group during her first few years in the classroom, and then later she took a job developing mathematics curriculum for a textbook company and then a software company. During that time, she continued her own professional development by attending meetings of the National Council of Teachers of Mathematics (NCTM), as well as the California Math Council's annual meeting at Asilomar, and by rereading books by Piaget and Constance Kamii, as well as Vanderwall's *Mathematics: Teaching Developmentally,* which she used to help her in her job as a math specialist.

Throughout her career, Sandy sought out professional development opportunities related to her interest in emergent literacy, as well as to learn more about teaching specific subject areas and instructional strategies in general. For example, as classroom teacher and then as a Title 1 Literacy Facilitator, Sandy was involved with the Emergent Literacy Institute and the California Literacy Project, and she regularly attended the Bay Area Writing Project and the California Reading Conference. Sandy attended the California Math Council's annual meeting at Asilomar and the Computer

Using Educator's (CUE) conference on a fairly regular basis throughout her teaching career. She also attended a summer institute in New Hampshire in 1999 at her own expense to learn more about teaching writing. This experience provided Sandy with both support and new insights into how she could and should teach writing. In addition, Sandy is a voracious consumer of educational literature and particularly likes the books published by Heinemann and Stenhouse. Some of her favorite authors are Nancy Atwell, Lucy McCormick Calkins, Anne Haas Dyson, Donald Graves, Shelley Harwayne, and Reggie Routman. Basically, Sandy approaches curriculum development by reading the latest books on whatever area she is working on, and she continuously reads children's literature. For example, she wrote in her final reflection for this book during the summer of 2000,

> *Right now I'm struggling with how to teach spelling. I've gone from not touching it at all to giving weekly spelling lists to appease the parents. This summer I've read many books and articles about spelling and am coming to a better understanding of what I can do to help students improve their spelling.*

Sandy also commented in 1999 that she needs the support of both books and people when she is trying to figure something out.

> *I have a lot of books and I can read them, but I don't think that they give you the full picture. So I can try to do what they say that they have done, but I think that going and actually hearing someone talk about it and practicing is really important for me. Talking about how things work with other teachers, so those are my resources . . . I can do a lot of learning by myself, but only up to a certain point. Then I need to go and practice with somebody else guiding me, saying, "Try it this way" or "Have you thought about this?"*

Ralph also reads and attends to his professional development by going to workshops and attending conferences. He is a regular attendee at the Bay Area Writing Project, the California Math Council's annual conference at Asilomar, the California Reading Conference, and the CUE conference for computer-using educators. In addition, he remembers attending presentations and reading books by Marilyn Burns, Donald Graves, and Vivian Paley. A personal favorite of Ralph's is an early childhood expert, Bev Bos.

Rick also learns from reading on his own, attending conferences, and his involvement with other professional development opportunities, such as the Developmental Study Center.

> *I guess the biggest thing that's changed is that our school got a grant to work with the Developmental Study Center, so they came out here. And I've been incorporating a lot of what happens in Developmental Study Center and a lot of the reading, that along with the cooperative adventures stuff that I've always done . . . and that's probably the biggest change.*

Books by authors like William Glasser, James Comer, Howard Gardner, and Alfie Kohn are among those that Rick mentioned to me, at Time 6 in 1999, as having a big influence on his thinking.

And then, just books. Books, books, always books. I'll get one author and then that author will lead me to some other author. Just some new take always on how to present this, how to think about it, how to frame it, make it easier for kids, or make it easier for me to understand and make it part of a life.

3. Reflection and Metacognition Can Influence Teachers' Pedagogical Development. The third factor that influenced development of pedagogical understandings of the teachers in this study was their propensity to regularly reflect on their teaching experiences and to think metacognitively about teaching and learning, and about children's behavior and development. My analysis of data collected from these four teachers across 15 years indicates that the ability to reflect and think metacognitively about one's thoughts and actions as a teacher is a key factor in being able to resolve problems and dilemmas that arise daily in teaching. It is the resolution of problems of practice, and the resolution of cognitive dissonance that arises when things do not go as planned in the classroom or with a student, that helps teachers continue to develop their pedagogical understandings.

All four of these teachers are reflective to a greater or lesser degree, and certainly all are capable of being reflective and thinking metacognitively. However, the level and degree to which teachers consciously engage in this kind of thinking appears to make a difference in their pedagogical development. Furthermore, the focus of one's reflection and metacognitive thinking also makes a difference. For example, because Julie has not taught in a classroom for over 8 years, we would not expect that her pedagogical understanding would continue to develop uniformly because she was not focused on teaching or on children's behavior in the classroom after she left teaching in 1993. Conversely, we would expect that the pedagogical understandings of Ralph, Rick, and Sandy should continue to develop if they focus their reflection and metacognitive thinking on resolving the problems, issues, and dilemmas that come up in their daily lives as teachers. In fact, data from the longitudinal study indicate that these three teachers have continued to develop their thinking about behavior, development, learning, and teaching over time, whereas Julie's understanding of these four areas within the pedagogical domain has not developed at the same rate.

A corollary to this factor (reflection and metacognitive thinking) has to do with teachers' intentions and actions. That is, if teachers do not have good intentions and a disposition to act on their reflections and metacognitive thinking, then they are not likely to develop more complex ways of thinking about pedagogy. In the case of these teachers, their intentions and dispositions to act on their reflections have remained important to them throughout their careers in the classroom as is evidenced in their own reflective writing found at the end of each of their case studies.

SUMMARY AND CONCLUSIONS

So what? So what have we learned from this study? First, I believe that the longitudinal case studies of four teachers from 1985 to 2000 provide information and offer insights into how these teachers' thinking about pedagogy—about children's behaviors and development, and about teaching and learning—changed over time. Essentially, their pedagogical understandings continued to develop from initial thinking that was quite global, and sometimes vague or confused, to increasingly better articulated understandings, which indicated better differentiated and eventually more integrated understandings of behavior, development, learning, and teaching. Furthermore, as their thinking about pedagogy becomes more sophisticated and complex, their thinking and actions become more congruent, as can be seen in observations of their classroom teaching. However, we also see throughout their case studies that each teacher's developmental trajectory is unique, and that their personal lives and professional contexts influenced how their pedagogical thoughts and actions develop. Second, I also believe, based on these four cases, that what they learned in their teacher education program did not wash out. It may not have been used much in their first few years of teaching when they were focusing mainly on their teaching, but their deep understanding of children's development continued to be foundational to their thinking and their classroom practice throughout their careers. This is evident in both the language they use to express their understandings of pedagogy and in the instructional strategies they use in their classrooms today. In all cases, their thoughts and actions convey a deep understanding of developmental and constructivist perspectives. Third, the way these teachers' pedagogical understandings changed over time was due to their efforts to solve and resolve the problems they perceived and the disequilibrium they experienced when their thoughts and actions were in conflict. In their various contexts, their resolution of the cognitive conflicts they experienced took place on both internal and external levels as they reflected on their problems and as they sought input from other sources about their problems.

Finally, as a result of this study, three rather obvious but important lessons emerged that those of us engaged in teacher education must remember: (a) Teachers need ongoing support if they are going to continue to develop, (b) teachers need ongoing professional development opportunities—they really do need to be lifelong learners—if they are going to continue to develop, and (c) teachers need to reflect and be able to think metacognitively if they are going to continue to develop.

APPENDIXES

APPENDIX A
Developmental Sequences of Teachers' Thinking about Pedagogy

Qualitative Level	The Goal of Instruction Is for Students to Attain:	To Obtain These Learning Objectives, Students Must:	Teacher Teaches by:
1. Naive Empiricism	A large store of facts and procedures.	Be able and receptive.	Showing and telling students what they need to know in ways that are appealing.
2. Everyday Behaviorism	Skills that are essential for attaining and using facts and procedures.	Practice the new skills in question, having first acquired whatever prerequisites are needed.	Giving students a lot of directed practice, with corrective feedback and positive reinforcement as needed; modeling and reinforcing.
3. Global Constructivism	Correct understanding of the concepts that underlie the facts, procedures, and skills in a given subject.	Explore and manipulate relevant aspects of the real world, having reached the stage of development at which the concepts in question can be correctly understood.	Giving students opportunities to explore and manipulate developmentally appropriate materials; providing hands-on experience.
4. Differentiated Constructivism	Conceptual understandings of a sort that are better than before and may improve still further.	Be actively engaged in their most advanced ways of thinking to construct understandings of the concepts in question at their present level of development; engaged in sense-making	Engaging student in thought-provoking activities and guiding their thinking toward better understandings within each domain.
5. Integrated Constructivism	Conceptual understandings that integrate the academic, social, and ethical dimensions of each concept, procedure, or skill to be mastered.	Be actively engaged in problem solving to construct understandings of the concepts in question at whatever the child's individual level of development.	Engaging students in challenging activities and guiding their metacognitive understandings of the academic, social, and ethical issues and concepts inherent across several domains.

Note. Adapted from A. Black and P. Ammon (1990), Developmental Teacher Education (pp. 4–9). *The Educator, vol. 4.* Copyright 1990 by University of California–Berkeley. Adapted with permission.

APPENDIX B

Clinical Interview Questions

I. A. If you had complete freedom to work as a teacher with any age group, which would it be?

    B. Why would it be that age group?

    C. Are there particular things you like about kids that age? Examples?

    D. Are kids this age different from kids who are a couple of years older or younger? Explain.

    E. Are there any special problems or challenges that come with children that age? Examples?

    F. How do you see this age group as the appropriate age for teaching the kinds of things you most want to teach? Why? Why not?

II. A. As you start out the year with a new class, would there be any information you would want about your students? Why? Why not? What kinds?

    B. From a teacher's point of view, what are some good ways to find out what sort of individual one is working with? (Specifics)

    C. How will you know what to expect of students—what they are capable of learning?

III. A. 1. Now we'll talk about some specific classroom activities. An activity commonly found in elementary classrooms is *sharing* time, when individual children are given opportunities to share experiences, objects, and so on with their classmates. Many teachers believe sharing is an important learning opportunity. Exactly what kinds of things might be learned from sharing in a second-grade classroom?

       2. Why would you expect those kinds of outcomes in particular?

       3. How about for sixth graders?

       4. Why are there (no) differences between second and sixth graders with respect to the kinds of learning you would expect to result from sharing?

       5. Are there particular ways in which a teacher handles sharing time so as to enhance the learning outcomes you have identified? Why might these details make a difference?

       6. Do you think that particular experiences are most likely to bring about learning? What kinds of experiences?

       7. In general, how would you describe the teacher's role in the learning process?

III. B. 1. In teaching history, some teachers make use of timelines to help children understand when various events occurred in relation to each other. Every inch on a timeline might correspond, say, to a certain number of years, and events are placed along the line according to their dates. At what ages (grade levels) do you think such timelines would be especially useful?

  2. Do you think that timelines would be less useful before or after the grade level(s) you have suggested? Why?

  3. Aside from grade level, are there other learning characteristics that might affect the usefulness of the timeline as a teaching tool?

III. C. 1. How would you go about teaching children the concept of a sentence so that they would be able to use periods and capital letters correctly when writing? Suppose the children in the class you were working with were third graders. What would you do and why?

  2. Would you do things differently if you were working with sixth graders? Why? Why not?

  3. In general, do you think it is important that a certain sequence or order of experiences be followed?

  4. How important is sheer repetition in school learning? . . . practice? . . . memorization?

  5. Do you think the same thing can be learned in different ways? Explain.

  6. Why do you think that some things take a long time to learn, whereas other things can be learned quickly? (i.e., What makes things either hard or easy to learn?)

  7. Have you ever considered grouping students within a class on the basis of their ability?

  8. Do you see such groups as pretty much fixed or changing?

IV. A. What goals do you have as a teacher? What do you most want to accomplish?

 B. Do you see students as being any different after being with you? How?

 C. How are these things learned or do people become that way?

 D. What kinds of feedback do you look for? How do you get it? Why choose these ways (or this way)?

V. A. Some people believe that part of the school's role is to train kids to be responsible, self-disciplined, and/or respectful of authority. Do you see any or all of these as part of the school's role? Explain.

 B. How are these things learned or how do people become this way?

VI. Do you foresee any obstacles to accomplishing what you want to as a teacher? Explain, specify relationship to teaching.

VII. A. We have talked a lot about teaching, learning, students, and so on. What do you see as your greatest resources or sources of information in your own development as a teacher?

B. What did you find yourself drawing on as you thought about and answered these questions?

APPENDIX C

Teaching Methods Likely to Be Found in a Developmentally Appropriate, Constructivist-Based Classroom

General Teaching Methods

1. More small-group than whole-group instruction.
2. More heterogeneous grouping than homogeneous grouping.
3. Interaction between students seen as an important source of knowledge.
4. Students offered choices in grouping and in the content of the lesson.
5. A functional basis for learning emphasized.
6. Students given reasons for learning particular lessons.

Literacy Instruction

1. Writing to read and reading to write emphasized.
2. Whole-language approach integrated into a balanced reading program.
3. Literature-based versus basal reading program.
4. Communication of meaning emphasized as a source of specific skill acquisition, not conversely.
5. Peer and teacher conferencing and editing of written products.

Mathematics and Science Instruction

1. Hands-on science and manipulative-based mathematics instruction emphasized.
2. Mathematics and science texts supplemental to teacher-organized curriculum.

3. Science as a reading activity deemphasized and science as observation, experimentation, and communication emphasized.

4. Mental mathematics, problem solving, and estimation emphasized over memorization of facts and algorithms.

Adapted from A. Black and P. Ammon (1990), Developmental Teacher Education (pp. 4–9). *The Educator, vol. 4.* Copyright 1990 by University of California–Berkeley. Adapted by permission.

APPENDIX D

Description of the Developmental Teacher Education (DTE) Program

M.A. and Multiple Subjects Credential
University of California at Berkeley
Graduate School of Education–Cognition and Development
Founded in 1980
Director: Dr. Paul Ammon
Coordinator: Dr. Della Peretti

Program Goals

- Preparation of elementary school teachers with an emphasis on deep understanding of the development of children's thinking and learning
- Developmental psychology treated as core knowledge
- Problem solving rather than apprenticeship model of learning to teach
- Integration of issues of equity, antibias curriculum, and second-language learning

Program Design

- 2-year graduate program leasing to M.A. and Multiple Subjects credential that qualifies graduates for CLAD certification (Cultural, Language, and Academic Development)
- Coursework and student teaching takes place in all four semesters
- M.A. research conducted under direction of Graduate School of Education faculty
- Gradual build up of teaching skills through five field placements selected to represent the full range of diversity in the Bay Area

- Fifth placement involves collaborative community service at schools serving low-income, linguistically diverse populations
- Employs doctoral students who serve as field supervisors

Students

- National pool of 120 applicants per year
- 20 students per cohort admitted each year, 40 students in program at one time
- Approximately 50% students of color and 30% males
- Strong subject matter backgrounds representing virtually all undergraduate majors

Contribution to Area Schools

- 100 student teaching placements per year
- Urban outreach community service during fifth placement (after-school program for 60 children)
- Graduates have high retention rate in teaching profession and assume leadership roles in their schools and districts

APPENDIX E

Recommended Professional Development Opportunities

The four educators who are the focus of this book recommend the following professional development opportunities for continuing one's pedagogical development. These experiences, which include conferences, workshops, and long-term professional development opportunities, were all valuable for their own growth as professional educators.

Bay Area Writing Project (BAWP)
5511 Tolman Hall #1670
University of California
Berkeley, CA 94720-1670
Telephone: (510) 642-0971
Fax: (510) 642-4545
http://www-gse.berkeleny.edu/outreach/bawp/bawp.html

BAWP is a collaborative program of the University of California at Berkeley and Bay Area schools. It is dedicated to improving writing and the teaching of writing at all grade levels and in all disciplines. As the flagship site of the National Writing Project, BAWP's program model and design are replicated at 160 colleges and universities throughout the country and at 5 sites internationally. Each year close to 4,000 teachers participate in BAWP summer and school-year programs. For many, BAWP remains a resource throughout their teaching careers. All four of the educators in this book have attended BAWP sessions throughout their career.

California Math Council
P.O. Box 880
Clayton, CA 94517-0880
Telephone: 1-888-CMC-MATH
http://www.cmc-math.org/

The California Mathematics Council is a professional organization of educators individually and collectively dedicated to the improvement of classroom instruction in mathematics at all levels. The annual Math Conference at Asilomar, which is organized by CMC, is hailed by many as the best mathematics education conferences in the nation. Over 8,000 teachers, administrators, and parents explore exciting, effective mathematics education at this conference. Ralph mentioned the Asilomar Conference as one of his favorite professional development activities, but all four of the educators in this book have attended this conference.

California Reading and Literature Project
Clarisa Rojas, *Co-Interim Executive Director*
University of California–San Diego
9500 Gilman Drive 0415
La Jolla, CA 92093-0415
Telephone: (858) 534-1600 or (888) 519-3165
Fax: (858) 534-2220
http://www.ucop.edu/csmp/crlp/index.html

The mission of the California Reading and Literature Project is to ensure that every California student achieves the highest standards of performance in reading and language arts. The California Reading and Literature Project supports teacher leadership and provides continuing professional development opportunities for teachers of reading and literature, including expository texts in K to 12 and university classrooms.

Sandy attended summer workshops sponsored by the precursor to the CRLP, the California Reading Project. She was also part of the Emergent Literacy Institute, an extension of CLP, with a training focusing on emergent literacy. CRLP also trains participants to lead workshops and classes.

There were follow-up meetings for a year, and most participants went on to teach or lead classes focusing on emergent literacy issues.

CUE—Computer-Using Educators Conference
1210 Marina Village Parkway, Suite 100
Alameda, CA 94501
Telephone: (510) 814-6630
Fax: (510) 814-0195
http://www.cue.org/

Computer-Using Educators (CUE, Inc.) is a professional organization of educators who support the use of technology in education. For 22 years, technology-using educators have been meeting at the CUE conferences to advance educational technology at all levels of education and address the use of educational technology in instruction, administration, curriculum, and management. All of the teachers in this book have attended CUE conferences.

Developmental Studies Center
2000 Embarcadero, Suite 305
Oakland, CA 94606-5300
Telephone: (510) 533-0213
Fax: (510) 464-3670
http://www.devstu.org/

The Child Development Project (CDP) is a comprehensive approach to elementary school restructuring that seeks to revamp teaching, learning, school organization, school climate, and teachers' work environments to more effectively promote the intellectual, social, and ethical development of students. Rick's school participated in the DSC program, and he felt it was an excellent match for his own classroom goals. Both Sandy and Ralph recommend several of the books published by the DSC.

Donald Graves
Heinemann Speakers Coordinator
361 Hanover Street
Portsmouth, NH 03801-3912
Telephone: (800) 541-2086, Ext. 148
Fax: (800) 354-2004
http://www.heinemann.con

Donald Graves is Professor Emeritus of Education from the University of New Hampshire. He has been a teacher, school principal, language supervisor, education director, and director of language in bilingual, ESL, and special programs. He also has been a codirector of an undergraduate urban teacher preparation program and a professor of an early childhood program. In addition to his writing, both personal and professional, he travels throughout the United States presenting keynote addresses, seminars, workshops, and inservice training sessions. Because of his extensive teaching background, he understands the real needs of educators.

Marilyn Burns Education Associates
150 Gate 5 Road, Suite 101
Sausalito, CA 94965
Telephone: (800) 868-9092 or (415) 332-4181
Fax: (415) 331-1931
http://www.mathsolutions.com/

As creator of Math Solutions inservice courses, Marilyn Burns is one of today's most highly respected mathematics educators. For more than 30 years, she has been teaching and writing for children, leading inservice workshops, and creating teacher resource materials. She formed Marilyn Burns Education Associates in 1984, working with a team of highly qualified inservice leaders to broaden the reach of her vision through workshops and courses. Created by Marilyn Burns and taught by a national team of more than 70 skilled inservice leaders with years of classroom experience, Math Solutions inservice programs help teachers improve how they teach mathematics in Kindergarten through Grade 8.

Dave Nettell
Cooperative Adventures
P.O. Box 1129
Sausalito, CA 94966-1129
Telephone: (415) 723-7112
http://www.nettell.com/ca1.htm

Cooperative Adventures are a series of increasingly complex and difficult challenges presented to groups in such a way so that success can only be achieved through communication and cooperation. The challenges are selected, presented, sequenced, and evaluated so that group and individual self-esteem is enhanced through the development of trust, risk-taking, and cooperation. Although originally designed for use with elementary (K–6) school children, the program has been successfully adapted and used with middle and high school youngsters, school staffs, community organizations, and corporate groups. Rick takes his students camping every year and has Dave Nettell work with them during this camping trip. He also considers Dave to be his mentor.

New Hampshire Writers' Project
P.O. Box 2693
Concord, NH 03302-2693
Telephone: (603) 226-6649
Fax: (603) 226-0035
http://www. nhwritersproject.org

The New Hampshire Writers' Project (NHWP) offers educational programs (mostly for adults), which include writing workshops and intensive writing courses in the spring and fall. The workshops bring professional authors together with aspiring writers for hands-on writing, editing, and peer review.

Sandy attended a 3-week summer writing program sponsored by the NHWP. She said, "It is similar to BAWP, I think, but with a major focus on the teacher's own writing. I learned a whole new way of thinking about writing here. This was an incredible experience."

National Writing Project
University of California
5511 Tolman Hall #1042
Berkeley, CA 94720-1042
Telephone: (510) 642-0963
Fax: (510) 642-4545
http://nwp.berkeley.edu/nwp.html

The mission of the National Writing Project is to improve the teaching of writing and improve learning in the nation's schools. Through its professional development model, the National Writing Project recognizes the primary importance of teacher knowledge, expertise, and leadership. The National Writing Project now includes 167 sites in 49 states.

Bev Bos
http://www.turnthepage.com/

This author's philosophy toward the creative use of materials and developing a sense of the child in your own thinking about art is an outstanding feature of her book, *Before the Basics: Creating Conversations With Children.* Her 10 rules for "getting the feel of it" help the adult focus on the child and the process rather than the end product. Presenting the materials and standing back is often the best approach in releasing the artist in young children. Ralph was especially influenced by Bev Bos' ideas.

APPENDIX F

Influential Professional Books

The four educators in this book suggest that the following books and professional journals were some of the main ones that influenced their thinking about pedagogy. They highly recommend them to others interested in continuing to develop thinking about teaching and learning.

Atwell, N. (1998). *In the middle: New understandings about writing, reading, and learning* (2nd ed.). New York: Boynton/Cook. (ISBN: 0867093749)

Atwell, N. (Ed.). (1990). *Coming to know: Writing to learn in the intermediate grades.* Portsmouth, NH: Heinemann. (ISBN: 043508500X)

Baratta-Lorton, M. (1994). *Math their way: Complete revised anniversary edition.* Palo Alto, CA: Addison-Wesley. (ISBN: 0201861534)

Bos, B. (1983). *Before the basics: Creating conversations with children.* Roseville, CA: Turn The Page Press. (ISBN: 0931540011)

Bos, B. (1990). *Together we're better: Establishing a coactive learning environment.* Roseville, CA: Turn The Page Press. (ISBN: 0931793017)

Burns, M. (1996). *50 problem-solving lessons: The best from 10 years of math solutions newsletters.* Sausalito, CA: Marilyn Burns Education Association. (ISBN: 0941355160)

Burns, M. (1998). *Math: Facing an American phobia.* Sausalito, CA: Math Solutions Publications.

Burns, M. (2000). *About teaching mathematics: A K-8 resource* (2nd ed.). Sausalito, CA: Math Solutions Publications. (ISBN: 094135525X)

Burns, M., & Tank, B. (1986). *A collection of math lessons from grades 3–6.* Sausalito, CA: Marilyn Burns Education Association. (ISBN: 0941355004)

Calkins, L. M. (1994). *The art of teaching writing.* Portsmouth, NH: Heinemann. (ISBN: 0435088092)

Calkins, L. M., with Harwayne, S. (1990). *Living between the lines.* Portsmouth, NH: Heinemann. (ISBN: 0435085387)

Child Development Project. (1996). *Ways we want our class to be: Class meetings that build commitment to kindness and learning.* Oakland, CA: Developmental Studies Center. (ISBN: 1885603800)

Dalton, J., & Watson, M. (1997). *Among friends: Classrooms where caring and learning prevail.* Oakland, CA: Developmental Studies Center. (ISBN: 1576211428)

Dyson, A. H. (1987). *Unintentional helping in the primary grades* (Technical Report 2). Berkeley, CA: National Writing Project. (ISBN: 9990083185)

Dyson, A. H. (1990). *Multiple worlds of child writers: Friends learning to write.* New York: Teachers College Press. (ISBN: 0807729728)

Dyson, A. H. (1993). *Social worlds of children learning to write in an urban primary school.* New York: Teachers College Press. (ISBN: 0807732958)

Dyson, A. H. (1997). *What difference does difference make? Teacher reflections on diversity, literacy, and the urban primary school.* Urbana, IL: National Council of Teachers of English. (ISBN: 0814156576)

Dyson, A. H. (1997). *Writing superheroes: Contemporary childhood, popular culture, and classroom literacy.* New York: Teachers College Press. (ISBN: 0807736392)

Dyson, A H., & Genishi, C. (Eds.). (1994). *The need for story: Cultural diversity in classroom and community.* Urbana, IL: National Council of Teachers of English. (ISBN: 0814133002)

Fox, M. (1993). *Radical reflections: Passionate opinions on teaching, learning, and living.* New York: Harcourt Brace. (ISBN: 015607947X)

Genishi, C., & Dyson, A. H. (1984). *Language assessment in the early years.* New York: Ablex. (ISBN: 0893912468)

Gibbs, J. (1994). *Tribes: A new way of learning and being together.* Santa Rosa, CA: CenterSource Systems. (ISBN: 0932762093)

Glasser, W. (1998). *The quality school: Managing students without coercion* (3rd ed.). New York: Harperperennial Library. (ISBN: 0060952865)

Glasser, W. (1998). *The quality school teacher: Specific suggestions for teachers who are trying to implement the lead-management ideas of the quality school in their classroom* (rev. ed.). New York: Harperperennial Library. (ISBN: 0060952857)

Goldberg, N. (1998). *Writing down the bones: Freeing the writer within.* New York: Pocket Edition. (ISBN: 1570624240)

Graves, D. H. (1982). *Writing: Teachers and children at work.* Portsmouth, NH: Heinemann. (ISBN: 0435082035)

Graves, D. H. (1994). *A fresh look at writing.* Portsmouth, NH: Heinemann. (ISBN: 0435088246)

Harwayne, S. (1992). *Lasting impressions: Weaving literature into the writing workshop.* Portsmouth, NH: Heinemann. (ISBN: 0435087320)

Harwayne, S. (2000). *Lifetime guarantees: Toward ambitious literacy teaching.* Portsmouth, NH: Heinemann. ISBN: (032500241X)

Kohn, A. (1996). *Beyond discipline: From compliance to community.* Alexandria, VA: Association for Supervision & Curriculum Development. (ISBN: 0871202700)

Kohn, A. (1999). *Punished by rewards: The trouble with gold stars, incentive plans, A's, praise, and other bribes.* New York: Houghton-Mifflin. (ISBN: 0618001816)

Kohn, A. (2000). *The schools our children deserve: Moving beyond traditional classrooms and tougher standards.* New York: Houghton-Mifflin. (ISBN: 0395940397)

Kohn, A. (2000). *The case against standardized testing: Raising the scores, ruining the schools.* Portsmouth, NH: Heinemann. (ISBN: 0325003254)

Nettel, D. (199). *The cooperative adventures handbook.* Send order to: Cooperative Adventures, P.O. Box 1129, Sausalito, CA 94966-1129.

Newkirk, T., & Atwell, N. (Eds.). (1998). *Understanding writing: Ways of observing, learning, and teaching, K–8* (2nd ed.). Portsmouth, NH: Heinemann. (ISBN: 0435084410)

Paley, V. (1987). *Wally's stories: Conversations in kindergarten.* Cambridge, MA: Harvard University Press. (ISBN: 067494593X)

Paley, V. (1992). *You can't say you can't play.* Cambridge, MA: Harvard University Press. (ISBN: 0674965892)

Paley, V. (1996). *Kwanzaa and me: A teacher's story.* Cambridge, MA: Harvard University Press. (ISBN: 0674505867)

Paley, V. (1998). *The girl with the brown crayon.* Cambridge, MA: Harvard University Press. (ISBN: 0674354427)

Paley, V. (2000). *White teacher* (with a new preface). Cambridge, MA: Harvard University Press. (ISBN: 0674002733)

Routman, R. (1995). *Invitations: Changing as teachers and learners, K–12.* Portsmouth, NH: Heinemann. (ISBN: 0435088378)

Routman, R. (1999). *Conversations.* Portsmouth, NH: Heinemann. (ISBN: 032500109X)

Routman, R. (2000). *Kids' poems: Teaching third and fourth graders to love writing poetry.* Scholastic Prof Book Div. (ISBN: 0590227351)

Routman, R., & Butler, A. (1991). *Transitions: From literature to literacy.* Portsmouth, NH: Heinemann. (ISBN: 0435084674)

Other Publications

Rethinking Schools: The Urban Education Journal is located online at http://www.rethinkingschools.org/ or 1001 E. Keefe Avenue, Milwaukee, WI 53212, Phone (414) 964-9646 or (800) 669-4192, FAX (414) 964-7220.

Starting Small is a training tool for educators of the early grades. The film, designed for inservice programs, and a 250-page text, designed for self-reflection or group discussion, profile exemplary pre-K through third-grade classrooms in which peace, equity, and justice are guiding themes. To order for FREE, send a written request on school letterhead, signed by a principal or administrator, by fax (334) 956-8486, or by mail to *Teaching Tolerance*, Order Department, 400 Washington Avenue, Montgomery, AL 36104.

References

Ammon, P. (1984). Human development, teaching, and teacher education. *Teacher Education Quarterly, 11*(4), 95–106.

Ammon, P., & Hutcheson, B. P. (1989). Promoting the development of teachers' pedagogical conceptions. *Genetic Epistemologist, 17*(4), 23–29.

Ammon, P., Hutcheson, B. P., & Black, A. (1985). *Teachers' developing conceptions about children, learning and teaching: Observations from a clinical interview.* Paper presented at the annual meeting of the American Educational Research Association, Chicago, IL.

Ammon, P., & Levin, B. B. (1993). Expertise in teaching from a developmental perspective: The Developmental Teacher Education Program at Berkeley. *Journal of Learning and Individual Differences, 5*(4), 319–326.

Ayers, W. (1993). *To teach: The journey of a teacher.* New York: Teachers College Press.

Ball, S. J., & Goodson, I. F. (1985). Understanding teachers: Concepts and contexts. In S. J. Ball & I. F. Goodson (Eds.), *Teachers lives and careers* (pp. 1–26). London: Falmer.

Berliner, D. C. (1986). In pursuit of the expert pedagogue. *Educational Researcher, 15*, 5–13.

Berliner, D. C. (1988). Implications of studies of expertise in pedagogy for teacher education and evaluation. In *New directions for teacher assessment. Proceedings of the 1988 Educational Testing Service Invitational Conference.* Princeton, NJ: Educational Testing Service.

Black, A. (1989). Developmental teacher education: Preparing teachers to apply developmental principles across the curriculum. *The Genetic Epistemologist, 17*(4), 5–13.

Black, A., & Ammon, P. (1990). Developmental teacher education. *The Educator, 4*(1), 4–9.

Black, A., & Ammon, P. (1992). A developmental-constructivist approach to teacher education. *Journal of Teacher Education, 43*, 323–335.

Bullough, R. V., Jr. (1989). *First-year teacher: A case study.* New York: Teachers College Press.

Bullough, R. V., Jr., & Baughman, K. (1997). *"First-year teacher" eight years later.* New York: Teachers College Press.

Bullough, R. V., Jr., & Knowles, J. G. (1991). Teaching and nurturing: Changing conceptions of self as teacher in a case study of becoming a teacher. *Qualitative Studies in Education, 4*, 121–140.

Bullough, R. V., Jr., Knowles, J. G., & Crow, N. A. (1991). *Emerging as a teacher.* London: Routledge.

Butt, R. L., Raymond, G., McCue, G., & Yamagishi, L. (1992). Collaborative autobiography and the teacher's voice. In I. F. Goodson (Ed.), *Studying teachers' lives* (pp. 51–98). New York: Teachers College Press.

California Education Policy Seminar and California State University Institute for Policy Reform. (1998). *Doing what matters most: Investing in quality teaching.* California State University Sacramento, CA: CSU Institute for Educational Reform. [Available online at http://www.csus.edu/ier/reports/LDHRpt.pdf]

Carter, K., Cushing, K., Sabers, D., Stein, P., & Berliner, D. C. (1988). Expert-novice differences in perceiving and processing visual information. *Journal of Teacher Education, 39*(3), 25–31.

Carter, K., Sabers, D., Cushing, K., Pinnegar, P., & Berliner, D. C. (1987). Processing and using information about students: A study of expert, novice, and postulant teachers. *Teaching and Teacher Education, 3,* 147–157.

Clandinin, D. J., & Connelly, F. M. (1996). Teachers' professional knowledge landscapes: Teacher stories—stories of teachers—school stories—stories of schools. *Educational Researcher, 25*(3), 24–30.

Codell, E. R. (1999). *Educating Esme: Diary of a teacher's first year.* New York: Algonquin.

Connelly, M., & Clandinin, J. (1990). Stories of experiences and narrative inquiry. *Educational Researcher, 19*(5), 2–14.

Csikszentmihalyi, M. (1975). *Beyond boredom and anxiety.* San Francisco: Jossey-Bass.

Denzin, N., & Lincoln, Y. (Eds.). (2000). *Handbook of qualitative research.* Thousand Oaks, CA: Sage.

Feiman-Nemser, S., & Buchman, M. (1989). Describing teacher education: A framework and illustrative findings from a longitudinal study of six students. *The Elementary School Journal, 89,* 365–377.

Freedman, S. (1990). *Small victories.* New York: Harper Perennial.

Fuller, F. F. (1969). Concerns of teachers: A developmental conceptualization. *American Educational Research Journal, 6,* 207–226.

Fuller, F. F., & Brown, O. H. (1975). Becoming a teacher. In K. Ryan (Ed.), *Teacher education* (Seventy-fourth Yearbook of the National Society for the Study of Education) (pp. 25–52). Chicago: University of Chicago Press.

Gibbs, J. (1994). *Tribes: A new way of learning together.* Santa Rosa, CA: Center Source Publications.

Glaser, B. G., & Strauss, A. L. (1967). *The discovery of grounded theory.* Chicago: Aldine.

Glassberg, S. (1979). *Developing models of teacher development.* Paper presented at the annual meeting of the American Educational research Association, Chicago, IL.

Glassberg, S., & Sprinthall, N. (1980). Student teaching: A developmental approach. *Journal of Teacher Education, 31*(2), 31–38.

Goodson, I. F. (Ed.). (1992). *Studying teachers' lives.* New York: Teachers College Press.

Goswami, D., & Stillman, P. R. (Eds.). (1987). *Reclaiming the classroom: Teacher research as agency for change.* Portsmouth, NH: Boyton/Cook-Heinemann.

Grossman, P. (1992). Why models matter: An alternative view on professional growth in teaching. *Review of Educational Research, 62,* 171–179.

Harding, S. (1987). *Feminism and methodology.* Bloomington, IN: Indian University Press.

Hollingsworth, S. J. (1989). Prior beliefs and cognitive change in learning to teach. *American Educational Research Journal, 26,* 160–189.

Hollingsworth, S. J. (1994). *Teacher research and urban literacy education.* New York: Teachers College Press.

Huberman, M. (Ed.). (1989). Research on teachers' professional lives. *International Journal of Educational Research, 13*(4), 343–466.

Hunt, D. (1974). *Matching models in education.* Toronto: Ontario Institute for Studies of Education.

Hutcheson, B. P., & Ammon, P. (1986). *The development of teachers' conceptions as reflected in their journals.* Paper presented at the annual meeting of the American Educational Research Association, San Francisco.

Hutcheson, B. P., & Ammon, P. (1987). *Teachers' cognitive development in the pedagogical domain.* Paper presented at the 17th annual symposium of the Jean Piaget Society, Philadelphia.

Johnson, L. (1992). *My posse don't do homework.* New York: St. Martin's Press.

Johnson, L. (1995). *The girls in the back of the class.* New York: St. Martin's Press.

Kagan, D. M. (1992). Professional growth among preservice and beginning teachers. *Review of Educational Research, 2,* 129–169.

Kane, P. R. (1991). *The first year of teaching.* New York: Walker.

Kidder, T. (1989). *Among schoolchildren.* Boston: Houghton-Mifflin.

Kohlberg, L. (1969). *Stages in the development of moral thought and action.* New York: Holt, Rinehart, & Winston.

Knowles, J. G. (1992). Models for understanding preservice and beginning teachers' biographies: Illustrations from case studies. In I. F. Goodson (Ed.), *Studying teachers' lives* (pp. 51–98). London: Falmer

Kohlberg, L., & Armon, C. (1984). *Three types of stage models used in the study of adult development.* In M. L. Commons, F. A. Richards, & C. Armon (Eds.), *Beyond formal operations.* New York: Praeger.

Kohn, A. (1993). *Punished by rewards.* Boston: Houghton-Mifflin.

Kroll, L., & Black, A. (1993). Developmental theory and teaching methods: A pilot study of a teacher education program. *The Elementary School Journal, 93,* 417–441.

Levin, B. B., & Ammon, P. R. (1992). The development of beginning teachers' pedagogical thinking: A longitudinal analysis of four case studies. *Teacher Education Quarterly, 19*(4), 19–37.

Levin, B. B., & Ammon, P. R. (1996). A longitudinal study of the development of teachers' pedagogical conceptions: The case of Rick. *Teacher Education Quarterly, 23*(4), 5–25.

Lidstone, M., & Hollingsworth, S. (1992). A longitudinal study of cognitive change in beginning teachers: Two patterns of learning to teach. *Teacher Education Quarterly, 19*(3), 39–57.

Lincoln, Y. S., & Guba, E. C. (1985). *Naturalistic inquiry.* Newbury Park, CA: Sage.

Loevinger, J. (1976). *Ego development.* San Francisco: Jossey-Bass.

Lortie, D. (1975). *Schoolteacher: A sociological perspective.* Chicago: University of Chicago Press.

Merriam, S. B. (1998). *Qualitative research and case study applications in education.* Thousand Oaks, CA: Sage.

Miles, M. B., & Huberman, A. M. (1994). *Qualitative data analysis: An expanded sourcebook* (2nd ed.). Thousand Oaks, CA: Sage.

National Commission for Teaching & America's Future. (1996). *What matters most: Teaching for America's future.* Woodbridge, VA: Author.

National Council for the Accreditation of Teacher Education (2002). *Professional standards for the accreditation of schools, colleges, and departments of education* (2002 ed.). Washington, DC: Author. (Available online at http://www.ncate.org/2000/unit_ stnds_2002.pdf].

Nias, J. (1989a). *Primary teachers talking: A study of teaching as work.* New York: Routledge.

Nias, J. (1989b). Subjectively speaking: English primary teachers' careers. *International Journal of Educational Research, 13,* 391–402.

Perry, W. (1970). *Forms of intellectual and ethical development.* New York: Holt, Rinehart, & Winston.

Piaget, J. (1952). *The origins of intelligence in children.* New York: International Universities Press.

Piaget, J. (1963). *Psychology of intelligence.* Patterson, NJ: Littlefield Adams.

Piaget, J. (1972). Intellectual evolution from adolescence to adulthood. *Human Development, 15,* 1–12.

Powell, R. R. (1996). Epistemological antecedents to culturally relevant and constructivist classroom curricula: A longitudinal study of teachers' contrasting world views. *Teaching and Teacher Education, 12,* 365–384.

Powell, R. R. (1997). Then the beauty emerges: A longitudinal case study of culturally relevant teaching. *Teaching and Teacher Education, 13,* 467–484.

Richardson, V. (1996). The role of attitudes and beliefs in learning to teach. In J. Sikula, T. Buttery, & E. Guyton (Eds.), *Handbook of research on teacher education* (2nd ed., pp. 102–119). New York: Macmillan.

Ryan, K. (1986). *The induction of new teachers.* Bloomington, IN: Phi Delta Kappa Educational Foundation.

Ryan, K. (1992). *The roller coaster year.* New York: HarperCollins.

Sabers, D., Cushing, K., & Berliner, D. C. (1991). Differences among teachers in a task characterized by simultaneity, multidimensionality, and immediacy. *American Educational Research Journal, 28,* 63–88.

Sears, J. T., Marshall, J. D., & Otis-Wilborn, A. (1994). *When best doesn't equal good: Educational reform and teacher recruitment: A longitudinal study.* New York: Teachers College Press.

Snyder, J. (2000). Knowing children—understanding teaching: The developmental teacher education program at the University of California–Berkeley. In L. Darling-Hammond (Ed.), *Studies of excellence in teacher education* (pp. 97–172). New York: AACTE Publications.

Sprinthall, N. A., Reiman, A. J., & Thies-Sprinthall, L. (1996). Teacher professional development. In J. Sikula (Ed.), *Handbook of research on teacher education* (2nd ed.). New York: Simon & Schuster.

Sprinthall, N. A., & Thies-Sprinthall, L. (1980). Education for teacher growth: A cognitive developmental perspective. *Theory into Practice, 29,* 278–286.

Sprinthall, N. A., & Thies-Sprinthall, L. (1983). The teacher as adult learner: A cognitive-developmental view. In G. A. Griffin (Ed.), *Staff development: 82nd Yearbook of the National Society for the Study of Education* (pp. 12–35). Chicago: University of Chicago Press.

Thies-Sprinthall, L., & Sprinthall, N. (1984). Perservice teachers as adult learners: A new framework for teacher education. In J. D. Raths & C. G. Katz (Eds.), *Advances in teacher education* (Vol. 2). Norwood, NJ: Ablex.

Stake, R. E. (1995). *The art of case study research.* Thousand Oaks, CA: Sage.

Strauss, A. S., & Corbin, J. (1990). *Basics of qualitative research: Grounded theory procedures and techniques.* Thousand Oaks, CA: Sage.

Turiel, E., & Davidson, P. (1986). Heterogeneity, inconsistency, and asynchRicky in the develoment of cognitive structures. In I. Levin (Ed.), *Stage and structure: Reopening the debate.* Norwood, NJ: Ablex.

Veenman, S. (1984). Perceived problems of beginning teachers. *Review of Educational Research, 54,* 143–178.

Vygotsky, L. S. (1986). *Thought and language.* Cambridge, MA: MIT Press.

Yin, R. K. (1994). *Case study research: Design and methods* (2nd ed.). Thousand Oaks, CA: Sage.

Zeichner, K., & Liston, D. P. (1987). Teaching student teachers to reflect. *Harvard Educational Review, 57,* 23–47.

Zeichner, K., & Tabachnik, B. R. (1981). Are the effects of university teacher education washed out by school experience? *Journal of Teacher Education, 32,* 7–11.

Zeichner, K., Tabachnik, B. R., & Densmore, K. (1987). Individual, institutional, and cultural influences on the development of teachers' craft knowledge. In J. Calderhead (Ed.), *Exploring teachers thinking.* London: Cassell.

Author Index

303

Subject Index